VATICAN II
REVISITED
by those who were there

VATICAN II
REVISITED
by those who were there

EDITED BY
ALBERIC STACPOOLE

WINSTON PRESS
MINNEAPOLIS, MINNESOTA

A Geoffrey Chapman book published by
Cassell Ltd
1 Vincent Square, London SW1P 2PN

Published in the United States of America by
Winston Press, Inc.
600 First Avenue North
Minneapolis, Minnesota 55403

Introductions and compilation © Geoffrey Chapman, a division of Cassell Ltd, 1986

Cover design: Koechel-Peterson Design

First published 1986

ISBN 0-86683-531-8

Library of Congress Catalog Card Number: 85-52188

Phototypesetting by Georgia Ltd, Formby
Printed in Great Britain by
Richard Clay (The Chaucer Press) Ltd,
Bungay, Suffolk

CONTENTS

III THE COUNCIL'S OBSERVERS

IV THE COUNCIL AT WORK

V CONCILIAR POSTLUDE

ACKNOWLEDGEMENTS

Some chapters in this book have appeared in other publications. The editor and the publishers wish to thank the following for permission to translate or reproduce:

Doubleday and Company Inc., for Chapter 2 from *Signposts for the Future* New York, 1978, pp.88–94; The Chancellor, Masters and Scholars of the University of Cambridge, and the University Orator, Dr J. Diggle, for the Address in Chapter 2.

Nouvelle Revue Théologique and the Centre de Documentation et de Recherche Religieuses de la Compagnie de Jésus, Namur, for Chapter 6 which appeared in volume 107, 1, 1985.

Beauchesne Editeur, Paris, for Chapters 8 and 23 from *Le Concile de Vatican II*, Paris, 1984, pp.7–32 and 49–72.

The Sacred Congregation for Divine Worship, for Chapter 11, a discourse given at the Meeting of Presidents and Secretaries of National Liturgical Commissions, Rome, October 1984.

PAUL BURNS translated Chapters 1, 6, 7 and 22.

JENNIFER JOHNSON translated Chapters 12 and 18.

AIDAN NICHOLLS OP translated Chapter 3.

EDWARD QUINN translated Chapter 2.

DAVID SMITH translated Chapters 8 and 23.

ENID STOYE translated Chapter 20.

As President of the English Benedictine Congregation I was originally invited to take part in the Ecumenical Council, 1962–1965. I had gone out to Rome with some fears, since the Council was a group of some 2,000 prelates of more than average age. What surprised and delighted me was the co-operation of the vast majority in a process to bring the Church 'up-to-date'. A turning-point was the decision, by the Secretary of the Council, that the thesis on the Liturgy would have to proceed, since the majority against the Liturgy Constitution was less than decisive. What really woke me up to a new outlook was the action taken by Pope John XXIII to revise the Liturgy with the help of some genuine 'progressives'.

From then onwards the great majority of the Council members were determined to bring the Church up to date – from Pope Pius X (1903–10) onwards there had been a strong conservative influence, revolutionised by John XXIII. The results were exhilarating – not least when they reached conclusions on the Nature of the Church, on the Vernacular Liturgy, and on a genuine and universal *Aggiornamento*. In the course of the Council I became a member of the Theology Commission, and was assisted by Fr Karl Rahner, S.J.

In 1966 at Oxford I delivered a course of seven Lectures on the Theology of Vatican II, and fourteen years later I published a revised edition of that Theology. The Council proved to be a remarkable step into a new era (though a small, largely insignificant, group of 'conservatives' tried in vain to go back to the period of Pius X and his successors). I warmly recommend this book on the Council edited by Dom Alberic Stacpoole. Let us hope that the Extraordinary Synod will confirm the Council's *Aggiornamento*.

St Edmund's College   + *B.C. Butler*
Ware, Herts   *23rd July 1985*

FOREWORD

JOSEPH CARDINAL BERNARDIN

The Second Vatican Council ended on December 8, 1965, and I was ordained a bishop the following April. Although I was not a participant at the Council, my entire episcopal ministry has taken place in its shadow. Perhaps, I should say 'in its light', for its various constitutions, decrees, and declarations have provided constant guidance for my thoughts and actions during the past twenty years.

For that reason it always has been fascinating, as well as illuminating, to sit at the feet of some of the major Council participants and learn more about the atmosphere, the struggles, the excitement, and the intricate processes which led to the development of certain conciliar documents. With the publication of this book, readers will have access to some of the more important actors in the drama which was the Second Vatican Council, to their reflections on the life of the Council, and to the Council's significance for the life of the Church in the last half of this century.

THE COUNCIL IN PERSPECTIVE

In reading this book it is important to recall that the Second Vatican Council represented the largest gathering of bishops in the Church's history. It also was the first Council whose participants truly represented the great cultural diversity of the local Churches in union with Rome. Twenty years later it is important to note that Vatican II was the first ecumenical council which did not ensue in some kind of schism. This was due, in large part, to the skill of Pope Paul VI in reconciling opposing factions and in providing for a careful implementation of conciliar teaching.

Although the Council did not result in schism, it is fair to say that the Council startled many people inside the Church and outside of it. On the other hand, those who were knowledgeable about trends and developments within the Church during the previous forty or fifty years were less surprised. They knew that the First Vatican Council had ended abruptly, with much of its business unfinished. Similarly, they were aware that there had been significant developments in biblical studies, patristics, liturgy, and catechetics. The pontificate of Pope Pius XII, in effect, had laid the groundwork for Vatican II. Thus, the Council was in continuity with the past.

Even though much had been taking place in the Church, the theological and pastoral currents of the previous decades needed a catalyst to channel them in the direction of building up the Church. Deciding that the thrust of the Council would be pastoral, rather than dogmatic, Pope John XXIII allowed the dynamic forces that were present within the Church to be unleashed with full creative and pastoral wisdom. The result was the documents of Vatican II.

IMPACT OF THE COUNCIL

The Council has had a powerful impact on the Church and on society throughout the world. In the past twenty years we have become much more aware that the Catholic Church can no longer be dominated by the particular Churches of the North Atlantic community. The Church is truly universal. Its most exciting growth is taking place in Africa and India. There is also a great surge of renewal in Latin America, where, in many places, the Church is identifying itself more and more with the people, with the poor.

The Council has also had significant influence in Church developments in the United States. I agree with the statement made by Bishop James Malone, President of the National Conference of Catholic Bishops. In his report in preparation for the Extraordinary Session of the Synod of Bishops, Bishop Malone states: 'Dispute about the meaning of Vatican II, and even failures in its interpretation and carrying-out, neither cancel nor outweigh what has been accomplished in these two decades. Overall, the Council still stands as the best, necessary foundation for Catholic renewal in the closing years of the twentieth century'.

Three examples of this renewal can be mentioned. First, collegiality among the U.S. bishops has made it possible for them to speak as one voice in public policy discussions such as those on the nuclear threat and the economy. Close collaboration and cooperation have enabled the bishops to minister more effectively. Shared decision-making has meant the establishment of many consultative bodies in which all the members of the Church can have input into the decisions which affect their lives.

Second, as someone who grew up and invested the early years of his priesthood in South Carolina, a state which remains two percent Catholic and in large measure a predominantly Protestant environment, I can appreciate the new ways in which the Council has helped us relate to those who are not Catholic. By giving great impetus to ecumenical endeavors, the Council brought important results to the Church in the United States. In addition to our interfaith dialogues, there is growing interfaith cooperation in addressing many of the moral challenges facing our society. The Church has learned how to be an active participant in the development of public policy in a pluralistic society.

Third, the Council's emphases on liturgy, on the scriptures, and on the nature of the Church have led to many programs of spiritual renewal. Renewed emphasis on the reading of Scripture and on the homily have enabled U.S. Catholics to become more familiar with the sources of our tradition and their implications for our daily Christian life.

FUTURE AGENDA

It is no secret that not everyone who participated in the Council was of the same mind or took the same approach to issues. There were opposing views. Members of the Roman Curia who had a major influence in the initial drafts of the early conciliar documents tended to be more conservative. Many of the theological experts who accompanied the bishops of the world to the council were more progressive. And in dealing with the resulting tension, much happened 'behind the scenes' in theological discussions, seminars, and commission meetings.

Those who favored renewal of the Church and the Church's adoption of a positive approach towards the world were in the majority. Nevertheless, some of the important conciliar documents remain compromises between opposing points of view. Perhaps that was inevitable. However, that the bishops were able to reach those compromises attests to the power of the Spirit guiding the Council Fathers in their task.

The compromises found in some of the documents mean that opposing – not contradictory – views are still in tension. People of good will can appeal to parts of the documents in support of their own opinion against other people of good will who appeal to other parts of the documents in support of an opposing position. This creates a certain amount of confusion in the Church and stirs up controversy.

Happily, the tension resulting from this confusion and controversy provides us with an agenda for the future. In many ways the agenda is marked by the same question that has confronted the Church throughout the centuries: How do we remain faithful to tradition while responding to qualitatively new problems with innovation and creativity?

In listing the problems that we must attend to, the first that comes to mind is one that I alluded to earlier. In the past several hundred years the Church has been primarily identified as a Western institution. The Council, however, has provided important new openings to the Eastern Churches as well as to non-Christian Eastern religions such as Islam, Hinduism, and Buddhism. Moreover, we now recognize that we are a *universal* Church. This recognition, in turn, raises a crucial question: How do we accomplish unity in the Church while adapting legitimately to a great diversity of cultures?

Although, as a community of faith, we often have been preoccupied by the task of implementing the vision and values of Vatican II, the world has not stood still while we went about our internal reform. In a world that is increasingly interdependent and marked by the threat of nuclear destruction, the Church has come to realize that it has an important role to play. The Church recognizes that it must work to develop an interdependence that not only provides for the physical needs of all but also serves the spiritual and moral needs of the human family. Although this role is a part of the Church's mission, and the Church is well equipped to play it on an international scale, the problem of accomplishing unity amid growing diversity remains primary on the Church's agenda. The Church must seek to reconcile the differences and to bridge the chasms between the Northern and Southern hemispheres, between the rich and the poor of the world.

A second item on the Church's future agenda has its origin in two of the major teachings of the Council. In its documents the Council repeated the traditional doctrine about the hierarchical nature of the Church, but it also insisted that the Church is the entire People of God. Many of the present tensions in the Church can be attributed to that twofold approach of the Council. We need to work out more clearly how these two truths are inter-related – not just on the theoretical level, but on the practical level as well.

In keeping with its affirmation of the imagery of the Church as the People of God, the Council made a major contribution in pointing out the rightful place of the laity in the Church. It also began the process of enabling them to assume that position. At the same time, however, some confusion has resulted about the appropriate role of an ordained priesthood. How to make our own a vision of Church that recognizes the distinctive charisms of all believers as well as the unique and essentially different charism of presbyteral ministry is another item on our future agenda.

Related to, but distinct from, the question mentioned above, is the question of the role of women in society and in the Church. In recent years there has been a growing awareness of the plight of women in society and in the Church – especially, but not exclusively, in the United States – as well as of women's individual and collective potential. The Church must take this issue seriously. To resolve it, the Church must work – within the framework of our Catholic tradition – to bring about appropriate changes in society and in the Church. Because of the deep feelings surrounding this current and future agenda item, the Church also needs to listen prayerfully and act decisively.

A final item on the Church's future agenda is social justice. Since the Council, the Church in the United States and elsewhere has taken some strong stands on issues of social justice. Unfortunately, many people were not prepared for this type of ecclesial teaching. Others have disagreed with it. If the vision of a just and equal society, which was so central to the work of the Council and to recent papal and episcopal teaching, is to be effective, then there is need for an ever deepening moral conversion of all believers. Such a conversion will make us more attentive to the social and economic needs of all of humankind. It will force us to examine how we relate to each other within the Church, and it will demand that our ecclesial life be an apt model of a just and caring community.

IN CELEBRATION

In the pages that follow, the reader will gain an overview of the life and work of the Second Vatican Council. It will be an overview given from the differing perspectives of those people who shared intimately in one way or another in that great ecclesial drama.

As we read their recollections and historical recountings and as we reflect on their observations and evaluations, we ought to celebrate the contribution which these people, and so many others, made to the life of the Council. As a bishop dedicated to the continuing implementation and development of the Council, I also want to celebrate the gift of the Spirit that guided the Council's work twenty years ago and continues to direct the Church today.

Archbishop's House
Chicago
October 1985

INTRODUCTION

ALBERIC STACPOOLE OSB

Our reasons for wanting this book written are fourfold. First because, like Mount Everest, the Second Vatican Council is there. Time has matured the Council's work and our understanding of its achievement. The twentieth anniversary is a good time to take stock and to ponder on the riches accorded to the Church and the world.

Secondly, there is a saying 'Where there is life, there is hope'. We still have among us the men who effected the Council, under the Holy Spirit. They are now for the most part old and retired, like Père Chenu who is about to pass his 91st birthday. We needed to catch their witness while there was yet time. We approached as many as we could find and the response has been generous although some, sadly, had to decline.

Thirdly, it is little realised by those who have lived through the evolution that has taken place in the life of the Church over the past twenty years what an overwhelming shock it was for the bishops and those others with high responsibility when the experience of this great Council was over at Christmastide of 1965, and the responsibility of communicating it in pastoral action was put upon them. For the most part, they went to the Council psychologically and theologically unprepared; who indeed could be prepared for so massive an experience, except a handful from the heart of Europe?

There is the example of William Gordon Wheeler who as coadjutor bishop of Leeds attended the last two Sessions. He remembers the continual and exciting development through to the end, the presentation of new documents and perpetual interventions throwing up modifications. There was 'a very precious and almost tangible presence of the Holy Spirit, most evidently in the daily liturgies and the wealth of prayer – about which none of us ever became blasé'. When he came home to Leeds, like all the Fathers

1

he brought back a gift from Paul VI, a copy of the life of St Charles Borromeo, Archbishop of Milan (d. 1584), who had, best among his generation's bishops, implemented the Council of Trent in his diocese. Of the initiatives Bishop Wheeler undertook, what stood out was his foundation of Wood Hall Conference Centre, venue of the first National Pastoral Council of England and Wales in 1967; and of the symposium of 1969 on 'The theology of spirituality', at which the main speakers included the Archbishop of York and the Bishop of Coventry (leading Anglicans). Leeds, in its quiet way, was the first too to set up its own diocesan pastoral council, and its own council of priests, very soon after the Council ended.

Another bishop who sent us recollections rather than a chapter was Augustine Harris, consecrated by Archbishop Beck of Liverpool in February 1966. His experience began where the Council ended. Jocularly he remarked that when the Conference of English Bishops gathered to wonder how best to implement the Council, their first thought was: 'How are we to persuade the laity not to kiss our episcopal rings any more?' He writes thus:

The Vatican Council ended in December 1965. In that same month I was appointed a bishop.

Being a new bishop who had not been party to the Vatican Council it was quite an experience to meet up with the English and Welsh Hierarchy who had to cope with the implementation of its Decrees. Having spent the previous thirteen years in prison work, I felt myself to be in the role of the observer. After the initial shock of being transferred from crime to collegiality, I was immensely impressed by the integrity of the bishops. They wanted to implement the Decrees of Vatican II but had not had time to digest the deeper meanings of the Council. One bishop said we will not really understand what Vatican II means for at least twenty years. It is interesting that after twenty years the Holy Father has called a Special Synod to reflect on the way forward. There was plenty of advice. Many strident voices were calling for radical reforms. Most of the Catholic community had not digested the new experiences, especially the liturgy. In the middle were the bishops trying to discern genuine reform and renewal, as distinct from superficial renewal. They were very conscious of the danger of moving in a false direction and being unable to return to the true path after the mistake had been recognised.

I remember some critics of the bishops questioning their faith. The faith of the bishops was never, in my mind, in question. They were going through the agony of any sincere person who is trying to decide what is the responsible way forward.

The late Bishop Ellis of Nottingham, a very dedicated pastor, told me that many bishops were bewildered by what the Holy Spirit was doing through them. He told me of bishops who had questioned their own response to the workings of the Holy Spirit. He mentioned some bishops who were physically ill as a result of the tensions. Too many people were claiming to know exactly what the Holy Spirit had in mind. But there was much wise counsel around and the bishops were quite prepared to take advice. The setting up of the Commissions in 1967 was a structural expression of their willingness to listen and when faults were found in the original structures they were quite prepared to adjust them.

Looking back on that period I cannot but admire the efforts of the bishops, trained before the Vatican Council and part of the Vatican Council, sincerely and sensitively attempting to apply the Vatican Council. The articulate Catholics voiced their commitment to renewal but with widely differing interpretations. The bishops were trying to serve everyone, including the silent majority and the one virtue which everyone saluted was integrity – and I found plenty of integrity in the Bishops of England and Wales.

The fourth reason for compiling this book is that much of that unbounded hope which stirred in the days of the Council has faded; we have forgotten how powerful it was. The days all began for the Fathers with their prayer, 'We are here before you, O Holy Spirit . . .' On the last day the papal brief was proclaimed: 'The Second Vatican Ecumenical Council, assembled in the Holy Spirit . . . must be numbered without doubt among the greatest events of the Church . . .' This hope is evident in the planning stages (as recorded by Cardinal Suenens, in Chapter 6 below) and especially in the witness of those who came close to the two Popes, and more especially to the dying Pope in his courage to 'throw the net in again' at the Lord's prompting. Pope John once said to his secretary Loris Capovilla: 'Only when a man has trampled his *ego* under his feet can he be truly free.' And that secretary pondered the super-human trust sustained by intense prayer, 'this unquenchable burning faith (by which alone) the Council could carry out its work, avoid the pitfalls, recognise the voice of the Spirit and light new pentecostal fires . . .' He wrote: '11 October 1962 is a date to enshrine in the annals of humanity . . . all had fuelled the lamp of hope . . .'

Complaining during the course of the Council about the drafts offered by the Theological Preparatory Commission, and especially the schema on Divine Revelation, Bishop Emile de Smedt of Bruges declared that this 'does not constitute an advance in dialogue with non-Catholics, but an obstacle . . . If the schemata are not drafted in a different manner, we shall be responsible for having crushed, through the Second Vatican Council, a great and immense hope. That hope is shared by all those who, with Pope John XXIII, in prayer and fasting expect that now finally some serious and notable steps will be taken in the direction of fraternal unity among all those for whom Christ our Lord prayed *ut unum sint.*' When the Bishop, a voice for the Secretariat for Promoting Christian Unity, left the microphone in the Aula, the assembly broke out in thunderous applause. Over the years that applause may seem to have diminished.

It is our hope that the contributions in this book will rekindle the early hope, demonstrate some of the fruits of Vatican Two, and help to penetrate the deeper meanings still to be explored in the Council documents.

As well as offering a witness to the Council this book is also presented as a tribute to those who took part. Many are eminent and need little introduction, but for the sake of those who have grown up since the Council, a brief background note is given on each contributor. In the course of compiling these and from correspondence and conversations with those who did not in the end write a chapter, a wealth of further detail emerged. Not all can be included, but historians of the Council may find valuable the following notes on two great popes, and two theologians.

JOHN XXIII

We know a good deal about Angelo Roncalli both as archbishop and as Pope John, largely through the writing of his secretary from 1953 till his death in 1963, Don Loris Capovilla (who gives his own witness, below); through the studies of Professor Giuseppe Alberigo, who has analysed particularly the opening speech of the Council as summing up Roncalli's whole life experience and view of history; and through the recent biography by Peter Hebblethwaite – who calls his own book 'an implicit commentary' on that speech. But we have not so far heard from Archbishop Bruno Heim, Apostolic Delegate and the Pro-Nuncio in London (1973–85), who had been secretary to Angelo Roncalli in a similar position in Paris during 1946–51, before Capovilla took over.

Archbishop Roncalli treated his secretaries as sons-spiritual, never losing their friendship. Mgr Heim took Roncalli to his own home in Switzerland several times; and equally Heim has been to Sotto il Monte to meet the Roncalli family. He remembers that all the villagers, from early days, regarded the archbishop as 'star quality', always knowing when he was expected home and turning out to the last child to greet him. Roncalli said to his secretary on an early occasion: 'Do not be upset at our village, it is not quite so clean as yours in Switzerland. But this is all part of my life; and if you would know me, you must see it. Do you see that woman over there looking like a gipsy? Well, that is my eldest sister! Tonight there will be little peace; they will all come around to talk.' That talk Roncalli considered as part of life's reality, which he – otherwise placed – considered himself privileged to be able to share.

As to talk, Mgr Heim tells a tale that seems to catch the future Pope's character well. As Nuncio, Roncalli was inclined to put kindness to others above punctuality towards his own staff. He came late one day to lunch, leaving the priests to discourse upon that point. When he did arrive a little late, their conversation ceased, and he was moved to remark: 'You are so silent: you may have been talking about your Superior. Talk on about me, do please. The priests have to give up so much – no families, no dancing, no drinking parties: their only pleasure is to talk about their parish priests and bishops, and that pleasure should not be taken away from them too!' His motto, it was said, was *omnia videre, multa dissimulare, pauca corrigere*: see all, say nought, leave well alone. He overlooked much and criticised little, complimenting when he could. His company was peaceful; he gave few orders and none that were useless, and was quick to abandon a course when it was proving fruitless or ridiculous.

Mgr Heim was invited to the pontifical coronation as part of the family. He was asked to design a coat of arms that added to the Roncalli tower the lion of Venice (which broke heraldic rules but had a precedent in Pius X). They corresponded together (in Italian), more than two dozen letters remaining in Mgr Heim's files. When they were together, a complete candour was expected on both sides – the mark of real friendship. Mgr Heim gives an early example of this gift for friendship. In 1947 in Paris they were talking together about the state of the realm, the secretary proffering his opinion: 'I think Rome is generally too passive towards other Christians. It seems to me that Popes should go out and invite those of other religions to meet them, even risking having them then spit in their faces. Instead what do they do? They sit on their thrones, waiting for such people to knock on the door and then enter tremulously on their knees; after which they say they shall think it over before they make any acceptance.' 'I know, I know', said Roncalli, 'but give it time'. Both wanted ecumenical initiatives, the secretary from his experience with Protestants, the Nuncio from his ten years in Bulgaria and ten more in Turkey with the Orthodox. So they kindled each other's hearts.

PAUL VI

Angelo Giuseppe Roncalli (1881–1963) and Giovanni Battista Montini (1897–1978) met first in Rome in 1924, there being sixteen years between them. One was fit, fat and earthy, the other was lean, frail and ethereal; one was pastoral and jovial, the other intellectual and reflective. The young Montini encouraged Roncalli over his seeming dismissal to Bulgaria for 'ten years hard'. A pattern developed, that Roncalli travelled to the periphery while Montini remained at the Secretariat of State, never out of Rome from 1924, beyond visits. Each quietly came to consult the other, the one bringing the robustness of the field, the other the precision of the head-quarters. When in 1944 Roncalli was precipitately posted to Paris, it was Montini who wrote to Cardinal Suhard, Archbishop of Paris to commend him. When some Frenchmen denounced Roncalli to Rome, it was Montini that they were addressing, who well knew Roncalli and quite well knew the French. When Roncalli wanted to plant an article in *Osservatore Romano* to defend worker-priests, he knew that he was in agreement with the young *sostituto* Secretary of State (promoted in 1937), so he did it through Montini. It was Montini who in 1953 told Roncalli that he was to be appointed Patriarch of Venice and raised to the Cardinalate; and when the new Patriarch then went to Rome, he found a sick and pre-occupied Pius XII and so chose to pour out his mind not to the older and senior *sostituto*, Domenico Tardini (later to become his own Secretary of State), but to the younger and more *simpatico* Montini.

While in Venice, Roncalli was soon writing to Montini in Rome about his initiatives in restoring the Benedictine island-abbey of San Giorgio; as well as about his involvement with the Christian Democrats. They then started writing more frequently, about Neo-Fascism in Italy, about Church politics in Rome and the wider world, about Montini's astonishing removal in 1954 to be Archbishop of Milan when Pius XII in his infirmity most had need of him. When Pope Pius finally died in 1958, it is said that the French Cardinals went to Rome with their minds divided between the old and known Roncalli and the younger and less familiar Montini, both tried as favourable towards the worker-priest movement pioneered by Henri Perrin in France. When Roncalli was elected, the first nominations he made for the Cardinalate were Montini and Tardini, the two *sostitutos* of Pius XII (in that order). Giovanni XXIII and Giovanni Battista continued to grow closer: in 1961 the Pope wrote to the Archbishop of Milan: 'I should write to everyone – bishops and Cardinals throughout the world.... But to reach them all I content myself by writing to the Archbishop of Milan; for through him I carry them in my heart, since for me he represents them all.' (At the Istituto Paolo VI there are filed some ninety communications between them.) When in 1962 Montini issued a Lenten Pastoral to his arch-diocese concerning the papal intentions for the coming Council, everyone knew that he knew the mind of the Pope, and so watched with the closest interest. They saw that the central theme would be the mystery of the Church, a Church given to renewal and dialogue.

Montini's Lenten Pastoral of 1962, entitled *Pensiamo al Concilio*, (translated in *The Church*, Montreal 1969) must have been very widely read. The copy I have used comes from the 13 box Vatican files of Bishop B. C. Butler, now in the archives of Downside Abbey; and it is one of two such documents – which suggests that many or all perceptive Council Fathers may have possessed their own such pamphlet. In his Introduction the Archbishop asks: why Rome? Because, he says, it is the city of the Church of Christ, it is the universal city, it is the city of hope (*città della Speranza*). In his *First Part*, he speaks of the universal calling: he speaks of the primacy of Peter as Pastor and Teacher with authority as Vicar of Christ; he speaks of the divine mystery of the Church, mystical body of Christ who is thereby continued in time and space in this instrument of salvific action. In his *Second Part*, he speaks of reforming the Christian life: of its radical concept (both *metanoia* and *aggiornamento*, root-change and heart-renewal); he speaks of faithfulness in the union between Christ and his Church, of the dignity of the lay vocation, the spiritual call of the people of God, and of the relationship of Christianity to society in the world. In his *Third Part* he speaks of the Church's universal salvific mission, of hope and love, of the need to be ever learning and ever praying.

The day before the Council opened (10 October 1962), Montini had given a discourse in the Campidoglio entitled *Rome and the Council*, where he had been able to eulogise Rome's vocation as both universal and eternal, and to speak of Catholic Rome's undoubted influence upon the forthcoming assembly. This is published with seven formal letters to his archdiocese from Rome during the First Session (Arcivescovado di Milano, 12 Dec 1963). He selects three themes for discussion: the Liturgy, sources of Revelation, and religious freedom. These should be considered in conjunction with his now famous letter of 18 October 1962 to the Secretary of State (and so to the Pope) on the uncontrolled conduct of the Council (see Cardinal Suenens' chapter below).

Montini held his hand in public until, on 2 December 1962, he wrote a decisive article in *L'Italia* and three days later spoke as decisively in the Aula; and after that he joined Cardinal Suenens in their virtual control of the Council's direction, in consultation with the by then evidently dying pontiff. On 1 June 1963 Montini was called to the papal bedside – a deathbed – returning that evening to Milan cathedral to pray with his people: 'Let us gather up his inheritance . . . Never before in our time has a human word rung out so loudly and won such recognition and affection throughout the whole world.' Those words, 'Let us gather up ...', were more ironic than Montini knew: the one Pope sowed, the other did gather up.

In his speech of the previous December, Montini had suggested that 'a vast amount of excellent material has been brought together, but is too disparate and uneven. A central controlling idea is needed to coordinate this immense material'. Now, as Pope Paul VI, he had to accept his own challenge; and his answer is set out in his first encyclical, *Ecclesiam suam* on The Church in the Modern World. There the new Pope set out a programme in three parts: first, *Awareness* through reflection and vigilance; secondly, *Renewal* through reform in obedience, poverty and love; thirdly, *Dialogue* through Christian presence in the world, modelling oneself on the dialogue of salvation but with a real approach to the world. These documents, from Lent 1962 to 6 August 1964, are all of a piece and should be studied as such: a full dress study is awaited (see Congar's chapter below on *Ecclesiam Suam*). Meanwhile, we might recall some words of Pope John on these same lines: 'First an approach, then a reconciliation, and finally perfect union.'

KARL RAHNER

When in mid-February 1984 'Pater Rahner' (as his friends were wont to address him) came to Heythrop College, London University to attend a lecture in his honour given by the Lady Margaret Professor of Divinity at Oxford, honouring his eightieth and last living birthday, he was called 'the world's most famous living theologian'. In tune with the insights of the Council, which he had so deeply influenced, Rahner's theological method had been to begin with a doctrine of man. From there he had coined a concept which brought him into much controversy, that of men and women who lived their lives existentially by values otherwise recognised as Christian; such people he called 'anonymous Christians'.

Born at Freiburg-im-Breisgau in 1905, Karl Rahner entered the Society of Jesus and was ordained a decade later in 1932. Studying under Martin Heidegger, he was appointed to lecture in dogmatic theology at Innsbruck, where he was Professor during 1948–64. After that, while the Council was in its last stages, he 'went home' (as he said) to succeed Romano Guardini as Professor of the Philosophy of Religion at Munich. As a working theologian, he has proven a kind of polymath; for he has made major contributions in the fields of the philosophy of religion, dogmatics, ecclesiology, hermeneutics, together with moral and pastoral theology. Naturally with

8

that range of enquiry, and being of an age to reach the height of his powers as the Council's preparation was *en train*, he made a profound contribution to Vatican II.

There are, as some say, three Rahners within the one Karl. There is the great and restless investigative theologian, whose monument is the twenty-volume collection, *Theological Investigations*; together with the five volumes of *Sacramentum Mundi* of which he was principal editor, and other such works as *Hearers of the Word* and his *Encyclopedia of theology*. Then, there is another Rahner whose influence on pastoral theology has been equally great. His distinction between the charismatic and the hierarchical elements in the Church, his defence of free speech among churchmen, his advocacy of a pastoral practice aimed at fostering personal decision rather than social conformity all attracted much attention before, during and after the Council. Then there is the priest-writer of small spiritual meditations for ordinary people.

It is the contention of Fr Ralph Wiltgen S.V.D. that two well organised groups tended to dominate Council proceedings, the German-Austrian Axis (represented as the Fulda Conference, i.e. the plenary meetings of all German bishops); and the concerted body of the religious orders, used to coordinating their efforts and easily able to communicate as bodies rather than individuals, with worldwide involvements. In his book, *The Rhine flows into the Tiber* (1967), Wiltgen takes a cool assessment. 'Since the position of the German-language bishops was regularly adopted by the European alliance, and since the alliance position was generally adopted by the Council, a single theologian might have his views accepted by the whole Council if they had been accepted by the German-speaking bishops. There was such a theologian: Fr Karl Rahner S.J. Technically, Fr Rahner was Cardinal König's consultant theologian. In practice, he was consulted by many members of the German and Austrian hierarchies; and he might well be called the most influential mind at the Fulda Conference. Cardinal Frings in a private conversation, called Fr Rahner 'the greatest theologian of the century'. The extent to which the bishops of Germany and Austria, and the entire Fulda Conference, leaned on Fr Rahner may be gauged by comparing his original observations with those submitted to the General Secretariat of the Council.'

At a later stage, Wiltgen returns to the effect of the German alliance on the process of the Council. He says of Cardinal Frings that 'except for the organisation which he had inspired and led, the Council might never have operated efficiently at all. He had leaned heavily upon the theologian Rahner; but by the end of the Council, he had come to be more cautious in accepting his proposals. Joseph Ratzinger, the personal theologian of Cardinal Frings and former student of Rahner, had seemed to give an almost unquestioning support to the views of his former teacher during the Council. But as it was drawing to a close, he too admitted that he disagreed on various points, and said he would begin to assert himself more after the Council was over.' Ratzinger had been wont to work in team with two Jesuit ecclesiologists, Aloys Grillmeier and Otto Semmelroth, both disciples of Rahner in the Society. The rest is told by another such disciple, Herbert Vorgrimler, Chapter 3 below.

YVES CONGAR

In Paris on 24 November 1984, on the occasion of the twelfth anniversary of the promulgation of the Decree on Ecumenism, the Franciscan Friars of the Atonement conferred on Père Yves Congar OP of Le Saulchoir-Couvent Saint-Jacques the Christian Unity Award for that year. It had gone to Cardinal Bea in 1965, to Archbishop Michael Ramsey in 1972 and to ARCIC I as a body in 1974. Frail as he was, Congar made a considerable speech from his Paris sick room, asking 'Quelles diversités sont possibles dans la communion?' He recalled that *Chrétiens désunis* had been the theme of his conferences delivered at Montmartre for the Week of Unity in January 1936. He might have recalled that in the summer of 1928 the subject of his lectoral thesis had been 'The unity of the Church'; and that from then on he had begun to dedicate himself, especially at his ordination in 1930, to the Church's unity, realising that that was his true vocation.

In 1935, Congar founded the series of publications, *Unam Sanctam* to elucidate current Church problems. (By 1964, fifty such volumes had been published, the latest by him.) In 1937, Congar's first book had such an impact that thereafter Catholic ecumenism had to have its record divided: 'before *Chrétiens désunis* and 'after *Chrétiens désunis*'! He became lionised, and for the sake of ecumenism responded: contributing to journals in France, Germany, England and America; participating in international conferences; preaching endlessly, especially in Unity Week.

At Saulchoir he organised a 'Groupe de Catholicité'; and from there many ecumenical meetings. The first and then most important occurred at Bièvres (Rochedieu) during 1–5 March 1937, preparing Catholics for the Oxford Life and Work Conference in July – to which he was, of course, invited. He did not go, being refused by Cardinal Pacelli, the future Pius XII: 'This was the first of a series of rebuffs I was to encounter'. Then he writes: 'From the autumn of 1946 onwards, I entered a danger zone of suspicion and supervision, together with my best friends and collaborators (notably Père Chenu O.P.). In point of fact, I had been in this position already as early as 1939.' In that year he had been called to account by the Master General of his Order for publishing a French text of Möhler's *L'Unité dans l'Eglise* (*Unam Sanctam*, Paris 1938) and for 'difficulties' in his own great book. When he wanted to bring out a revised enlarged edition, he was clearly discouraged.

Congar found himself imprisoned by the Nazis, indeed in Colditz for a while. He returned in May 1945. With the Church in France 'in one of its finest moments', he rediscovered that the future of the Church is linked with the future of the world – a presage of *Gaudium et Spes*. He caught up the lost years and drafted *Vraie et fausse réforme dans l'Eglise* (*Unam Sanctam* 72, Paris 1950; 2 ed 1969), an ecclesiological survey of sixteenth-century Reform. He began looking eastwards with Istina, to the Orthodox and then 'from the beginning of 1947 to the end of 1956 I knew nothing from (Rome) but an uninterrupted series of denunciations, warnings, restrictive and discriminatory measures and mistrustful interventions'. Articles were withdrawn and ecumenical meetings cancelled. Making a hundred changes to *Chrétiens désunis* and rewriting two chapters, Congar submitted his new edition for censorship to his General, who waited two years until the encyclical *Humani generis* (1950) on False Teaching and then returned it with a warning about 'false eirenism'.

In the mid fifties three French Provincials were dismissed, Chenu and other scholars were warned, and Congar was summoned to his Master General. He was 'sent' to Jerusalem where he wrote *Le mystère du Temple* (Cerf 1958), which required seven censors and over three years before it could be published. On return in September 1954, Congar was summoned to Rome, and then in November he was dismissed to Cambridge for a year, suffering 'odious restrictions on my ministrations and movements, especially to houses of study; I could not entirely avoid contact with Anglicans but they had to be restricted to a minimum and no ecumenical questions could be discussed'. A tale is told in Oxford of Congar sitting on the wall at the other end of St Giles from St Benet's Hall (where I now write) – on the wall, that is, of St John's College -- eating his meagre sandwich lunch. He looked across that boulevard to Blackfriars, where he was to reside but not to trouble the Dominican student friars or use their library. He reflected: *Et Lazarus similiter mala.*

He returned to France in December 1955 'and was assigned to a monastery at Strasbourg in which I am now writing these memoirs. I must confess that for the last ten years (to 1964), my contributions to ecumenism have been meagre . . . The chief work (now) to be done is that of an inner renewal, ecclesiological, anthropological and pastoral . . . More and more I am combining theology with history . . . Deficiencies in our ecclesiology will not be discovered and overcome till we have made a thorough historical study of doctrines and patterns of behaviour that have become habitual to us all. This has been my main contribution to the cause (of the Church) in the last ten years'.

Congar's influence upon the process of the Council was considerable: at least five of the Decrees bear his mark. Among his books, one that particularly influenced the Council Fathers was *Lay People in the Church* (1953 and 1964; reissued Geoffrey Chapman 1985). Many books and articles have appeared since.

'Vatican II' was the twenty-first of the General Councils. Beyond Catholicism it has been argued that there have been no Oecumenical Councils since the Photian Schism divided the East from the West, the last such – of the *Oekumene*, 'the whole inhabited world' – being the Seventh, Nicaea II in 787. Vatican II was fundamentally different from the others: it was in no way secret, but open to Observers from the rest of Christendom, and to guests of the Secretariat for Promoting Christian Unity, and partially to the world's very curious press. It had the active participation of up to 2540 prelates and that is about four times the number of any other Council save Vatican I. It was professionally prepared by ten Preparatory Commissions and two Secretariats: and fuelled by experts drawn from the Church's great scholars who were crucially able to affect, if not direct, events. It was conducted in a blaze of publicity, all four Sessions in 1962, 1963, 1964 and 1965 being subject to detailed narrative and analysis in contemporary books, articles and debate; and to studies afterwards. It covered a far greater mass of issues, doctrinal and pastoral, than any Council before it; and, in so doing, it dealt not combatively or correctively with heresies and crises, but congenially and reflectively with the growth subjects of the age, attending to 'the signs of the times'. Its deliberations were promulgated to the whole world in every language of serious thought, *The documents of Vatican II* becoming a *vade mecum* for study alongside the new translations and commentaries upon holy Scripture. Two Dogmatic and two Pastoral Constitutions, nine Decrees and three Declarations became the best known documents of the living Church – and not without cause, for they were among the finest teaching that any one generation had been privileged to receive from its pastors.

Rather than try to gauge the shifts of thought that this Council represents, from a juridical Church to a mystery/sacrament Church, from obedient faithful to co-responsible faithful, from *contemptus mundi* to sanctification of matter, from salvation as fidelity and moral excellence to salvation as involvement with Christ as creating the whole of his world, let us look lastly and more lightly at other 'goings on' in Rome at the time. Dr Donal Kerr from St Benet's Hall, Oxford, now Professor of Church History at St Patrick's College Maynooth, was present on the fringes. This is the picture of vast stimulation that he gives from his memory of it all:

The importance of the fringe activity was never greater. At one stage many of the Council Fathers had to go to school again to acquaint themselves with the new terminology that theology was using. Experts real and pseudo thronged to Rome to listen and give their own opinion on the great debates; and by their comments they undoubtedly influenced the decisions of the Council. In the last three Sessions every single document was debated at these meetings. When the Eucharist was debated I went one day to hear Fr Francis Clarke give a conservative exposé of the doctrine. The next night it was to hear a brilliant exposé of the progressive view. This time it was Edouard Schillebeeckx OP, who put forward the idea of 'transfinalisation' and 'transignification', attributing this new theological breakthrough to de Bacciochi, then sitting next to me, of whose presence at the lecture Schillebeeckx was unaware.

A few days later we went to hear Henri de Lubac SJ enthuse about the first chapter of *Dei Verbum* – the crown jewel of the Council's documents. A while later it was a brilliant exposé of Indulgences by, I seem to recollect, Gregory Baum OSA. Was it he who at that conference, when questioned about such things as forty days and forty quarantines, dismissed them with the answer that they had had a good innings? One of the most crowded meetings I attended was for a conference given by Hans Küng whose winning and persuasive manner captivated the audience. Rahner was speaking elsewhere and perhaps Ratzinger too. The trouble was to fit in all that one wanted to hear: some wise organisations, especially those of the progressive wing circulated lists of forthcoming talks. Rome was one big theological 'think-in' or at least 'listen-in'.

Very many of the Council fathers attended these meetings. Indeed when I drove down from Monte Verde it was always in the company of three or four bishops, unless a Session was on. The fringe-activities formed an important part of Vatican II – providing the fathers with an insight into new theological jargon and both influencing daily opinion and, of course, being influenced by it. Though we did not realise it then, we were present at perhaps the greatest and most comprehensive theological concourse the Christian world has seen.

Lastly, let us return light-heartedly to the ecumenical dimension. There is a tale told by Margaret, widow of Canon Bernard Pawley, who was one of the Anglican Observers at the Council, as the Archbishop of Canterbury's first representative in Rome. She developed a sound test of the progress of ecumenism in those years: the progress of the clergy wives. At the opening of the First Session on 11 October 1962, no wives were invited at all. At the closing of that Session wives were indeed invited, but they were given seats far in the distance and neither books nor kneelers. At the opening of the Second Session on 29 September 1963, wives were invited, and markedly further forward. At the closing of that Session, they were further forward still and granted a kneeler. 'Thereafter', she told me 'we moved further forward – as in grandmother's footsteps – and were progressively given kneelers and then books'.

The prayer, *Adsumus* 'We are here before you, O Holy Spirit' perhaps equally applies to the gathering up of these chapters on the Council twenty years later. The result, the reader will surely agree, is a benign accident of balance and depth; and the more is this apparent when one recalls those who were asked to contribute but found themselves unable, for various reasons: pressure of work, poor health, a certain diffidence.

Letters of regret came from Cardinals Alfrink of Utrecht, Dearden of Detroit, Martini of Milan and Volk of Mainz; from Rome Cardinals Hamer of the Congregation for Religious and Ratzinger of the Congregation for the Doctrine of the Faith and Piero Rossano of the Lateran University; from Archbishop Sir Guilford Young of Hobart; Bishop Alan Clark of East Anglia, Mgr Joseph Baker of St Louis, Fr Pierre Duprey, recently promoted Secretary of SPCU, Rabbi Marc Tannenbaum of the American Jewish Committee, Dom Godfrey Diekmann of St John's Abbey, Collegeville, Minnesota and Abbé René Laurentin.

Of those who had earnestly hoped to contribute, Bishop Christopher Butler, at the time of the Council Abbot of Downside, and President of the English Benedictine Congregation wrote: 'I am quite doubtful whether at my age (I am now in my eighties) I can recover the situation as you would wish it to be: Vatican II was a turning point in my life . . .' He has however, graciously recommended our book in the Introductory Letter we reproduce. Bishop Gerard Mahon M.H.M. proposed an article on the lines of 'Partners in mission'; but he found that much of his thunder had been stolen by Bishop Donal Lamont's fine account. He had asked himself (and his paper might have given answers): 'How shall ecumenical collaboration actually be practised in the real situations on the mission field? What is the relationship between dialogue and evangelisation? Where should the Church stand in the struggle for liberation?' *Ad Gentes* had at least made it possible, he said, to ask these questions; and twenty years ago perhaps that was already an achievement. Fr John M. Oesterreicher of the Institute of Judaeo-Christian Studies, New Jersey chose to send a privately printed treatise he had had published on his eightieth birthday: 'The rediscovery of Judaism: a re-examination of the Conciliar Statement on the Jews', quite excellent but at sixty pages, too long. A visit to the 89-year-old Cardinal Henri de Lubac S.J. at the rue de Grenelle, Paris brought an exciting and most animated hour of discussion, a general enthusiasm and then a later regret that someone entering his tenth decade should talk, yes, but not write.

Others who have helped in gathering these chapters together should also be thanked: Mrs Marly Soltek of Cologne (who knew Karl Rahner, with her family); Karl-Heinz Weger S.J. of Munich, familiar with the Rahner papers; Dom Philippe Bär, now Bishop of Rotterdam; the late Mgr Richard (Dick) Stewart of SPCU; Fr Michael Sharkey, Congregation for Catholic Education, Rome; Fr Gerald O'Collins S.J., Dean of Theology at the Gregorian University; Anne Boyd, Chief Editor of Geoffrey Chapman, who made the initial invitation and sustained it.

St Benet's Hall
Oxford
October 1985

PART ONE

THE TWENTY-FIRST
ECUMENICAL COUNCIL
OF THE CHURCH

1

A COUNCIL FOR ALL PEOPLES

MARIE-DOMINIQUE CHENU OP

Perhaps it takes a theologian born in the last century to feel how great have been the changes in the Church from a theology of man that saw men and women patiently waiting for redemption in an alien world, to one that sees them in the homeland of their redeeming – becoming redeemed and sharing in the work of the Redeemer. For instance, if we cast our eye upon the last and longest of the conciliar Constitutions and Decrees, Gaudium et Spes, *we find a whole new mood: 'The joys and hopes, the griefs and anxieties of the men of this age [are those] of the followers of Christ.' The part that deals, for instance, with fostering the nobility of marriage and the family has a section on 'The sanctity of marriage and the family' (sec. 48) and another on conjugal love (sec. 49): these alone represent the first occasion on which a General Council has vindicated the goodness of the physical state of married life. The Council documents are full of these great innovations. Père Chenu does us a service in extolling them.*

The depth of his appreciation is evident if we recall a little book he wrote in 1937, Une école de théologie: Le Saulchoir, *which found its way on to the Index of Prohibited Books just twenty years before the Council. In it, Père Chenu insisted on the value of historical studies in interpreting theology and dogma. He wrote: 'Understanding a text or doctrine is inseparable from knowing the setting in which they originated, for the simple reason that the insight which produced them is encountered in the context, literary, cultural, philosophical, theological, spiritual, in which they take shape.' He went on: 'It is the human condition to have mind only in a body, and to express unchangeable truth only in the history where it becomes incarnate.' Recognizing the anti-Protestant and anti-rationalist character of a Catholic theology too long shaped in apologetic and polemic, he called for 'le retour aux sources', what the Council was to advocate especially in relation to Scripture and the Fathers (cf.* Perfectae caritatis, *sec. 2). In his own discipline, Thomism, he asked that the historical context should be reconstructed, so as to understand thinker and thought in its proper context: 'It is good Thomism to do the history of Thomas's thought – to see his soul united to its body.' Early Council schemata failed to perceive that; later ones took the message.*

Père Chenu was born at Soisy-sur-Seine on 7 January 1895. He studied at the Angelicum in Rome under Garrigou-Lagrange then taught at Le Saulchoir, the French Dominican House of Studies, at that time in Belgium. He was particularly interested in the historical context of Thomas Aquinas and Thomism but the small book Le Saulchoir *which presented these ideas was suspected of Modernism and withdrawn. In 1962 he was invited to advise the French-speaking African bishops at the Council. His best known work in English is* Towards understanding St Thomas *(1964).*

19

There are, I find, a large number of Christians who are very well informed on the content and proceedings of Vatican II, and who assent to its decisions, but who nevertheless say that, in their view, the Council had too little to say on the subject of God. There is something in this statement, but it is clearly somewhat ambiguous. It stems from a particular, explicit or implicit, conception of Christian doctrine as focused on God as God, rather than on the Man-God Christ, upon God as involved in the history of humanity. Such a conception leads to a certain dismissiveness toward the earthly setting in which the Christian 'economy' is worked out, coupled with an over-valuation of a supernatural which does not concern itself greatly with specific analyses of human situations, and for which such analyses are seen as already a contamination of doctrinal purity. Of course Vatican I, which took place in the climate of deism then widespread in the world and in the Church, accorded better with such a conception. For example: the word 'Gospel' (*evangelium*) and its derivates 'evangelize', 'evangelization', appear some two hundred times in the texts of Vatican II, but only three or four times in those of Vatican I – a shift in vocabulary that provides a striking illustration of the difference between the two Councils. There is a definite pluralism of theologies and spiritualities within the homogeneity of doctrine in the abstract.

If the humanization of God is the constant axis of the theology of Vatican II, it is natural that man should be the common denominator of its analyses and decisions. Once God becomes man, man becomes the measure of everything (as Karl Barth said), including the Word of God, since God now speaks the language of men. We can now, with careful reading, perceive the nerve centres of the deliberations and pronouncements of Vatican II. There are many of these, but let us take a few examples.

The first and most notable is the way the Pastoral Constitution *Gaudium et Spes* (on the Church in the Modern World) is headed by a long psychological and sociological analysis of the situation of mankind in the modern world. This is the first time in history that a Council has 'introduced' (the text is called an 'Introductory Statement') its doctrinal and institutional position by referring to the actual situation of the world. This is because this Constitution is built not on recourse to the eternal verities come down from heaven, but on constant reference to the dynamic of a 'new age' that calls the statements of faith into question. For the first time, the Church defines its own mystery through and in the movement of the world, in which it finds the setting for its existence and its self-understanding. By seeking the world, the Church comes out of itself in order to be itself: the then Cardinal Montini made this undertaking clear from the first session of the Council, and the Council made its overall intention quite plain in this Introductory Statement: 'Hence the pivotal point of our total presentation will be man himself, whole and entire, body and soul, heart and conscience, mind and will' (n.3). This can be seen quantitatively, in that the words *homo* and *humanitas* occur more than two hundred times in this great text. So even one of the most conservative prelates at Vatican II, Cardinal Colombo of Milan, was moved to state: 'Vatican II is the Council of man'.

The plan for this Constitution had originally been worked out by starting from faith in the Christ Man-God; from where, by deduction, the properties that should constitute human perfection according to this divine model were defined. But this first draft was promptly rejected, since it went against the general drift, which began with man. What is this 'man' for the Council?

Without trying to extract a coherent treatise on the subject from the conciliar texts, we can, I think, find some key points, which will immediately be seen to be an expression of the characteristic features, sensibilities, aspirations and utopian hopes of mankind in this period, 1950–1970.

Man is not presented primarily in his psychological and moral individuality, but in his congenital commitment to the whole universe, whose energies he is gradually discovering and exploiting. Through the will of the Creator, he plays an active and conscious role, a role that is constantly increasing, in the building-up of the world, of which he is both manager and tenant, an enterprise in which he finds his own perfecting. This is the benefit of industrial society, whose spread has transformed working conditions as well as expanding man's cultural horizons. Previously, the Church had based its diagnosis and teaching on social matters on considerations of an artisan and peasant society alone, thereby, as Paul VI was to complain at the Council, losing touch, distancing itself from communion on the human and the Christian level, with the 'new man' and both his achievements and his failures. Now, at least in principle, this gap is to be bridged: man is exalted, given a dignity that associates him with the Creator. Instead of the resigned pessimism which imbued both mainstream teaching and pastoral practice, a newly confident optimism radiates from the very words and phrases of this Christian sociology, strengthening the hopes and prayers of the Assembly.

Today, twenty years later, the socio-economic depression has overturned this diagnosis and forced both the Church and the world in general to be more cautious in their exaltation of man, to have a lively mistrust of the effects of technocracy. Yet we can still echo the words of John Paul, in his address to UNESCO (3 June 1980): 'I want to proclaim my admiration in

21

the face of the creative richness of the human spirit, of its unceasing efforts to understand and affirm the identity of man, of that man who is always present in every manifestation of culture.'

It is thanks to the extraordinary efficacy of this meeting between man and nature that the earlier conception of man, atrophied in a spirituality that divorced matter from spirit, body from soul, has been overthrown. This dualism, inherited from the followers of Augustine and nourished by Cartesian philosophy, had for several centuries dominated the prevailing forms of spirituality, the ordinary teaching of the Magisterium and clerical preaching. At the height of scholasticism, Thomas Aquinas had reacted against this idealism and taught the dignity of matter, of the body, of sexuality: this alas without much success, despite his official approval, as witness the history of spirituality and Christian morality in the West. Leaving aside Teilhard de Chardin's *Hymne de l'univers*, and without making reference to Thomas Aquinas, the Council has done better to place man at a point of consubstantiality of matter and spirit. A benefit that has not only reconciled faith and technological culture, but has gone right to the roots of popular spirituality. This is perhaps not the least of the Council's achievements.

A second effect of industrial civilization is that the intensive socialization of production, distribution and ownership of goods, in mutual loyalty, in cultural sharing, in the relations between rich and poor nations, sheds an intense light on the fact that man is social by nature, in his very being. After several centuries of individualism, which included Christian personalism, a lively consciousness of the collective needs which henceforth will condition human perfectibility and which already affect human security, has grown up. Old-style liberal régimes have had to give way to this pressure, and the Magisterium of the Church has embraced this process of socialization, previously condemned by Pius XII (so late as that). For Christians, the notion of 'neighbour' has been transformed, now going beyond the interplay of interpersonal relationships to an understanding of the overall common good. The Council took note of this evolution and analysed the reasons for it and its consequences in a fine chapter in the Constitution *Gaudium et Spes* (Part I, ch. II) under the new heading 'The Community of Mankind'. The breadth of this view of humanity, throughout the growth of history, is ratified, so to speak, at the summit, consecrated by a theology of the incarnate Word, who took part in the dynamics of this human solidarity. Here, as Pius XI said earlier, the theological virtue of charity takes on its political dimension, as we can see in practice every day.

In a logical sequence, it is the Church's evangelizing mission itself which finds its setting and its guidelines in this meeting with the world and the riches of human civilization. Faith will now be transmitted through and in a communion of living exchanges between the world and the Church. What governs human affairs becomes the law of evangelization. The Constitution devotes a whole section (sec. 44) to a description of this process of mutual benefit: taking on the mental attributes of various forms of human culture, it says, will enable the people of God to hear, distinguish and interpret the many voices of the age, so that revealed truth can be set forth to greater advantage. So, in opposition to a false apostolic supernaturalism, the Council sees the infinitely varied and contingent development of human communities becoming, for both individuals and societies, the ground in which the seed of the Good News is to be sown. Anyone who promotes the human community, even if he is antagonistic to the Church, is contributing indeed to the coming of the Kingdom (sec. 44).

And so on, throughout the insights and directives of the Council. The process was not carried through without provoking scruples and misgivings on the part of some who saw this exaltation of man as tinged with naturalism. This is why, in the closing session of the Council, Pope Paul VI, who had constantly supported the elaboration of this teaching, devoted one of his last addresses to a reaffirmation of the theme (7 December 1965):

> The Church of the Council has not rested content with reflecting on its own nature and the ties that link it to God: it has also devoted a lot of attention to man, to man as he really is in our time: living man, man entirely bound up in himself, man who sees himself not only as the centre of all his concerns, but who dares to claim to be the underlying principle and final reason behind all existence . . . The religion of the God who made himself man has met with the religion (for it is that) of man who has made himself God. And what has come out of it? A collision, a struggle, an anathema? This could have happened, but it has not. The old story of the Samaritan has been the model for the spirituality of the Council. A limitless sympathy has quite taken hold of it. The discovery of human needs (which become greater as the sons of earth become greater) has absorbed the attentions of our Synod. At least, you modern humanists who deny the transcendence of the supreme realities, recognize this merit in it, and learn to recognize our new humanism: we too, we more than anyone, pay homage to man.

By way of conclusion, a word from Pope John Paul II's first encyclical: 'Man, actual man, is the way of the Church.' For more than a century, we had been told the opposite!

2

CATHOLICS AND PROTESTANTS: AN ECUMENICAL INVENTORY

HANS KÜNG

In 1962, on the eve of the Council, an Oxford journal, The Old Palace, *ran a special number asking views from non-Catholics. The Anglican, Canon Roger Greenacre; the Baptist writer, Rev Ernest Payne CH; and the Congregationalist, Rev John Huxtable, all warmly cited one book – The Council and reunion by Hans Küng (Sheed & Ward Stagbook 1961). The then Archbishop of Canterbury, Geoffrey Fisher, said of it: 'You should look at it! I have never read such a book in my life!' The Church Times called it 'a noble book'. Introducing the German edition, Cardinal Dr Franz König had written: 'It is a happy omen to find a theologian responding to the stimulus provided by the Holy Father ... to see, with his help, in all loyalty to the Church, the perspectives that are opening before us concerning the divisions in Christendom and the hopes offered by the coming Council.' Introducing the French edition, Cardinal Achille Liénart had written: 'There are many Christians of all communions who long for that unity which Jesus Christ willed, and who place in the coming Council their hopes that a way may be opened to it. They will be happy to discover from this book how the Catholic Church, working throughout for her own renewal, can usefully contribute to the return of unity, in common adherence to "the truth which frees".'*

The fortunes of the harbinger of the Council have fluctuated since 1961. It might be best – on the principle, nihil nisi bonum – *to remind ourselves that, while Fr Küng has recently encountered disapproval from the Sacred Congregation for the Doctrine of the Faith, Dr Küng has more recently met the approval of the University of Cambridge, who on 13 June 1985 gave him the signal honour of its highest honorary degree, that of Doctor of Divinity. This is an English paraphrase of the Greek and Latinity of the Cambridge Orator:*

> 'And there appeared a great wonder.' Not least among the wonders of our irreligious age is a scholar whose numerous lengthy and learned works of theology have become best-sellers in many languages and whose lectures have held audiences of thousands enraptured in all parts of the globe. Born in Switzerland, educated for the priesthood in Rome, author at twenty-nine of a book on the teaching of Karl Barth which showed so profound an understanding of its subject that the elder theologian could scarely believe that its author was a man so young; appointed professor of theology three years later, then consultant theologian to the Second Vatican Council, which he prayed would be the harbinger of a new era for his Church; thereafter, by his writings, issued in unbroken stream during more then twenty years, he has sealed his reputation in the eyes of scholars and gladdened and illumined the hearts of believers. He has that supreme gift of expressing clearly what others feel but cannot so well express; he has helped those of his own faith to see their Church in a clearer light and those of other faiths to look with fresh

hope to the reunion of all Churches. Some call him controversial: but in his controversy is a deep engagement with the questions which most urgently confront mankind. Some call him radical: but in his radicalism is an unswerving desire to reach to the roots, to see the truth of the Gospel unclouded by false tradition. Some call him a rebel: but in his rebellion is the expression of his loyalty to his faith. I should say of him, rather, that he has taken as his watchword this precept of St Paul: 'Examine all things: hold fast that which is good.'

I present to you

HANS KÜNG

Professor Ordinarius of Ecumenical Theology and Director of the Institute for Ecumenical Research, University of Tübingen.

The pressures of other work prevented Dr Küng from contributing a new article to the present volume but he expressed his good will by directing us to an article published (by Doubleday N.Y.) in 1978 in a collection entitled Signposts for the Future. *Since Küng's 'ecumenical inventory' is still relevant we reproduce it here.*

We hear complaints in the churches today that an increasing number of Christians are not at ease in any of the Christian churches and tend to form a kind of 'third denomination', without attachment to a church. But how are we to cope with this ecclesial 'homelessness' if the churches themselves are not becoming more impartial, more flexible, more hospitable also toward each other? For most people today the denominational differences arising from the Reformation have become completely irrelevant. Formerly Catholics knew Protestants only from hearsay and vice versa, while now the members of different denominations are in more or less close contact with one another. Under these circumstances many Christians ascribe the maintenance of the schism to unenlightened, inflexible ecclesiastics and their theologians intent on retaining power. Are they completely wrong in this opinion?

Certainly we cannot ignore *what has hitherto been achieved*. A survey of the ecumenical movement provides scarcely a hint of the labour, tenacity, hope against hope, which were necessary for decades in order merely to get the World Council of Churches established (1948). From a survey of Catholic ecumenism also we can only surmise what efforts and personal sacrifice it cost a few Catholic lay people and theologians, undaunted by the anti-ecumenical attitude of the popes up to Pius XII, to prepare for the breakthrough of the Catholic Church to ecumenicity under John XXIII and the Second Vatican Council (1962–65).

It is due to all these untiring efforts – against the background of cruel nationalistic experiences of 'Christian' peoples in two World Wars – that relations between the churches claiming to follow Jesus Christ have been turned into something positive. And if we look even further back, to the Reformation period, we can see how much the Catholic view of Martin

Luther's personality has changed. We can also note the change of temper in Catholic and Protestant 'controversial theology': the early polemic gave way to attempts to bring out the differences in the official teaching of the denominations, with the result that subjective polemics were overcome and an 'ecumenical' theology emerged. Which means that the churches and their theologies have travelled a long way from denunciation and inquisition to communication and discussion, from denominational coexistence to ecumenical co-operation.

It is true that the Catholic Church in particular has not yet joined the World Council of Churches and presents special difficulties for an ecumenical agreement because of its tradition, teaching, and organization (and especially the primacy and infallibility of the pope). But the fact cannot be overlooked that, in comparison with the post-Tridentine, Counter-Reformation Church – despite all compromises – the basic trend of the Second Vatican Council amounted to a turn of 180 degrees in the direction of ecumenicity. Despite all the remaining unresolved problems (birth control, divorce, ministry, mixed marriages, celibacy, primacy, and infallibility), the concrete *positive results* must not be underestimated. They also provoke *further questions* – to be at least briefly indicated here – to the other churches.

1. Since the Second Vatican Council, what has changed *for Christendom as a whole*?

a. The Catholic *share of guilt* for the schism is now recognized. At the same time the necessity of continual *reform* is accepted: *Ecclesia semper reformanda* – continual renewal of our own Church in life and teaching according to the gospel. But the further question arises: May the other churches then regard themselves as in no need of reform (Orthodox Church) or even as already reformed (Lutheran and Calvinist churches), or are they also still to be reformed?

b. The other Christian communities are *recognized as churches*. In all churches there is a common Christian basis which is perhaps more important than everything that divides them. But again the question arises: Ought there not to be a more intense effort to find the common Christian basis and 'substance' also in the other churches?

c. An *ecumenical attitude* is required from the whole Church. There must be an inward conversion of Catholics themselves, a growth of mutual understanding between the churches and a readiness to learn by dialogue, a recognition of the faith, the baptism, the values of other Christians, finally a theology and church history worked out in an ecumenical spirit. But there is a further question: Will the other churches then, for their part, also recognize and realize the numerous Catholic concerns in theology, liturgy, and church structures?

d. *Co-operation* with other Christians is to be promoted in every way. There must be practical collaboration in the whole social field, but also prayer together and increasingly a united worshipping community – especially in the liturgy of the word – and finally discussion between theologians of equal standing. Here, too, a further question must be faced: Ought not the other churches also to develop more strongly a readiness to co-operate?

2. What has changed in regard to the *churches of the Reformation* since the Second Vatican Council? A whole series of concerns which were central to the Reformers have been accepted at least in principle by the Catholic Church.

a. *A new appreciation of the Bible:* (i) In worship: Proclamation, prayer, and hymns should all bear the imprint of a biblical spirit; a new and more varied cycle of Scripture readings covering a number of years has been produced. (ii) In the life of the Church as a whole: Instead of insistence on the Latin Vulgate translation there is now a demand for modern translations of the Bible from the original text; instead of the former prohibition of Bible reading by the laity there are now repeated invitations to read the Bible frequently. (iii) In theology: The Church's magisterium is not above God's word but exists to serve the latter; it is no longer the universal teaching of the Church that revealed truth is contained 'partly' in Scripture and 'partly' in tradition; the study of Scripture must be the 'soul' of theology (and of catechetics), the justification of the historical-critical interpretation of Scripture is recognized, the inerrancy of Scripture is claimed not for statements on natural science but only for truths of salvation.

b. *Genuine people's worship:* the realization of the concerns of the Reformers can be seen in a number of examples: (i) As against the former clerical liturgy, there is a service involving the whole priestly people through an intelligible structure and active participation of the whole congregation in common prayer, singing and meal. (ii) As against the former proclamation in the alien Latin language, there is a new attention to the word of God proclaimed in the vernacular. (iii) As against the standardized, uniform Roman liturgy, there is adaptation to the different nations; national episcopates with shared competence instead of the formerly exclusive papal competence. (iv) As against the former proliferation and concealment, there is now simplification and concentration on essentials: revision of all rites and thus a greater similarity between the Mass and the last supper of Jesus. (v) There is reform also of the liturgy of the sacraments, of the church year, of the breviary. (vi) Included in all this is a positive settlement of classical points of controversy (vernacular and the chalice for the laity are likewise permitted in principle).

c. *Revaluation of the laity:* Direct access of the laity to the Scriptures and the realization of the people's worship are themselves an important fulfilment of this third concern of the Reformers. In addition, there are numerous theological publications on the importance of the laity in the Church, with an implicit criticism of clericalism; every bishop is expected to set up a pastoral council consisting of priests and lay people.

d. *Adaptation of the Church to the nations:* As against a centralized system, the importance of the local churches and the particular churches (dioceses, nations) is stressed; national and continental conferences of bishops are to promote practical decentralization; the Roman Curia itself is to be internationalized.

e. *Reform of popular piety:* There has been a reform of fasting regulations, of indulgences and devotional practices. Restrictions have been imposed on the excesses of Marian devotion (the Second Vatican Council set up clear limits in this respect by rejecting a separate document on Mary); nor was any additional Marian dogma promulgated.

This largely completed realization of the concerns of the Reformers again raises further questions. Should not the Protestant churches now make it their business to approach Catholics effectively with more self-critical understanding? To put it quite concretely –

appreciation of the Bible, certainly: but where does Protestantism stand in regard to its neglect of the common tradition of the early Church and of the Middle Ages?

genuine liturgy of the word and people's worship, certainly: but what of the celebration of the eucharist, thrust into the background or even practically excluded in Protestant churches?

revaluation of the laity, certainly: but what of the importance of ordination and the Church's ministry (also beyond the limits of a particular region)?

adaptation to the nations, certainly: but what of the international and universal character of the Church, so often put in question by Protestant provincialism?

reform of popular piety, certainly: but what of the closeness of the Church and its worship to the people, often imperilled by Protestant intellectualism?

3. What has changed in regard to the *Eastern churches*, which have often been regarded as merely an appendage of the Latin Church? Since Vatican II the churches of the East have been expressly recognized as enjoying equal rights with those of the West. Rebaptism is not required of Orthodox Christians who become Catholics, nor are Orthodox priests expected to be reordained, and celibacy is not imposed on them. If they want to do so, Orthodox Christians may receive the sacraments in Catholic churches; on the other hand, if no Catholic priest is available, Catholics may receive the sacraments in Orthodox churches. Mixed marriages between Catholics and Orthodox are valid, even if they are not contracted in Catholic churches. Ought not all these things to hold also with reference to the Protestant churches? Immediately before the close of the council there took place simultaneously in Rome and Constantinople the solemn revocation of the mutual excommunication of 1054, which had inaugurated the schism between East and West, lasting almost a thousand years. But does not this very act require both sides to face its consequences, particularly in regard to the eucharistic community? The Orthodox Churches remained far too static, rigidly holding to the position not of the primitive Church but of the Byzantine centuries. Ought not they also to have roused themselves to a serious reform of their liturgy, theology, and church structures? But on the other hand the Catholic Church rigidly upheld the primacy of jurisdiction and papal infallibility in its relations with the Orthodox churches. Ought we not honestly to re-examine both questions in the light of the New Testament and the common early church tradition, instead of refusing to discuss these points of doctrine?

In fact, as even Pope Paul VI has admitted, the *papacy* with its absolute claim is the main difficulty in the way of ecumenical agreement. But is an agreement on this subject possible at all? Yes, if (a) the papal *primacy* is understood less as a primacy of honour or jurisdiction and more as a pastoral primacy in the service of the unity of the Church as a whole; (b) papal infallibility is understood as the function of witnessing and proclaiming in the service of the 'infallibility' or, better, 'indefectibility' – that is, of the indestructibility – of the Church in truth, despite all errors in detail.

The rest of the doctrinal differences with reference to Scripture and tradition, grace and justification, Church and sacraments may be regarded as largely settled in theological terms. The situation can be summed up briefly and systematically. Today the primacy of *Scripture* as the original Christian testimony (normative norm) prior to all later *tradition* is acknowledged also by Catholic theology and, on the other hand, the importance of post-biblical tradition (regulated norm) is admitted at least in principle by

29

Protestant theology. Justification in virtue of faith alone is affirmed by Catholic theologians, just as the necessity of works or deeds of love is affirmed by Protestant theologians.

Fortunately, much more has happened among the ordinary people in the churches. Mutual understanding today in a large number of Catholic, Protestant, and Orthodox congregations has increased to an extent formerly inconceivable. There is intercommunion already among many groups. This actually living ecumenicity at the base is more important for the future than all theological controversies and all finely spun ecclesiastical diplomacy. Nevertheless, a more intensive support for ecumenical efforts must be expected from the leadership of the churches, particularly in regard to urgent *ecumenical imperatives* such as (a) reform and mutual recognition of church ministries, (b) common liturgy of the word and open communion, (c) common building and common use of churches and other structures, (d) common fulfilment of service to society, (e) increasing integration of theological faculties and religious instruction, (f) drawing up of concrete plans for union on the part of church leaders at national and universal levels.

Ecumenicity is more than mere activism in reform. It can be found and realized only if all the churches concentrate afresh on the one Christian tradition, on the gospel of Jesus Christ himself. Only in that light can denominational fears and uncertainties be reduced, ideological fanaticism and bitter prejudice be overcome, the economic, political, cultural entanglements with a particular society, social stratum, class, race, or state concealed behind theological differences be discerned, and an advance be made towards a new freedom. This of course means that there can be no ecumenical agreement without renewal in the Church, but also no renewal in the Church without ecumenical agreement.

But what then is 'Catholic' and what is 'Protestant'? In the future the differences will continue to find expression only in diverse traditional *basic attitudes* which have developed from the time of the Reformation but can be integrated today into a true ecumenicity.

a. Who is *Catholic*? Someone who attaches special importance to the Catholic – that is, *entire*, universal, all-encompassing, total – Church. In the concrete, to the *continuity* of faith in time and the community of faith in space, maintained in all disruptions.

b. Who is *Protestant*? Someone who attaches special importance in all traditions, doctrines, and practices of the Church to constant, critical recourse to the gospel (Scripture) and to constant, practical *reform* according to the norm of the gospel.

c. But from all this it is clear that 'Catholic' and 'Protestant' basic attitudes, correctly understood, are by no means mutually exclusive. Today even the 'born' Catholic can be truly Protestant and the 'born' Protestant truly Catholic in his mentality, so that even now in the whole world there are innumerable Christians who – despite the obstructions of the churches' machinery – do in fact realize a genuine ecumenicity finding its centre in the light of the gospel. Being truly Christian today means being an *ecumenical Christian*.

Such an ecumenical Church of the future certainly must not dissolve into disparate, unorganized groups. But, despite the fact that it must also have an institutional character, it would not be a single party organization, an absolutist religious Roman Empire. This ecumenical Church of the future would be marked by more truthfulness, freedom, humanity, by more broad-mindedness, tolerance, and magnanimity, more Christian self-confidence, supreme composure, and courage to think and to decide. Such a Church would not always be behind the times but as far as possible ahead of them. It might be the avant-garde of a better humanity.

3

KARL RAHNER:
THE THEOLOGIAN'S CONTRIBUTION

HERBERT VORGRIMLER

The last volume of Rahner's Theological Investigations *(20, Darton, Longman and Todd 1981) carries two papers under its Part IV: Future of the Church, which are both germane to our interest. The first is 'Basic theological interpretation of the Second Vatican Council' (pp. 77–89), where Rahner emphasized the historical nature of the Church and the fact that its 'living space' is now the whole world; and 'The abiding significance of the Second Vatican Council' (pp. 90–102), where he dealt with the 'Council of the World-Church', the relationship with the world, the theology of transition and of liberation, the ecumenical change of mind and the optimism of universal salvation. As a tribute to Karl Rahner who died in 1984, we have asked Herbert Vorgrimler to write about Rahner and the Council.*

Professor Herbert Vorgrimler has known Rahner as a working friend since before the Council. Born in Freiburg (as Rahner too) in 1929, he followed Rahner to Innsbruck. Ordained in 1953, he became Editor of the Lexikon für Theologie und Kirche *and the* Konzilkommentar *during 1958–68 (i.e. including the Council years). After four professorial years at Lucerne, he succeeded Rahner at Münster in 1972 as Professor of Dogmatics and the History of Dogma. Editor of numerous works, including Festschriften for both the sixtieth and seventy-fifth birthdays of Karl Rahner, and for the sixtieth birthday of Hugo Rahner his brother, and for the French Jesuit Cardinal Jean Daniélou, he is the author of a dozen books and over two hundred articles. He is a member of the dogma section of* Concilium. *His books in English translation include* Karl Rahner: his life, thought and work *(Burns & Oates 1965; Paulist Press 1966);* One, holy, catholic and apostolic: studies in the nature and role of the Church in the modern world *(Sheed & Ward 1968), six essays written for and dedicated to Rahner on his sixtieth birthday, from whose work several of them begin; Ed* Commentary on the documents of Vatican II *(Herder & Herder; Burns & Oates 1967–9 in five volumes); Ed with Karl Rahner,* Theological dictionary *(Herder & Herder 1965).*

Right up to the very last days of his life, Karl Rahner regarded the Second Vatican Council as a great event, full of blessing, and at any rate 'the beginning of a beginning' for the Church on her way forward into the future. In a collection of essays aimed at keeping alive the memory of that Council his voice is one that should not be missing from the *ensemble*. His death, on 30 March 1984, meant that he could not contribute personally to this book, any more than he could contribute to the present journey of the

Church, a journey about which one can't be wholly sure that it is really directed towards the future. If I myself, as Rahner's oldest pupil and one of his closest friends, am to make an offering in the present context to this momentous event in modern Church history, even though I did not actually take part in the Council's proceedings, I cannot avoid some personal reflections on the work which Rahner and I together devoted years of our lives to carrying out.

HOW THE GREAT COMMENTARY ON THE COUNCIL AROSE

In 1955 Rahner agreed with the Catholic publishing house *Herder* in Freiburg im Breisgau that he would take over the editorship of the *Lexikon für Theologie und Kirche*. From the start of 1956 onwards he gave over half of his working time to this enterprise. The *Lexikon* in question had a richly influential past in German-speaking countries. The first edition appeared in thirteen volumes beginning in 1847. The last edition, a mere ten volumes, came out between 1930 and 1938. The encyclopaedia enjoyed the support of the episcopal hierarchy, and wielded a considerable authority among the ordinary clergy. It is easy to understand, then, that the task of producing the new edition was attractive to Rahner.

From 1948 on, Rahner had been professor of dogma and the history of dogma at the University of Innsbruck. After the end of the Second World War he had begun to work in earnest for the renewal of theology. By this I do not mean that he wanted to replace the Church's official teaching with private theses and theological opinions of his own. It was ever his concern to preserve what was permanently valid in Christian believing, but he distinguished between the substance of the content of faith and the mode and manner in which one expresses that substance. And so it was his wish to translate the Christian message anew for today, to formulate it in a language that would strike home to contemporary people and intersect with their experience. Not that Rahner was alone in committing himself to such a programme. He lived in a period marked by a multiplicity of break-throughs, theological and spiritual. One thinks of the ecumenical movement, not least in Great Britain; of the liturgical renewal, in Belgium and Austria *inter alia*; of the movement of theological *ressourcement*, intensively cultivated in France in particular through the activities of men like Yves Congar and Henri de Lubac. Rahner's own colleagues in Innsbruck had their share in such movements, not least his own brother Hugo Rahner, and the liturgiologist Josef Andreas Jungmann.

But this wave of theological renewal broke against the barrier constituted by the scholastic theology of the Roman schools. The Roman theologians, especially those of the Angelicum and the Lateran University, disposed of considerable influence over the Church's highest doctrinal authorities, the so-called Holy Office, and shared in some sense in the authority of the Pope himself. In their Neo-Scholastic perspective, the attempt to translate the truths of faith into a new language for the men of today was superfluous and fraught with dangers. In their view, one had to do with eternal, unchangeable truths for which a permanently valid linguisticality had been found in Rome itself. This ahistorical manner of thinking also extended to the sphere of ethics. According to these theologians, the divine will for human behaviour could be read off from nature, from the order of the animal creation. Moreover, theological specialists were accorded by them no independent knowledge and competence. Their task was to be auxiliaries to the Roman magisterium, to the Pope; they were to be 'his' theologians. In various countries supervision over theological activity was exercised through a system in which the decisive roles were played by nuncios and bishops. Once particular theologians became suspect in Roman eyes, tough administrative measures were taken against them. Free discussion of theologians' opinions was forbidden.

This situation Rahner took as a challenge. It was not his desire to achieve a renewal of theology by way of collision with the doctrinal jurisdiction of Rome or of the bishops. His way was one, rather, of peaceful persuasion. In his eyes the work on the highly-respected theological *Lexikon* was tailor-made for the purpose. In the first place, one could set forth the generally received and certain teaching of the Church. After that, one could indicate – carefully and prudently – what questions were still open, and where difficulties in the expression of doctrine stood in the way of right comprehension. The *Lexikon* had the advantage of two episcopal protectors who were answerable for the 'tendencies' of the encyclopaedia vis-à-vis the nunciature and Rome. In the protracted but eirenic negotiations with both men during the publication of the ten volumes, Rahner preserved his reputation for rootedness in the theological tradition, his sure sense for new ways and not least his diplomatic dexterity. Thus Rahner took upon himself an enormous burden of work. The *Lexikon* was to have thirty thousand articles, produced by two thousand scholars. Rahner read all the principal articles in manuscript and corrected them, where necessary, with his own hand. He read every article without exception at the stage of galley-proofs.

Obviously, Rahner could not have got through this gigantic workload unaided. When the *Lexikon* began to appear, he asked the present writer, who was on the spot in Freiburg, to take a share in his theological concerns. I had been with him in Innsbruck in the years after 1950 and had served in part as his private assistant. Between 1958 and 1968 I helped him with his work on the encyclopaedia, so that all in all I had direct contact with Rahner during a period of eighteen years. The *Lexikon*, for ecclesio-political reasons, boasted a second editor. This was Monsignor Josef Höfer, a long-standing friend of the *Herder* publishing house. A born dogmatician and ecumenist he had entered the papal diplomatic service after the War, and was by now First Counsellor at the embassy of the Holy See to the Federal Republic of Germany. Höfer had countless Roman contacts, with cardinals, theologians of the papal *Athenaea* and other influential personalities. Especially valuable for the *Lexikon* was his amicable relationship with Augustin Bea SJ, the later cardinal, at that time an adviser to Pius XII. At Höfer's request Bea wrote some positive articles about the *Lexikon* for *Osservatore Romano*.

Of the ten projected volumes of the encyclopaedia two had already appeared when John XXIII announced the holding of an ecumenical Council. Although this news was a happy surprise, it was also for us – understandably – a harsh blow. How could a theological encyclopaedia continue to be produced when a Council was in the offing and might promulgate new dogmas and doctrinal judgements which would inevitably entail alterations in our articles? After long reflection, we decided to carry on with the job and to add to the ten alphabetically arranged volumes a further one on the Council itself. This supplementary volume would then contain all the modifications the Council had introduced. But once the Council had got into its stride, and had begun to develop in quite a different direction from what the Roman theologians had projected, showing no sign of wanting to produce fresh dogmas or doctrinal determinations, we were obliged to change our plan. And at this point we drew new inspiration from the German bishops, who wanted *Herder* to publish the first official conciliar texts, finalized in 1963, in as fine and worthy a form as possible, in both Latin and German. But this episcopal velleity was not to be realized in a twinkling: as far as the official Latin text was concerned, we had to await its publication in *Acta Apostolicae Sedis*, and as to the German translation, countless versions, mostly bad, were in circulation so that here a quite fundamental revision was necessary.

In the December of 1964 Rahner and I discussed the new situation in Munich. We realized that the conciliar texts were of such a quality (and quantity!) that it would not suffice simply to add a supplementary volume to the *Lexikon*. We decided therefore to aim for a full-dress commentary on the conciliar documents, to be published in parallel with the (Latin-German) texts. We set up a group of consultants, consisting of ten persons who were to work directly on the Council texts. Their remit was to make the Commentary as authoritative as was humanly possible. Rahner invited me to take over the editorship itself. I tried to lay down guidelines for the Commentary. I introduced the principle that each document was to be portrayed genetically, in its origins and subsequent history. I wanted it to become obvious in what precise context its affirmations were to be interpreted, what they said and what they consciously didn't say. We would utilize the speeches of the bishops in the Council's sessions, the 'relations' and debates, and take into account the various proposed amendments ('modi'). With Rahner's assistance I worked out a list of collaborators. They were to be theologians who broadly welcomed the Second Vatican Council and had worked constructively on its documents; they should be men committed to a positive exposition of the Christian faith, in the spirit of John XXIII, and free from the tendency to anathematize one's opponents. We had no prejudices about their nationality. Thus in the upshot forty-one individuals joined our team, eighteen of them non-Germans. They included among their number men who had taken a notable part in the Council such as Gérard Philips, Yves Congar, Josef Ratzinger. The 'Roman' theologians were represented by Paolo Dezza, Giovanni Caprile and above all Pietro Pavan, John XXIII's personal theologian and the principal author of *Pacem in Terris*.

But as soon as the team set to work on the Commentary a problem raised its head. How far ought one to respect the privacy of the Council? What counted as due discretion about its internal discussions? How could one get hold of the many papers that had served as drafts for the documents and so should be borne in mind by us? Our Commentary threatened to grind to a halt. In this dilemma I availed myself of the help of the *Lexikon*'s co-editor Höfer with his first-rate Roman contacts. In an audience with Paul VI on 28 March 1966 he filled in the Pope about our problems, outlining to him the projected edition of the Council texts and commentary. Paul VI said to him, 'I welcome it wholeheartedly, and I will make all the documents accessible to you.' And so it fell out. The Pope also made it possible for the Roman Jesuit Giovanni Caprile to note down in his chronicle of the Council all the interventions of 'higher authority', i.e. of the Pope himself, for the benefit of our Commentary. The Pope was very content with the result. In an audience on 14 March 1968 he told Monsignor Höfer that our Commentary was the best scholarly project on the Council so far. He expressed his gratitude and warm recognition of their efforts to the publishing house and the editorial team.

In January 1966 the German bishops entrusted me with the task of gathering together the extant German translations of the Council documents and revising them. This undertaking lasted well into 1966, and Rahner, who had been for some years a Latin master, helped me with it. The outcome received the approbation of the German, Austrian and Swiss episcopates.

Thus it was that our edition of the Council's texts and the commentary thereon came into being: three whole volumes of it, published by Herder of Freiburg between 1966 and 1968, comprising altogether one thousand nine hundred and four pages. Soon afterwards the Commentary (minus the texts) appeared in an English translation under the title *Commentary on the Documents of Vatican Two*: five volumes were published by Herder & Herder (New York) with Burns & Oates (London) between 1967 and 1969, a total of eighteen hundred and ninety-five pages. The magisterial quality of the Commentary was internationally acknowledged. It was a 'resounding success'.

KARL RAHNER IN THE PREPARATORY PHASE OF THE COUNCIL

Karl Rahner had become a widely celebrated theological figure, thanks to his extensive lecturing activity in Europe and also to his publications, above all the *Schriften zur Theologie* (1954–   ), Englished as *Theological Investigations* (Darton, Longman & Todd 1961–84). When John XXIII announced his Council there was a general expectation in many quarters that Rahner would be invited to participate in its preparatory work. But Rahner had made himself unpopular in some circles of ecclesiastical officialdom and, above all, among the theologians of the Roman colleges. As early as the immediately post-war years he had started to express himself in highly critical terms where the Church and the deportment of Church officers were concerned. The background for this was the deafening silence and compromising attitude of official Church circles to the Nazi régime. In a theological perspective Rahner spoke not only of a 'Church of sinners' but of a 'sinful Church'. Naturally enough, this sort of language was in clean contradiction to a triumphalist view of the Church such as dominated the pontificate of Pius XII, for instance in his encyclical *Mystici Corporis* of 1943.

In addition, Rahner had some special theological difficulties with Rome.

In 1951 a bulky manuscript on the history and theology of the dogma of the Assumption had been despatched by him to Rome, because the local ecclesiastical censors could not decide whether to give it an *imprimatur* or not. The Roman censor was quite definite in his denial of the *imprimatur*. In the typescript Rahner had set forth his theories on the development of dogma, the theology of death and especially on the idea of 'resurrection *in death*'. In 1954 Pius XII in one of his *allocutiones* rejected the idea of a eucharistic concelebration in a way which, though Rahner's name was never mentioned, left little doubt that he had in mind Rahner's theology of concelebration, put forward some years previously. The so-called Holy Office then forbade Rahner from writing any further on that topic. In 1960 Rahner published an article on *Virginitas in partu* in which he said that virginity is a theological concept, referring to a person's total availability before God (*Fiat voluntas tua*), rather than an attempt to give anatomical or biological facts a theological pertinence. This article aroused a furore among the Roman theologians. The prefect of the Holy Office, Alfredo Cardinal Ottaviani, who was a canonist rather than a theologian, and his assessor Archbishop Pietro Parente, endeavoured from that moment to keep Rahner out of the preparations for the Council.

Karl Rahner was a Jesuit, but that was not of much help in the situation. The Jesuits in the neighbourhood of the Holy Office were either his enemies, such as the dogmatician S. Tromp and the moral theologian F. Hürth; or they were cautious tacticians like Augustin Bea. The General of the Society, Janssens (who died in 1965), was an amiable and benevolent enough man, but quite helpless in the face of the Holy Office. Rahner knew a number of bishops who were well-disposed towards him but of these there was only one who really set himself to work for Rahner energetically and from conviction. This was the then bishop of Berlin, Julius Cardinal Döpfner, soon to be Archbishop of Munich and President of the German Bishops' Conference [and quite soon to die so tragically young].

Cardinal Döpfner discussed the matter thoroughly with John XXIII in an audience on 24 January 1961, defending Rahner and his theology against the suspicions which the Roman theologians had aroused in his regard and asking the Pope to include Rahner in the preparatory work for the Council. John XXIII agreed. But this did not in itself mean that the Pope would have his way: the Holy Office and the Roman theologians not infrequently opposed the papal will. I can illustrate this with the following example. Of the many proponents of theological renewal persecuted in the pre-conciliar period by the groups I have mentioned, Père Henri de Lubac, presently a Cardinal, was one, as is well-known. In the years from 1961 to 1967 I had a number of contacts with him, and he told me of the difficulties he and others had to endure from this direction, not least on account of their support for Père Teilhard de Chardin SJ. One day, during the preparations for the Council, he visited Father Janssens, about whom he related:

> Là, une fois je l'ai vu dans sa chambre, il était à son fauteuil, moi j'étais en face, et il me montrait la fenêtre. Et la fenêtre indiquait justement la direction du Saint-Office. Et il disait: 'Mon Père, ces gens-là, ces gens-là, ils n'obéissent pas au pape. Quand ce n'est pas contre le pape, nous sommes bien obligés de leur obéir tout de même. Mais ces gens-là, ils n'obéissent au pape.'

It was in such a way that Roman circles prevented Rahner from joining any of the more important preparatory commissions for the Council. However, so as to give John XXIII at any rate a *pro forma* obedience they allowed Rahner, on 22 March 1961, to be named a consultor for the preparatory commission on the administration of the sacraments, and more especially as an expert on questions touching the diaconate.

A vigorous movement in favour of the restoration of the permanent diaconate had gathered momentum among those associated with the Church society *Caritas* and, later, among those who in the Church's name had opposed the National Socialist régime from out of the concentration camp of Dachau (not far north of Munich). Rahner first came into contact with these ideas in 1948. In 1957 he published a first article on the topic, in which he made known his warm support for the idea. He had great expectations of a restored permanent diaconate, looking to it for a new, effective mode of the presence of the Church in the world, a more differentiated image for the clergy and an inspiration for later structural reform. From the start, Roman circles had not looked wholly askance at the notion of a renewal of the diaconate. They supposed the deacon to be a sort of helper with distributing communion, or a catechist in mission territories. So they regarded Rahner's part in this particular question as harmless enough. From lack of funds, he was never invited to any of the Roman sittings. Instead, he, along with the Archbishop of Zagreb, Francis Šeper, the later Cardinal of the Holy Office, was invited to submit a written report on the diaconate. This he did in the summer of 1961.

At the same time Rahner began to work out a major book on the diaconate with contributions from various hands. It appeared in the summer of 1962 under the title *Diaconia in Christo*, edited by K. Rahner and H. Vorgrimler, a book of six hundred and forty-six pages, dedicated to Cardinal Franz König of Vienna and Cardinal Stefan Wyszynski of Warsaw. It served as a foundation for the work of the theological commission that produced the text now found in *Lumen Gentium* 29. As is well-known, the Council created the possibility of restoring the diaconate as a permanent office in the Church, not least for married men, and Paul VI laid down guidelines for this restoration in a *motu proprio* of 18 June 1967. By 1984 there were ten thousand and twenty-nine permanent deacons throughout the world. Seldom has a movement in Church history enjoyed so remarkable a success in such a relatively short time. Karl Rahner's share therein was considerable. But I am running ahead of events: I must retrace my steps to the year 1961.

In October of that year the Archbishop of Vienna, Cardinal König, asked Rahner to look over the conciliar drafts and write a critical report on them. In this way Rahner became the personal theologian of the Vienna Cardinal at the Council. König had known Rahner since the War years, when König himself was a simple chaplain in Vienna, and Rahner, who had been expelled from Innsbruck (Austria) by the Nazis, was employed by a pastoral institute of the Vienna Archdiocese. Since those years Rahner and König had often been in contact. When König, as a professor of religious studies, was editing a dictionary on his subject in 1956 he asked Rahner for a number of articles. König was an enthusiastic and knowledgeable contributor to the *Lexikon für Theologie und Kirche* on his own specialist subjects: the history of religions and religious science. Cardinal Döpfner of Munich joined himself to Cardinal König's request that Rahner help with the conciliar drafts, and Rahner consequently forwarded his report to Döpfner also.

Rahner was shocked by the drafts that had been prepared for the Council in Rome itself. He gave particular attention to the drafts on the fundamental dogmatic and moral theology. They had been treated in the conventional Neo-Scholastic style. A treatise *De deposito fidei pure custodiendo* highlighted the plenary authority of the ecclesiastical magisterium over eternal truths. Another, *De fontibus revelationis*, spoke of the two sources of divine revelation, the written and the oral, ascribing to the latter a doctrinal content of its own. The inerrancy of Holy Scripture was discussed in such a way that in practice the use of the historical-critical method in biblical exegesis would have been impossible. The draft *De ecclesia* contained a triumphalist ecclesiology, orientated on the 'mystical body' and 'perfect society' models of the Church, and attributed to a 'Church' defined in terms of the Pope and, above all, his curial organs, the highest possible competence in secular concerns. Another draft, *De beata Maria virgine*, represented a 'Mariology of privileges'. *De castitate* and *De ordini morali* preserved natural law principles in an ethic that was both unhistorical and fundamentally sub-human. Egregiously bad was a *votum supremae sacrae Congregationis Sancti Officii*, already printed and bound on fine paper, which began by demanding the solemn condemnation of fifteen contemporary theological errors or 'isms': in effect these amounted to everything that had been proposed in the Church by way of renewal since the First Vatican Council!

In a series of quite fundamental Latin reports Rahner sought to oppose these Roman positions. He devoted particular effort to showing that where the Roman theologians wanted the Council to define new dogmas, for instance on the existence of limbo or the correctness of Monogenism, the necessary foundations for a dogmatic definition were in fact lacking.

Rahner also tried, through his own publications and by encouraging the work of other theologians, for instance in his series *Quaestiones Disputatae*, to pick up different themes of the Council and to steer them in a new direction. He wanted to show at the very least how open many questions were and how far from ready we should be to utter a definitive dogmatic word about them.

While he was working for the by now imminent Council, Rome dealt him a severe blow. On 7 June 1962 the General of the Jesuits informed Rahner that everything he might write from now on was to be subjected to a special preliminary scrutiny by the Roman censor. This measure emanated from Cardinal Ottaviani. Neither the General nor Rahner were informed of the grounds for taking the step. One may assume that it was intended to warn the bishops against using Rahner's services, and to put obstacles in the way of any publishing activity Rahner might have in mind before the Council opened. He dubbed it 'the muzzle-measure'. But he did not submit to it without a fight.

He apprised Cardinals Döpfner and König of what had happened, along with Bishop Volk of Mainz (now a Cardinal) and Monsignor Höfer in Rome. König spoke that same month (June) with John XXIII and asked him for help. Volk won over the then President of the German Bishops' Conference, Cardinal Frings, Archbishop of Cologne, to the idea of a written petition to be sent by the Cardinals to the Pope. German academics, especially scientists in the universities, started to gather signatures. Professor Paul Martini who was medical adviser to the Federal Chancellor, Dr Konrad Adenauer, gained the latter's adhesion to the document. In the upshot, a note bearing two hundred and fifty signatures was forwarded to the Pope via diplomatic channels. Cardinal Bea also interceded with the Pope on Rahner's behalf. The Pope promised to 'find all ways and means', but at first nothing transpired. However, it must have given the Holy

Office food for thought that the Cardinals and bishops I have mentioned did not abandon Rahner, but remained determined to stand by him.

KARL RAHNER DURING THE COUNCIL

In October 1962 a list of some hundred and ninety theologians nominated by the Pope as official Council experts, *periti*, was made public. Rahner's name was on it. Not that this necessarily meant very much. A *peritus* received a pass with which he could get in to attend the solemn sessions of the Council in St Peter's basilica; but the really decisive work was done in the Council commissions, where the bishops sat together with chosen experts. Rahner was not nominated for such a commission. Nevertheless, at Cardinal König's request he travelled to Rome and when the Council opened put himself at its disposal.

John XXIII solemnly inaugurated the Council on 11 October 1962 with that signpost of a speech in which he spoke of the prophets of doom who whispered daily in his ear, asking for condemnations and the pure repetition of dogmatic formulae. The Pope's own wish, was, on the contrary, to encourage the forces of renewal. Could these be mustered, scattered as they had been hitherto across the world? Would they find the moral courage to speak? The Roman theologians were of the opinion that their prepared texts were so perfect that everyone should be able to approve them after the briefest conciliar discussion, thus enabling the Council to be dissolved at the earliest possible date. They moved heaven and earth to cover their brain-children with the authority and glory of the Pope himself.

In this *first phase* of the Council, the theologians of renewal – among whom Rahner must certainly be accounted one of the most prominent – had one determined purpose: to prevent the adoption of the Roman texts. A most important effect of the countless gatherings, lectures and conversations which went on *pari passu* with the official sessions was that bishops and theologians learned to know each other. The open exchange of views got going. Rahner spoke, during the first weeks of the Council, to the German, Austrian and Swiss episcopates. He met with the French theologians, and conveyed his ideas to the French bishops. He noticed with some astonishment that the Latin American Cardinals and bishops showed deep interest in him and his views. Into such circles he brought his own critique of the text *De deposito fidei pure custodiendo*. Together with Josef Ratzinger, he formed the audacious plan of composing a new draft on divine revelation to set against the Roman text *De fontibus revelationis*, ensuring thereby that the forces of renewal at the Council would not just negate everything put before them but contribute positive counter-proposals. Cardinal Frings sanctioned this new draft in the name of the German bishops and had it delivered to the other episcopal conferences.

On 14 November 1962 there began the official discussion of the preparatory Council text on the sources of revelation. The course of the debate was in part a stormy one. A vote was taken on 20 November. The opponents of the official text failed to reach the necessary majority for ditching the document, but their numbers were such that John XXIII withdrew the prepared text and empowered a commission to formulate a new one. This was the 'breakthrough': it meant that the official Roman drafts were not sacrosanct. The sixteen conciliar documents which we possess today were all of them freshly minted during the Council.

Rahner worked during these weeks for individual bishops and for episcopal conferences, offering more and more argued criticism of the other prepared texts, especially the two on which interest now centred: those on the Church and on Mary. On 5 December 1962 there took place his own decisive personal 'breakthrough'. Cardinal König simply escorted Rahner into a session of the commission that was working on the new text on divine revelation. This commission was co-chaired by Cardinal Ottaviani and Cardinal Bea. Ottaviani would have had the right to eject Rahner, as he was not an accredited *peritus* of this particular commission. But he didn't eject him. And this pattern was repeated on 7 December.

After the end of this session of the Council, on 8 December, the work continued in the home countries of the participants. Rahner busied himself over the winter months with the themes of revelation, the Church and Mary, and also with a new draft document on the Church in the world. In February 1963 he was named as a commission *peritus* and member of a seven-strong group of theological experts for the next text on the Church. In this official capacity he was now obliged to take part in the Roman sittings. Later on, Rahner looked on this period as the *second phase* of the Council's work. Those theologians intent on renewal now saw it as their duty to keep the newly forged texts 'open' in such a way as to exclude further dogmatic determinations, for instance in regard to the relation between Holy Scripture and oral tradition.

During this period Rahner acquired a high reputation among those Roman theologians who were, objectively speaking, his opponents. He had a perfect mastery of the Latin language. He possessed an enormous knowledge of the patristic and Scholastic traditions. He could understand his opponents' arguments from within. He opposed them with a striking logical sharpness. He left no doubt in anyone's mind that he was concerned to serve the pastoral needs of the Church. And so he moved towards a resolution of his conflict with the Holy Office. In February 1963 during a break between sessions he talked with Cardinal Ottaviani about the censorship measure taken against him. Ottaviani explained to him that the measure had been taken out of friendship for him, that it had been wrongly interpreted, that it was for his defence, in short that it should be regarded as a privilege. Rahner replied that he would willingly renounce such a privilege. In May 1963 the Jesuit General told Rahner that in future he, the General, would choose Rahner's censors, as before. With this the Holy Office retreated, and from then on until his death Rahner was spared further canonical penalties. In fact he came to have a genuinely friendly relation with his former enemies, and contributed essays to the *Festschriften* for Ottaviani and Parente.

The continuation of the Council under Paul VI opened what Rahner saw as the *third phase* of its work. At this stage it was possible to introduce some small, carefully selected portions of a renewed theology into the conciliar texts. Closest to Rahner's heart lay the hope that the Council would do something of real practical usefulness for the life of the Church. To this realm belong the renewal of the diaconate, and the structural recognition of episcopal collegiality through a re-evaluation of the standing of bishops' conferences and through reform of the Curia. Also to be mentioned here are the declaration of religious and conscientious freedom, and the acknowledgement that Catholics might well have differing opinions in political matters. All of these achievements Rahner summed up in the phrase 'a beginning of the beginning'.

If we ask ourselves today, in which conciliar texts traces of Rahner's influence are to be found, it is not altogether easy to give an answer. Rahner made himself an integral part of the intensive and laborious team effort which led to the Council's texts. He had a large part in the making of *Lumen Gentium*, marked as that document is by his favourite themes: the sacramentality of the Church and its eschatological character, the collegiality of the bishops, the meaning of the local Church community, the ecclesial rather than individualistic nature of the sacraments, the salvation of non-Christians, the diaconate and not least Mary's membership of the Church. *Dei Verbum* owed much to him, especially in regard to the relation of Scripture and Tradition, and the limits of the inerrancy of the Bible. He gave *Gaudium et Spes* its fundamental impulse even if later on he came to regard its theological argumentation as inadequate. He worked in the commission which produced the decree *Perfectae caritatis* on the renewal of the religious life. And further traces of his influence can be found in many other conciliar documents – for instance in what the Liturgy constitution has to say about concelebration.

In an essay written fifteen years after the end of the Second Vatican Council Rahner wrote about 'The abiding significance of the Second Vatican Council'. He noted here five features of the Council which made it in his eyes a great and greatly significant event:

1. The Council was in Rahner's eyes the first event in Church history in which the Church really understood and actualized itself as a *world* Church. In other words, at the Council the Church ceased to think of itself in purely European or Anglo-Saxon terms. For Rahner an important indicator here was the renouncing of Latin as the language of worship.

2. The council expressed a desire for a new relation between the Church and the world. Here one should mention the giving up of political means to succour religion, the recognition of the rights of an erroneous conscience, the acknowledgement that the ordinary secular world was not to be moulded according to the norms of the Church.

3. The Council included in its documents embryonic traces of a renewed theology. Where these traces may be found can best be identified by asking at what points the Congregation for the Doctrine of the Faith found it necessary after the Council to express itself in anguished or defensive tones.

4. The mind of the Council was an ecumenically-orientated mind, and this led to a changed attitude on the part of the Catholic Church towards non-Catholic Christendom (and also to non-Christian religions and to secular humanism). The Church admitted that outside her borders lay things of genuine, positive worth sometimes lacking in the Church herself.

5. The Council expressed itself in favour of an optimism about universal salvation. That entailed a recognition of the all-encompassing grace and activity of God, and therewith a relativization of the importance of ecclesial activity. The Church can be a sign of salvation without God being obliged to limit his salvation exclusively to the Church and its sacraments. The manifestly pessimistic view of humanity and the destiny of history which had been in possession since Augustine underwent revision.

Karl Rahner remained convinced that the Church must continue further along this path which the Second Vatican Council opened. It is in this way that the Church will foster and propagate the Christian faith in the future. I myself was in a position closely to observe Rahner's optimism about the future of Christianity, from 1968 onwards. We worked together right up to his death, for example on the collection he founded, *Quaestiones disputatae*. And frankly I also experienced that the 'developments' of the last years in the Church, in Rome itself, filled him with dismay and pessimism. He could discern no further steps being taken on that way forward, and spoke often, even publicly, about a 'wintertime' ['winterlichen Zeit'] that has fallen on the Church of Rome.

BIBLIOGRAPHICAL NOTE

During both the preparatory work on the Council and the Council itself I received very many letters from Rahner describing his work and the difficulties he encountered. Because this correspondence possesses real documentary value, I have published extracts from ninety-nine letters of Rahner first of all in the Swiss journal *Orientierung* and secondly in the new edition of my biography of Rahner, *Karl Rahner verstehen* (Freiburg-im-Breisgau 1985), pp. 171–220. The above essay leans heavily on this authentic material.

PART TWO

CONCILIAR PRELUDE

4

THE COUNCIL
COMES OF AGE

THOMAS HOLLAND

Here are memories from a seventy-seven year old former Bishop of Salford in England, who brings out the flavour of senior clergy, an international brotherhood of like-trained men who continued to live (not too far from the yew-tree) their lives of significant toil. His memories are of people, not theologies; and picnics en route, not turmoil after arrival. The enthusiasm was there, and that hid the hard work.

Educated at Upholland seminary, Thomas Holland achieved a PhD at Valladolid in 1929, and a DD at the Gregorian University, Rome in 1936. After teaching in Lisbon, he became a naval chaplain during the War (awarded a Distinguished Service Cross in 1944). He was with the Catholic Missionary Society during 1948–56 and then secretary to the Apostolic Delegate to Britain, Archbishop G. P. O'Hara. He was ordained Bishop of Portsmouth in 1960 and the following year he was made a member of the Secretariat for Promoting Christian Unity (until 1974), and in 1965 a member of the Secretariat for Non-Believers (until 1973). He attended the Synod of 1974. In 1980 Salford University made him an honorary LlD.

People in this part of the world [northern England] not unreasonably identified Pope John's 'Ecumenical' Council with ecumenism and logically assumed the whole exercise would stand or fall by what it achieved in the cause of Christian unity. Cardinal Godfrey I remember deploring this amiable simplicity. He was not alone. More shrewdly, others fastened on to the title 'Vatican II' and saw the main objective as the completion of unfinished business left over from Vatican I. In particular they were thinking of what was often traded as Vatican I's image of the Church: a single peak soaring aloft from a flat plain. They saw Vatican II going exclusively, or at least in a very big way, for bishops.

In *Lumen Gentium* on the Church, surely the greatest of the Council documents, bishops and their collegiality do have their place – a very significant place, *after* the chapter on the People of God. For many of us this was the pivotal point of the whole Council – supremely Johannine, though the Constitution was elaborated under Paul VI and largely in response to

49

the vision of the Church he presented to us in his inaugural address of 29 September 1963. I remember particularly the moving comparison of himself with his predecessor Honorius III 'as he is depicted in the apse of St Paul's-outside-the-walls in splendid mosaic, adoring Christ. He, the Pontiff, a tiny, shrunken figure, lies prone kissing Christ's feet. Christ towers above him, a majestic, royal teacher presiding over the congregation in the Basilica which is the Church . . .'

In response to an implicit appeal Pope Paul seemed to make in that address, a suggestion came later in the name of the bishops of England and Wales to hold regular meetings of Pope and bishops. It was the first mention in the Council of World Synods.[1] Cardinal Suenens and others came forward at once to express warm approval.

Returning, however, to preconciliar visions of Vatican II's main purpose, I have no doubt Pope John's hopes embraced both the 'ecumenical' assumption of the less wise and the shrewder analysis of the Church historians. As revealed in *his* inaugural address (11 October 1962), his dearest concern was much more with sheep than shepherds. A more accessible and nourishing diet of divine truth – something akin to a break-through in contemporary presentation of the Faith – engaged his thoughts and launched a People of God's Council on a course free from anathemas, tempered with compassionate insight and void of gloom.

A document (recently published by the Istituto Paolo VI of Brescia and signed by Archbishop Montini on behalf of the Lombardy bishops)[2] shows considerable distress at the very beginning of the Council over the failure in the preparatory stages to produce a programme in which schemata would be discussed in logical sequence culminating in the Constitution on the Sacred Liturgy. Could one conclude that *his* main hope from the Council at that point was liturgical reform? So far from that being the final document crowning the whole work, we cut our conciliar teeth on it!

My own experience as a Member of the Secretariat for Promoting Christian Unity (SPCU) left me with a pronounced list to starboard, i.e. towards the side of the less wise and their assumption that ecumenical means 'All about ecumenism', always! Not that one scamped any of the sessions or failed to grapple with any one of the other schemata! Yet for two preconciliar years, four during, and seven after the Council, SPCU work steadily absorbed one's nights and days with a constant flow of working-papers and meetings.

Pope John's creation, the SPCU, has of course become a permanent organ of Central Administration. Is it the only ad hoc Council structure to survive more or less in its original form? More remarkably, Church government itself could scarcely survive now without SPCU. In making that point (perhaps forcing things a bit), I would go on to argue that the simplist assumption of the less wise was not altogether wide of the mark. Judged by the single criterion of service in the cause of Christian unity, Vatican II comes through more than handsomely.

Divided Christendom now finds (and 'full in the panting heart of Rome!') a bond of union, not yet, alas, in fullness of faith, but in warmest charity, mutual understanding and ever-ready service. Ecumenical traffic now ranges to and from the Vatican as wide as Christendom. It was already moving during the Council with the return of St Andrew's head to Constantinople and the mutual liftings of ancient anathemas. That, if I am not mistaken was the grand finale of Pope Paul's first session. And who could ever forget his own return from the United Nations General Assembly in New York? His message, formally eirenical, nonetheless, in truly pontifical style, built all manner of ecumenical bridges.[3] Council Fathers gathered around TVs to watch his approach to the podium with bated breath. So motionless was he until then, he seemed to be his own wax-work figure, incapable of speech.

Secretary General, Pericles Felici, prefaced the following morning's work with the news that the Pope intended to come straight from Rome airport to St Peter's to be welcomed home by us. Business finished as usual about 12.30. Our turn to sit motionless – all 2,000 of us! Towards 1 p.m. Peter's great doors parted. We rose and there he was! Our applause even rivalled UNO's response to his: 'Jamais plus la Guerre!' In bitter days to come, did he still find sweet relief in remembering that moment? He looked radiant!

Pope John's famous flair for opening doors and windows was not confined to the Vatican. It was complemented by an inspired choice of plenipotentiaries acting in his name, and surely none more *indovinato* than Augustin Bea's as first president of the SPCU. Spiritually he was and remains the corner-stone of that enduring edifice. His progress from Scripture Professor Emeritus to Cardinal and Conferencier[4] on the grand scale in capital cities astonished even former students as percipient as the late Father Alexander Jones of *Jerusalem Bible* fame. Bea was responsible for the basic emphases in *Unitatis Redintegratio*: e.g. conversion of heart and prayer the soul of ecumenism; the evil of false eirenicism, the adoption of the key-note scriptural phrase *veritatem facientes in caritate* Ephesians 4:15. (Did he by the way, adopt it as his own motto as Cardinal? That, too, would have been *indovinato* – he lived it!) He insisted in and out of season on all who engaged in ecumenical dialogue being *vere competentes*. If only these principles had been honoured as much in practice as they were notionally welcomed!

51

Bea could at first pass for a desiccated scholar brim-full of *wissenschaft*, but not after his first smile and the witty phrase that often accompanied it. The SPCU gathered once at a convent (of which more anon) near his native village. I happened to be with him at a coffee-break. He opened up on his youthful background with great charm and vivacity. He recalled with boyish delight his father, family, farm etc. The family name, I gathered, had contracted to Bea from Beam, or was it Beamt?

He rose one day in the Aula to remind us of due respect for our Eastern brethren's legitimate tradition of married clergy. There was fire in his words: so there was occasionally too in the SPCU after half-baked interventions. *Crede experto*!

The Cardinal's first-lieutenant, Secretary Jan Willebrands, had visited us at the Catholic Missionary Society's Headquarters in London back in 1950. He was already then a big wheel in European ecumenics. I fear he had miscast the CMS as the spearhead of a British equivalent. We saw ourselves rather as the spearhead of the Conversion of England which in the hands of the then Superior, Father J.C. Heenan was not always an instrument of peace.[5] He believed also in disturbance . . . Anyway, a presence was invited from the CMS at the next European Ecumenical Conference to take place shortly in Paris. A number of future consultors of the SPCU were there. My main memory, however, is of an animated disagreement between fathers Congar and Bouyer. Neither yielded an inch. Sparks flew. What it was all about I now have no idea!

How often, on the completion of a difficult piece of work, one was to hear Cardinal Bea wind up with: 'Special thanks to our Secretary (Willebrands) . . . We shall not find a better one!' He spoke for all of us.

Members of SPCU with one or two exceptions were in episcopal orders, half a dozen of them later to become Cardinals. One such, Lorenz Jäger of Paderborn, had also visited CMS Headquarters with his trusty theologian Edward Stakemeier, later Director of the Johann Adam Möller Institute, of which the Archbishop was President.[6] As an SPCU Consultor he became a very dear friend, despite the constraints of our only common tongue, Latin. I received a copy of the *Festschrift* his fellow intellectuals published for him. Next came the little card recording his death. *Requiescas care Eduarde, post tot et tantos labores!* Archbishop Jäger's predecessor at Vatican I, Konrad Martin, was a member of that Council's all-important *Deputatio de Fide* and in effect the architect of its crucial texts. Clearly a strong sense of noblesse-oblige moved his successor to take up his pen and produce at Paderborn in 1960 his *Das ökumenische Konzil, die Kirche und die Christenheit* which caught the preconciliar English market in a translation.[7] It is undoubtedly one of the best of its kind. There were many. Jäger's tribute to his predecessor's work in Vatican I runs: 'a masterpiece of clear exposition and beautiful, easily understood Latin'. He quotes Dom Cuthbert Butler on Konrad Martin: 'a learned theologian, an agreeable controversialist and a truly apostolic bishop'.[8]

When SPCU was in session, Stakemeier always sat behind his chief and fed him with slips of paper from which the Archbishop made significant contributions to the debate. Dare I wonder how much of his excellent book was devilled by Monsignor Stakemeier?

It alerted me to a long-forgotten detail with its reference to Pio Nono's letter to Manning on the eve of his Council: 'The Pope was quite prepared to invite Protestant Observers . . . would give them a good opportunity to bring forward their doctrines and their reasons for them. Even if they were not in a position to do this themselves during the Council, they would certainly find men of their own choosing, skilled in theology, to whom they could present their arguments for examination and discussion. Lastly he expressed his wish that many might be present at the Council for this purpose.' (*op cit* 63f, a quotation from Granderath.) I fear it was a forlorn hope in those times. It is at least clear, though, that there is nothing new under the sun.

This then is the place to salute our own Vatican II Observer Corps – 'our own' in the sense of being SPCU's special responsibility and a 'Corps d'élite'. Bishop Moorman of Ripon gave a return-of-hospitality dinner at the Columbus Hotel in the Via della Conciliazione to which he also invited Hans Küng. He made a bee-line for me after making his number with our host. 'You are Archbishop Heenan?' 'Sorry!' 'Where is he?' 'Not here!' Some time before this Dr Küng had spoken in Oxford. Our J.C.H. followed him there with a vigorous counter-blast. Two cheers for the spunk of the Tübingen trouble-shooter! If only J. C. H. had been there! A collector's piece?

The first time Cardinal Bea paraded his troops J.C.H. found England in a minority of one among the Members. Whatever the reason, (could it have been the old persuasion that Anglicans are better understood on the continent?) with one bound our man was in to see Pope John. A second English bishop, just ordained, became a Member [i.e. this writer]. Consultors (no vote but plenty of voice) represented a kaleidoscope of interests, disciplines, and countries. Pope John had annexed to the main duty (*Unitatis Redintegratio*) Religious Liberty and the Jews.

Gus Weigel SJ, a pioneer ecumenist from one of the American universities, quickly won attention with such phrases as: 'I deny the allegation and defy the allegator!' From then on he supplied steady light relief in the grimmest sessions. He also did tough crosswords in 'no time flat', and died before the Council finished. RIP.

Our three English Consultors (Maurice Bévenot, SJ, Gerard Corr, OSM and Frank Davis of Oscott) were established practitioners, respectively, in Ecclesiology, Mariology and Newmanology. For Continentals, perhaps even more than for us, this last was and is a supreme ingredient. Didn't Jan Willebrands do a doctorate thesis on Newman? Cardinal Döpfner of Munich likewise? Gerard Corr began briskly (and spontaneously) with a questionnaire on Marian outlook and practice which he circulated to Anglican Bishops. Most of them replied not only courteously but, in the continental sense, very positively.

I have so far left two remarkable men unmentioned: Jerome Hamer, OP, third in the SPCU hierarchy, a polyglot; and Hermann Volk of the University of Mainz, a determined monoglot – or so it seemed.[9] Latin was *de rigueur* in all the Commissions. Hermann was the only one always to get away with his vernacular. The day he was preconized Archbishop of Mainz, Bea saluted him on behalf of us all in his flawless Latin: 'Optime Praesul Moguntine!' (Cheers!) Volk was author of a considerable number of theological *opuscula* which had a wide influence.

Jerome Hamer, Regent of Studies for the whole Dominican Order, had just published his seminal treatise: *The Church is a Communion*.[10] Vatican II would have been the poorer without it – SPCU immeasurably so without *him*. Of Belgian origin he appeared to be perfectly at ease in any language. He made a pair in this with Willebrands. Bea of course read but hardly spoke English. So he had made doubly sure his Secretary and Vice-Secretary spoke it perfectly.

There were occasional heated encounters in camera. Heenan (who spoke German after a fashion) on one occasion rose in wrath to accuse Volk of heresy. Poor Volk of the long-winded interventions (accompanied perhaps by a manual ritual of lifting water in the palm of his right hand from his right boot, and transferring it overhead into his left hand for downward transit into his left boot) sat smiling as J.C.H. tiraded away, too *distrait* to speak either Latin or German. But for once, it seems, quick wits had skated too quickly over an essential phrase. Peace was restored – not Volk's: he continued throughout to smile uncomprehendingly.

Heenan tangled, this time in Latin, with Willebrands over certain innovations in Holland which he denounced in a way that clearly stung our Secretary. He bridled, beginning with: *Utique! sunt multa peccata in Holland!* and going on to put Heenan in his place with a heated mise-au-point. I, who carried such a name, intervened in the ensuing silence with: '*Agnosco humiliter esse multa peccata in Holland attamen propono –*' It worked! Jan dissolved in laughter, the others joined in, even Heenan who normally didn't find me funny.

Undoubtedly the chain-horse of the SPCU members was the Belgian Emile-Joseph de Smedt, Bishop of Bruges. He was entrusted with the text of the Declaration on Religious Liberty (*Dignitatis Humanae*). He wrote and rewrote it no less than seventeen times as the *modi* rolled in. War-horses like Cardinal Ruffini of Palermo thundered against it. Even our dear SPCU Consultor, Charlie Boyer SJ, expressed fears that the difficulty of squaring it with Pio Nono's *Syllabus* would kill it in the end. The day was won, however, thanks in large measure to a distinction, worthy of the best scholastic tradition, between error and people: error has no rights, but people in error do!

I think it was about this time 'Mil' of Bruges made his famous assault on Triumphalism, Clericalism and Juridicism, for ever fuelling left-wing Vaticanologists all around the world. The feeling even among bolder bishops was: 'Brilliant but over-done!' Nonetheless he got and deserved his accolade for guts. All who congratulated him received a copy from his well-filled Greg-bag: 'Mil' was never a quitter!

Happily 'Mil' and I recently, on Saturday 18 May 1985, found ourselves seated side by side at Pope John Paul's sixty-fifth birthday luncheon given in Belgium by the Cardinal of Malines (+ Godfried Danneels). I took the opportunity to check with 'Mil' whether Cardinal Bea had ever given the green light to his famous triple attack on 'Clericalism, Juridicism, Triumphalism' (see appendix). He reflected a while, then firmly said: 'No.' He remains an unblushing father of his triplets – and indeed he is happy to see acknowledged as his brain-child 'Triumphalism' (his favourite) in a recently published Flemish dictionary. He recalls that the word came to him as he shaved one morning after he had struggled late with this text the night before. I always wondered why 'Mil' had never been given the red hat; but at this luncheon he was given better. Though there must have been three score at the table, Pope John Paul got up at the end and purposefully strode along the line to 'Mil' to give him, now enfeebled by age and illness, a loving embrace. The years fell away from him, and there he was again, the young man I had known in 1935 on journeys home from Rome via Brussels.

I wonder how far I am justified in the present context in recalling earlier memories of this remarkable man to whom I would, within the area of work confided to the SPCU, apply all that Jäger wrote about his predecessor Konrad Martin of Paderborn? In 1936 I travelled from Rome to Belgium with five students from the Belgian College. (Three became bishops: two Vicars-General.) We took our time enjoying Lago Maggiore, Righi Mountain, Lake Lucerne etc, singing all manner of 'carmina burana' on the way. We had all passed our finals in good shape. 'Mil' put me up for a night at his home in Opweik. It was near enough to Brussels for getting to my sister's final profession at Uccle the following morning. His patriarchal father, I remember, formed the sign of the cross on our foreheads as we went to rest that night.

Long years later I was in Lourdes with a workingmen's pilgrimage to pray for the conversion of England. 'Mil' had just been elevated from auxiliary at Malines to the diocese of Bruges. I spotted that Bruges pilgrims were in Lourdes: Yes, they said, their new bishop was with them staying at the Chaplains' Residence. He was out when I called but the concierge courteously invited me to wait in his room. I allowed 'Mil' the time in which I smoked one of his cigars and left, to assure our pilgrims at lunch I would be bringing a bishop to dine one evening. As I left, the concierge politely asked how I came to know the bishop since I was English. 'We were students together.' 'He's done much better than you, hasn't he?' he said, not so politely! I ran 'Mil' to earth giving his blessing with other bishops at the end of the torchlight procession. My warm, first-name approach, loaded with dates and details, drew no more than a brief request for prayers in view of his enormous new responsibilities in Europe and Africa. Total brush-off!

The next time we met was early in 1961 at the Paulist Conference Centre on Lake Albano at my first SPCU plenaria. Of course he had no recollection of our encounter at Lourdes and, worse than ever, still no recollection of our trip in 1936. I solemnly conjured him to sound out his family when he got home. Mother and brothers came to the rescue and saved my sanity! It was his turn to eat humble-pie at our next plenaria.

For a meeting a year or so later in Germany he met J.C.H. and me at Brussels Airport. His car drew from Heenan the NT indictment: 'Recepisti *Mercedem* tuam!' 'Mil' had his revenge with a strong Belgian cigar. After a mile or so the discomforted archbishop tossed it furtively through the sunshine roof. 'Mil' however had his eye on him and at once pulled off the road in some alarm. He knelt up with his back to the windscreen sniffing hard at the space between the roof and the sliding panel. Negative! but a chastened prelate learned for the first time the likely destiny of objects tossed through the sunshine roof.

Supper was awaiting us in Ghent at Bishop van Callewaert's (known to

one and all as 'Kilowatts'). For me it was elysium re-visited. He had kept
open house for chaplains during the war. The last time I sat at his table (in
naval rig)[11] I marvelled at the ingenuity with which in hard times he
managed to replenish the board. Evacuated to England a jump ahead of
Kaiser Bill's lot in 1914, he continued his studies for the priesthood at
Upholland College, Lancs. Of all continental bishops he was England's best
PRO man. Alas! during the Council he caught a liver infection. He was as
yellow as a guinea when last I saw him. However, the gentle smile still won
through. He was greatly missed on the Liturgy Commission. RIP.

Was it pure coincidence that robbed Sacred Liturgy of three outstanding
Members? Along with 'Kilowatts', and victims of the same fell disorder,
went Archbishop O'Hara's successor in Atlanta Georgia, and a young
Spanish bishop from the Balearic Islands with whom I had struck up an
acquaintance. He had bitter reason to deplore the harm done to his people
by certain female *veraneantes* or summer visitors from mainland Northern
Europe.

'Mil's' house in Bruges caused us certain pangs. A new lift was being
installed *at the expense of the municipality*! Indeed that august body had
responsibility for total maintenance! After Mass the following morning we
were off at the crack of dawn on a journey of 800 odd kilometres, J.C.H.
blithely intoning his parody of a German marching-song: 'Wir fahren,
wir fahren, wir fahren, nach Willebrands!' Around midday 'Mil's' ever
sharp eye spotted a perfect picnic spot among the pines. Out came the
hamper, the solids and two magnificent clarets lovingly chosen by 'Mil's'
VG (later a bishop, Maurits de Keyzer, one of the famous five companions
on the trip from Rome twenty-five years ago).

Let me honour at this point the foresight of Belgian seminarists. Each
year of their progress adds (or added?) to their personal bin in the vintner's
cellars one or two chosen crus apt for long laying-down. When at last they
got their own place, hospitality is (or was) assured for their guests on the
noblest scale. So it was in the pine-woods that summer's day. 'Mil'
demanded the driver's right to siesta. We stretched our legs on a soft
upward path of pine-needles. We arrived at the huge Bavarian Convent for
late evening Mass followed by dinner. It was my introduction to haunches
of venison impaled with miniature models of the parent-beast.

Of that hard-slogging week, memory retains lighter moments, e.g.
entering with J.C.H. a neat little gasthaus to find Volk seated behind a stein
with a fellow theologian; on deeper penetration into the interior, what
looked like a Deanery Conference of local priests similarly installed (what a
good idea!); Gus Weigel dogging me at speed as I hared around the garden

57

in the evening, saying the rosary. Or finally, Jan Willebrands and his staff hauling themselves out of a short breather to tackle the heart-breaking task of writing up the protocol of the week's deliberations.

Paulo maiora canamos! vid. the super-session in the Vatican Palace when for a long evening the Commission *de Doctrina Fidei* and the SPCU met behind locked doors for a crucial part of the debate *De duplici fonte Revelationis*. Cardinals Ottaviani and Bea sat at the head of the long table, the senior to the right, Bea on his left. Members of both teams flanked it either side. Consultors, as usual, crowded the wall seats. Very courteously, the senior Cardinal invited our man to open the batting. Bea had cleverly chosen Karl Rahner as first man in (both being Jesuits).

Audio-mechanics at the Vatican were still in the chrysalis stage. There was only one microphone. Rahner moved purposefully forward. For the next ten minutes or so all that could be said in favour of combining Scripture and Tradition intellectually into a single medium of divine truth as against the traditional concept often parodied as 'parallel pipelines', poured out in passionate Latin. Rahner put down the instrument. There was no applause. He must, however, have sensed the general appreciation: nobody could have done better, or so it seemed.

The Cardinal of the 'Suprema' (i.e. the former Holy Office) called his champion into the lists, Father Sebastian Tromp SJ, one time (and long time) professor of fundamental theology at the Gregorian University, and specialist (*inter alia*) on the Mystical Body in the Greek Fathers. Years ago I had followed his course on that pregnant theme. He had kindly accepted to be obstetrician to my doctorate thesis and when, in the first session of Vatican II, the Gregorian University gave a reception for former alumni among the Council Fathers, he singled me out for his heaviest broadside. Useless to point out to him that the Holy Spirit was guaranteed to be at work in the Aula! 'He works through human agents! Look at the mess you are making of your collaboration, caro!'

On that dramatic Vatican evening my *cher maître*, dear Trompy, stood fearlessly up to the microphone. (At the Gregorian reception he used the privilege of age to sit throughout.) After the ritual salutes, he went straight to the point on which Rahner had balanced part of his argument, triumphantly claiming it was in direct contradiction of a well-known principle of St Cyprian. Rahner sprang instantly to his feet demanding the other Jesuit's microphone. He got a hand to it. Trompy held on and for an unforgettable moment or so the mike swayed between them. This was, however, one encounter Rahner failed to win.

The event calls, I feel, for comment in heroic vein. So! I have often marvelled at the highlights life, like a lighthouse, has periodically beamed over my piebald theological background. They remain a permanent enrichment, available for illumination and joy indefinitely. Among them a microphone sways to and fro against a background of crimson tapestry while Cardinals, and prelates of every degree along with some of the sharpest thinkers in the Church of God, look at one another with a wild surmise ...

*   *   *

The moment comes when the cherry-stones have been carved and the mind can no longer refuse an effort to unify and universalize. What *was* Vatican II, at least for this one Council Father? It was the experience of a lifetime, not to be missed at any price, and, (*misericordia!*) not to be repeated in anyone's lifetime, be he Pope, Prelate, Peritus or most brilliant of Secretaries General!

It was a *liturgical* experience. Not just for the Mass which began the Sessions and the prayers that closed them. The space between: speeches (*'Venerabiles Patres! Mea humili opinione...'*); voting (*'Vota nulla duodecim; Defecerunt scrutantes scrutinio!'*), even the visits to Bars-Jonah and -abbas, integrated a solemn service of homage to our Via, Veritas and Vita, Christ the Lord. We wore choir dress throughout despite inept pressures to adopt 'clergyman'. Pope John in fact had suggested that we should super-impose mozzettas over our mantellettas. Not on! Anyway we boiled like lobsters.

It was a *pastoral* experience. Each bishop – in the Aula, in commission meetings, struggling with texts at his desk – was accompanied by his people for whom he was both witness and judge.

It was a massive *human and humanizing* experience. Not just the Rhine! All the world's rivers flowed into the Tiber! Provincial minds broadened, naive reactions met their challenge, gas-bags were deflated. It was a *debunking* experience, revealing how easily and perseveringly world opinion misses the point. The conciliar process seeks neither victory nor defeat, only *consensus*. (Once only did we vote on the parliamentary model of win or lose and that was for a purely procedural decision: where best to treat of Our Lady: within *Lumen Gentium* or separately? A narrow win for König of Vienna and *Lumen Gentium*!) All the schemata were worked and re-worked until moral unanimity was more than assured.

Last of all, it was a *controlled* experience. At the human level superbly staged, logically and firmly paced despite running four times the length wishful thinkers in Rome (Pope John, I fear, among them) had bargained for. At another level, the deepest, Vatican II was a striking confirmation of

59

Pio Nono's monitum to the Fathers of Vatican I: 'You will find the Holy Spirit within the Council, not outside!'

Poor Volk came very near to arrest by Vatican Police for distributing *outside* the Basilica a document blasting the Decree *Inter Mirifica* (on the Instruments of Social Communication) on the very day the text came up for the vote. Secretary General Pericles got wind of the irregularity. Out came the *sbirri* (policemen), in a very marked manner, to relieve Hermann and companion of their armfuls of seditious(?) literature. Other documents in tidal waves flowed round us from the regions of the Meuse and elsewhere. Partisan gatherings appeared here and there. No doubt some bishops were in sympathy. The experience of years of occupation must have predisposed younger minds towards a very existentialist view of faith and life within Church and State. Yet even the disgruntled Peasant on the Garonne, Jacques Maritain, after searching with lamps through every text of Vatican II, eventually paid handsome tribute to their scrupulous fidelity to the deposit of Faith.

NOTES

1. It was in fact made in a short speech by Bishop Holland himself on 16 October 1963 [Ed.].
2. Cf Cardinal Suenens' chapter: this refers to the Archbishop of Milan's letter of 18 October 1962 to the Cardinal Secretary of State.
3. 'The Pope's Appeal for Peace', address of 4 October 1965, English text CTS S270, 1–12 [Ed.].
4. He was the centrepiece of the first Heythrop College Ecumenical Conference, August 1962, delivering a paper on 'The priest, minister of unity'. English text in *Christian Unity* (Sheed & Ward 1963), 51–81; and *The Unity of Christians* (Geoffrey Chapman 1963), 73–93 [Ed.].
5. In fairness to the CMS let it be recorded that the first high-level ecumenical colloquy to be held in England in our time – it was held behind closed doors and without press detection – occurred at CMS HQ in Hampstead in the summer of 1951. Fr Heenan had become Bishop of Leeds, but he initiated the arrangements. Fr Charles Boyer S.J. of *Unitas* Rome was present; and from the Anglicans Canon Leonard Prestige of St Paul's, Austin Farrer of Oxford and Ian Ramsey [Author].
6. The Institute was founded to provide information about confessional matters, with a view to reunification in Germany [Ed.].
7. *The Ecumenical Council, the Church & Christendom* (Geoffrey Chapman 1961); see also his *A stand on ecumenism: the Council's Decree* (Geoffrey Chapman 1965) [Ed.].
8. *The Ecumenical Council*, 66f.
9. Both became Cardinals, the Dominican on 24 April 1985 as Prefect of the Congregation for Religious & Secular Institutes. Both were asked to contribute to this book.
10. *L'Eglise est une communion* (Cerf 1962); ET Geoffrey Chapman 1964.
11. Chaplain Royal Navy, 1943–6. Port Chaplain, Bombay, 1946–8 [Ed.].

APPENDIX:
BISHOP EMILE-JOSEPH DE SMEDT
ON THE INITIAL SCHEMA *DE ECCLESIA*

'I accuse the *Schema* of three faults – "triumphalism", clericalism, juridicism.'

On 'triumphalism': in the way in which it is composed, in this pompous style, which we are used to in *L'Osservatore Romano* and other documents of that ilk, in which the Church is presented as moving from triumph to triumph and receiving universal admiration for the words and actions of her leaders.

On clericalism: a pyramidical notion, at the base the laity who count for nothing, at the summit the Pope, who counts for everything. By contrast, the Bishop of Bruges reminds us that the whole Church, laity, priests and bishops, form one people of whom the bishops are the servants; he points out the danger of falling into 'episcopalism', 'episcopolatry' and 'papolatry'.

On juridicism: there is nothing on the Motherhood of the Church.

Bishop de Smedt made several striking speeches, perhaps the most notable on 19 November 1962, in the name of the SPCU upon *dialogue oecuménique*, where he set out nine conditions. See also Y. Congar, H. Küng, D. O'Hanlon, *Council speeches of Vatican II* (Sheed & Ward 1964), I.4: 'The priesthood of all believers', 25–8; IV.2 'Religious freedom', 157–68. [Ed.]

5

THE FOUNDATION OF THE SECRETARIAT FOR PROMOTING CHRISTIAN UNITY

THOMAS F. STRANSKY CSP

In The Wiseman Review (The Dublin Review *under other colours*) 236.493 *(Autumn 1962), 203–16, a young Paulist priest from the United States and a member of SPCU since its inception two years earlier, published what was regarded as a most exciting curtain-raiser for the Council: 'The Vatican Council 1962'. He began: 'When a Roman prelate faced a barrage of questions on how the Vatican had been preparing the Second Vatican Council, he responded: "It's a mystery – known to God alone!" That answer is too absolute, and this article attempts to survey the important dates and detail the evolving working methods used for a Council that has no predecessor in the vastness and thoroughness of its preparations.' The Paulist Father finished his article by quoting Pope John. This is how he put it: 'Exactly one month before the Council Fathers convened, the Holy Father broke the silence of his private retreat in order to give a radio/television message to the Catholic world. He said: "In the course of three years of preparations, an array of chosen minds assembled from all parts of the world and every tongue, united in sentiments and in purpose, has gathered together so abundant a wealth of doctrinal and pastoral material as to provide the episcopate of the entire world, when they meet beneath the vaults of the Vatican Basilica [the Aula], themes for a most wise application of the gospel teaching of Christ which for twenty centuries has been the light of humanity redeemed by his blood." ' What would the world episcopate do with such a mountain of documents? Then, neither Pope John nor Fr Stransky knew. Now he reconsiders.*

The author found himself free and avid in Rome the day the Secretariat for Promoting Christian Unity began its promoting in 1960; so he was called to its permanent staff (1960 till 1970, when he went home to USA to become President of the Paulist Fathers for eight years) together with Cardinal Augustin Bea SJ, Mgr Jan Willebrands and Mgr Jean-François Arrighi of Corsica, and then Rev Don Salzmann. They resided – perched precariously – in the via dei Corridori 64 (suitably named), accumulating luxuries like file cabinets, voting members (from Britain, Bishops Heenan and Holland and Fr Gerard Corr OSM; from America, Fr James Cunningham; from Belgium, the great Bishop Emile De Smedt; from Germany, Archbishop Lorenz Jäger...), and consulting members (among them future Cardinals Hermann Volk and Jerome Hamer OP). With a confrère, he has edited Ecumenical Documents I: Doing the truth in charity *(Paulist Press NY 1982). He is presently editing and commenting on 'every single piece of correspondence between Rome and Constantinople, 1958 to 1982 (about 700 items!)'. He is also director of Paulist novices at Oak Ridge, NJ, and a member of the Joint Working Group between the Roman Catholic Church and the World Council of Churches.*

'Youth, what man's age is like doth show;
We may our ends by our beginnings know.'
Sir John Denham (1615–1669), Of Prudence

In late May of 1958 my Paulist superiors sent me to Europe with glorious freedom, generous trust, and an almost carte blanche assignment. I was for a few years to sniff and sift out the gentle breezes of Church renewal in wide-ranging areas of theology and practice. I was interested in the mission renewal, with its focus on Europe itself (is only France pagan?); and I was eager to experience, first-hand, the beginnings of the Catholic response to the ecumenical movement which had already in 1948 been institutionalized within the World Council of Churches. In a positive use of the phrase, I detected in Europe's tired skies the happy cloud of Vatican II, small as a child's hand.

Within seven months of my arrival, Pius XII had died (9 October 1958), his old, unknown 'transitional' successor was elected (28 October) and John XXIII announced his intention to convoke 'an Ecumenical Council for the Universal Church' (25 January 1959).[1]

That previous June I had disembarked from a Dutch liner at Rotterdam. I visited the headquarters of the Grail in Tiltenberg. These missionary lay women told me of, and introduced me to Monsignor Jan Willebrands. The forty-seven year old rector of nearby Warmond seminary was the Dutch bishops' representative for ecumenical concerns – the first such appointment anywhere in the Church.

My notes from our conversation outline Willebrand's description of Europe's only trans-national organization of Catholic scholars: the Catholic Conference for Ecumenical Questions.

In 1950 Jan Willebrands and his fellow countryman, Frans Thijssen, had travelled Europe to enlist the interest of Catholic theologians, historians, biblicists, liturgists and missiologists in taking seriously Protestant and Orthodox ecumenical efforts. The Vatican Holy Office had recently permitted Catholic experts, under strict conditions, to participate in ecumenical discussions,[2] and Pope Pius XII himself had approved the existence of the Catholic Conference.

Annual meetings began in 1952, Willebrands as acting secretary. Over the years the themes were those which were predominating in the World Council of Churches, especially in its Faith & Order Commission. By fortunate coincidence, both Jan Willebrands and the WCC general secretary, Willem A. Visser 't Hooft [cf. *Times* obituary, 6 July 1985], were Dutch. They met frequently, and in their chats did not have to exercise their multi-lingual skills. After each such meeting Willebrands and Thijssen headed south and reported to Pius XII's designated contact-man, a consultor to the Holy Office since 1949 and former rector of Rome's prestigious Biblical Institute (and also the Pope's confessor) – the Jesuit Father Augustin Bea.

The last conference meeting was in 1963. During the eleven years, on the fluctuating list of seventy to eighty within this unique fraternity were France's Yves Congar, Irenée Beaupère, Christophe Dumont; Belgium's Jerome Hamer, Lambert Beauduin, Emmanuel Lanne, and Louvain's Charles Möller, Gustave Thils, Roger Aubert; Hubert Jedin, Edward Stakemeier, Baltazar Fischer, Josef Jungmann, Karl Rahner, Hermann Volk, Hans Urs von Balthasar, John Vodopivec, Hans Küng, Johannes Feiner; England's Bernard Leeming, Maurice Bévenot, Henry Francis Davis; the USA's sole Gustave Weigel; the Middle East's Pierre Duprey, Jean Corbon, Robert Clément; Rome's Jean-François Arrighi, Jan Witte, Josef Höfer, and Charles Boyer.

It was this network of scholars, facilitated in their prudent, forward steps by the diplomatic, quietly zealous Jan Willebrands, that would shape the original staff of the Secretariat for Promoting Christian Unity (hereafter, SPCU) and much of its original body of consultors.[3]

The SPCU ushered in the official entrance of the Roman Catholic Church into the one ecumenical movement. Twenty-five years later I risk to judge that the period from 1 January 1960 to the opening of Vatican II on 11 October 1962 was far more critical than the Council itself for the future official *modus operandi* of the Church in that movement. 'What-if?s' are not the stuff of history, yet in what follows I ask myself, with the reader, that question at almost every step into those thirty-four months of the early 1960s.

II

Already in his original 1959 announcement, John XXIII envisaged the Council to be of service 'not only for the spiritual good and joy of the Christian people but also an invitation to the separated communities to seek again that unity for which so many souls are longing in these days throughout the world'.[4] The announcement perplexed other Christians. Was this a papal attempt to reunite all Christians in the fashion of the Councils of Lyons (1274) and of Florence (1438–42) – a common table, presided over by the Pope, at which 'reunion formulae' could and would be signed? Pope John gradually clarified his intention, perhaps even to himself.

His language shifted attention from a reunion Council to one of the internal renewal of the Roman Catholic Church; from other Christians' joining the Catholic leaders for debate and, one hopes, eventual consensus, to their more distant watching of the Roman Catholic Church renewing itself through its own exclusive gathering.

Then a middle way emerged – between a reunion council and an exclusively Catholic event. Its principal architects and pavers were the elderly Pope John and equally elderly Cardinal Bea: both were born in 1881. Together they taught so many of us 'the art of the timely answer from old men' (Eccles 8:9).

Pope John's second slate of cardinals included Father Bea (14 December 1959). The Pope had met the Jesuit scholar only once, very briefly, during his March 1959 audience with the staff and consultors of the Holy Office. He was made a cardinal, one surmises, in order to give recognition to the Jesuits and to offer traditional respect to Pope John's predecessor;[5] Bea had been a close advisor to Pius XII and, since 1945, his confessor. In Father Schmidt's words, already at the first audience Pope John granted Cardinal Bea (6 January 1960), 'they understood each other perfectly'. The 'close spiritual sympathy between the two was altogether confirmed by later events in connection with the Council . . . Few people understood Pope John's idea of the Council and worked so hard to put it into practice as did Cardinal Bea.' Dr Vittorino Veronese, former Director-General of UNESCO, told Bea that in his last audience with Pope John (20 April 1963), two months before the Pope's death, John XXIII had confided to him: 'Imagine what a grace the Lord has given in making me discover Cardinal Bea.'[6]

As the record has now uncovered, in early 1960 Bea was not inactive, one who was only, as he describes himself in his spiritual diary, a quietly working, praying cardinal in Rome.[7] Two weeks into wearing the red, the Cardinal wrote to Edward Stakemeier, director of the Johann-Adam Möhler Institute in Paderborn, established by Archbishop Lorenz Jäger.[8] Bea suggested that the Paderborn ecumenical institute consider making its own a proposal to have the Holy See establish as an organ of the Roman Curia 'a commission for the ecumenical movement'; Bea would be willing to make suggestions to the draft. Stakemeier quickly sent the draft. On 20 January Bea responded with suggested omissions and additions, e.g., the title should be 'for ecumenical affairs' (in re ecumenica). He urged Stakemeier to address the letter directly to the Pope, but send it first to Cardinal Bea who would act as intermediary. A month later Bea again wrote to Paderborn. Because of his experience of the Curia, with its peculiar susceptibilities, Bea now preferred to drop the word *ecumenical* with its various interpretations, and to use instead, 'A Papal Commission for the Promotion of the Unity of Christians.' The new title would also 'avoid the question of "return" and the like'.

Without any changes in Bea's draft, Archbishop Jäger now owned the proposal, and he sent it to Bea on 4 March.[9] Cardinal Bea added his own supporting elaboration, then forwarded it to Pope John on 11 March 1960. Bea's elaboration is not in the public record; following the strict Vatican rules, immediately after the Cardinal's death all his private papers were moved to the Vatican Secret Archives. The Jäger proposal made no direct reference to the upcoming Council, except that it alludes to Pope John's first encyclical *Ad Petri Cathedram* (29 June 1959). Did Cardinal Bea make a tighter connection between the proposed Commission in the Roman Curia and the preparations for the Council?

To Cardinal Bea's surprise, the answer came within forty-eight hours, and over a weekend. On Sunday, 13 March, the Pope's private secretary, Monsignor Loris Capovilla, telephoned to Cardinal Bea that John XXIII 'agrees in principle' with the proposal and wants to see him the same day. Bea did so, and Pope John asked him to draft statutes for the new commission.[10] What Bea did not know was the hand-written note John XXIII put on the margin of the proposal the next day: 'Cardinal Bea will be president of the proposed Pont(ifical) Comm(ission). Answer and reach accord with the Bishop of Paderborn [Jäger]. Prepare everything, but wait until after Easter for the official publication; this will bring it into line with the other commissions which will be named on various other matters of the Council.'[11]

But within the week the Pope became preoccupied with possible opposition within his Curia, and so he directly told Cardinal Bea on 20 March that 'secretariat' rather than 'commission' would be a more prudent name; the low-keyed title would offer 'more freedom of movement in a rather new and unique field'.[12] It should be a preparatory body restricted to the Council preparations. Prudence about the present, one step at a time. Bea submitted his final draft of statutes on 23 April 1960.

I have detailed this because until late 1981, with Bea's own silence, the taken-for-granted history had been different. Even Cardinal Jäger, whom I heard relate the history at Bea's funeral in 1968, stated that Paderborn had taken the initiative, Bea agreed with the proposal and sent it on to Pope John.[13] The correct version has the original idea and gentle provocations and serious revisions coming from Cardinal Bea. It reveals once more to those who worked closely with the Cardinal how his four decades of experience of Rome and the Curia would guide us during the eight remaining years of his life.

On 30 May 1960, after a more public event, John XXIII brought the Curial cardinals into his study. He told them he was soon to announce the preparatory commissions of the Council, to establish also a 'Secretariat for the Union of Christians', and to have Cardinal Bea as its president.[14] That completed SPCU's pre-history.

III

In that same late May of 1960 I was in Rome. I had just begun my temporary summer asignment – helping out during the tourist season at the Paulist parish of Santa Susanna. Monsignor Willebrands was passing through the City. He had just come from Geneva, where Dr Visser 't Hooft had asked him to inquire from Vatican authorities if Catholic Observers could be sent to the WCC meetings of Faith & Order and of the Central Committee (St Andrews, Scotland, 16–24 August 1960). Willebrands invited me to the mid-September Catholic Conference for Ecumenical Questions. What the Dutch ecumenist did of course not tell me was that Cardinal Bea had confided in him what Pope John would soon announce, and that Bea had asked him, upon return to Holland, confidentially to relay the same news in Geneva to Visser 't Hooft and to ask if Bea could soon meet the WCC general secretary.[15]

Pentecost is our highlighted religious community feast. Two of us Paulists participated in the Pentecost Vespers at St Peter's Basilica (5 June). Pope John was presiding. To my surprise, at the end of the service he read his *Superno Dei Nutu* (his *motu proprio* establishing the Secretariat): the preliminary (ante-preparatorial) stage of the Council is over; the preparation of drafts (*schemata*) shall begin in the autumn through ten drafting commissions and three secretariats; among these organs is a secretariat which would enable 'those who bear the name of Christians but are separated from this Apostolic See . . . to follow the work of the Council and to find more easily that path by which they may arrive at the unity Jesus Christ sought from His Heavenly Father with fervent prayers'.[16]

Nothing, nothing ever flitted across my imagination that I, a thirty-year-old priest, could or would ever be directly involved in that startling, active symbol of Pope John's loving concern to promote Christian unity.

The day after Pentecost, Cardinal Bea was publicly appointed the SPCU president. He submitted to the Pope three names for the SPCU secretary. On the list was Jan Willebrands, and John XXIII appointed him on 29

June. During July the first list of SPCU members and consultors was drawn up and submitted to higher authorities. Many of their names, plus some from other sources, formed the approved list of sixteen members (with right to vote) and twenty consultors. The *Osservatore Romano* published the names on 3 September.[17]

In August Willebrands as an observer joined the WCC Central Committee meeting in Scotland.[18] In its published report, the Committee considered Pope John's SPCU 'an important development in the Roman Catholic Church . . . It will no longer leave all initiative in this field (of ecumenical conversation) to individual Roman Catholics but begin to speak and act itself in relation to other Churches and to ecumenical organizations'.[19] As Visser 't Hooft later put it, they finally had 'an address at the Vatican'.[20]

Willebrands's Catholic Conference gathered at Gazzada in northern Italy, during 19–24 September. Years later Cardinal Willebrands remarked that 'since the work of the Conference, like all ecumenical work, had hitherto been often regarded with suspicion, those who came to Gazzada were a little surprised to find there Cardinal Bea, Cardinal Montini, Archbishop of Milan [later Pope Paul VI], and Cardinal Alfrink [Utrecht]'. Bea met at length with those who were already designated as SPCU consultors this being – 'although limited to those who happened to be present, the first meeting, however unofficial, of the SPCU'.[21]

Before that, when at August's end Willebrands returned from Scotland to Rome and reported to Bea, he also contacted me. He asked, whether I would come aboard the new little Bea/Willebrands boat in Vatican waters as one of the two crewmen (the other being Jean-François Arrighi, a Corsican with many years of ministry in Rome and in the Curia, much of it as Cardinal Tisserant's private secretary). It seems my primitive ecumenical knowledge, my enthusiastic commitment to the movement, my youthful energy, and my mother tongue, along with abilities in German, French and Italian, were sufficient assets. My superior-general in New York quickly approved. Only then, in mid-September, did I first meet the SPCU helmsman.

Until then I had never met a bishop (except my confirming and ordaining ones), let alone a cardinal. In his most simple quarters at the Brazilian College, I now saw in that seventy-nine year old, with hooded eyes and bent shoulders, the mark of one long huddled over a desk, his slender back like a 'frail tree exposed to a constant gale of scholarship'. We talked at length, in the hope, I guess, that first impressions would be accurate, needing later confirmation by day-to-day experience. I judged immediately that Cardinal Bea lived by his borrowed principle, which he later called 'the ecumenical motto': 'Do the truth in charity' (Eph 4:15).

What I did not perceive then would be revealed in those next eight years with him: a churchman who never lost his nerve or his calmness – an obvious charismatic quality in those first SPCU years of understandable jitters. To this often impatient American, Bea possessed an extraordinary sense of timing: when to push whom for what, when to lie back and wait (and this quality I appreciated more after the fact). In his judgements one saw dove-like simplicity *and* serpentine wisdom. With us originals and later staff additions, the Jesuit was, as he resolved to be in his private retreat notes of 1960: 'with subordinates: always friendly, patient, kind, but not familiar: firm and clear'.[22] And his 1962 diary entry: 'Towards all who work with me: show confidence in them, prove my love for them whenever I can, be patient with them – making allowances for the character of each individual – and make sure that it is a joy to work with me. Pay tribute to the work they do.'[23] Cardinal Willebrands well remembers that when he became the SPCU secretary, the Cardinal advised, 'I shall not mind if you sometimes make mistakes, but I shall mind if you don't do something practical'.[24] So the foursome was set, the papal mandate in hand, and, as the Cardinal wryly remarked in that initial chat, 'No one will tell us, "This is the way we did it last year".'

The first minor headache was office space. The SPCU was a local name without a habitation. The Vatican administration had designated rooms of the second floor of an old and large palazzo on the Via dei Corridori, two blocks from Piazza San Pietro. But we were to wait until the former occupants, a Vatican employee's family, had moved out and the painters and masons had done their frescos. Weeks went by while in often bizarre ways of efficient team-work, we four were preparing for the first plenary meeting of the SPCU's members and consultors, papally convoked for 14–15 November 1960. Only on 21 October did Willebrands, Arrighi and myself walk into the completed office. In that space were cramped a midget entrance parlour, three small rooms, and by a still inexplicable shift of interior walls, four bathrooms. No lightbulbs or stationery or soap, no filing cabinets were in evidence; only two desks with chairs. Our sole typewriter I borrowed from Santa Susanna, and for two years bathtubs served as holy archives.

Many SPCU visitors over the next months were under the impression that the entire palazzo was the Holy See's gift to unity. And when two prelates came to look over the facilities in preparation for Pope John's visit to each of the curial offices, they decided that to avoid the *brutta figura* of the milieu, we four would have to meet His Holiness elsewhere – in the largest room, with ornate cushioned furniture and damasked walls, of the Oriental Congregation, which dominated most of the palazzo (that visit, 9 January 1961). But we did move in. The overarching image, I recall, was from P. G. Wodehouse: once you climb on a tiger's back, you should carefully consider your next moves.

IV

On that back, I will describe the six major steps, intentional or not so planned, over the next two years.

PUBLIC RELATIONS OR ALSO DRAFTERS?

Superno Dei Nutu (5 June 1960) directed the SPCU to help other Christians to 'follow the work of the Council'. Nothing is stated about its internal functions, as, for example, how the SPCU shall proceed at its plenary sessions. Had we the right to draft *schemata* and to present them to the Central Preparatory Commission? I heard rumours that some in the Curia, especially in the Holy Office (Cardinal Ottaviani, also president of the Theological Commission), in the secretariat of State (Cardinal Tardini), and on the Central Commission's staff (Archbishop Felici) preferred the SPCU to be only a public relations and quasi-press office for the needs of the 'separated brethren'; leave *schemata* to the more competent – the Commissions.

Cardinal Bea and Pope John were quite aware of this counter-pressure. Bea needed a decision before the November plenary session. Rather than press the issue too forcibly by a public act, John XXIII gave Cardinal Bea the nod to proceed with the drafts. Thus for the next two years, juridically the SPCU in fact functioned like the Preparatory Commissions.

But these commissions were only preparatory. They would cease once the Fathers had convened and the Council had set up its own working tools. The SPCU became the exception. On 6 August 1962 the SPCU was simply confirmed as an organ of the Council itself, with the same structure and functions it had enjoyed during the preparatory stage.[25] But still, some jurists understandably pressed, could the SPCU present drafts on the Council floor and co-operate in joint commissions with themes common to both? Cardinal Bea took the ambiguity directly to John XXIII, who himself decided yes by a rescript he promulgated a few days after the first Council session had begun (19 October 1962).[26] The SPCU was protected!

The SPCU could now prove itself before the Council Fathers by the presentations and contents of its drafts.[27] At the Council's end, we would hear no murmuring objections to Paul VI's confirmation of the SPCU as a permanent office of the Holy See.[28]

WESTERN CHRISTIANS OR ALSO ORTHODOX?

Superno Dei Nutu did not distinguish between the two major groups of other Christians, those of the Orthodox Churches (including the pre-Chalcedonian)[29] and of the Protestant Communions. Would the SPCU be responsible for contacts with the Orthodox, or would that be the competence of the Preparatory Commission for the (Catholic) Eastern Churches (Cardinal Amleto Cicognani)?

Cardinal Bea had told the Pope that he considered himself little qualified to handle the problems of the East; he had enough work with the West. Pope John would have it otherwise but conceded: Cardinal Cicognani's Commission shall be responsible for the other Christian Churches of the East.[30] When in July of 1960 Bea drew up his list of recommended SPCU members and consultors, no Eastern-rite bishop was on the members-list, and only two consultors had acknowledged competence for Orthodox concerns (Christophe Dumont, OP of the Istina Centre in Paris; Pierre Dumont, OSB of Chevetogne); these two consultors should help in whatever collaboration would be forthcoming with Cardinal Cicognani's Commission.

Although that Commission at the First Session would present its own *schema* on principles, ways and means of achieving reunion with the Eastern Churches, it had never exercised its initial competence of direct contacts with Orthodox leaders. Through consultation, especially of several SPCU loyalists, Bea began to realize that the Orthodox did not wish to have contact with the Oriental Commission but did desire such with the SPCU. After the first SPCU plenary meeting he reported this to Pope John. The Pope replied, 'All right, Your Eminence, take them by all means'.[31]

This inclusive ambit of 'all other Christians' gave the SPCU the unequivocal right to contact the Orthodox Churches on the possibility of delegated Observers to Vatican II. And because of these direct contacts with Patriarch Athenagoras, the SPCU prepared for his meeting with Pope Paul in Jerusalem (December 1964), and for the mutual lifting of the 1054 anathemas between the Sees of Rome and of Constantinople (7 December 1965).[32] Enjoying its drafting rights, the SPCU was the eventual sole author of the Decree on Ecumenism, which considered the restoration of full unity as one and indivisible.[33]

CHRISTIANS ONLY OR ALSO JEWS?

Left out of any direct consideration by the Council's preparatory structures, as outlined in *Superno Dei Nutu*, were the Church's relations with non-Christians. One presumed that both the Theological and the Missions Commissions would treat the subject, but without direct consultation with people of other faiths. Dialogue was not yet a word on Catholic lips.

Since Pope John had first announced Vatican II, several Jewish leaders were vocally hoping that the assembled bishops would at least not reinforce theological supports for anti-semitism, but instead, out of integrity, the Council should try to face head-on Catholic understandings, attitudes, and relations with the Jewish people in the post-Holocaust common era. Other Jewish leaders, more quietly, were worried that Vatican II would, by its statements, even increase Jewish fears.[34]

The topic was not in the Jäger/Bea proposal and did not come up in the Pope John/Cardinal Bea discussions prior to *Superno Dei Nutu*. In fact, according to Monsignor Loris Capovilla, the Pope's secretarial confidant, until a week after *Superno Dei Nutu* 'it never entered Pope John XXIII's mind that the Council ought to be occupied also with the Jewish question (*questione ebraica*) and with anti-semitism'.[35] The Jewish theme reached the Pope's consciousness at a private audience on 13 June 1960.

Upon recommendation from the French ambassador to the Holy See,[36] John XXIII talked with Professor Jules Isaac. This Jewish scholar had been the director of education in France, the author of French textbooks, a noted historian, and promoter of the Paris-based society of Jews and Christians, *Amitié judéo-chrétienne*. Isaac presented to Pope John a lengthy memorandum about the history of Catholic attitudes and actions towards the Jews, especially as these were expressed in the Church Fathers, the liturgy, and catechisms. But at the private audience Isaac had time only to outline his report.

'How in a few minutes', Isaac reminisced,[37] was he 'to make (the Pope) understand that at the same time as a material ghetto, there has been a spiritual ghetto in which the Church gradually enclosed old Israel'; that there had always been a Catholic 'teaching of contempt (*mépris*)' towards the Jews, but now that tradition faces a growing counter-pressure, 'a purificator' in the Church, so that between the two contrary tendencies, Catholic opinion is divided, 'remains wavering'; that the head of the Church, 'a voice from the summit', could show the good path by solemnly condemning 'the teaching of contempt, in essence, anti-Christian'?

Towards the end of the conversation, Isaac suggested that the Pope set up a committee to study 'The Jewish Question'. 'I thought of that from the beginning of our meeting', replied Pope John, and smilingly added, 'You are right in having more than hope . . . I am the head (*chef*) but I must also consult . . . Here is not an absolute monarchy.' He then asked Capovilla to have Isaac contact Cardinal Bea, 'whom the Pope trusted and on this subject had confidence in the Cardinal's wisdom'.[38]

Two days later, on 15 June, Isaac met Bea, and could discuss with him at length his memorandum already in the Pope's hands. The record is now silent until three months later. On 18 September Pope John received Cardinal Bea in audience, and 'formally charged the SPCU with the task to prepare a declaration dealing with the Jewish People'.[39] At the SPCU plenary session in mid-November, Bea communicated this special papal mandate, but told us that unlike other topics, even the fact of initial discussion on what he called 'The Jewish Question' and the later drafting of our reflections had to be, at John XXIII's request, *sub secreto*. Had both the Pope and the Cardinal already anticipated the delicate, often twisted path this topic would follow over the next six years?

Upon insistence of the Council Fathers during the Second Session (1963), the SPCU enlarged the *schema* to include all non-Christians (*Nostra Aetate*). After Vatican II Paul VI continued to confide Catholic/Jewish relations to the SPCU,[40] which, in turn, became a partner in establishing the International Catholic/Jewish Liaison Committee (December 1970). In late 1974, Pope Paul created a Commission for the Church's religious relations with the Jews, with at least for the time being, the SPCU president and secretary having the titles of president and vice-president.[41] The Commission promulgated 'Guidelines for the Implementation of *Nostra Aetate*, sec. 4 (the paragraph on the Jews)' on 1 December 1974 and on 24 June 1985, 'Notes on the Correct Way to Present Jews and Judaism in Preaching and Catechesis'.[42]

LEADERS KEPT AT A DISTANCE, OR NOT?

The SPCU broke through the ancient walls of distance and suspicion by arranging visits of Christian leaders with the Pope. The first *tête-à-tête* since the Reformation of a Pope with the head of another Christian Communion was that of John XXIII and the Archbishop of Canterbury, six months after *Superno Dei Nutu*. The arrangements for Archbishop Geoffrey Fisher's visit (2 December 1960) were not without difficulty and, in hindsight, humour.[43]

On the occasion of Monsignor Willebrands's presence at the WCC meeting at St Andrews (mid-August, 1960), Archbishop Fisher, one of the six WCC presidents, asked him to inquire in Rome if a visit with John

XXIII would be feasible upon the Archbishop's return from a late November visit to the Ecumenical Patriarch Athenagoras in Constantinople. On 9 September Cardinal Bea directly asked Pope John, who replied, 'Why not?'

Most of the ensuing obstacles came, I suspect, from a miffed Cardinal Tardini, Secretary of State. The papal decision bypassed 'proper consultative channels'. And in the main steps for arrangements, the SPCU was dealing directly with Lambeth Palace in London (the Archbishop's official office and residence), not through the Secretariat of State and the British Legation to the Holy See.

I was drafting and typing the first letters to Lambeth at home, on my rattling seminary typewriter with exhausted vowels; the SPCU doors were still closed. I knew by heart almost every word of the growing Lambeth/SPCU file. This preparation occasioned the first SPCU experience of Vatican 'leaks'. As December drew near and the upcoming visit was receiving enormous publicity – accurate or not, Cardinal Bea asked me to prepare for the Secretariat of State a long memorandum on the step-by-step background of the visit, with summaries of our internal memos, of Fisher's and Bea's letters, etc. Two days after Cardinal Bea had sent the final text (in English) to the Secretariat of State, *Il Tempo*'s vaticanologist, without his mentioning source or using quotations, reproduced that memorandum almost verbatim in the daily newspaper. It seemed to be my first article in Italian.

The visit was also my first experience of the scrupulosity of Vatican protocol, especially 'compromise-protocol' if some wanted to display official coolness and to cut the visit's import down to size.

The historical break-through was to be called a mere 'courtesy visit'. The only title to be used throughout was *Dottore* Fisher (we had even to struggle to have approved for the *Osservatore Romano*'s official notice of the cold fact, 'Anglican Archbishop of Canterbury'). Archbishop Fisher was most hospitably received in residence at the Venerable English College, but the limousine which would bring him to and from the Vatican should have no Vatican license plates (so our Arrighi rented a car from a nearby agency). Bea was not allowed to be present at any stage of the audience. No photographs of the Pope and Archbishop together were taken, and Cardinal Tardini forbade even private cameras at the post-audience, afternoon lawn-tea at Cardinal Bea's residence in the Brazilian College.[44] Thus, the only extant Vatican proof of that visit is that short notice in the *Osservatore Romano* afternoon edition of 2 December 1960.

My own protocol contribution on the day before the visit was very modest, very proper, and most welcomed. I invited Colonel Robert Hornby, Archbishop Fisher's recently appointed press officer who had already been in Rome several days, to come to the Paulist apartment with his shaking, bewildered head, in order to share with me a wee glass or two of the pastor's black label scotch (Hornby called it whisky).

Nevertheless, what most struck me before, during and after the entire event was the humble calmness of Pope John and Cardinal Bea. They realized that the visit was cracking the rock of previously negative Roman Catholic/Anglican relations at the highest levels in England and in Rome. For the two the visit was a bold success, despite the humiliating compromises accepted to satisfy the hesitant. The occasion was also one more happy link which was forging the bond between the Pope and the Cardinal, both approaching fourscore years. And the visit provided us fledgelings with a splendid opportunity widely to publicize what the SPCU was about (indeed it was my first attempt at a SPCU background paper for reporters' use).

Although the SPCU could arrange no further visits of other Church leaders with Pope John until after Cardinal Tardini's death in July 1961, the precedent had been set for what have since become normal acts of Christian courtesy among Churchmen and women: doing the truth in charity. As Cardinal Bea reflected, 'With a meeting between heads of Christian communions . . . we must realize that we are treading on most holy ground'.[45]

The visit also moved Archbishop Fisher, in February 1961, to appoint Canon Bernard Pawley of Ely Cathedral as his personal representative to the SPCU. He came to Rome from time to time to check in, broaden his contacts, and report back. With that arrangement as a precedent, in March 1962 the Council of Evangelical Churches in Germany, the birthplace of the Reformation, assigned the same task to Dr Edmund Schlink, professor of theology at Heidelberg.

OBSERVERS TO VATICAN II?

The most public symbol of Rome's deliberate distance from the World Council of Churches had been the Holy Office's refusal to have Roman Catholics present in any role, no matter how 'unofficial', at the first two General Assemblies – Amsterdam (1948) and Evanston, Illinois (1954).[46]

But now John XXIII was Pope, Vatican II was on the horizon, the SPCU was the WCC's 'address in Rome', and already the SPCU and WCC officers were in direct if unofficial contact. Visser 't Hooft invited the

SPCU to delegate Observers to the Third General Assembly, convoked for 18 November–5 December 1961, in New Delhi. One presumed a warm green light was finally glowing in the Vatican. We wrote in confidence to a selected five, would they be willing and able to be free for the Assembly, if so designated as official Observers? Three of them were already SPCU consultors; their New Delhi participation would be a valuable asset to the SPCU as it progressed with its *schemata*. The five accepted with enthusiasm. In June 1961 Cardinal Bea sent the list of the names to Cardinal Ottaviani for 'clearance'.

Without even informal consultation with Bea, Ottaviani responded: the Holy Office claims the right to decide the principle, and that decision is that no official RC Observers shall go to India. Although a copy of Bea's protest to Ottaviani had gone to John XXIII's desk, the Pope did not have to intervene. In early July the two Cardinals reached a compromise: five SPCU delegated Observers, yes; but none of them to be members, consultors, or staff of the SPCU.[47]

This was a most critical decision. If the Catholic Church had not sent official observers to this jealously cherished meeting of Anglican, Protestant and Orthodox Churches, then in understandable reciprocity those Churches would not even have considered the possibility of their similar participation in Vatican II a year later.

Even before the SPCU had existed, in August 1959 Pope John publicly alluded to the 'reasonableness' of our separated brethren's presence at the Council, if they wanted.[48] In late January 1960, Cardinal Tardini expressed the same view on French television.[49] Father Antoine Wenger, a French journalist with so many Curial contacts at that time, commented that 'the idea itself seemed to be quite audacious in Roman circles. The Holy Office, notably, was not very favourable to it.'[50]

One of the freedoms of movement for the SPCU was its rightful ability, without 'clearance from above', to move into other Christian circles and there, with informality and without publicity, to sound out the 'Observer question'. The SPCU second plenary session had already raised it in February 1961. In April the SPCU staff, in consultation with the Preparatory Commission on the Eastern Churches, drafted a working document on the subject.

On 1 September 1961, Pope John mandated that the 'whether, how, and under what title non-Catholics be invited to the Council' be treated at the second session of the Central Preparatory Commission (November).[51] Then Cardinals Bea and Cicognani presented their case. The Commission overwhelmingly approved the proposal.[52] But the only comment in the

Commission's official press communiqué was that a 'simply consultative vote' was taken; 'the final decision on such an important matter belongs exclusively to the Holy Father'; and 'premature would be any conjecture one way or the other'.[53]

We in the SPCU presumed 'a New Delhi reverse': how in reciprocity could we expect the WCC and the world confessional bodies, such as the Lutheran World Federation and the World Methodist Council, to invite the Roman Catholic Church to send Observers to their future major meetings, if our Church would not invite such to Vatican II?

Six weeks later Pope John publicly settled the question in his allocution, *Humanae Salutis* (25 December 1961), which formally convoked Vatican II: many other Christians 'happily hope to be able to send to the Council, in the name of their Communities (*Coetuum*), their own representatives who will make it possible for them to follow the Council proceedings more closely. This is a great hope and consolation to us. And precisely in order to facilitate these contacts, we have already instituted a Secretariat for this specific purpose.'[54]

The public decision had been worked out in confidential detail: delegated Observers can attend the closed assemblies where *schemata* are presented for open discussion; the Observers are excluded from commission work meetings, unless with the president's permission for special reasons; they have no right to speak or vote at the general assemblies; the SPCU has the task 'to mediate between the organs of the Council and the Observers whatever information is necessary for following more closely and competently the Council work. To such sessions competent people, including Council Fathers, can be invited, in order that the Observers are exactly informed on the Council themes'.[55]

With this decision and these statutes in hand, Monsignor Willebrands frequently packed his travel bag for personal contacts with other Christian leaders. They, in turn, would follow their different juridical ways in determining if there were reasonable hope that a formal SPCU invitation would receive a positive answer. Dr Visser 't Hooft, and others, had already strongly advised us that if the Holy See were to extend invitations, they be sent directly to the Churches and to the world confessional bodies, and not through the WCC.

The SPCU secretary travelled first to the Ecumenical Patriarchate in Constantinople and to the Church of Greece in Athens (14–20 February); then to Archbishop Michael Ramsey, who presided over the Lambeth Conference of Bishops, and to Dr Scharf of the Evangelical Church of Germany (March); then to a Geneva meeting of the secretaries of the world confessional bodies (3 April 1962). At this last gathering were present, besides Dr Visser 't Hooft, representatives from the Lutheran World Federation, the World Presbyterian Alliance, the World Methodist Council, the Baptist World Alliance, the International Congregational Council; the World Convention of the Churches of Christ (Disciples), the World Society of Friends; the Old Catholic Church (Union of Utrecht), the Pentecostals; the Patriarchates of Constantinople and of Moscow.

From 13 May to 2 June 1962 Willebrands travelled eastwards for similar contacts with the 'non-Chalcedonian' Churches: the Coptic Church of Egypt; the Orthodox Church of Ethiopia; the Armenian Orthodox (Catholicate of Cilicia); and the Syrian Orthodox. On the way back (1 June) he again visited Patriarch Athenagoras.

The favourable responses slowly arrived in our office. From late May into July, Cardinal Bea was signing the formal invitations: first to Archbishop Michael Ramsey (Anglican Communion); then to the world confessional bodies; then to the above non-Chalcedonian Churches. Lastly, on 24 July, Cardinal Bea formally invited Patriarch Athenagoras to delegate Observers, and similar letters went directly to the other Orthodox Churches: Alexandria, Antioch, Jerusalem, Cyprus, and Greece. These invitations requested a response, with the names, before 15 September.[56]

During August and September the silence from the Orthodox was perturbing. More than two decades later, no one has still been able completely to unravel the tangled mass of events and intentions. 'Messy, messy, messy' were my mutterings on the evening of 11 October 1962, despite my grateful image of that morning's presence of thirty-eight delegated Observers in the two front rows which faced the high altar of St Peter's and the presider, Pope John XXIII.

Already the first Pan-Orthodox Conference (Rhodes, 24 September–2 October 1961) had resolved that in future relations with other Churches, the Orthodox would adopt a common stance. In that spirit, for example, relations with the Roman Catholic Church and its coming Council would be decided together, and not by individual Orthodox Churches of their own. Patriarch Athenagoras, more than all others, wanted to send Observers. He had sent this position and an account of Monsignor Willebrands's February visit to the other autocephalous Churches, including the Moscow Patriarchate. But unanimity of decision was the condition, and Athenagoras was nervous over the previous unofficial negative stances towards Vatican II from Athens and Moscow.

In May 1961 *The Journal of the Patriarchate of Moscow* had published an unsigned article which caricatured Pope John's intentions for Vatican II and excluded 'any participation whatsoever by us in the work of the new Vatican Council'. The article ended, 'The Patriarchate of Moscow replies to Cardinal Bea, *Non Possumus*' (we are not able).[57] In the SPCU we presumed *Non Possumus* was already a reply; no invitation had been mailed to Moscow. But in August 1962, on the occasion of the WCC Central Committee meeting in Paris, Monsignor Willebrands spoke with Archbishop Nikodim, president of the Moscow Patriarchate's Department on Religious Affairs. Willebrands returned to Rome with the ambivalent results: in principle, he could personally inform the Holy Synod in Moscow on Vatican II, and the SPCU could transmit an invitation *if* the Synod later found it possible to accept one. Take the risk! In strictest secrecy, Willebrands, with clearance from Pope John and the secretariat of State (and a visa from the USSR embassy), flew to Moscow on 27 September and returned on 2 October with the answer: send the invitation. On 4 October Cardinal Bea did so, by telegram and by express-letter.

Constantinople was already aware of the visit. On 6 October Athenagoras telegrammed to Bea: any news yet?, and to Patriarch Alexis: any decision yet? The Moscow patriarch answered him the next day: nothing new to communicate. So on that same day, the 7th, Patriarch Athenagoras made his decision: because of a presumed lack of unanimity, he could not delegate Observers to Vatican II. He telephoned his representative to the WCC in Geneva, Bishop Emilianos Timiadis: go to Rome and communicate the sad news to Pope John and to Cardinal Bea.

The fact of the secret Moscow visit reached the press on 7 October through the *France-Presse* agency's release from the Russian capital. Rome was abuzz. A first-ever visit of a Vatican official to Moscow had political repercussions, as the Italian press is wont to perceive in every Vatican gesture. 'What secretly went on?' I composed a simple factual press release for 10 October; otherwise, we all kept mum. The release concluded: 'As far as the sending of Observer-delegates is concerned, it must be pointed out that the final decision belongs to the Holy Synod of the Church of Russia.'

The delegated Observers from other groups were already arriving, and we were getting them settled with their lodgings, council passports, and documents. One of them had already had his pocket-book deftly picked during his first visit to St Peter's (four years later he told me that was his 'only mistake of Protestant naïveté in the Holy City'). On 9 October, Bishop Emilianos saw Cardinal Bea and Pope John. Not even the eagle-eyed journalists noticed his one-day stop-over.

On the day Vatican II opened, 11 October 1962, the SPCU received the Moscow cable, dated the 10th. The Russians were coming. The next afternoon Archpriest Vitalyi Borovoi and the Archimandrite Vladimir Kotliarov arrived for a most delicate assignment. They joined their fellow Observers for the closed general assembly the next morning. Of all Eastern Orthodoxy, on both sides of what Churchill had dubbed the Iron Curtain, only the Church of Russia was present.

In those few overloaded months of 1962 misunderstandings of intentions, even inexact chronology of events, caused tensions first between Moscow and Rome, then Constantinople and Moscow, then Constantinople and Rome. A careless, public judgement from any official Vatican source would have been disastrous. In all this muddle and its aftermath, Monsignor Willebrands, Cardinal Bea, Pope John and Patriarch Athenagoras exercised holy diplomacy: all four uttered not a public word. Constantinople's delegated Observers attended the Third and Fourth Sessions.[58]

Although in no way foreseen in 1962, these contacts with other Christian Communions had initiated the personal and organizational relations which in the post-Vatican II years led to the active presence of SPCU-delegated Observers at confessional and inter-confessional gatherings, to a variegated series of international and national bilateral dialogues with Orthodox, Anglicans and Protestants, and to ongoing collaboration with the World Council of Churches and with the world confessional bodies, such as the Lutheran World Federation, the first to have with the SPCU a joint dialogue commission (1966).

Relations with the Church of Russia had so improved during the first session that negotiations were successful for the release of Ukrainian Metropolitan Josyf Slipyi from a Siberian prison camp; Monsignor Willebrands met him in Vienna and accompanied him to Rome in February 1963.[59] Post-Vatican II contacts with the Moscow Patriarchate are numerous, and include the theological conversations which had already begun in Leningrad in 1967. The most vivid symbol I cherish is the image of Metropolitan Nikodim who led his Church's delegation to the inauguration of Pope Paul VI's successor on 3 September 1978. Two days later in the papal study, Nikodim suffered a massive heart attack, and before he died there, he was held, alone and briefly, in the arms of another servant of unity, the short-lived Pope John Paul I.

WHAT FIVE THEMES FOR THE CENTRAL PREPARATORY COMMISSION?

Cardinal Bea's first press conference was to the powerful media of New

York City the day after the Vatican had announced his appointment as SPCU president. The Cardinal continued to welcome the opportunity to mount lecture podia, grant television and radio interviews (often on the occasion of his addresses), pursue writing – any media to communicate his ecumenical commitment and reflections. Before the Council began, he had lectured in Genoa, Turin and Milan, Bern, Basle and Zurich, Paris, East and West Berlin, Tübingen, Munich, Vienna, Oxford [Heythrop College] – to name less than half of his European cities. In the nine months which preceded Vatican II, he had given twenty-five talks or printed interviews.[60] His small staff followed his example, although we three were not so ubiquitous or prolific. If some in the Vatican wanted the SPCU to be only a press office, we were obedient at least to being one.

One of my first SPCU obediences was the perusal for pro-or-con ecumenical 'wishes and desires (*vota et desideria*)', which the Vatican Press had already published *sub secreto*, from bishops, superiors general, Catholic universities, and the Curial Congregations – 9,520 pages in fifteen thick volumes. My general impression, very disheartening, was of a collection of such disparate views of what Vatican II should or could be and of how it would treat Pope John's *aggiornamento*, that who and what would win out was unanswerable. If I am now allowed an arrogant touch, my notes had copied, without judgement, Cardinal Montini's prediction: 'This will be the greatest Council the Church has ever convened, the grandest because of the Church's spiritual and numerical confluence and because of the complete and peaceful unity of its hierarchy. It will be the greatest by the catholicity of its dimensions, of greatest interest to the entire geographic and human world.'[61]

In our offices we were filling the bathtubs, like Cana jugs, with articles, memoranda, books and lengthy letters, from both Catholics and other Christian sources, on their ecumenical *vota et desideria*. But our primary responsibility was to condense and channel all this raw data as servants to the members and consultors as they proceeded with drafting *schemata*.

Our first plenary meeting, on 14–15 November 1960, was held in a subdued, stuffy and ill-lit room in the Vatican, adjacent to a junkroom of precious sculptured fragments called the Hall of Broken Heads. The experience of the meeting led Cardinal Bea and his staff to suggest future meetings of five to six days outside Rome. All of these six preparatory sessions but one were held in an isolated retreat house at Ariccia on Lago di Nemi, far enough removed from Rome to prevent the bishops' skipping out during the meetings for Vatican business or for visits with city friends. Ariccia provided an atmosphere which quickly bonded members, consultors and staff into a community of intense work, shared liturgy and recreation. The August 1961 session took place in the summer cool of Bühl, Germany. Some local folk were amused, perhaps edified, to witness an international group of eight to ten of us priests and bishops – no one could distinguish who was which, splashing in the village swimming pool between the afternoon session and vespers.

Cardinal Bea presided over each session. He allowed 'the utmost freedom of discussion, gently keeping it to the point'.[62] With twenty-five years of all sorts of meetings now on my roster, I do not recall any SPCU work session as a disaster of aimless repetition, spinning theological wheels, and long ego-centred speeches. Chairmanship is indeed an art.

Our autumn 1962 copying machine was a cheap one, with blue ink that would not endure. My fading copy of that first plenary session's assignments, divided into ten subcommissions, now shows a blend of astute and naive prophecy. Translated from the Latin:

1. The relation of the separated baptized to the Church (The Mystical Body). Members of the Church: in what sense? Definition of heresy and the ways of handling them. The formula of abjuration in conversion.

2. Hierarchical structure of the Church. The source of power of the ministers of the Church. The Relation between Patriarchs, Bishops and the Supreme Pontiff.

3. The conversion of individuals and of communities. Conditions to be placed upon them. Also: the question of the restoration of the deaconate: usefulness, duties, powers, celibacy, required studies and preparation?

4. The priesthood of all the believers and the condition of the laity in the Church. This question is joined to others: religious freedom and tolerance.

5. The 'Word of God' in the Church; its importance in doctrine and life, in preaching: in the Mass (Epistle and Gospel in the vernacular language), and in catechesis.

6. Liturgical questions: the vernacular in the Mass and in the administration of the Sacraments. Communion under both species, at least on special occasions, e.g., first Communion, marriage, etc.

7. Mixed marriages: conditions for permission; pastoral care in the preparation of the spouses and after the marriage.

8. The Octave of Prayers for Unity. New formula (Wattson, Couturier).

9. The central ecumenical problems according to the orientation today of the World Council at Geneva, and especially according to that Council's concept of unity.

10. Questions concerning the Jews.[63]

As the drafting proceeded, all themes were whittled down to five schemata. Cardinal Bea presented these to the Central Preparatory

Commission which, in turn, had eventually to settle for seventy projects within 119 booklets from all the commissions. The SPCU's five themes were these: the Word of God; the need for prayer for the unity of Christians; ecumenism; relations with the Jews; religious freedom. The complex itineraries of these themes through the Council, outside or inside the SPCU ambit, have seen detailed descriptions and commentaries in later books and encyclopedias.

V

But my outline here of the SPCU's first two years remains, I repeat, the far less known and the far more critical for the determination of the Church's ecumenical journey, insofar as the SPCU has been one of its primary institutional pilgrims.

On 13 October 1962, the assembled delegated Observers, SPCU members and consultors, language interpreters, Bea and his small, haggard staff met with Pope John XXIII. The Pope ended his almost off-the-cuff, familial talk, à la Newman: 'Blessed be God for each day, each day is enough for us'. That day was certainly enough for Cardinal Bea. Usually so cautious with superlatives and with more in mind, I then judged, than our presence together, the first SPCU president exclaimed, 'A miracle, a miracle!'

> *What we call the beginning*
> *is often the end.'*
> T. S. *Eliot*, Gerontion

NOTES

1. *Acta Apostolicae Sedis* 51 (1959), 69 (Hereafter, *AAS*).
2. *Ecclesia Catholica* 20 December 1949, *AAS* 42 (1950), 142–147.
3. Years later Cardinal Willebrands entrusted to the Chevetogne monastic library the complete archives of the Catholic Conference. Its history has yet to be written.
4. *AAS, op cit*
5. Cardinal Bea himself admitted this motive. Cf Stjepan Schmidt's 'Epilogue' in his edition of the Cardinal's diary, *Augustin Cardinal Bea: Spiritual Profile*, ET E.M. Stewart (Geoffrey Chapman 1971), 276. The Jesuit Father Schmidt was Bea's loyal private secretary and best knew his person and activities. He has published several articles on Cardinal Bea's earlier life as providential 'preparation for ecumenical mission'. He is currently preparing a full-scale Life. The only extant biographies are E.M. Jung

83

Inglessis, *Augustin Bea, Kardinal der Einheit* (Recklinghausen: Paulus Verlag, 1962); Bernard Leeming, *Agostino Cardinal Bea* (Notre Dame: Notre Dame Press, 1964); Mgr W. A. Purdy, *Cardinal Bea* (CTS B533 1981), 1–17.

Born in the village of Riedböhringen at the edge of Germany's Black Forest, Bea was educated as a Jesuit in the Netherlands, Austria and Germany. Ordained priest in 1912, he studied Oriental philology under Protestant scholars at Berlin University. After a three-year term as Jesuit provincial in Munich, he was called to Rome to supervise Jesuits who specialized in philosophy and theology and to teach biblical theology and exegesis. From 1930–1949 he was rector of the Pontifical Biblical Institute, as well as consultor to several Roman Curia congregations. He was the principal author of the encyclical *Divino Afflante Spiritu* (1943). He died on 16 November 1968, and is buried in the village church of his birth. He once remarked, 'In Rome visitors tend only to stare at cardinals' tombs; in my village, all will pray for me before mine'.

6. *Spiritual Profile, op cit*, 276.
7. *Ibid*, 53 (1960 entry).
8. The following Bea/Stakemeier correspondence has first come to light in 1981 through Heinrich Bacht, 'Kardinal Bea: Wegbereiter der Einheit', *Catholica* 35 (1981), 173–88.
9. The German translation of the Latin original in Lorenz Jäger, *Einheit und Gemeinschaft* (Paderborn, Bonifatiusdruckerei, 1972), 139–142.
10. Cardinal Bea, 'Il Segretariato per l'Unione dei Cristiani', *La Rivista del Clero Italiano* 46.11 (November 1965), 4.
11. Giovanni XXIII, *Lettere (1958–1963)*, with appended documents and various notes. Edited and published by Loris Francesco Capovilla (Rome, 1978), 496.
12. Bea, 'Il Segretariato . . .' *op cit*.
13. The older version is still so presented, e.g. by Peter Hebblethwaite in his *John XXIII* (Geoffrey Chapman 1984), 375.
14. In the official text of this talk, Bea's name is not mentioned, but here, S. Schmidt, 'L'opera del Cardinale Bea per la creazione del Segretariato', *L'Osservatore Romano*, 3 February 1984, 6.
15. Jan Willebrands, 'Introduction', in Augustin Bea and W. A. Visser 't Hooft, *Peace among Christians*, ET Judith Moses (Association Press NY 1967), 10. Bea and Visser 't Hooft did meet three months later, and this was kept secret until after the Council. Cf Augustin Bea, *Ecumenism in Focus* (Geoffrey Chapman, 1969), 2.
16. *AAS* 52 (1960), 436. Cf A. Bea, *The Unity of Christians* (below, note 45), 166.
17. *AAS* 52 (1960), 855–856. Three lists of additions were announced during the Council years.
18. The Holy Office had given permission to Willebrands and Bernard Leeming, SJ; and for the Faith & Order meeting, to Irenée Beaupère, Jerome Hamer, and Leeming.
19. *Ecumenical Review* 12 (1960), 46.
20. W. A. Visser 't Hooft, 'The General Ecumenical Development since 1948', in *A History of the Ecumenical Movement*, vol 2, ed Harold E. Fey (Philadelphia: Westminster 1970), 16. J. Willebrands observed, 'How often had the complaint been made, and in particular to Dr Visser 't Hooft, that there was no office in the Catholic Church to which one could turn concerning ecumenical problems', *Peace among Christians, op cit*, 10–11.
21. Cardinal J. Willebrands, 'Il Cardinale Bea: il suo contributo al movimento ecumenico', in *Simposio Card Agostino Bea (16–19 Dicembre, 1981)*, ed SPCU (Rome: Pont Univ Lateranense, 1983), 5–6.
22. *Spiritual Profile, op cit*, 50.

23. *Ibid*, 245.
24. J. Willebrands, *Simposio, op cit*, 8.
25. *Ordo Concilii*, promulgated by John XXIII, *Appropinquante Celebrandi, AAS* 54 (1962), 614.
26. *Acta Synodalia*, the Vatican Council archives (Vatican Polyglot Press, 1962) vol. 1, pars 1, 78. The rescript also required the SPCU to enlarge its body of members, eventually to thirty for the Second Session, and this helped us to fill in the gaps for adequate geographical representation and for Eastern-rite bishops. Cf vol II, pars 1, 78–79.
27. *The Decree on Ecumenism*, promulgated 21 November 1964; *The Declaration of the Relation of the Church to Non-Christians*, with its longest paragraph (n.4) on the Jews (28 October 1965); *The Declaration on Religious Freedom* (7 December 1965); and often forgotten as a joint work with the Theological Commission, *The Constitution on Divine Revelation* (18 November 1965).
28. *Finis Concilio*, 3 January 1966. *AAS* 58 (1966), 40. Later Paul VI specified the structure and competence of the SPCU in *Regimini Ecclesiae Universae*, which reorganized the Roman Curia, *AAS* 59 (1967), 918. Without the SPCU as a first model, would Paul VI have established the Secretariats for Non-Christians and for Non-Believers?
29. Those who did not accept the Council of Ephesus (431) later formed the Church to which the name Nestorian is sometimes given. Those who rejected the Council of Chalcedon (451) have organized Churches more along national lines – the Coptic (Egypt), Ethiopian, Syrian and Armenian Churches, and the Syrian Church of India. These all are sometimes called 'pre-Chalcedonian' or 'non-Chalcedonian' Churches; more recently, 'oriental Orthodox', to distinguish them from, simply, the 'Orthodox' Churches of the Byzantine (both Greek and Slavic) tradition.
30. J. Willebrands, *Simposio, op cit*, 6.
31. A. Bea, *Ecumenism in Focus, op cit*, 35, note 32.
32. Cf *Doing the Truth in Charity*, Ecumenical Documents (Statements of Popes Paul VI, John Paul I, John Paul II, and of the Secretariat for Promoting Christian Unity (1964–1980)), Edd Thomas F. Stransky, CSP and John B. Sheerin, CSP (Paulist Press, NY, 1982), 178–182.
33. The Commission for the Eastern Churches presented, as the fourth schema of the First Session, *That They May Be One*. The Fathers were aware of the last chapter of the Theological Commission's *On the Church* which dealt with christian unity, and knew of the yet unseen SPCU *schema* on the same theme. The Fathers voted (1 December 1962) in favour of a single conciliar document on Church unity. Cf Thomas F. Stransky, CSP, *The Decree on Ecumenism*, history, text and commentary (Paulist Press, NY 1965), 8–10.
34. Cf Arthur Gilbert, *The Vatican Council and the Jews* (Cleveland: World Publishing, 1968), 41–64.
35. Archbishop Capovilla's signed memorandum (22 March 1966) of his recollections of the Isaac visit. Father S. Schmidt graciously gave me a copy (April 1985). [Cf Ed H. Vorgrimler, *Commentary on the documents III* (1969), 2–4 = 'The visit of Jules Isaac'.]
36. *Ibid*.
37. The conversation is according to Isaac's unedited account, published in *SIDIC* (Service International Documentation Iudéo-Chrétienne), 1981, n.3, 10–12.
38. Capovilla memo.
39. A. Bea, *The Church and the Jewish People* (Geoffrey Chapman, 1966).
40. *Regimini Ecclesiae, op cit*, 919.
41. *Osservatore Romano*, 23 October 1974. This document has never appeared in *AAS*.

42. *AAS* 67 (1975), 73–79. English, cf *Doing the Truth in Charity, op cit*, 342–7. *Notes* in ed Helga Croner, *More Stepping Stones to Jewish–Christian Relations, Christian Documents (1975–1985)* (Paulist Press, NY, 1985), 220–232.

43. The only previous contact of a Pope with Anglican bishops was Benedict XV's audience with a delegation of U.S. Protestant Episcopalians (of whom three were bishops) in May 1919, concerning possible Vatican representation in an exploratory world conference on faith and order. The Pope's answer was negative. For details, cf Thomas F. Stransky, CSP, 'A Basis beyond the Basis', *Ecumenical Review*, April 1985, 213–215.

44. Contrary to Hebblethwaite's account, *op cit*, 383, Bea did meet Fisher.

45. Ever pastoral as a teacher, Cardinal Bea wrote a theological reflection on the visit in the next issue of *La Civiltà Cattolica*, 1960, 561–8. The English text in Bea, *The Unity of Christians*, ed Bernard Leeming, SJ (Herder and Herder, 1963; Geoffrey Chapman, 1963). Here, 69.

46. On 5 June 1948, the Holy Office issued its monitum *Cum Compertum* which drew attention to Canon 1325, prohibiting 'mixed meetings' without previous permission of the Holy See. Visser 't Hooft had already invited to Amsterdam ten 'unofficial' Catholic Observers, but each would have to make arrangements to secure canonical permission. Upon directives from the Holy Office, the Dutch bishops had their pastoral letter read in all their churches on the opening day of the Assembly. Cf the text in 'The Roman Catholic Church and the First Assembly', *Ecumenical Review*, 1 (1948), 197–201. On the occasion of the 1954 Evanston Assembly, Cardinal Stritch of Chicago promulgated a harsher, less nuanced statement with the same conclusion. Cf *Ecumenical Review*, 7 (1955), 169.

47. The final five observers: T. Edamaran and I. Extross of India; Edward Duff, SJ (USA); J. C. Groot (Netherlands); M. Le Guillou, OP (France). The appreciation for the presence of these five Observers and for the new contacts with Roman Catholics 'in an atmosphere of mutual good will', and for the establishment of the SPCU are recorded in the Assembly minutes. Cf the official *New Delhi Report*, ed W. A. Visser 't Hooft (SCM, 1962), 6, 29, 151, 175.

48. Sunday audience at Castelgandolfo, as published by a reporter who was present, *La Croix*, 1 September 1959. *Osservatore Romano*, in its account, did not include this papal comment.

49. Later published in *Acta et Documenta*, Series I (ante-preparatoria), Vol 1, 160.

50. A. Wenger, *Vatican Council II: the First Session*, ET Robert J. Olson (Westminster, Md: Newman, 1963), 143.

51. The SPCU proposal, *Acta et Documenta*, series II (preparatoria), Vol 2, pars 1, 165f, 450–57. Bea's report, 458–63; Cicognani's, 464f; votes and comments, 466–95.

52. *Ibid*, 419.

53. *Osservatore Romano*, 10 November 1960.

54. *Enchiridion Vaticanum* (Bologna: Ed Dehoniane, 9ed, 1971), 16.

55. The same points eventually in *Ordo Concilii, AAS* 54 (1952), 618.

56. The first publicly to accept the invitation was the Anglican Communion through Archbishop Michael Ramsey, on 5 June 1962. The SPCU did not send an invitation to the Baptist World Alliance, which agreed to disagree and preferred no invitation. For details, cf Thomas F. Stransky, CSP, 'A Roman Catholic Perspective on Baptist Ecumenism', in edd W. Boney and G. Iglehart, *Baptists and Ecumenism* (Valley Forge, Pa.: Judson, 1980), 130. We still lack a comprehensive history of the discussions within the other Churches which led up to the decisions to accept the invitation, the appointment of Observers, their (then) confidential reports during the four sessions, etc.

57. *The Journal of the Patriarchate of Moscow*, 1961, n.5, 73–75.
58. Over the four sessions 186 official Observers attended, for longer or shorter periods or were present at one or more of every session. For details and all names, cf *Observateurs-Délégués et Hôtes du Secrétariat* (Vatican Polyglot Press, 1965); and see p. 359 below.
59. For the most detailed account of the Slipyi release, cf Wenger, *op cit*, 173–176.
60. The best of these in Bea, *Unity of Christians, op cit*. Somewhat of a best seller, at least in English, it appeared in seven languages.
61. *Acta et Documenta*, Series I, Vol 1, 119–21.
62. J. Willebrands, *Simposio, op cit*.
63. Cardinal Bea later presented these major titles, with some alterations and omissions of detail, to the Central Preparatory Commission, 12 June 1961. He added to subcommission 10: 'Since not a few Jews have submitted wishes and suggestions for the Council, our Secretariat, by special mandate, shall treat these in a special section'. *Acta et Documenta*, Series II, Vol 2, Pars 1, 164f.

APPENDIX:

CONCILIAR WRITINGS OF AUGUSTIN CARDINAL BEA, SJ

Ed Bernard Leeming, SJ, *The Unity of Christians* (Herder and Herder/Geoffrey Chapman, 1963): twenty collected texts from the period 1960–62.

The Church and the Jewish People: a commentary on the Second Vatican Council's Declaration on the relation of the Church to non-Christian religions (Geoffrey Chapman, 1966). An appendix incorporates four addresses to the Council during 1963–65.

The Way to Unity after the Council: a study of the implications of the Council for the unity of mankind (Geoffrey Chapman, 1967).

Ed Stjepan Schmidt, SJ, *Augustin Cardinal Bea – Spiritual Profile* (Geoffrey Chapman, 1971): edited from the diaries and private papers of the Cardinal, by his secretary.

Simposio Card Agostino Bea (16–19 dicembre 1981), Communio N.S. 14 (Pontificia Università Lateranense, Rome, 1983).

[Ed.]

6

A PLAN FOR THE WHOLE COUNCIL

LÉON-JOSEF CARDINAL SUENENS

The German theologian Fr Joseph Ratzinger (personal peritus to Cardinal Frings of Cologne) judged that the failure of the Council to approve any text in its First Session was 'the great, astonishing and genuinely positive result' of that Session. He rightly attributed this result to 'the strong reaction against the spirit behind the preparatory work' – a reactionary spirit indeed which is now being termed 'restorationism', but was then called 'integralism'. Ratzinger called this circumstance 'the truly epoch-making character of the Council's First Session'.

But there was another major reason why the First Session failed to reach the goal of a promulgated text; a failure, despite a plethora of plans and preparatory papers, to formulate a radical strategy, a single main plan. Something of the evidence for this has been emerging recently through the colloquies held at the Istituto Paolo VI in Brescia (Pope Paul's birthplace), and notably a colloquy held on 23–25 September 1983, entitled: 'Giovanni Battista Montini, Arcivescovo di Milano, e il Concilio Ecumenico Vaticano II; preparazione e primo periodo'. Among the Testimonianze was the Cardinal Archbishop of Malines/Brussels, Léon-Josef Suenens, who narrated that in a conversation in March 1962 – half a year before the Council opened – Pope John asked him, 'Who is attending to the making of an overall plan for the whole Council?' The Cardinal replied that, though some seventy-two schemata were in preparation, no one was thinking at that scale: 'Ça c'est le désordre total!' The Pope, reflecting, asked him: 'would you then like to make a plan?' So the Cardinal suggested that, before plans were made, one had to ask what a Council is and what it is not; then ask what it should concentrate upon; then make that more precise. Here he tells of that process.

Léon-Josef Suenens (b. 16 July 1904) was the son of a brewer, who died when he was not four years old. Educated by the Marist Brothers in Brussels and then at the Institut Sainte-Marie, run by diocesan priests, he was called to the priesthood. Cardinal Mercier sent him to do his studies at the Gregorian University, Rome, where he achieved doctorates in both philosophy and theology with a baccalaureate in canon law. Throughout his time in Rome he kept up a steady and intimate correspondence with Mercier, who had a lasting influence upon him. Ordained in 1927, he studied on until 1929, when he returned to his Institute in Brussels to teach. Then for ten years he was Professor of Philosophy at the Malines Seminary, teaching the history of philosophy and pedagogy, consolidating his own under-standing and influencing the lives of future priests.

In 1940 he was appointed Vice-Rector of the University of Louvain. This is important, for its connection: there is a saying that the Council showed clearly that behind every great prelate is a great university – Vienna, Munich, Nijmegen, Louvain... Soon his Rector was imprisoned by the Nazis, and he quietly took on the task if not the office for the duration of the War. Among his initiatives was the foundation of the Institut des Sciences Religieuses there, since he had for a while shared the view that the religious education of the laity was never given sufficient attention at university levels.

On 16 December 1945 Suenens was consecrated bishop and made auxiliary to the then aging Cardinal van Roey. During this time the young Bishop Suenens discovered the international movement emanating from Dublin, The Legion of Mary. At once he saw the apostolic potential of such a movement for the laity; so on several occasions he journeyed to the Legion's headquarters in Dublin to confer with its founder, Frank Duff and to study the implications of the movement throughout the world. He then wrote a commentary on its promise, The theology of the apostolate of the Legion of Mary; *and later he wrote a biography of one of the Legion's outstanding early members, Edel Quinn. He went on in 1956 to publish* The Gospel to every creature, *his own dominant ideas about the pastoral mission of the Church, ideas that he later developed piecemeal into other books – such as* The nun in the world *(1962, revised 1963), which engendered a strong renewal of apostolic activity among the women's orders.*

In 1959 the Auxiliary represented the Cardinal of Belgium at the Catholic World Congress of Health. Addressing some three thousand members of the medical and allied professions, he asked them and their colleagues to devote their time to solving the problem of birth control. Equally he asked universities to pursue studies into the question of human fertility, so that Catholics might be better able to fulfil their marital duties while responding fully to their dignity and obligations as Christians. From this initiative there ensued a series of annual international meetings at Louvain, where in 1962 an Institut Universitaire des Sciences Familiales et Sexologiques was established. The Bishop's contribution was a book entitled Love & control *(1961, revised 1962).*

In December 1961 Léon-Josef became Archbishop of Malines, and the following March a Cardinal. During the Council he was closely involved as the paper below indicates. Since the Council he has been one of its most ardent protagonists and continues so today.

I have been asked to shed light on a historical matter involving the origins of the Council. It concerns the initial plan which I submitted to Pope John XXIII, and to which the then Cardinal Montini [Milan] referred in a letter to John XXIII (18 October 1962), a letter I gave to the Paul VI Institute in Brescia, which has published it in its Bulletin.[1]

This is how it came about. During an audience with the Pope in March 1962, I complained to John XXIII about the number of schemata prepared for discussion at the forthcoming Council, which seemed quite excessive. There were, I believe, seventy-two of them, very uneven in value, and in any case so overwhelming in volume that *a priori* they prevented fruitful and worthwhile work at the Council itself. John XXIII asked me to clear the ground and submit to him a plan based on the prepared schemata.

After studying these documents, I sent him a preliminary note designed to cut out a lot of dead wood and set the Council on a truly pastoral course. The note was both negative and positive: *idem nolle* as well as *idem velle* were both needed as a basis for more detailed work to follow. This note is given below as Appendix I. John XXIII approved this verbally to me; and it then paved the way for future work.

The plan was ready at the end of April 1962. I had included, as far as I could, the themes dear to me, with a constant care to put forward the pastoral adaptations that seemed to me to be the most important considerations. Being confidential, the document remained strictly personal till I judged it appropriate to share it with some Cardinal friends of mine, including Cardinal Montini. In my files I have found a letter from Cardinal Liénart, who put his agreement in writing (Appendix II); the others expressed their agreement verbally.

For his part, John XXIII told the Secretary of State, Cardinal Cicognani, to send photocopies of this plan to a number of Cardinals, by way of information. This was done in May 1962.

John XXIII wanted to rally certain influential Cardinals behind the plan, so as to be able to present it with their support when the right moment came. To this end, he asked me to discuss it with certain Cardinals, whom he named to me.

An initial meeting was held at the Belgian College in early July 1962. I gave a report of this meeting to John XXIII in a letter dated 4 July (Appendix III). A second meeting took place, also at the Belgian College, shortly after the opening of the Council, at which Cardinal Montini was present, as were Siri [Genoa], Lercaro [Bologna] and others. Support for the project was general, since what was at stake was no more than establishing a general framework for subsequent discussion in the Council.

Appendix IV gives the final version of the plan I proposed. John XXIII had in the meantime thoroughly assimilated its general thrust. Hints of it can be seen in the memorable radio message of 12 September 1962,[2] announcing and presenting the Council that was to open a few weeks later. The *Osservatore Romano* of 12 September 1962 introduced the Council under the heading '*Ecclesia Christi, lumen gentium*'. John XXIII introduced it as a continuation of our Lord's commandment: 'Go, therefore, make disciples of all the nations; baptize them in the name of the Father and of the Son and of the Holy Spirit, and teach them to observe all the commands I gave you' (Mt. 28:19–20). These words formed the subject matter of the plan, and the Pope's speech also took over the distinction proposed between the Church '*ad intra*' and the Church '*ad extra*', on which the plan hinged.

The Council opened on 11 October 1962. John XXIII had said: 'In Council affairs we are all novices', and he left the Council to work out its first steps on its own. He had said to me: 'The Pope's first duty is to listen and keep silent to allow the Holy Spirit free play', and, showing me the plan in his desk drawer, told me he would use it at the appropriate moment. That, then, is what happened before the Council opened.

During the first few weeks, as we know, the Council had some difficulty in finding its way and direction. The state of the Pope's health, which was beginning to give cause for alarm, should also be remembered as bearing on the way things went. On 18 October 1962, Cardinal Montini, also worried about the general lack of direction, wrote a letter to John XXIII [through his Secretary of State] asking for a more definite structure and greater coherence in the Council proceedings, and at the end of this letter, he alluded to the plan I had prepared. The Pope sent me a photocopy of this letter (Appendix V): it is now public knowledge, and of particular interest to historians, as it already gives indications of certain aspects of Montini's forthcoming pontificate [the letter should be linked, as a study, with Paul VI's first encyclical, *Ecclesiam suam* (6 August 1963), discussed by Père Congar (below p. 129) and see editorial addendum [Ed.]].

With the state of the Pope's health becoming worse, I had a problem of conscience: should I take the initiative and put the plan forward officially, or keep quiet and wait, since John XXIII had said that he would choose the moment to make it public? As the ill Pope could not be approached direct, I sent him a letter of affection and sympathy without raising such questions, but I sent his secretary, then Mgr Loris Capovilla, a copy of the speech I was proposing to make the following day in the Council, in which I would put forward the basic elements of the plan. I told Mgr Capovilla to do as he saw fit with this, not imagining that the Pope would be in any state to take cognizance of it. To my surprise, Mgr Dell'Acqua [Archbishop Angelo Dell'Acqua of the Secretariat of State] called me to the Vatican early the following morning to tell me that John XXIII was not only fully in agreement with my text, but that he had read it and annotated it, writing some complementary observations in the margin in Italian. I asked Mgr Dell'Acqua to have these translated into Latin, so that I could be sure of not betraying the Holy Father's thoughts, and so I was able, with a completely clear conscience, to make the speech in the Aula which set out the central theme to which the Council rallied. This was on 4 December 1962. Support for the plan was greatly strengthened by the fact that the following day Cardinal Montini, who had been very reserved during this First Session, pronounced himself warmly in favour, as did Cardinal Lercaro.

This, as objectively as possible, was the sequence of events. The verdict of history will, I am sure, be that Vatican II was a Pentecostal blessing for which John XXIII did not pray in vain, and for which he offered up his sufferings and his life itself.

LÉON-JOSEF CARDINAL SUENENS

APPENDIX I: A NOTE ON THE SUBJECT OF THE COUNCIL
(from Cardinal Suenens to John XXIII, March 1962)

Subjects to be chosen

The announcement of the Council has raised great hopes among the faithful and in the world at large.

It must respond to this double level of expectation: this, it seems to me, means that it must deal with a double range of subjects.

The first would deal with the Church *ad extra*, that is the Church as it faces the world of today.

The second would deal with the Church *ad intra*, that is the Church in itself, but with the aim of helping it better to respond to its mission in the world.

Criteria of choice

May I, in all filial loyalty, be allowed to suggest what I believe should be criteria that should govern the choice of subjects to be brought forward for discussion:

Positively
It seems to me that the subjects to be studied by the Council should be:

matters of *major* importance
matters of *vital* importance
matters of importance *for the whole Church*
matters that relate to the desired *pastoral renewal.*

Negatively
It would be a great and painful disappointment for the Church and the world if the Council were to get bogged down in minor matters, when the world and the Church are anxiously awaiting the Council's response to problems of burning actuality.

The result of this would be that the wood could not be seen for the trees and that the Council would be stifled, in its vital outreach, by an excessive growth of secondary branches.

Cut out dead wood

So it seems to me that we must mercilessly cut out everything that is secondary, minor, of local concern, purely canonical or administrative in import. Specifically, may I say, in all filial frankness, that eight tenths of the schemata, in their present form, do not strike me as 'Council material'. One only has to read them to see that they abound in secondary matters.

Referral to Commissions

I think examination of these texts – on which, it must be said, there was wide disagreement in the Central Commission – should be referred *either* to the Commission for the Reform of Canon Law, *or* to special post-conciliar Commissions, of which more later.

92

A PLAN FOR THE WHOLE COUNCIL

Mark out avenues

It seems to me that if the Second Vatican Council wants to avoid the painful hesitations which marked the first acts of Vatican I, it has to mark out some wide avenues through the forest and to bring certain major matters to the forefront of the Fathers' consideration.

Usefulness of a restricted Commission

In order to proceed to a first selection of these matters – the final and definitive choice belonging in the last resort to His Holiness the Pope – it would seem opportune and practical for the Holy Father to set up, for his personal and private use, a restricted Commission – a sort of 'brains trust' – of a few members whose task would be to suggest to him what these major concerns – according to the criteria set out above – are.

Choice in terms of length of time available

The choice of these questions must inevitably be limited according to how long it is envisaged that the Council should last. At all costs, we must avoid the bishops having the impression that they did not have time to deal seriously with the matters put before them because the Council had got bogged down in details.

Post-conciliar Commissions

Whatever the outcome, and however long the Council lasts, there would seem to be a need to envisage, and to announce fairly quickly, the setting-up of post-conciliar Commissions.

Aim:
These Commissions would, after the Council, be charged with:

1. continuing examination of matters not tackled or unresolved by the Council, or even new questions;
2. monitoring the practical outcome of the decisions taken by the Council on different subjects.

Composition:
These post-conciliar Commissions would de-congest the Council; and setting them up would give the feeling of serious intent to our endeavours that the whole world expects to see. These post-conciliar Commissions should be made up of bishops representing the various continents, to be named by the Holy See. They should not be too numerous. Experts could be called in in a consultative capacity.

These Commissions could carry on the work of the pre-conciliar Commissions, on a new basis, taking account of the basic directives emerging from the Council itself.

Attachment to various Congregations
It would seem to be of extreme benefit for the good of souls if these Commissions became permanent bodies, attached to each Congregation of the Roman Curia. This would create a sort of breath of life blowing between the Centre and the periphery at the heart of each Congregation, and would allow the diocesan bishops to make their pastoral concerns known, and so to rethink the problems tackled by each Congregation in a pastoral way,

while at present the Congregations are by the nature of things more attuned to the canonical and administrative aspects of their work.

Furthermore, these Commissions could receive from the Holy Father the mandate to work out the reform of the Roman Curia that the bishops of the whole world want and which is essential if a real, specific, lasting pastoral renewal is to be achieved.

A Council which proclaimed a few great truths without setting up the means to oversee their implementation after the Council would be like a short spring not leading to a summer or to any harvest.

Decentralization through Bishops' Conferences

One of the Council's great difficulties, not on the dogmatic level, at which absolute unity is easy, but on the pastoral level, will be to set out rulings that are at one and the same time applicable to all and supple in their implementation.

Would it be possible to hope that, for the good of the Church, some specific adaptations, on the level of pastoral application, should be reserved to the Bishops' Conferences, naturally subject to the final approval of the Holy See?

The danger of immobilism

Efforts at pastoral renewal have not been felt with the same intensity in different countries. There are grounds for fearing that the bishops who have most experience in these matters will not be sufficiently numerous to make their wishes prevail within the Council. The experience of what has happened in the Central Commission shows that there is a strong current of integralism opposed to any pastoral renewal of any real importance. May the Holy Spirit enlighten His Holiness the Pope so that the immobilist tendency, even if it proves numerically stronger, may not in the end prevail.

A pastoral Council

If I might be permitted to express one wish at the end of this note, it is that the Council may be above all a pastoral, that is an apostolic Council. What an immense benefit it would be for the Church if it could define the broad outlines of how the whole Church could be put into a state of mission, and at all levels: lay people, clergy, bishops and Roman Congregations! What a splendid Pentecostal grace this would be for the Church, just as our beloved Head wished for with so much heart and Christian hope!

APPENDIX II: LETTER FROM CARDINAL ACHILLE LIÉNART

Diocese of Lille
68 rue Royale
Rome, 14 June 1962

His Eminence Cardinal Suenens,
Archbishop of Malines-Brussels

Your Eminence,
I have just learned of the plan you have drawn up to fuse all the valuable elements brought together by the Preparatory Commissions into a whole capable of showing the modern world what the true Church of Jesus Christ is and what response it can make to that world.

I am absolutely delighted by your project and don't want to wait till this evening to tell you so just on the telephone. I fully approve the apostolic spirit in which you have conceived the project, the appreciation of the various main topics you have made and the breadth of the perspectives you have opened up.

At a time when the Church is really the matter under discussion, I believe the Council cannot do better than concentrate on showing it in all its reality, its rich complexity, its constructive dynamism and its broad openness to all mankind.

There is still much to do if this wish of the Holy Father's is to be carried out by the Council. But I keenly hope your plan will be accepted and that we can resolutely set out on this road without further delay.

Your Eminence, please accept my thanks and the assurance of my respectful and fraternal devotion.

(signed) Achille Cardinal Liénart
    Bishop of Lille

APPENDIX III: LETTER FROM CARDINAL SUENENS TO JOHN XXIII

Malines, 4 July 1962

Most Holy Father,

Your Holiness asked me to inform you directly of the reactions of the various Cardinals who have studied the general plan I submitted to you.

We have had a very friendly and relaxed meeting at the Belgian College. At the beginning of this, Cardinal Döpfner [Munich] proposed that it might perhaps be better to let the schemata go forward for discussion at the Council without an overall plan, but he quickly agreed to the unanimous and insistent views of Cardinals Montini, Siri and Liénart, who very warmly supported the plan put forward and strongly underlined the need for a broad and coherent overall plan.

All agreed in wishing that the Council should start with a doctrinal section that would form the matter of the first session, with the pastoral section occupying the further session or sessions.

Everyone wanted this doctrinal section to start with a study of the Church: '*De Ecclesiae Christi mysterio*', that is the Church in its essence, in its specific components.

We were unanimous in not wanting the Council Secretariat to send the different schemata already prepared out to the bishops pell-mell: it would make a bad impression on the world outside to see the Council beginning with secondary matters which failed to allow the central idea to be seen.

This concern to begin with a constitution on the Church – in the hope that the second Vatican Council might really be the Council *De Ecclesia* – is even shared in the Orthodox world. On a separate sheet I have transcribed a recent text by Professor Florovsky, who is one of the most noted Orthodox theologians of the present time. A Catholic would put things differently, but the convergence on the central idea seems striking to me, and this is why I am drawing it to your attention.

We now need to work out a more detailed plan showing where and how the finished schemata could find a place in the overall framework as set out. As the Cardinals I have mentioned wanted me to do this, I have set to work on my return here, using the existing schemata to the greatest practical extent. On a separate sheet I attach some considerations on the general picture by way of clarification and indication of the overall tenor.

After which, Most Holy Father, I shall only have to deliver all this to Your Wisdom and pray that the Holy Spirit will guide you in setting out the final guidelines.

I have just read Fr Dehon's *Il diario del Concilio Vaticano I*, which your Holiness recommended me to do: it is full of interest and life and at the same time indications of what should be done . . . and what should not be done. It is throughout a glorification of the Holy Spirit, who works through human instruments who are always defective and often so poor in their humanity.

With, Most Holy Father, my feelings of deepest filial piety, with which I have the honour to be Your Holiness' humble and obedient servant.

APPENDIX IV: THE PLAN SUBMITTED TO JOHN XXIII

Introduction

The plan which follows has been conceived in such a manner as to give the Council a pastoral, coherent overall direction, and one that all can easily grasp. It is put together like a triptych, its three parts being: a basic introduction, the major themes grouped under four main headings, and a final message which would be a sort of apotheosis of the Council.

Response to expectations
The themes highlighted are, we believe, those that most concern the faithful and the world. We have tried to respond to expectations and situate the Council fully in the life of the Church and the world, and not in a closed vessel.

Convergence around four centres of interest
These subjects gather around four centres of interest the subjects which the schemata drawn up by so many different people dealt with in discontinuous order and sometimes from opposing viewpoints.

Use made of work done
These themes allow maximum possible use of the schemata drawn up: a massive and important amount of work has been done which we must take advantage of, while removing its fragmentary and mosaic character, breathing a soul into it. Most of these schemata are lifeless skeletons due to their juridical, canonical and sometimes repressive approach. [Cf the 'dry bones' (of Ezekiel) so well applied by Bishop Donal Lamont (p. 270) [Ed.].] We will try in our plan to give them some life and breadth of approach and make them contribute to an overall whole.

Suitable for the learned and the faithful as a whole
The themes which stand out and are easy to remember are as appropriate to bishops and theologians as to ordinary Christians who, thanks to this easily popularized plan, will be able to follow the phases of the Council, and respond to the rhythm of the Church [*suivre les phases . . . vivre au rhythme*]. They will be totally suited to the preaching of pastors; they are such as to strike the imagination through their simplicity and clarity.

An instrument of pastoral progress
These themes will allow us to deal, as we go, with the chief errors of the time, either *ad intra* in the bosom of the Church, or *ad extra* in the world. But they deal with them in a positive and constructive way, without anathemas. They thereby allow us to take account of certain gaps in our own pastoral teaching and to remedy these.

Overall approach of the plan

Schema 'De Ecclesiae Christi mysterio' as a starting-point
As a start, it seems necessary to link the Second Vatican Council to the First. The best way of doing this would be to begin the Council with discussion of a schema *De Ecclesiae Christi mysterio*.

Reasons
(a) *Continuity with Vatican I*. The First Vatican Council had prepared a schema *De Ecclesia*, of which it was able to define only one part: papal primacy and infallibility. It did not have time to 'place' the bishops or the laity in the mystery of the Church.
(b) *Better doctrinal balance*. This would be both a work of continuity and the achievement of a better balance, since the mystery of the Church would thereby appear in its fullness and in complete harmony.
(c) *A step towards our separated brethren*. The Orthodox reproach the Church with not giving bishops their due place; the Protestants reproach it for not giving the laity their proper place. In this schema *De Ecclesiae Christi mysterio* we could well reply to their objections in a positive manner by showing the link between the Papacy and the Body of the Church, by demonstrating the place and meaning of the episcopal college and by stressing the role of the laity (all this will be dealt with in more detail later).
(d) *Operari sequitur esse*. Before devoting the Council's efforts to 'the Church at work', it would seem essential to preface these efforts with a major doctrinal declaration on the Church in itself: *operari sequitur esse*. The Church must define: *quid dicis de teipso?*
(e) *The Church is Jesus Christ 'communicated and spread'*. We would thus straight away put the stress on the essential: the Church is Christ living today in his mystical body; it is Christ, our contemporary.

The one question that sums up all the others for the bishops of 1962 is whether or not we are faithfully continuing the work our Master entrusted to us, the work He wishes to carry out, through us.

The basic idea
The Council falls naturally into two main fields:

that of the Church *ad intra*;
that of the Church *ad extra*.

The schema we propose introduces the collective examination of conscience on their mission which the bishops want to make. The basic question they face, and which could be the central question for the whole Council, the cross-roads from which its main avenues open out, could be this:
How is the Church of the twentieth century measuring up to the Master's last command:

Go, therefore
Make disciples of all the nations
Baptize them
in the name of the Father and of the Son and of the Holy Spirit
And teach them to observe all the commands I gave you.

Which leads naturally to the following plan:

Section A: *Ecclesia 'ad intra'*
As a basis for division into parts, one could take the text from St Matthew just quoted:

Go, therefore: *Ecclesia evangelizans* (or *salvificans*)
Make disciples of all nations: *Ecclesia docens*
Baptize them: *Ecclesia sanctificans*
In the name of the Father . . .: *Ecclesia orans*.

Section B: *Ecclesia 'ad extra'*

Under this general heading several major problems (detailed later) could be grouped together, falling comfortably into the scope of 'and teach them to observe all the commands I gave you'.

Making use of the schemata already prepared

This schema *De Ecclesiae Christi mysterio* already has some groundwork done in the shape of existing schemata, such as *De Ecclesiae militantis natura* and *De membris Ecclesiae* . . . (Prepared by Cardinal Ottaviani, Holy Office). It would be enough for these to be re-worked according to the observations of the members of the Central Commission. Because they would serve as an introduction to the whole, the existing texts could be amplified here and there, but once they have been re-worked they would be substantially usable as an introduction.

Section A
Ecclesia 'ad intra'

I. Ecclesia evangelizans (or salvificans)

Go, therefore. To respond to the Saviour's command, the whole Church must be put 'on a mission footing'. This is the sector of *missionary pastoral work*.

A doctrinal declaration

The Central Commission has, virtually unanimously, adopted the wish expressed by one of its members to see the Council work out a major declaration on the missionary duty of the members of the Church, both *ad extra*, in relation to non-Christian peoples, and *ad intra*, in relation to those who minimize or even seek to eliminate all efforts directed toward 'conversion', claiming that 'life witness' is enough, that the apostolate is an intrusion into and an assault on the consciences of others, that all opinions are valid if they are sincere, that good faith in itself makes up for lack of theological faith. This is of course the opposite [*contre-pied*] of the Gospel and undermines all efforts to 'carry the Good News to all creation'.

Let us now take the *Ecclesia evangelizans*, on its different levels:

A. On the episcopal level

It is natural for the examination of conscience and of pastoral renewal of any apostolate to start with those who are apostles as of divine right and, as such, heads of the pastoral work in their dioceses.

Major questions:

1. There is a need for a major declaration on the subject of the apostolic college and the role of bishops at the heart of the Church. This schema *de episcopis* would, in passing, be of the greatest use *vis-à-vis* our Eastern separated brethren, who reproach the Church with strongly minimizing their [bishops?] role in the Church. This schema *de episcopis* exists under the

title *De episcopis residentialibus* (prepared by Cardinal Ottaviani). This would need to be re-worked according to observations made by members of the Central Commission, particularly those of Cardinals Richaud [Bordeaux], Döpfner and Bea [SPCU].

2. There is a need for a clear statement of the role proper to the bishop as head of the overall pastoral work in his diocese.

3. There is a need to study the 'care of souls' [Cf the Bishop of Lancaster's chapter *De Cura Animarum* (p. 255) [Ed.]] from the viewpoint of the duties of a bishop. This schema exists: *De Cura animarum in genere*, first part (prepared by Cardinal Marella [S. Congregation for maintenance of St Peter's]).

4. In the light of the principles stated, the following would emerge as practical corollaries:

(a) The strengthening of the powers of bishops *in se* [in themselves, as such]. The Schema *de episcopis* prepared by the Bishops' Commission would have to be put together with the schema prepared by the Eastern Commission, since they complement each other.

(b) The strengthening of the powers of bishops *quoad religiosos exemptos individualiter* [in relation to individual exempt religious].

(c) The strengthening of the powers of bishops *quoad religiosos exemptos collective prout adunantur in Unionibus Superiorum Maiorum* [in relation to exempt religious collectively, in that they are incardinated in congregations under major superiors].

B. *On the level of secular and regular clergy*
This is the place to deal with matters affecting the clergy: vocation, seminary and scholastic training, after-ordination care, and the eventual help provided by a permanent diaconate, and so forth.

(a) The Council of Trent set its seal on *Seminaries*. St Charles Borromeo [1538–84] gave them a lasting form. Unfortunately, as time went by, seminaries became more and more centres of piety and study, so losing a certain practical pastoral aspect which the Council of Trent had intended them to have.

We must create a new type of seminary, or, more precisely, fill out the idea of seminaries conceived exclusively as places of piety and study, by giving them an additional role as centres of practical pastoral initiation – the methodology of which can be worked out later.

This reform would have incalculable consequences, since apostolic renewal of the clergy affects everything.

On the more specialized question of religious, this would be the place to examine all questions of adaptation to the apostolate raised for the active orders by the rules of the religious life, and also questions relating to better collaboration between regular and secular clergy in the framework of present-day apostolic needs. Several existing schemas could be used here, such as: *De sacrorum alumnis formandis, De vocationibus ecclesiasticis fovendis* (both by Cardinal Pizzardo [Prefect, S. Congregation of Seminaries & Universities]), and *Quaestiones de religiosis, Disciplina de renovatione vitae et spiritus* (Cardinal Valeri [President of the Commission on Religious]).

(b) On the question of *permanent deacons*: would it not be possible to leave open the possibility, in some countries at least, of trying out the experiment of permanent deacons, who would be so useful if we really want the message – and the sacraments – to reach everyone?

A special Commission could look into the conditions for this. If the Council does not want to see permanent deacons as a universal feature, then let it allow experiments on a limited basis. The question would in any case seem to merit examination by the Council.

C. On the level of nuns and lay brothers

The Church has more than a million nuns and a large number of lay brothers. These huge resources are not being used a hundred per cent for apostolic purposes. They could benefit from a re-appraisal which would ask for a great effort at *aggiornamento* of nuns' rules and habits (and those of lay brothers), bringing them into line with the needs of the present-day apostolate. And strong stress should be placed on the role they could play – with proper formation – as animators of the adult laity.

D. On the level of lay people
(a) A doctrinal declaration

There is a need for a major statement on the position of lay people in the Church. The Code of Canon Law devotes a mere three lines to them! A schema *de laicis* has been prepared [Cf the Archbishop of Liverpool's chapter, 'Toil in the Lord' (p. 237) [Ed.]] but it needs rewriting to give it some life and breadth of vision. It should also be brought into line with that prepared by the Commission for the lay apostolate.

Our separated brethren reproach us for sins of clericalization, for stifling the laity. They believe in the 'priesthood of the faithful' and assign an important role to them. Often, when a Catholic leaves the Church and joins a sect, he will say that he has found there a religion in which he is more respected and finds more to do.

In view of all this, we need to work out a major statement, warm and fatherly in tone towards lay people, recognizing their rights and duties by virtue of their baptism, which incorporates them into the Church.

(b) A 'catholic' terminology for Catholic Action

We should tackle the question posed to the World Congress on the Lay Apostolate by Pope Pius XII in 1957 on the 'generic' meaning to be retained for, or as Pius XII said, 'restored' to the term 'Catholic Action'. After the Pope's explicit appeal to this Congress we cannot, it would seem, leave the question unanswered.

Existing schemata could be used: *De laicis* (Cardinal Ottaviani) and those on the lay apostolate prepared by the Commission presided over by Cardinal Cento [Roman Curia].

II. Ecclesia docens

We must go out to those who do not know the Saviour and take them his message, the whole content of his message, so as to make 'the whole of the Gospel' available to 'the whole of life'. This is the purpose of *pastoral catechesis* in the broadest sense of the term.

We must make the Gospel known to people of every condition by every possible means.

Of every condition

– We need to study the religious teaching given at the different levels of education, up to and including university.

– We must study the question of a universal *catechism*. Should there be just one catechism or would a simpler 'directory' do? And what would we want to see as the content of such a directory, from the apostolic point of view for example?

– We must look carefully at the transmission of the Word of God through preaching.

These questions are dealt with in various schemata, such as: *De catechismo et catechetica institutione* (Cardinal Cicognani i.e. Secretary of State Cardinal Amleto Cicognani. His brother, Cardinal Gaetano Cicognani, was President of the Liturgical Preparatory Commission [Ed.]), *De catechetica populi christiani institutione* (Cardinal Ciriaci) and *De Verbo Dei* (Cardinal Bea).

By every possible means

Here would be the place for examining the various communications media: press, radio, TV, cinema, and incorporating the usable portions of the schema prepared on social communications [Cf also the Bishop of Limburg's chapter (p. 195) [Ed.].]

III. Ecclesia sanctificans
This would be the place to discuss major matters concerning the *pastoral aspects of the sacraments*. Cf for example, the schemata: *De Ecclesiae sacramentis* (Cardinal Cicognani), *De sacramento poenitentiae* (Cardinal Marella), *De sacramento ordinis* (Cardinal Marella), and so forth.

IV. Ecclesia orans
This is the place for the whole question of *pastoral liturgy*.
    We could use the schema *De sacra liturgia* drawn up by the Commission on the subject, clearing away some of its accretions in order to examine some major questions selected for their importance for the whole Church, both Western and Eastern. Cf the schemata: *De usu linguarum vernacularum in liturgiis* (Cardinal Cicognani), *De officio divino* (*idem*).

Section B
Ecclesia 'ad extra'

This section could be placed under the text from St Matthew following the words 'Go, therefore . . .': 'And teach them to observe all the commands I gave you'.

The world's expectation

The Church should carry Christ to the world. This world has its own problems, and is in anguished quest for solutions to them; some of these problems are obstacles to the spread of truth and grace.
    Here are a few major problems that can be put together in this way:
    – What do men look for? Answer: they look for love in the bosom of their families, daily bread for themselves and their families, peace within and between nations. These are basic aspirations. Can the Church bring them anything on these different levels?

Answers

We might suggest that the Council should concentrate its attention on the following four questions:
    (a) The Church and *family society*, particularly conjugal society.
There is a particular threat to the state of grace of souls in the matter of conjugal morality. We are here faced with a crucial problem: that of birth control. In the light of new problems, the essence of *Casti Connubii* needs to be recast, using certain pronouncements of Pius XII and balancing the duties of spouses with their parental responsibilities.
    What could be done with the encyclical *Casti Connubii* [1930] is what was done for *Rerum Novarum* [1891] in its review in *Quadragesimo Anno* [1931] and its bringing up to date by *Mater et Magistra* [1961].
    There are several schemata prepared, such as *De matrimonio et familia* (Cardinal Ottaviani).
    (b) The Church and *economic society*
The Church is expected to condemn atheistic *Communism*. What is most important is that it

101

should pick out the *true part* of Communism, and strongly condemn injustices and social inequalities in the distribution of wealth. In the eyes of the underdeveloped countries, the Church must appear to be the Church of all and above all of the poor. Moralists have devoted thousands of volumes to every detail of the sixth commandment: there is practically nothing written on the obligation to give one's surplus to others, nor the social application of goods created for the use of everyone. The social and communitary implications of genuine Christianity must be vigorously pointed out.

(c) The Church and *civil society*

We are faced with a new political world. This poses particular problems for Church-State relations. One of the main problems in this respect is the religious freedom which the Church claims for itself. What should its attitude be toward the religious freedom of others?

Cf e.g. the schema *De libertate religiosa* (Cardinal Bea). [Cf chapters by Cardinal König and Mgr John Tracy Ellis (pp. 283ff.) [Ed.].]

(d) The Church and *international society*

The world of today, which has known the horrors of two world wars, has a deep aspiration to *peace* on the international level and is very sensitive to anything that threatens this. It would be good to show the world that the Church is, above all, an instrument of peace.

The Church is expected to take a stand on war, the atom bomb, the use of nuclear energy for peaceful purposes, and so forth. These are delicate problems, but they must be tackled, without fail, one way or another.

Message to the World

It would seem desirable for the Council to address a final and solemn message to the world. This message, in brief, could be addressed:

first to our separated Orthodox brethren;
then to our separated Protestant brethren;
next to all those in the world who believe in God;
finally to atheists, pointing out the meaning of God and his presence.

It could end by evoking Christ in glory, King of humanity and Master of the universe, 'Pantocrator', Beginning and End of the whole cosmos, in a vision dear to men of today.

Its final words could be a sort of collective act of faith in Christ living in his Church, according to his promise: 'And know that I am with you always; yes, to the end of time.'

An eschatological vision in which the Church takes stock of its state as 'a pilgrim Church, on the way', and in which it addresses itself to the Lord vowing to be humbly and courageously faithful, 'Till he come, till the day of the coming of the Lord.'

APPENDIX V: LETTER FROM CARDINAL J.-B. MONTINI TO
CARDINAL AMLETO CICOGNANI, SECRETARY OF STATE

The Vatican, 18 October 1962

Your most reverend Eminence,

It is with the deepest humility, that, at the instance of other bishops whose wisdom I cannot doubt, including my venerable brethren of the bishoprics of Lombardy, I venture to draw your attention to something that seems very serious to me and to other Council Fathers: the lack, or at least the failure to announce the existence of, an organic, thought-out and logical programme for the Council which has happily been inaugurated and which is followed by the eyes of the whole Church, as well as by those of the secular world. It has been announced that the schema on the Sacred Liturgy will be discussed first, whereas in the volume distributed, this schema did not have any precedence over the others, nor would there seem to be any need to put it first; this seems to me to confirm the fears that the Council has no pre-set programme of work. If this is the case, as it would seem to be, its development will be decided, and perhaps compromised, by arguments outside the subjects the Council should be concerning itself with; there is no organic structure to reflect the great aims the Holy Father has assigned, by way of justification, to the holding of this extraordinary event. This is dangerous for the outcome of the Council; it diminishes its significance; it makes it lose, in the eyes of the world, that vigour of thought and intelligibility on which its efficacity will to a large extent depend. The material that has been prepared does not seem to have a harmonious and unified overall form; it hardly shines out like a beacon over the age and the world.

This is why I, the least, dare to remind your Eminence that several months ago and at your personal invitation, a few Cardinals met to discuss the need for the Council to form not an accumulation of loose, disconnected blocks, but a monument whose construction would respond to a guiding thought. We reached certain conclusions which seemed to me right, and which in the judgement of other judicious ecclesiastics, were excellent.

So I make equally bold to point out to you what the programme for the Council that has just opened *must*, if I may say so, still be.

1. The second Vatican Council should be centred around one sole theme: Holy Church [*la santa Chiesa*]. This is required to give continuity with the first Vatican Council, which was interrupted while dealing with the subject. This is what all the bishops want, so as to know exactly what their powers are, following the definition of papal powers, and what the relations are between one and the other. It is what is needed, it seems to me, in view of the maturity reached by the doctrine on the Church since the encyclical *Mystici corporis* [1943], and the extraordinary riches offered by this doctrine not only to theologians and canonists, but also for the prayer and present life of the Church. It is what men of our time seem to want; they regard the fact of the Church above all else in our religion and often to the exclusion of all else. Holy Church: this should be the one and all-embracing theme of this Council; and the vast body of material prepared should be organized around what is obviously its sublime centre.

2. In view of this, the Council should begin by turning its thoughts to Jesus Christ, our Lord. It is He who should appear as the principle of the Church, since this is both his emanation and his continuation. The image of Christ, like the Pantocrator in the ancient basilicas, should dominate his Church gathered around Him and before Him. The act of faith has already been pronounced, and this is good. But the hymn addressed to Christ should attach his mystical and historical body to the celestial and invisible Head, as this body goes through a time of total plenitude. A prayer would perhaps suffice, an act of praise from the whole Council to Christ the Lord, but a deliberate, solemn, conscious act, which would determine the whole further development of the Council.

3. The Council should also, still at its outset, perform a unanimous and joyous act of homage, faithfulness, love and obedience to the Vicar of Christ. After the definition of the primacy and infallibility of the Pope, there were some defections, some hesitations and then some docile acceptances. Now the Church rejoices to recognize in Peter, in the person of his Successor, this fullness of powers which constitutes the secret of its unity, strength, and mysterious power to defy the times and make mankind into a 'Church'. Why not say so?

103

Why does the Council not give expression to this certainty that has been achieved? Why, when it is due to discuss the powers of bishops, does it not put any sort of temptation away from itself and remove any sort of doubt from the minds of others, as to the slightest possibility of seeing the sovereign grandeur and solidity of this truth called into question once more? Here again, a simple, short act would suffice, but it must be solemn and from the heart.

4. Then the Council concentrates on the 'mystery of the Church'. That means that it orders, elaborates and expresses doctrines concerning itself: bishops, priests, religious, laity, the various forms of ecclesial life, the different ages of life, young people, women, etc. If indeed it needs to go as far as this. The Church takes full cognizance of itself, shows that it genuinely stems from the Gospel, renews the composition of its cadres, its organs, its hierarchies; in other words, it defines its constitutional laws, not only in its juridical aspect as a perfect society, but also in other aspects proper to it, those of a humanity living on faith and charity, animated by the Holy Spirit, loved as the Bride of Christ, one and catholic, holy and making holy. I think this was the Pope's original intention in announcing the Council. And it is on this chapter, 'What *is* the Church?', that the First Session should close, bringing together the numerous schemata that exist on this subject.

5. The Second Session should then consider the mission of the Church: what the Church *does (Operari sequitur esse)*. And in my view it would be both good and easy to take up the various activities of the Church in different chapters: *Ecclesia orans* (this would be the place to deal with the Sacred Liturgy); *Ecclesia regens* (that is, engaged in the various tasks of pastoral life); *Ecclesia patiens*, and so forth. All questions of morals, dogma (related to the needs of our age), works of charity, missionary activity, etc, could be studied in their due place in this second stage of the Council.

6. Finally, a Third Session will be needed, to deal with the relationship between the Church and the world which surrounds it, which is outside it and removed from it. This comprises: 1. relations with our separated brethren (discussing this question at the beginning of the Council seems to me to risk compromising the outcome); 2. relations with civil society (peace, dealings with States, etc); 3. relations with the world of learning, art, science . . .; 4. relations with the world of work, the economy, etc; 5. relations with other religions; 6. relations with the enemies of the Church, etc. These subjects, of the greatest interest to men of our time, believers and unbelievers alike, cannot be dealt with in the same style as the preceding ones, but should take the form of 'Messages'[3] sent by the Church to humanity living and acting outside its ambit, messages in which the Church's own principles would ring out strongly, and which, with a certain prophetic spirit, would sound an appeal, in each sector of humanity to which they were addressed, to welcome in a new and sympathetic way the light and salvation of which the catholic Church is the only source.

7. The Council should as a conclusion celebrate the communion of saints (through a canonization, or a ceremony of propitiation) and some charitable gesture (an offering, help to the Missions, a pardon, a foundation, or whatever) should be found to round off all the good words of the Council with good deeds. Post-conciliar Commissions should be set up shortly, so as to assure the actual execution of the decrees and good intentions produced by this great effort of renewal.

Perhaps all this is a fantasy, to be added to those that abound at this time of great spiritual ferment. Your Eminence will be the judge of that. Sending it to you spares me the remorse that would have come from keeping silent, and gives me the occasion to confirm my feelings of devotion to the Pope, to the Church and to the Council. And to humbly kiss your hand while remaining your most devoted servant.

J.-B. Cardinal Montini, Archbishop

PS

1. The plan set out above is in very summary form and does not take the content of the schemata into consideration. They need to be looked at again, to see what should be added or cut out or modified. What I was aiming at here was an ideal scheme and the order to be followed in distributing the material.

2. The structure, following the suggestion made by H.E. Cardinal Suenens, could be derived from the last words of Christ in St Matthew's gospel 28:18–20: 'All authority in heaven and on earth has been given to me...'

J.-B. M.

NOTES

1. *Istituto Paolo VI. Notiziario* no 7, November 1983, 11–18. *Ibid*, Pubblicazioni 3 (Brescia 1985), 181–4. The Italian text was also published in a special supplement in *Osservatore Romano* of 26 January 1984. The version at Appendix V is translated from that together with the French version given by Cardinal Suenens in *Nouvelle Revue théologique*, 107/1, Jan–Feb 1985, 18–21. [This letter is discussed in Peter Hebblethwaite, *John XXIII, Pope of the Council* (Geoffrey Chapman 1984), 442–4. Ed.]

2. For the substance of this radio message, cf. L. Capovilla, 'Thoughts on the opening of the Council...' in this volume; for fuller portions of the text cf. his note 20.

3. The closing messages of the Council [8 December 1965] in fact followed this suggestion fairly closely. Cf. Ed W. M. Abbott, SJ, *The Documents of Vatican II*, 728–37. [Paul VI to the Council Fathers. To Rulers (read by three Cardinals). To Men of Thought & Science (*ibid*). To Artists (*ibid*). To Women (*ibid*). To the Poor, the Sick and the Suffering (*ibid*). To Workers (*ibid*). To Youth (*ibid*).]

7

REFLECTIONS ON THE
TWENTIETH ANNIVERSARY

LORIS F. CAPOVILLA

These thoughts are very personal, and they come from close to the centre. In 1953, when he left his secretary, Bruno Heim, in Paris and went on to become Patriarch of Venice, Angelo Roncalli took as his secretary Don Loris Capovilla, a priest of thirty-eight years who had served as an army chaplain, as a journalist and broadcaster, and was then editor of the diocesan La voce di San Marco. *Faithful to the end – he had been taken on to the Vatican in 1958, even though he was not familiar with Rome – Capovilla became Pope John's literary executor, and in his own careful way his biographer. We might recall, for instance, that* Souvenirs d'un Nonce Cahiers de France (1944–1953) *(Edizioni di Storia e Letteratura 1963; ET Mission to France, Geoffrey Chapman 1966), is a mass of Roncalli's documents edited by Loris Capovilla (with forty-one photos). He has been an assiduous editor rather than a historian or biographer. The Pope's papers have come to print through his good offices; and that includes the now famous* Journal of a soul *(Geoffrey Chapman revised ed 1980). Of these, we might recall* Papa Giovanni XXIII, Gran Sacerdote, come lo ricordo *(Ed S e L, Rome 1977), which includes unpublished diaries from the pontificate, also the material he provided for Peter Hebblethwaite's biography* John XXIII, Pope of the Council *(Geoffrey Chapman 1984).*

On 28 January 1963 (the year of his death), Pope John, who saw his secretary daily, wrote him a letter, clearly for posterity. It read: 'Dear Monsignor, At four this morning I was awake and looking over conciliar material when it struck me that it would be good to think of a future "historian" of the great event that is under way, and that he will have to be chosen with care. I think that the obvious witness and faithful exponent of "Vatican II" is really you, dear Monsignor: and insofar as a mandate can come from me – Pope of the Council, alive or dead – you should be authorised to accept this task as the Lord's will, and do honour to it, which would also be an honour for holy Church, a pledge of blessings and a special reward for you on earth and in heaven.' John was not quite 'Pope of the Council' in the end, and Archbishop Capovilla, now Guardian of the Shrine at Loreto, has not quite been its historian. The Council was too great for both bishops and any single scholar; but Mgr Capovilla continues to redeem that mandate.

A PERSONAL NOTE

The surge of memories and images overwhelms me and frightens me somewhat. Rather than setting out to write about that time, I should prefer merely to relive its old hopes and fears, as I felt them through the words and actions of that great man 'whose name was John'. I close my eyes, and see him; I open them, and hear and feel the comments, ideas, worries, fears and expectations. The twenty years that have passed have raised many questions, seen many developments, which we should now be able to consider without partiality or mitigation.

I too, as have many others, have come a long way since then, and hope to have done the Church 'some service' – though less than others, no doubt. And now, even though I am sure of the great truths of the faith, and I believe am not prey to destructive melancholy, I hope I can trust myself not to be overcome by timidity or dazzled by the flashes of light my eyes have seen, not to hold back from opening my heart, not to hold *secretum meum mihi* and in doing so betray the truth:

> From remotest earth we hear songs, 'Honour to the upright one'.
> But 'Enough, enough!' I say.
> 'Woe to the traitors who betray,
> to the traitors who treacherously betray!' (Is. 24:16)

For some, young people especially, perhaps, such detachment may seem like an evasion, or a convenient retreat into personal ascesis, a passive acceptance of situations and institutions, a 'withdrawal' in short, virtually a denial and an instinctive fear of the prophetic word, a rigidity in the face of the questions raised. It could be this, I admit, but it can also be something different, and something positive: a feeling of unease in the face of situations that are, to say the least, confused, but accompanied by a renewed need for deeper study in the spirit of evangelical hope; the promise of spring felt, against all probability, by the 'remnant of Israel', made up of the faithful whose faith is none the lesser for respecting the opinions of others, for noting different possibilities in social and political affairs, while remaining convinced that the leaven will not fail to permeate the mass.

NEW MEN

It is commonly held that the Sixties marked a sort of watershed: the end of an age, the passing of the 'Constantinian era', *la fin d'une chrétienté*,[1] the end of a certain way of being Christian and embodying the message. This went with another basic phenomenon: we Europeans began to confess our faults of omission, to recognize the limits of our culture and civilization; we stopped bandying our own interests across the world under the spurious pretext of 'advancing' the poorer peoples of the earth. We also saw how easy it is to protest and knock down, compared to the difficulty of building a new and better *civitas* in the perfect freedom of the children of God. Let us not, however, be too categorical about those times; let us simply say that for believers, events produced a need for radical changes, for personal conversion, for a decisive shift away from a triumphalist past and to a mission of service.

Let us open the gospels. One spring day, between the Resurrection and Pentecost, 'Simon Peter, Thomas called the Twin, Nathanael from Cana in Galilee, the sons of Zebedee and two more of the disciples were together. Simon Peter said, "I'm going fishing". They replied, "We'll come with you". They went out and got into the boat but caught nothing that night' (Jn. 21:2–3).

So they went back to their fishing as though nothing had happened, yet they felt they were not the same people they had been. They caught not a single fish and yet their hearts were full of joy. Christ, truly risen, had not abandoned them, had not dragged them into an adventure with no meaning and no outcome. From now on it was always to be like that. These men were no longer to be what they had been before. They were to travel the roads of the world, constantly adopting the apostolic and prophetic stance of Peter, who, in the house of the centurion Cornelius in Caesarea, received the most dazzling insight of his life: 'God has made it clear to me that I must not call anyone profane or unclean . . . The truth I have now come to realize . . . is that God does not have favourites, but that anybody of any nationality who fears God and does what is right is acceptable to him' (Acts 10:28, 34–5). Peter became a new man from that moment; not that he was without sin or weakness, but new in his faith and openness to others. Later, on the Vatican Hill, it was not the timid yet rash fisherman from Galilee who was crucified, but the witness to the Risen Christ; just as on the Via Ostia it was not Saul of Tarsus, the Roman citizen, who was beheaded, but the Apostle of the Gentiles.

These wonderful deeds, which we associate with the mysterious coming of the Spirit at Pentecost, do not mean that henceforth every problem is clarified, every difficulty removed. But this is where we start from: a disconcerting call, a road that led to Golgotha, a fishing trip that caught nothing, a revealing dream (of Peter and Cornelius), a meeting in the home of a pagan. From these beginnings we have moved and will move onwards, till Christ comes the second time, and these inspirations are enough to justify recalling the Second Vatican Council, from its opening on 11 October 1962 to its closure on 8 December 1965.

TUESDAY 9 OCTOBER 1962

It is fifteen days since we learned the news of the unexpected and worrying sickness that is affecting the Pontiff's life. He has gone on with a programme of intense activity, interrupted only by consultations with eminent doctors. He seems calm when he asks for clarifications about the gastric disorders he is suffering from, and about the X-rays. His pilgrimage to Loreto and Assisi on 4 October has given him the impression that the anti-religious feelings that have often characterized Italy in the past have been left behind. The crowds lining the roads of Lazio, Umbria and the Marches, and thronging the railway stations, have given him the measure of a dialogue without intermediaries, between father and children, showing a mentality profoundly altered for the better. He was on foot throughout the journey, seemingly oblivious of the pain that went with him from early morning till his return to Rome in the depths of the night.

Today is the fourth anniversary of the death of Pius XII. The Pope has decided to hold the memorial service in St Peter's, instead of the Sistine Chapel, so that more people can be present. Those who were beginning to guess something about his illness, remarked on his pallor and air of tiredness. But these were just the effects of having got up at 3.30 in the morning! His voice was clear and his steps brisk. He told the hundreds of bishops present: 'Through my example I have wished to increase the respect shown to the dear and blessed memory of this *Servus servorum Dei*, my inspiration for total dedication to the Church of which he was so worthy and edifying a Pontiff.'

He gave audiences to the Hungarian bishops Hamvas and Kovacs and the Yugoslav prelate Zazinovic, talking long to each one alone. Towards evening he handed a note to the Secretary of State, on which was written in his neat hand: 'Bishops from China, if and how to receive them. *Idem* for bishops from the *silenzio*.' This was a constant concern: what to do to re-establish and improve contacts with the Communities in countries whose political regimes have virtually abolished freedom of religion. Concern for the Church in the world, how it should keep its freedom to proclaim the Gospel without protection from political powers of one colour or another, '*flectar non frangar*' ('I will bend but not break') as opposed to the opposite proclaimed in the confrontations of the time of the *Risorgimento*: he saw all this as true to the Gospel, concerned not with the advantage or honour of the individual, but with the common good, and requiring the courage and burning faith that Christ not only justifies, but demands when he tells Peter to throw the net in again (Jn. 21:6). So John XXIII often said that applause or agreement mattered little to him; in his heart was the duty to watch prudently, and to sow widely. This provided the unaltering texture of his whole life.

WEDNESDAY 10 OCTOBER

This morning he gave a final look over the definitive version of his addresses for tomorrow and the following days, before dispatching copies to the Press Office. He saw Mgr Dell'Acqua [Secretariat of State] – whom he liked to refer to in the words of St Paul: 'The man dedicated to God, fully equipped and ready for any good work' (2 Tim. 3:17) – then his friend and confessor Mgr Alfredo Cavagna and finally Cardinal [Amleto] Cicognani, [Secretary of State].

During his evening rosary, in a repetition of his gesture on the eve of his announcement of the forthcoming Council (24 January 1959), he placed his address for the following day on the altar and piously entrusted it to the mediation of the Holy Family, a picture of which, from the school of Veronese, decorated the chapel. On the way out, he said: 'We are at the foot of the holy mountain. God has given us this hour of grace. It is up to us to accept it with humble trust.'

THURSDAY 11 OCTOBER

All night long the rain hammered down on roofs and pavements, with thunder and lightning. I rose at 5.30 and from my attic window saw St Peter's Piazza polished by the rain in preparation, as it were, for the opening procession. Towards 6.30 the sky cleared. The Pope celebrated mass then, in memory of the holy motherhood of Mary. As usual, I assisted him, admiring his complete immersion in God, and worrying about the sickness that was gnawing increasingly at the Pope's stomach, but . . . 'Unless a grain of wheat falls on the ground and dies, it remains only a single grain; but if it dies, it yields a rich harvest' (Jn. 12:24).

The Council was about to begin: the bishops all summoned individually by the successor of St Peter, under the guidance of the Holy Spirit but still requiring intense preparation and prayer and effort from men and women of good will throughout the world.

At breakfast the Pope did not speak. He did not open the papers either, but merely glanced at the headlines. Then he walked up and down the room in silence for a while, looking out of the window at every few steps. Outside, groups of faithful and onlookers were gathering under the colonnades; snatches of hymns and sacred music floated in through the windows. During the night, a huge basket of roses had arrived by air from the Mexican sanctuary of Our Lady of Guadalupe, which the Pope at once had placed by her statue in the Vatican gardens. At 8.45 he went up to the Hall of Consistories. In the lift and along the corridors we exchanged only a few words, carefully articulated as though the pontifical rites had already begun. To the words of *Ave maris Stella*, which he intoned in the Pauline Chapel, the procession began descending the Scala Regia. The Pope was carried in the *sedia gestatoria* and as the cortège moved out into the Piazza, I saw that his pale features were relaxed, but his smile came less often and showed traces of the physical pain which he was carefully hiding.

The crowds, conscious of the momentous occasion, applauded the Pope, and through him the important event that was being inaugurated. At the door of the basilica, John XXIII signalled that he wished to get down from the *sedia*, while the cantors intoned the *Tu es Petrus*. But the bearers took him part of the way down the nave, to save him the fatigue of the long walk. Then he continued on foot, a brother amongst brothers, majestic under the pontifical cape, which seemed to weigh heavy on his shoulders. He looked from side to side two or three times, as if seeking for a known face, or to give the bishops a first sign of his interest and encouragement. In their places, the bishops all bowed; the Observers from separated Christian Churches and Communities and the invited guests all shared in the same gesture. The *Veni Creator Spiritus* rang out high and vibrant, followed by the mass sung by the Dean of the College of Cardinals, Eugène Tisserant.

The most moving part of the ceremony was when he, the Pope, John XXIII, first and most qualified among the faithful, knelt alone facing the congregation, and made his profession of faith in a high, clear voice: '*Ego Ioannes, Ecclesiae catholicae episcopus . . .*' The articles of the Apostles' Creed thus set the seal on three years of intense preparatory work and lighted the journey of the Church towards new shores of peaceful evangelical conquest.

The *Adsumus* (prayer to the Holy Spirit), recited by the Pope, the singing of the Gospel and the greater litanies preceded the address, which was the dominant note of this first movement of the conciliar symphony.

It was past midday when John XXIII pronounced his discourse *Gaudet mater Ecclesia*.[2] 'Mother Church rejoices that, by the singular gift of Divine Providence, the longed-for day has finally dawned . . .' The attention of the whole assembly was fixed on him, and his clear diction of the elegant Latin made for immediate understanding. The official guests and Observers had translations in their hands. The message they heard and read was on these lines: The opening of the Council is a cause for joy; the Council seeks to be a representation of the message of salvation. The still audible voices of ancient and recent conciliar assemblies testify to the perennial fecundity of the Church. Now there is a need for prudent updating and reordering. Turning our back on the 'prophets of doom', we should recognize that Providence is leading us towards a new order of human relations. Finally, the Church can hold a Council without any interference from earthly powers. The Christian family and the human family are one, and a Church vowed to poverty will become a credible Church.

One o'clock had gone when the Pope concluded this extraordinary and long celebration, without showing any signs of fatigue. He took the lift up out of the Basilica, and after thanking Archbishop Felici [Secretary General of the Council], went out on to the balcony to receive the plaudits of the crowd. At lunch, all he said was: 'I had to struggle to stay calm, to hold myself in from the beginning to the end. While reading the address, I asked our Lord to speak to every one of that huge assembly individually.' I read him some messages that had come in during the morning, indicative of the vast amount of interest that his opening address had aroused.

He rested for an hour. When I went into his room at 3.30, he was not there. I found him at his usual place in the chapel, and asked how he was feeling. He replied, 'After what the Lord has given me this morning, I should be feeling fine. More than ever, I see the need for interior dialogue, for long prayer, for silence. We are nothing. He has done it, has done everything.'

At six o'clock he received Mgr Dell'Acqua, and they talked of the subjects to be discussed by the Council and recalled their common sojourn in Istanbul, when any small gesture of courtesy between Catholic and Orthodox was something miraculous. At seven, it was the turn of the Secretary of State, after which I reminded him that the town council had organized a torchlight procession in his honour and that of the Council Fathers, and that he was expected to give his blessing from the balcony. He cut me short: 'No, what I have done and said this morning is enough for one day. It's not a good thing for the Pope to show himself in public again, let alone speak again.' None of us dared to contradict him, but eventually the Secretary of State pointed out that the crowd was waiting: five hundred thousand people singing and holding their torches aloft, an impressive spectacle. I asked him at least to look out through the curtains, which he did. Obviously amazed by the scene, he said: 'Open the windows, draw the curtains. I will give a blessing, but I will not speak.' When he saw the crowd outside, however, he was moved to speak: 'Dear children, dear children', he cried. 'I hear your voices. My voice is an isolated one, but it echoes the voices of the whole world. Here, in fact the whole world is represented.' He went on to wax lyrical on the subject of a rose-coloured moon which, he pointed out, was 'also enjoying this spectacle'; and reminded everyone that what united them was Christ himself, casting his glow over them all like the moon.[3] Coming back into the room, he sat down, and with his inimitable simplicity said: 'I hadn't expected so much. It would have been enough for me to have announced the Council. God has allowed me to open it.'

From seven to eight he watched the special television programme on the Council, and pronounced himself pleased with it: 'A fine programme that makes it easier to understand and arouses interest. *Christus annuntiatur, in hoc gaudeo*: however Christ is proclaimed, that makes me happy' (Phil. 1:18). He kept me talking for another half hour on the programme for the days and months ahead, showing no sign of exhaustion after such an intensive day, perhaps justifying the optimism of his specialist Antonio Gasbarrini, who was convinced that what was troubling him was not a cancer but ulcers.

FRIDAY 12 OCTOBER

He rose at 4.30 and celebrated mass at seven. During breakfast, he glanced through the papers and the Press release from the Secretariat of State, composed by his good friend Professor Federico Alessandrini. Then he called me to his study and read me a note he had just composed, entitled *ad perpetuam rei memoriam*. It expressed his feelings and his inner peace after the celebrations of the previous day:

> Today marks the solemn opening of the Ecumenical Council. The account of it is written in all the papers and in Rome also in the exulting hearts of all. I give thanks to the Lord who has made me not unworthy of the honour to open in his name this source of great graces for his holy Church. He disposed that the first spark that led to the preparation of this event during three years should have come from my mouth and my heart. I was ready to give up even the joy of this opening. With the same calm I repeat the *fiat voluntas tua* about whether I shall stay at this post of service for all the remaining time and in all the remaining circumstances of this my humble life or whether I shall be called upon to stop at any moment, so that this commitment to go forward to the end may pass to my successor. *Fiat voluntas tua sicut in caelo et in terra.*

At ten o'clock he received the eighty-five 'extraordinary delegations' which had been summoned to Rome for the opening of the Council; then the auxiliary bishop of Sofia, the Czech prelates Necsey, Lazik and Tomasek, the Papal Nuncio in France, Archbishop Paolo Bertoli, and others. The audiences took place in the Sistine Chapel, and, taking his inspiration from Michelangelo's *Christ in Judgement*, Pope John told the representatives of the nations before him: 'We must indeed render an account to God, we and all the heads of State who bear responsibility for the fate of nations. Let them give ear to the anguished cry of 'peace, peace' which rises up to heaven from every part of the world, from innocent children and from those grown old, from individuals and from communities. May this thought of the reckoning that they are to face spur them on to omit no effort to achieve this blessing, which for the human family is a blessing greater than any other.'[4] Audiences went on in this way without a break till 2.30, when he lunched and rested. Despite the tiring morning he felt well, and told his colleagues so. The other day, when Gasbarrini had affectionately encouraged him, he replied: 'Don't you worry about me, doctor. I've always got my bags packed.'

That evening, when he took his leave, he assigned me the final reading for the day: '*Imitation of Christ*, book three, chapter five, number four', and I puzzled over the words: 'The lover flies, runs, and rejoices; he is free and is not bound. He gives all for all, and has all in all; because he rests above all created things in the one Supreme Being, from whom flows and proceeds every thing that is good. He does not regard the gifts, but transcending all good things betakes himself to the Giver.'

THE DAWN OF THE COUNCIL

Our lives are marked by certain dates which bear the unmistakable imprint of the Holy Spirit. Some are individual, such as the day of our baptism, or of our first conscious encounter with Christ; some affect our circle of family or friends, some the whole of humanity.

The eleventh of October 1962 was one of these latter, not so much for the exceptional event that took place, one repeated only twenty times before in the course of history, as for its implications and outcome, which have gone beyond what anyone could have imagined at the time. Those who took part in the events of that day surely still feel its resonance; those who then took part in the Council with their prayers, studies, reflections, in obedience to the Spirit, have borne fruit in abundance; from it they learned to overcome their past anxieties, to face the present in an ecumenical dialogue carried on without fear or presuppositions, to reject the subtle suggestions of the world to follow novelty for its own sake, or come to facile accommodations.

The Pope, who had first presented the idea of a Council on 25 January 1959 as an 'unexpected spring flower', and who had then assiduously promoted the idea for nearly four years; who had canonically convoked this apostolic endeavour, open to Christian brethren of all denominations and to the whole of humanity, on 25 December 1961,[5] inaugurated it now with the revealed words whispered in his ear: 'Very soon now, I shall be with you again, bringing the reward to be given to every man according to what he deserves' (Rev. 22:12).

A MILESTONE

There are those who still ask what Pope John meant by calling the Council; others ask whether the whole thing was not rushed; whether something untoward did not happen during the debates, like a gun going off in inexpert hands; whether simplicity and innocence didn't play ugly tricks; whether the prudence evident in the preparations didn't lose its place of honour as first among the cardinal virtues once the first spark had been struck.

So as not to leave these questions in the air, I should like to refer to three texts, produced by three Popes at the outset of their papacies. First, Paul VI:

> As the opening of the Second Session of the Second Vatican Ecumenical Council draws near, I cannot but feel profoundly moved by the grandeur of the holy inheritance bequeathed to me by my predecessor John XXIII: an inheritance which I received, as you well know, with fear and deference, but determined not to give in to any pressures that would prevent the most precious treasure of example, works and teachings, with which that great pontiff has enriched the Church, from remaining absolutely intact.[6]

Then Pope John Paul I:

> My programme will be to continue his (Paul VI's), on the lines already mapped out by so many indications from the great heart of John XXIII: that is, I wish to continue carrying into effect the inheritance of the Second Vatican Council, whose wise teachings have still to be guided to fulfilment, watching out for the imprudent though well-meaning impetus that can traduce their content and meaning on the one hand, and on the other, for timid and restraining forces that might slow down this magnificent impulse for renewal and new life.[7]

And finally, Pope John Paul II:

> I wish to point to certain directions which I consider to be of first importance and which, as such, will not only receive my attention, with, I trust, God's help, but also my continuing efforts, so that they may become embodied in the reality of the Church. Above all, I wish to stress the permanent importance of the Second Vatican Council, and I see it as my formal duty to put it into practice. Is the Council not in fact a milestone in the bi-millenary history of the Church, and, on reflection, in the religious and cultural history of the world? But the Council, just as it is not enclosed in its documents, is still not finished in its application, in what has been done in these post-conciliar years.[8]

ARCHBISHOP LORIS F. CAPOVILLA

In one of his frequent familiar conversations with groups of the faithful, John XXIII described his first inspiration for the Council as, 'a grace of intense perception of the Lord, as the two disciples felt on the road to Emmaus, with the same notes of surprise, stupefaction, commotion. It came out like a humble wild flower hidden in a meadow: you hardly see it, but you sense its perfume.'[9]

The time had been set by Providence. But it would perhaps be out of place to stress the presumed improvisation of the decision, and to suggest that enthusiasm covered up the difficulties in the Pope's mind. He was not just a man of 'simple good nature' as was often made out, as is shown by the profundity of a text dating from 28 June 1961:

> The Ecumenical Council seeks to embrace, under the outstretched wings of the Catholic Church, the entire inheritance of Christ. God wills that, besides its work on the conditions and concerning the *aggiornamento* of the Church, after twenty centuries of life – this is the scope of the task – it may also produce another result . . .: the coming together in one body of the whole of Christ's mystical flock. We must set aside easy illusions, since, when the time comes for this ideal to be realized, it will really be that blessed time when we close all our doors, and advance together, singing 'Hosannahs', to paradise. It will be a long time, however, before all the nations of the world perfectly understand the gospel message; and furthermore it will take not a little toil to change the mentalities, tendencies and prejudices of those who have a past behind them; and we shall need too to examine, somehow, what time, traditions and usages have managed to superimpose on reality and truth.[10]

My mind goes back to the first time Pope John spoke to me about the somewhat difficult and controversial idea of a Council: 2 November 1958, when he had been Pope for only five days. He spoke of it again on 21 November, travelling from the Vatican to Castelgandolfo, and a third time on Christmas Eve. No, I can't say I was exactly enamoured of the project then! It seemed to me that at the age of seventy-seven, John XXIII could have been content just to advance a little farther along the lines marked out by his predecessor, just to give evidence of his undoubted talent for being a father-figure. One evening, coming out of the chapel after evening rosary, I got the reply my doubts and fears deserved: 'You haven't yet shed your self; you're still concerned with the impression you make and you're projecting this concern on to your superior. Only when a man has trampled his *ego* under his feet can he be truly free. You're not free yet.' He was. He had put his *ego* under his feet and kept it there, at the time when some were acclaiming him, some just supporting him, and others still doubting.

On 11 October 1962, my thoughts went back to this radical humility of his, this super-human trust sustained by intense prayer, this unquenchable and burning faith, and I came to the conclusion that only with men, Christians, priests made in this mould could the Council carry out its work, avoid the pitfalls, recognize the voice of the Spirit and light new Pentecostal fires, so that it could carry out the vast task assigned to the Church by its divine Founder, who called it to shed its light on the nations: *Ecclesia Christi, lumen gentium*.[11]

CHRISTIAN THINKING AND THE MODERN WORLD

It is generally recognized that the beginning of the Sixties not only marked the end of an era, but was a time full of new hope. A widespread sense of dissatisfaction impelled the different elements of the human family towards a quest for new ways of escape from the blind alley of rigid and obstinate confrontation that had produced the climate of the 'cold war'. Illusory? Perhaps; yet the general tendency was away from fossilized situations to seeking solutions which might lead to a new order in the world.

So the President of the United States met the Soviet leader; there were splits in the Communist bloc; there was de-colonization (at least partly initiated by the colonial powers); there was a longed-for (or feared) spread of democracy in many countries; ideologies shattered; systematic doubt at all levels of teaching produced anguished speculation. Christians could not remain outside these aspirations or temptations, but became conscious of the need to equip themselves with renewed understanding and more effective means of spreading their task of witness and service. They saw the need to bring humanity the richness of the Gospel message, intact in its attractive originality and perennial vitality. Apostolically-minded pastors saw the need for a new *summa* of Christian thought, presenting the most debated and burning issues in a form accessible to the age, as had happened at various times in the past through councils and synods.

Pius XII had in fact understood both the possibility of destructive storms that could lay waste the whole of humanity, and the possibility of a new springtime for the Church,[12] and applied himself diligently to shedding the light of revealed truth on the risks facing mankind. In his place, the new Pope came to the waiting people in late 1958 – '*le maître qu'on n'attendait pas*', the man of works of mercy, of evangelical simplicity.[13] He himself gave an account of the original inspiration for the idea of a Council coming to him in a conversation with Cardinal Tardini [Secretary of State] about the troubles of the modern world and what the Church could do to help the cause of peace and harmony.[14]

The Council documents have a valid import for all time, since though their expression is conditioned by their time and place in history, they deal with eternal truths. But these are inevitably clothed in the garments of a particular epoch, in which the current spiritual climate necessitated the particular formulation of a thought, the stamp of a certain word, which could then become the sure possession of the Church and remind it of the precise moment at which that thought and that word took shape.[15]

If the task of councils has always been to bend man's intolerant intellect to 'obedience to Christ' (2 Cor. 10:5) by making use of the spiritual weapons offered by the times, so that all may 'come to unity in our faith and in our knowledge of the Son of God, until we become the perfect Man, fully mature with the fullness of Christ himself' (Eph. 4:13), this was pre-eminently the task of the twenty-first Council, a task defined by Pope John himself as being (and which still is) the *aggiornamento* of the Church. He set this out unequivocally in his first encyclical letter, *Ad Petri cathedram* (29 June 1959): 'For one who knows how to read the innermost feelings and thoughts of men; for one who has seen most of the world, who recognizes old and new experiences, and who knows how to distinguish between sacred principle in the eternal gospel and changeableness of climate, of temperament, of local contingencies, it comes naturally to think not of what divides souls, but of what is capable of uniting them in mutual understanding and reciprocal esteem'.[16]

SIGNS OF THE TIMES

Anyone who is capable of expressing his ideals in such terms is not going to build them into an ivory tower isolating him from the concerns of the mass of humanity, but make them the 'living substance' of his thinking and action, designed to place himself in the midst of everything that is vital in the order of human relationships. The biblical phrase 'signs of the times' (Mt. 16:3) is a clear and concise expression of this commitment to the various concerns and anxieties of the modern world, this overriding pastoral concern, based on a view of the *vis christiana* operating in the history of the world, not parallel to it.

Pope John used this phrase in the Apostolic Constitution *Humanae salutis* with which he convoked the Fathers in 1962, but he had often, in earlier documents, urged the need to know and understand the real situation in which men live and work. 'Making our own', the Constitution says, 'Jesus' recommendation to learn to distinguish the ''signs of the times'', we seem to perceive, in the midst of so much darkness, not a few indicators of hope for the Church and for humanity. Even the bloody wars which have taken place in our time, the spiritual ruination caused by many ideologies and the fruits of so many bitter experiences have not failed to produce useful lessons. Technological development itself, which has produced the possibility of creating weapons of mass destruction on a catastrophic scale, has also raised anguished questioning, forced human beings to become more thoughtful, more conscious of their own limitations, more desirous of peace.'[17]

The emergent phenomena of the modern age were later systematically singled out in the encyclical *Pacem in terris* (1963) – and they are no less actual now than they were twenty years ago:

> the economic and social advance of the working classes; the advent of women into public life; the deep transformation of the human family in its socio-political aspects: no longer dominator and dominated nations; all nations have formed themselves or are forming themselves into independent political communities; there is no longer seen to be any justification for racial discrimination; the juridical arms of political communities are tending to set out the basic rights of human beings in clear and concise terms; through the means of *constitutions*, juridical terms are being established to determine the ways in which public authorities are formed, as well as their relations with their subjects, their spheres of competence, the means by which they are to put their laws into effect; that is, the relationship between individuals and States is being established in terms of rights and duties; and public authorities are being assigned the primary task of recognizing, respecting and harmoniously arranging, watching over and promoting the rights and duties of citizens. Human beings are becoming more generally convinced that disputes between nations should not be resolved by recourse to armed conflict, but rather through negotiation.[18]

CITIZEN OF THE WORLD

These same 'signs of the times' were invoked in the televised radio message of 11 September 1962, in which Pope John set out the broad lines of what he hoped for from the coming Council. The message was a prophetic appeal, which was subsequently overshadowed by the – equally inspired and important – pronouncements made in October. Today it stands as perhaps the most complete indication of John's thinking on the direction the Council should take. Those who expected simply a renewed exhortation to prayer and penitence were forgetting that eight earlier documents issued under Pope John's signature during the year had more than amply covered this aspect.[19]

The radio message was, as it were, a culmination of the extensive catechesis of 1962, and it deliberately avoided any discussion of the six *schemata* sent to the Fathers. It concentrated rather on speaking of the activity of the Church *ad extra*, activity which, being wholly apostolic, undoubtedly contributes to the overall good of the human race. It also emphasized what would increasingly become the heart and centre of the council: *Ecclesia Christi, lumen gentium*, in order to make clear that the Church, bride of Christ, the *salvator mundi*, would, through this ecumenical gathering, show itself as the Church of humanity, for humanity.[20]

On this subject, he wrote on 5 June 1960: 'This is henceforth a principle written into the spirit of all the faithful belonging to the Roman Church: to be truly and consider themselves, as Catholics, citizens of the whole world, just as Jesus is the adored Saviour of the whole world. This is a good exercise in true catholicity, and all Catholics should take account of it and make it a precept, in the light of their own mentality and as a guide for their own conduct in both religious and social affairs.'[21] So, in the anxious days before the Council, John XXIII outlined the salient features of this catechesis for the Church in the modern world, more than ever determined to proclaim freedom, peace and justice, and to defend their principles and execution.

The Church itself claims for itself a freedom that cannot be circumscribed within the narrow ambit of worship or be reduced to just this. Christ, who entrusted his Church with the mission of leading mankind to everlasting salvation, at the same time gave it the powers and means to carry out this mission, and no earthly power can legitimately deprive it of these. Besides, truth and freedom are the twin foundation stones on which the whole of human civilization is built.

Making use of the freedom that belongs to it, and conscious that no one can be allowed to 'chain up God's news' (2 Tim. 2:9), the Church will openly denounce all injustice; the Council was to remind those who hold power, and particularly economic power, that they are obliged to share their riches with the underdeveloped countries. To those who, from malice or any other motive, continue to perpetuate the image of a 'class Church', a 'Church of the rich' or 'State Church', John replies with pontifical solemnity, almost *ex cathedra* one might think: 'Where under-developed countries are concerned, the Church presents itself as it is, and wishes to be – as the Church of all and especially as the Church of the poor.'[22] On the basis of this quotation, one can see that the radio message of 11 September prepared the way for the work of the Council, and set the tone for the Constitution on the Church in the Modern World, *Gaudium et spes*, which did not exist even in embryonic form at that time, not being promulgated till 7 December 1965 [i.e. the last day of the Council].

A French journalist, engaged in following the work of the Council, asked a Roman prelate who was deeply involved with the preparatory work what interpretation should be placed on the very 'open' tone of this message compared with the first communications given out about the *schemata* submitted to the Fathers for their consideration. This prelate, well aware of the implications, replied: 'It also behoves public opinion in the Church to help the Pope make the Council what he wants it to be'. 'Which Council?' asked the journalist. 'We'll know that the day it opens.'[23]

PROPHET OF HOPE

11 October 1962 is a date enshrined in the annals of humanity. Men saw in their midst the presence of an inspired and passionate interpreter of their widest hopes, whose voice Paul VI was rightly to call prophetic, 'certainly inspired by a special impulse from the divine Providence which "orders all things for good" (Wis. 8:1) and with consummate wisdom provides for the good of the Church according to its needs.'[24]

This voice did not cry out in the desert. It was heard by Catholics recalled to a livelier sense of responsibility in the field of witness and missionary activity; it awoke a longing for unity among the 'separated brethren', giving new impulse to specific initiatives aimed at fulfilling Christ's wish '*ut unum sint*' (Jn. 17:21). It awoke curiosity and sympathy among believers of all religions, sincerely moved by the ecumenical language used by the Bishop of Rome. It brought pleasure to all men of good will, of whatever ideological or political persuasion, who were seeking brotherhood and peace.

Seen from the threshold of the Vatican Basilica, the great procession of bishops from all over the world recalled the vision of the first Pentecost when the message was miraculously spread to the simple and the humble, the little ones and the poor, those to whom God preferentially reveals himself (cf Mt. 11:25). The little ones and the poor had waited for the unfolding of a love capable of piercing laws and customs; priests had waited for the return of that apostolic zeal that had previously given so much light to the world; the bishops, for the collegial charity that encouraged each of them to participate in the service, struggle and sacrifice of all; the Pope himself – as he had written in his *Journal of a Soul* – 'to be able to pursue his great aim, scarcely understood, of pouring himself out over everything that was ministry of faith, grace, pastoral spirituality, while holding himself apart from all involvement in political affairs of whatever sort and at whatever level'.[25]

All had fuelled the lamp of hope; theologians and pastors, politicians and trade unionists, rich and poor, conservatives and progressives, the discouraged and the uncertain, the timid and the rash. Nothing had been lost. No one had been deceived. Humanity had not come to a sudden halt. Rather, the faithful had become more open in listening, more resigned to losing what was ephemeral, to renouncing 'things' while remaining obstinately faithful to their baptismal Creed and respecting the best traditions of their native lands.

The inaugural address to the Council set out the main lines of the task to be undertaken, without giving the least ground for speculation about what might be said on particular themes of faith, evangelization or the dialogue with humanity. It would be a good idea for all of us to re-read that address now: reflecting on it is a great help to understanding the inspiration and aims of Vatican II, and to avoiding false polemics from either side which can lead either to fidelity to the 'deposit of faith' impeding apostolic dynamism on the one hand, or pastoral innovation compromising the truth on the other.[26]

AGGIORNAMENTO

On 11 October 1962 John XXIII expressed above all his measured optimism and his positive view of the meaning of history, which meant rejecting, from the start, the view derived from a certain sort of integralism. Then, repeating what he had said on many occasions before, he went on to outline the eminently pastoral scope of the Council: 'The salient point of this Council is not, therefore, a discussion of one article or another of the fundamental doctrine of the Church which . . . is presumed to be well known and familiar to all.' The salient point is rather a more effective presentation of this doctrine, 'which should be studied and expounded through modern research and modern scholarly disciplines'. In other words, an *aggiornamento*, a bringing up to date. And the Pope did not hesitate to say that there could be homogeneous development of doctrine and new formulations of truths whose substance remains unchanging: 'The substance of the ancient doctrine of the deposit of faith is one thing. The way in which it is presented is another.'

Avoidance of condemnation of errors that in themselves tend to disappear was the next guideline: 'Often errors vanish as quickly as they arise, like fog before the sun. The Church has always condemned these errors. Frequently she has condemned them with the greatest severity. Nowadays, however, the spouse of Christ prefers to make use of the medicine of mercy rather than that of severity. She considers that she meets the needs of the present day by demonstrating the validity of her teaching rather than by condemnations.' He did not list all such self-evident errors of the modern world, but made it clear that he included all forms of totalitarianism, militant atheism, the idolatry of technocracy, 'violence inflicted on others, the might of arms and political domination'. All such, he said, 'are of no help at all in finding a happy solution to the grave problems which afflict (mankind)'.

The young cripple, calling on apostolic help from the threshold of the Temple, evokes an un-idyllic view of man, and, at the same time, the widespread desire of humanity to escape from the bonds of error and conformism, to open up to the light of truth, to 'arise, and walk'. How much that was positive and young in spirit was occasioned by this address, particularly by its final call for unity, the 'great mystery Jesus Christ petitioned with fervent prayer from his heavenly Father on the eve of his sacrifice'.

There is no discernible break between successive stages from the first announcement of the Council on 25 January 1959 and the end of the First Session on 8 December 1962, or the succeeding Sessions presided over by Paul VI. In his Apostolic Constitution *Humanae Salutis*, John had spoken of the Council meeting 'at the right point in time', a time when the Church felt the need to give greater efficacy to its own vitality, to promote the sanctification of its members and the greater diffusion of its revealed truth. The Council was to be a demonstration of a Church, 'ever living and ever young, which feels the rhythm of the age, which in every century adorns herself with new splendour, irradiates new light, realizes new conquests, while remaining always faithful to herself, to the divine image impressed on her countenance by her Bridegroom who loves and protects her, Christ Jesus'.[27] At a distance of years from that opening of the Council on 11 October 1962 and from its closure on 8 December 1965, we still have the guidance of the Council documents and their subsequent interpretations that have come from the altar of St Peter's into our hands.

Faithfulness to the authoritative teaching contained in the sixteen Council documents and later documents which apply them and interpret them would seem to be an ineluctable duty for all Catholics. This means staying in the tracks of truth and freedom with openness and courage, not being afraid to call black black and white white, never compromising with those who presume to meddle with the deposit of faith or capriciously alter the outlines of moral law, liturgy and Church discipline, as formed, clarified and expounded in Catholic tradition over the course of centuries. On 29 August 1959, John XXIII had forcefully stated:

> It is a question of saying 'No' to evil in all its forms. Simply because he proclaimed a *non licet*, the head of John the Baptist was cut off and placed on a dish . . . In daily life we often hear: The Church could be more indulgent, could agree to some small compromise. Never, we say! The Pope can be as good-natured and magnanimous as one wishes, but faced with the tragedy of reality with unfulfilled wants, he will be firm, clear, unmoveable, in obedience and homage to the truth.[28]

There is another quotation I should like to recall at this most evocative time, a powerful and even prophetic one: 'St Ambrose has written that, even after his head was cut off, the dead eyes of John the Baptist condemned all that is disorder and contradicts the law of the Lord.'[29] Pope John's eyes, too, could become hard when faced with obvious manifestations of evil, disorder, mocking wrong-doing. Those eyes implored! The imploring was for the biblical concept of justice invoked by the faithful and by the prodigal son returned home; it asked for ardent efforts to provide for all in peace, in accordance with the dictate of the beatitudes and the teaching of the pastoral and social magisterium of the popes in this century, from Leo XIII to John Paul II, from *Rerum Novarum* to *Laborem Exercens*.

NEW HEAVENS AND A NEW EARTH

From the moment the Council was first announced, through the years of preparation and into the first session, there were uncertainties, equivocations, delusions and confusion. Some saw the Council as just a magnificent show, a splash of colour, a display of charitable organization; there were those who insisted, with apologetic fervour, on its secondary elements; others saw it as simply a continuation of a régime of presence and service, even an increase, but without anything new; others again looked for novelty in a break with the past.

For the 'remnant of Israel' the Council meant an occasion for the most attentive listening and a motive for theological hope. This is what it should have been and should still be for all those who know how to recognize salvation in obedience to the Spirit. From the first announcement, the Council was proposed as an act of humility, an invitation to communion, an indication of service. It was to be, as the Pope said, both an effort to make the message of salvation more accessible to mankind, and a preparation of the way towards the final unity of the human race. He looked to the future

with an optimism and enthusiasm that have carried down the intervening
years.

From the steps of St Peter's, like Peter and John on the steps of the
Temple at Jerusalem, the Church continues to preach Christ risen from the
dead. To tired afflicted humanity, disorientated, trusting excessively in
progress, in politics, in laws; to men seeking help, support, guarantees, the
Church says more decisively than ever: ' "I have no silver and gold, but I
give you what I have: in the name of Jesus Christ of Nazareth, rise and
walk." The Church offers the men of today no fading riches, no mirage of a
happiness to be enjoyed only on this earth: she pours out a wealth of supernatural grace which, raising men to the dignity of children of God, offers
them a firm protection and assistance to a more human life.'

Shortly before the Council opened, committing some thoughts on the
Letters of St Peter to paper, John paraphrased the prophecy concerning
'new heavens and a new earth': 'New heavens and a new earth! When will
we see them? . . . First of all we shall see the triumph of justice brought
about by the offering up of our lives and the cultivation of a spirit of peace.'

New heavens and a new earth! John XXIII could well aim at these with
his adamantine faith and extraordinary readiness to serve. And in obedience
to the Spirit and in the light of this eschatological hope, he could put
forward the three basic aims of Vatican II: inner renewal of the Catholic
Church; re-presentation of its *essence* 'without spot or wrinkle'; ecumenical
inspiration, witnessed by the bishops of the whole world, called together by
Peter, united round him and like him concerned above all with the effective
and integral well-being of humanity, making their own, in the opening
words of *Gaudium et spes*, 'The joys and hopes, the griefs and anxieties of the
men of this age, especially those who are poor or in any way afflicted'.

He could put forward these aims because he himself was totally detached
from outside conditioning and personal ambition. Even clad in cardinal's
purple, he introduced himself to the Venetians as 'of humble birth and
trained to a contented and blessed poverty, which makes few demands and
fosters the growth of the most noble and lofty virtues, a good preparation
for the higher ascents of life'.[30] At the age of just thirty, he already showed
the balance that was to sustain him through the various stages of his
ministry, as he moved from place to place, inside Italy and outside, never
losing his composure or changing tone: 'The Lord has deigned to make me
understand once more the full importance, for me and for the events of my
priestly ministry, of that spirit of sacrifice, with which I wish ever more to
inform my conduct, 'as a servant . . . a prisoner of Christ' (Eph. 6:6; 3:1).
May all my works . . . be marked with this seal: that everything is done in

and by the Lord, with much enthusiasm, but with no concern for their greater or lesser success.'[31]

He could put forward these aims because, as soon as he had been elected Pope, he had immersed himself in reading the history of the Councils, taking account of Paul III's definition of the coming Council of Trent as 'the best and most opportune remedy in the recurrent crises of the Church'. He knew the details of the tortuous history of the Councils, the decade of uncertainty Paul III had to suffer before the work of Trent could begin, so that he could in his turn bequeath his testimony to the historians: 'No anxiety on my part and no desire to be there myself at the finish of the Council. What the Lord wills is more than enough for me. Whatever the Lord might impose on me in the way of sacrifice of my *amour propre*, sacrifice of my life itself, I gird myself with and count as a blessing, for however *Christus annuncietur et clarificetur, in hoc gaudeo et gaudebo*.'[32]

The Second Vatican Council was not just an exercise in inner renewal of the Church, in re-statement of its essence, in ecumenical endeavour. It was the creation of new men and new women, renewed by the Father, through his Son Jesus Christ, in the Holy Spirit. It was a revelation of the will of the Father; a pressing appeal to conversion of life; an encouragement to set out on the most tremendous journey. At the end of the first year of his pontificate, at a general audience on 28 October 1959, John XXIII spoke of his own hopes and thoughts in terms that earned him, among other titles, that of 'Pope of the *Pater noster*':

> The good wishes for the aims, prosperity and success of the pastoral work we have begun, which are expressed to us with so much kindness and affection, certainly touch our heart. But they do not distract us from the thought of the other world which awaits us, and from which there comes to our ears, as we trust in the Lord's mercy, the invitation to join the Church Triumphant, which is the constant hope of all souls who believe in Jesus, Saviour and glorious and immortal King, world without end . . .
>
> So, venerable brothers and beloved children, when we consider the first experiences which the Lord during the past year has permitted us to enjoy in our contacts with the episcopate, the clergy, people of every nation and every sort, and also with all those, who, under another name, still bear the sign of Christ on their brows, we must say that never before so vividly, as on this first day of our second year, have we been aware of the general design of the great mission of the Pontificate, as the guardian of Christ's testament. This is what we perceive as we contemplate once more the salient points of the prayer which Jesus on the mount taught his followers, almost as if he were tracing the shining paths of the apostolate of Holy Church.[33]

This extract surely contains all Pope John: it is his Council, his testament, his immortality. He often used a phrase which all of us would do well to recall under the most varied circumstances: 'Without and beyond the name, kingdom and will of the Lord, there is nothing desirable for me, nothing of interest for my ministry.'

NOTES

1. 'The main subject of Vatican II is the Church, meditating on its own essence, mission and modes of being in the light of the fundamental mystery; seeking to renew itself in such wise that all may recognize that it was for the Church that Christ pronounced his priestly prayer, and that the Church is the community of the faithful followers of the double commandment of love ... The Church would be too much *of this world* if it sought to see itself primarily in juridical terms of unity. Of course the Church is in the world, and so needs a visible structure. It needs laws and an administration. But if it wishes to be faithful to its essence and to give its witness in a comprehensible and authentic manner, it can only do so through revealing its innermost mystery. Were a Church to use the power structures of this world to conserve its unity and integrity of faith – inquisition, temporal power and privilege are essentially not service but a means of being served – it would be weak; it would also obscure its mission. The Church of Vatican II has firmly decided to set aside all these *trappings* and legal usages which no longer seem appropriate for spreading its message in the world of today.' (Bernhard Häring, *Vatican II in the Sign of Unity*, Rome, 1963, 23f.) Of this book, which is really an extended commentary on his opening address at Vatican II, Pope John said: 'In these pages my soul can really be found'.
2. Extracts in Robert Kaiser, *Inside the Council* (London, 1963; US, *Pope, Council and World*, New York, 1963), pp. 81–4. Full text in Ed. W. M. Abbott SJ, *The documents of Vatican II* (New York & London 1966), 710–19.
3. Cf. Kaiser, *op cit*, 85f. The full text of this speech is also in Ernesto Balducci, *John, 'the Transitional Pope'* (London & New York, 1965), 196–8.
4. Kaiser, *op cit*, 87.
5. John XXIII, *Discorsi, messaggi, colloqui* (DMC) (Rome, 1960–63, 5 vols), II, 819; Apostolic Constitution *Humanae salutis*, AAS 54 (1962), 1–13, ET Abbott 703–9.
6. *Acta Apostolicae Sedis* (AAS), 7 October 1963, Paul VI, Apostolic exhortation *Cum proximus* of 14 September 1963, 729f.
7. John Paul I, radio message 'A dawn of hope rises over the world', in *Insegnamenti di Giovanni Paolo I*, (Vatican), 15.
8. John Paul II, first broadcast, 'Fidelity to the Council', in *Insegnamenti di Giovanni Paulo II*, I (Vatican, 1978), 13f. Cf Karol Wojtyla, *Sources of renewal*: study on the implementation of the Second Vatican Council (Krakow, 1972; revised ET London, 1980).
9. DMC, II, 652.
10. DMC, III, 574–5.
11. 'The world indeed has need of Christ and it is the Church that must bring Christ to the world.' Radio message of 11 September 1962. Excerpts in Kaiser, *op cit*, 72f; Balducci, *op cit*, 311f; full (Italian) text in DMC, IV, 519ff.
12. Warning about the dangers of nuclear weapons, in AAS 36 (28 May 1954), 213; address to young people, in AAS 50 (28 April 1958), 216.

13. Madeleine Delbrel, *Nous autres gens de rues* (Paris, 1966), 318–20.

14. *Journal of a Soul* (London & New York, 1965), final note. The statement 'without having thought of it before' has given rise to some controversy. Pope John (as all his later writings and speeches indicate) was referring to the period before he was elected Pope, when he made it an absolute rule not to concern himself with projects outside his competence. It is a fact that he mentioned the idea of a Council to a few people close to him before 20 January 1959, but only tentatively, without giving away exactly what was in his mind So he said that the first time he spoke about a council was on 20 January to Cardinal Tardini, five days before making the official announcement in the Benedictine monastery of St Paul in Ostia. There is nothing insincere in this account of events. Tardini, the Secretary of State, was his principal aide and the executor of his decisions; so it was natural to tell him first, in 'audience', the decision he had made, and he did it so naturally and persuasively that he obtained not only his consent in obedience, but also his enthusiastic collaboration. [Kaiser places this conversation in 'the second week in January' and comments: 'Tardini's assent to this proposal was "immediate and exultant", according to John's first recorded report of that meeting, and, according to another, later report given by John, "restrained but nevertheless positive". Tardini told persons in the Curia that John would soon forget he had ever mentioned a Council.' *Op cit*, 14 – *Transl.*] Finally, it is on record that at the time of this meeting, John had already prepared the first draft of his address for the following Sunday, the homily at Mass in which he made the historic announcement of the Council. [See Hebblethwaite, 312ff, who suggests that 'the actual date of decision could well have been the night of 8 January 1959'. Ed.]

15. Cf. Various, *Concilio Ecumenico Vaticano II* (Genoa, 1962); Cardinal Joseph Frings, *The Council and modern Thought*, 147–76.

16. DMC, I, 812; AAS 51 (1959), 497–531; CTS S254, 'Truth, unity and peace', 5–40.

17. DMC, IV, 867–76; AAS 54 (1962), 1–13.

18. DMC, V, 521–66; AAS 55 (1963), n5; CTS S264, 'Peace on earth'.

19. These documents were: Apostolic Constitution *Sacrae laudis*, 6 January; Apostolic Letter *Consilium*, 2 February; Pastoral Letter *Quanti siete*, 8 April; Letter *Omnes sane*, 15 April; Apostolic Letter *Oecumenicum Concilium*, 28 April; Encyclical *Paenitentiam agere*, 1 July; Exhortation *Il Tempio massimo*, 2 July; Apostolic Letter *Appropinquante Concilio*, 6 August 1962.

20. Cf. Kaiser, *op cit*, 72f; Balducci, *op cit*, 311f.

21. DMC, II, 394.

22. Cf. Kaiser, *op cit*, 72.

23. Antoine Wenger, *Vatican II – Première Session* (Paris, 1963), 32.

24. AAS, 55 (20 September 1963). Lettèr *Horum temporum*, 14 September 1963, 734.

25. *Journal*, 'July and August 1962'.

26. Cf. Paul VI, Encyclical *Ecclesiam suam*, AAS 56 (20 August 1964), n10; CTS Do 354, 'The Church in the modern world', 5–64. Cf also Kaiser, *op cit* 81–4.

27. DMC, IV, 870f; cf. Balducci, *op cit*, 308.

28. *Scritti e Discorsi di Giovanni XXIII*: July-August 1959 (Siena, 1959), 120f.

29. DMC, I, 624.

30. Balducci, *op cit*, 157.

31. *Journal*, 'Spiritual Exercises . . . 13–19 October 1912.'

32. *Ibid.*, '24 March 1960'. The Latin quotation is from St Paul, Phil. 1:18: 'Whether from dishonest motives or in sincerity, Christ is proclaimed; and that makes me happy'.

33. DMC, I 504f; excerpts in Balducci, *op cit*, 40f.

8

MOVING TOWARDS A PILGRIM CHURCH

YVES CONGAR OP

This chapter had its beginning at an International Colloquy in Rome during 24–6 October 1980 organized by the Istituto Paolo VI, and entitled 'Ecclesiam Suam: première lettre encyclique de Paul VI'. The Colloquy issued its Proceedings, Pubblicazioni dell'Istituto Paolo VI, Brescia 1982, Père Congar's paper being 'Situation ecclésiologique au moment de Ecclesiam Suam *et passage à une Eglise dans l'itinéraire des hommes', 80–102. He has since republished it in* Le Concile de Vatican II *(Beauchesne 1984), 7–32; and in view of his present infirmity he has suggested that it appears in English in this book. It admirably shows the theologian's mind at work upon the Council.*

When the new Pope, Paul VI, opened the Second Session on 29 September 1963, he affirmed that 'The Church is a mystery. It is a reality imbued with the hidden presence of God. It lies therefore within the very nature of the Church to be always open to new and greater exploration'. Three ideas have steadily emerged as expressions of that mystery: that the Church is a koinonia/communio, *a* participatio in Deo *and its members a* participatio in corpore Christi; *that the Church is a pilgrim society, as a caravan of folk in via, 'man on his way'; that the Church is 'the new people of God' (and* Lumen Gentium *II is entitled* De Populo Dei). *These ideas Père Congar has called 'une ecclésiologie en gestation'. He has written much about them, propagating the new vision from before the Council ended. See his essay, 'L'Eglise comme peuple de Dieu', in* Concilium *1 (1965), 15–32; and his two chapters in* Le Concile de Vatican II, *109–36 which complement this study. Such writings confirm his greatness as an ecclesiologist.*

Something happened at the Council and the dominant values in our way of looking at the Church were changed by the Council. That will become clear in the course of my analysis; but I am bound to stress that such a plan is simplistic. Vatican II was intentionally in continuity with the previous councils of the Church and with Tradition.[1] Paul VI himself insisted on its continuity with Vatican I.[2] As every historian knows, everything is always changing and at the same time there is in many ways a deep continuity. There was also tension between the ideas that were dominant in Rome and the movement of ideas in other cultural environments. There is, after all, a geography of ideas. When I consider the way in which the Council developed, I am very conscious of that obvious tension between those other cultural environments and the Roman Curia or what is associated with it. But even there I have to be careful not to be simplistic. All those who took part in the Council were united by their Catholicism.

If I were to say that at the opening of the Council the official ecclesiology was dominated by a juridical view, I would only be singling out a basic inspiration and general orientation and leaving aside other facts, without overlooking them. When he intervened on 5 December 1962, one of the criticisms made by Cardinal Montini himself of the schema prepared by the Theological Commission was that 'In the same schema the primary elements of canon law are set out; the truths however are not fully expounded, those truths which refer more explicitly to the mystery of the Church, to its mystical and moral life, truths by which the Church's vitality in the real sense of that word are achieved.'[3]

The first chapter of the schema was in fact entitled: *De Ecclesiae militantis natura* ('The Nature of the Church Militant'). It began by discussing the plan of God the Father (sec. 1) as carried out by the incarnate Son who sanctifies and directs (*gubernat*) the people of God towards eternal salvation 'not only by himself, but also by the leaders chosen by him' (sec. 2). A short paragraph on the images of the Church (sec. 3) was followed by one on the image of the body, envisaged in the sense of *Mystici Corporis*. The schema concluded with the statements that 'the Church as a society is the mystical Body of Christ' (sec. 6) and that 'the Roman Catholic Church is the mystical Body of Christ' (sec. 7).[4]

It is clear, then, that this preparatory schema incorporated the teaching of *Mystici Corporis*. The Archbishop of Milan himself frequently quoted from this Encyclical, but his references were for the most part to its mystical aspects. Among the new elements contained in the schema was Chapter XI on ecumenism, but as a whole it was, as Antonio Acerbi has noted, 'a summary of the pontifical teaching of the past one hundred and fifty years'.[5] The language, which presents us with a total view, is juridical. This is strikingly apparent, for example, in Chapter X: *De necessitate Ecclesiae annuntiandi Evangelium omnibus Gentibus et ubique terrarum* ('The need for the Church to proclaim the Gospel to all nations and everywhere on earth'). This arose because of the struggle that the Church – and above all the Popes – had conducted against the absolute and lay claims made by the secular powers. That struggle had led Popes and theologians working in Rome to give priority to, and to regard as a key concept of ecclesiology, the idea that the Church was a society and even a *societas perfecta*, a 'complete society'. It should not be forgotten that these ideas have not been eliminated by Vatican II and that they continue to be valid in Catholic ecclesiological teaching.

The really important question, then, is: What concepts will enable us to approach the whole question? What are the dominant concepts? They are, I believe, the concepts of *societas, societas perfecta* and *societas inaequalis, hierarchica.* I would like to examine each of these concepts in turn.

Societas

L. Billot, *Tractatus de Ecclesia Christi* . . . (1898, 3 ed, Prato 1909): 'The present tractate is concerned with the society of the Church as such, insofar as it is a society.'[6] Billot looked at the body of the Church as conceptually separated from its soul of grace. He saw that body as existing as such independently of the grace and virtues that are found in its members, namely as a 'society which is a collection of members under a hierarchy set up with twofold power', a society of jurisdiction and order.

Confronted with this brutal choice, one is reminded of a statement made in *Lumen Gentium*, 14: *'Illi plene Ecclesiae societati incorporantur qui, Spiritum Christi habentes . . .'* ('They are fully incorporated into the society of the Church who, possessing the Spirit of Christ . . .'). I can bear witness to the fact, as the one who edited this, that there was a general conviction that what was expressed here in the question of the members of the Church was a concrete conception of the Church. In its own way, the Encyclical *Mystici Corporis* was a critical questioning of Billot's point of view in that it reintroduced the aspect of grace and charisms into the reality of the social body of the Church. It did this, however, by satisfying the request made in 1940 by Fr Przywara not to define the Church in terms of the mystical Body, but rather to define the mystical Body in terms of the Church, that is, in terms of a society.[7]

Several other treatises which have taken the idea of *societas* as their point of departure could be mentioned in this context. Perhaps the most notable are C. Pesch, *Praelectiones dogmaticae De Ecclesia* (1894ff, 4 ed, 1909); M. d'Herbigny, *Theologica de Ecclesia* (3 ed in 2 Vols, 1920–25) and J. V. Bainvel, *De Ecclesia Christi* (Paris, 1925). Bainvel's treatise begins his Thesis 1 with the words: 'Christ himself founded the Church after the fashion of a distinct visible society, in which there would be, and outside of which there would not be, the Christian religion.' After having defined society in purely philosophical terms, another author, A. M. Vellico, applied this definition to the Church and stated that 'We have the Catholic doctrine which held and holds firmly that Christ the Lord while on earth founded his Church as a true and properly so-called society; an unequal society – and thereby called a hierarchical society'.[8]

Societas perfecta

This concept goes back to Aristotle's *Politics*. Thomas Aquinas used it for the *civitas*, but did not apply it to the Church; that was something that happened later.[9] The concept was, however, already implicit in the statements made by Gregory VII.[10] It was applied to the Church only in a very discreet way, for example by Bellarmine[11] before the eighteenth century, when the theories of public law, which attributed the entire external organization of the Church's life to political power first began to appear.[12]

French bishops made use of this concept to criticize the civil constitution of the clergy in 1790.[13] This became one of the themes of the great struggle conducted by the papacy and the Roman jurists against the claims made by the state to limit and control the Church's freedom of action. This happened from the time of the pontificate of Gregory XVI onwards (1839).[14] The claim that the Church was an original, autonomous society which by divine right possessed all the powers that it needed to obtain its supernatural end was given a juridical foundation first by Tarquini (1862) and later by Cavagnis. This claim was made again and again by Pius IX in various consistorial allocutions, including *Singulari quadam* (9 December 1854), *Multis gravibusque* (17 December 1860) and *Maxima quidem laetitia* (9 June 1862). The concept also occurred in the same Pope's Syllabus of Errors 19, condemning the thesis 'The Church is not a true and complete society, clearly free; and it does not enjoy its own proper and permanent rights conferred on it by its divine founder: but it is for the civil power to define what are the rights of the Church and the limits within which it can exercise those same rights' (*DS* 2919). Finally, the notion reappeared towards the end of the pontificate of Pius IX in the Encyclical *Vix dum a Nobis* of 7 March 1874.

The thesis was taken up again by Vatican I in Chapter III of the schema *Supremi Pastoris*. This schema was distributed on 21 January 1870, but it was neither voted on nor debated by the Council.[15] It was a frequent theme in the teaching about civil society and the relationships between the Church and the state so carefully worked out by Leo XIII. There is evidence of it in many of his encyclicals: *Diuturnum illud* of 29 June 1881, *Immortale Dei* of 1 November 1885 especially (see *DS* 3167), *Libertas praestantissimum* of 20 June 1888, *Sapientiae christianae* of 10 January 1890 and *Praeclare gratulationis* of 20 June 1894. In this Pope's pontificate, it was given juridical support by Cavagnis and Zigliara. Pius X, Benedict XV and Pius XI each provide at least one reference to the theme of *societas perfecta*[16] and, together with them, the classical authors of treatises on public Church law[17] and those like Rudolf

Sohm who wrote criticisms of false spirituality[18] also dealt with it. The theological writings of Pius XII and Charles Journet, for example, have also shown that, far from being incompatible, the visible and the juridical aspects of the Church can themselves be regarded as spiritual.

Societas inaequalis, hierarchica

This became a fundamental affirmation of official ecclesiology in the period between the First and the Second Vatican Councils. Long before Vatican I, Gregory XVI wrote: 'No one can overlook the fact that the Church is an unequal society in which God has destined some to command and others to obey. The latter are the laity, while the former are the clergy.'[19] I have already referred to the schema *Supremi Pastoris* that was distributed at Vatican I. In Chapter III of this document, we read: 'The Church of Christ is not a society consisting of equal members, as though all the faithful who form part of it had the same rights. It is, on the contrary, an unequal (hierarchical) society in that some of the faithful are clergy and others are laity. It is above all such a society because there is in the Church a power that is divinely instituted which some have received in order to sanctify, teach and govern and which others have not received.'[20]

This theme was later reiterated by Pius IX,[21] Leo XIII[22] and Pius X.[23] It was finally included in the 1917 edition of Canon Law. Canon 107 states that 'Ex divina ordinatione sunt in Ecclesia clerici a laicis distincti'. It was even echoed much later in the preparatory schema (No. 5): 'The Church, by the very fact that it is a body, is perceived by the eyes. It is a collection, moreover, of many members, clearly not equal, since some are subject to others and since clerics and lay, superiors and subjects, teachers and disciples, and diverse statuses exist within it.'

The theological manuals, which almost without exception had an apologetic aim, attempted to prove that, during his ministry in this world, Christ founded a Church as a society. They also set out to show that this society was perfect (or complete), in other words, that it was provided with power to legislate, govern and restrain by means of penalties. Secondly, the authors of these manuals described the Church as an unequal or hierarchical society, incorporating by divine right a difference between those who governed and those who were governed. There was a pyramidical view of the Church which was expressed in many different ways.

The term 'hierarchology', which I coined in 1947, has since been used by many authors. At that time, I also cited what Möhler had written about the juridical form of ecclesiology with which he had been confronted, namely that 'God created the hierarchy and in this way provided more than sufficiently for the needs of the Church until the end of the world'.[24] Christ was seen essentially as the founder of this society rather than as its actual foundation. This led Cardinal Montini to make the following criticism of the schema of the Theological Commission:

> Further, the doctrine which deals with the relation existing between the Church and Christ should be declared more forcibly. It should be said, and it should be made clear to everyone, that the Church is well aware that it can do nothing of itself, but receives everything from Jesus Christ and functions precisely insofar as Jesus Christ is present and active in it. The Church is not only a society or community founded by Christ the Lord, but is an instrument in which he is present undisclosed (*arcane*) so that he might bring about the salvation of the human race by teaching, by sacramental sanctification, by pastoral care, all of which should be fed by his spirit – who is the Good Shepherd of souls.[25]

This reminds me vividly of the emotional and even passionate way in which Paul VI said on 29 September 1963, at the very beginning of his pontificate, when he was opening the Second Session of the Council: 'There are three questions, essential in their extreme simplicity, but only one reply: . . . Christ. Christ is our principle. Christ is our hope and our end.' *Lumen Gentium*, 3, contains an almost literal echo of these words.

To this I would add that the hierarchy was entirely centred on the Roman pontiff and existed in a perspective of spiritual monarchy. Not all the classical theological manuals were as brutally frank as that of Domenico Palmieri, who entitled his work *Tractatus de Romano Pontifice cum Prolegomenis de Ecclesia* (Rome, 1877; 2 ed, 1891; 3 ed, 1902). But after the so-called Gregorian reform, which marked a decisive turning-point in Catholic ecclesiology and has since that time been reduced to its Latin part, the Church has appeared as a kind of deduction from or expansion of its Roman head. As the place at which a *De Ecclesia* was formulated, Rome had considerable significance. The preparatory schema of Vatican II was edited on the basis of a *Schema Compendiosum de Ecclesia* by men who in one way or another all belonged to the Holy Office.[26] It was accompanied by a *Symposium Theologicum de Ecclesia Christi*, sponsored by the Lateran. Although this was not an official glossary, it was quite significant.[27]

One of the aims of Vatican II was to complete the work of Vatican I and in that way to make it more balanced by formulating a theology of the episcopate, both as a body or college and as a formal element in the local Churches. The first of these two aspects was quite unsatisfactorily treated in the schema of the Preparatory Commission. Cardinal Montini spoke about this in his intervention in the Aula on 5 December 1962, when he suggested an order of chapters beginning with the college of apostles as the origin of the college of bishops.[28] Two days later, celebrating the feast of Saint Ambrose at Milan, he pronounced these powerful words: 'Yesterday, the theme of the Church seemed to be confined to the power of the Pope. Today, it is extended to the episcopate, the religious, the laity and the whole body of the Church. Yesterday, we spoke of the rights of the Church by transferring the constitutive elements of civil society to the definition of a perfect society. Today, we have discovered other realities in the Church – the charisms of grace and holiness, for example – which cannot be defined by purely juridical ideas. Yesterday, we were above all interested in the external history of the Church. Today, we are equally concerned with its inner life, brought to life by the hidden presence of Christ in it.'[29]

Later, as Pope Paul VI, he returned to this theme of the theology of the episcopate on at least two occasions. In his discourse given on 4 December 1963 at the close of the second period of the Council, he referred to the five orientation questions of 30 October, the implications of which had been vigorously debated by those who opposed collegiality. He also alluded to this question again when he addressed the Council at the opening of the third period on 14 September 1964.

Everything that I have said so far is directly relevant to my subject. But I think that I shall come much closer to the heart of the subject as I have defined it at the beginning – 'the movement towards a pilgrim Church' – in the two sections that follow. The first of these is 'what has become of the values known as the "perfect and unequal society" '. The second is 'the change in our view of the temporal reality of the world'.

WHAT HAS BECOME OF THE VALUES 'PERFECT AND UNEQUAL SOCIETY'

These ecclesiological values have not been rejected or forgotten, but they are no longer regarded as the door by which we enter into the reality of the 'Church', nor are they the dominant values.

Societas

The Council speaks of the 'mystery' of the Church. It traces that mystery back to the mystery of Christ insofar as the latter is itself more than simply an external work like creation and is an involvement on the part of God himself in the world's destiny. By this I mean an involvement on the part of the Trinitarian God. This accounts, for example, for the opening paragraphs of *Lumen Gentium* (Church) and *Ad Gentes Divinitus* (Missions). It accounts for the quotation from Cyprian in *Lumen Gentium*, 4: 'Sic apparet universa Ecclesia sicuti "de unitate Patris et Filii et Spiritus Sancti plebs adunata" ' ('Thus the universal Church shines forth as "a people made one with the unity of the Father, the Son and the Holy Spirit" ').[30] It also accounts for a declaration made at the end of sec. 2 in *Unitatis redintegratio* (Ecumenism) which could hardly have been made at Vatican I: 'Hoc est unitatis Ecclesiae sacrum mysterium, in Christo et per Christum, Spiritu Sancto munerum varietatem operante. Huius mysterii supremum exemplar et principium est in Trinitate Personarum unitas unius Dei Patris et Filii in Spiritu Sancto' ('This is the sacred mystery of the unity of the Church, in Christ and through Christ, with the Holy Spirit energizing a variety of functions. The highest exemplar and source of this mystery is the unity, in the Trinity of Persons, of one God, the Father and the Son in the Holy Spirit').

In these conditions, the most suitable concept is undoubtedly that of 'communion' and Paul VI loved it. I well remember the way in which he spoke to me about it, quoting from J. Hamer's book, *The Church is a communion* (1962)! It is true, of course, that the Council did not go as far as it might have gone in working out this idea. As Antonio Acerbi has pointed out, it retained some elements of a juridical ecclesiology. According to *Lumen Gentium*, for example, the Church is 'ut societas constituta et ordinata' in this world ('constituted and organized in the world as a society') (sec. 8) and a 'societas hierarchica ordinata' ('a hierarchically structured society') (sec. 20, 14). This is still true.

To return to Paul VI. It is well worth while examining the deep insights that he had into the Church as a communion, combined with his insights into the mystery of Christ. Here I can do no more than recall one aspect, to which Dom Emmanuel Lanne has already drawn attention in his excellent article in memory of the late Pope.[31]

Paul VI was orientated towards ecumenism, particularly with regard to the Orthodox Church. What I have in mind was his pilgrimage to the Holy Land with (according to an autographical note dated 21 September 1963) two intentions: 'to give honour to our Lord Jesus Christ' and 'a fraternal meeting, as the prelude to a more stable reconciliation, with the different separated Christian denominations that are represented there'. I also remember the visit to Phanar and the breve *Anno ineunte* in which he spoke of the Orthodox and the Catholic Churches as 'sister churches'. According to Lanne, this name 'was employed not with a socio-political intention in mind, but in a genuinely Christian and evangelical perspective. The theological basis of the term "sister churches" is the brotherhood of the children of the Father in Jesus Christ and their communion with one another, since we have communion with the Father and the Son'. The text is formal and an ecclesiocentric approach is avoided together with an imperious concentration on the Roman Church as *mater et magistra* by the author's taking the mystery of Christ as his central point.

'Communion' is a key concept in the ecumenism of Vatican II and Paul VI continued to use it again and again after the Council. It allows us to clear the way blocked by *Mystici Corporis* and the strict identification of the members of the mystical Body with the members of the Roman Catholic Church. It avoids the situation of all or nothing. We are already in communion with non-Roman Catholic Christians, even though that communion is imperfect. But our communion with Orthodox Christians is almost perfect. The modest but very important word used in *Lumen Gentium* 8, the Decree on Ecumenism and the Declaration on Religious Freedom – *subsistit in* – enabled the ecclesiology of *Mystici Corporis* to be corrected, or rather perfected. This was, of course, something that Cardinal Liénart had called for from 1 December 1962 onwards, the time when the preparatory schema was first debated. I can even go further and say that the last word has not yet been spoken about this ecclesiology of 'communion'!

The approach of Vatican II was tentative. No one guided the Council in a systematic way. But a *mens concilii* or *mens pastorum* emerged from it which frequently enabled juridical terms that were close to natural reason to be replaced by positive Christian expressions. The vocabulary of 'power' was not employed. The participants spoke rather of mission and service.[32] And they used such words consciously and deliberately. It is quite instructive to compare Vatican II with Vatican I simply on the basis of a word count of key terms. For the sake of example, I would, with reference to the relevant publication,[33] list in alphabetical order only some of those words that were used in the documents of Vatican II, but never in those of Vatican I. They include *amor* (113 times), *dialogus* and *evangelizatio* (31 times each), *evangelizare* (18 times), *fraternus* (49 times), *fraterne* (12 times), *fraternitas* (26 times), *historia* (63 times), *laicus* as a noun (200 times), *ministerium* (147 times), *ministrare* (31 times), *missionalis* (75 times), *novitas* (39 times), *pauper* (42 times), *servire* (17 times) and *servitium* (80 times). Other terms occur in the documents of both Councils, but in very unequal proportions, even if the great inequality in the total number of pages is borne in mind. Let me give only one very significant example: *evangelium*. This word appears only once in the texts of Vatican I. Even the excellent Evangelium of the Tridentine chapter on Scripture and traditions (*DS* 1501) is replaced in the

chapter on Revelation of the Constitution *Dei Filius* of Vatican I by
'*supernaturalis revelatio*' (*DS* 3006)! The same word occurs 157 times, on the
other hand, in the texts of Vatican II.

Societas perfecta

This term never meant that the Church was without fault; but, before
Vatican II and Paul VI, it was never said at such a public and official level
that the Church is constantly in need of reform. From then onwards,
however, that has been said again and again.[34] This presupposes a greater
consciousness of the distance that separates the Church from the kingdom
of God and from the historicity of the Church. (I shall have something to
say about this below.) The term *societas perfecta* had two meanings for
Vatican II. The first is that the Church has of itself everything that it needs
to achieve its end. Vatican II speaks in a very discreet way about mission, care
and duties[35] and, without insisting on it, as the official texts and the manuals
used to, about the right to coerce and punish. The second meaning refers to
the theme of the *libertas Ecclesiae* and the demands made by it. This second
sense in which the term is used by Vatican II is all the more important in
view of the freedom taken by the Council with regard to the rules of
'Christianity' or the 'Catholic state'.[36] The theological context in which
this proud assertion of apostolic freedom is made is different from what it
used to be after the endemic struggles between the two 'Powers', in other
words, after the eleventh century. This has to do, as we shall see, with a
new understanding of what is 'temporal'. The Church has to find support
for its freedom less in juridical agreements with the secular Powers and
more in the dignity of the human person and the freedom to believe
which is permanently linked to it.

Vatican II, then, respected the idea of a *societas perfecta* by keeping to these
two meanings. From the time of the Catholic restoration in the nineteenth
century until the period in the present century when Catholic Action was
fully developed, however, this theme of a *societas perfecta* represented something quite different in the concrete. The Council did not let itself be
confined to this meaning, which implied that the Church, as Catholics
living together and forming a cultural world of their own, was quite self-
sufficient. I was personally familiar with that Church, which undoubtedly
had a certain power and grandeur. It constituted a Catholic replica of the
framework and structures of the whole of life, having its own schools,
universities, hospitals, clubs, trade and professional associations, newspapers, journals and books. Catholics had a defensive, siege mentality. They

thought that the world was conspiring against them and were therefore closed to everything that came from outside.[37] From the time of Leo XII onwards (1823–29), the number of specifically Catholic societies and activities increased enormously. The clergy protected themselves by apologetics that were always triumphant. I was very familiar with all that!

Paul VI's attitude and that of the Council were very different. The Council knew and said publicly that the Church was not the same as the world and that Christian life made certain distinctive claims,[38] but it formulated a programme for the Church within the world no longer restricting it to the Christian world. The Council was not a self-enclosed group of men living in its own separate world. It was the meeting place of pastors who had come from every part of the world. It opened with a message to that world (20 October 1962) and ended with the publication of a Pastoral Constitution on the Church in the Modern World (7 December 1965), together with seven messages sent out under the vault of heaven to various categories of humankind (8 December 1965). What was the attitude of Paul VI himself? We have to hear what he said or read what he has written to know that. A few months after the worker-priest movement had been suppressed, he wrote, for example:

> Christian assemblies have often been no more than élite groups. There have been no crowds and the great majority of the people seem to have been absent from them. Will they come back? They will not.
>
> Priests have to go to the people. It is useless for the priest to ring the church bell. No one listens to it. He has to hear the sirens sounded by the factories, those temples of technology where the modern world lives and breathes. He has to become a missionary again if he wants Christianity once more to become and to remain a leaven within civilization.[39]

Then, ten years later, there was *Ecclesiam Suam*, proclaiming that the distinction of being with the world was to be not separated from the world,[40] to oppose a retreat from the world (sec. 70). Here, I would simply recall these words of the text:

> The world will not be saved from outside. Like the Word of God who became man, we have to some extent to assimilate the forms of life of those to whom we want to take the message of Christ. Without claiming privileges that will put us at a distance from others, without preserving the barrier of an incomprehensible language, we have to share the customs that are common to all, provided that they are human and honest, and especially those of the least of men . . . We have to become brothers of our fellow-men.[41]

A month after this, opening the Third Session of the Council on 14

September 1964, the Pope said: 'The Church is not an end in itself. It wants to be entirely Christ's, through Christ and in Christ and entirely men's, among men and for men.'[42]

This led to the idea of the Church in the ecclesiology of Vatican II as the 'sacrament' of salvation, the 'sign and instrument' of 'intimate union with God and of the unity of all humankind'.[43] What a dynamic idea! It points to a destination beyond the Church, to a being for all, to mission as 'being with' and as 'dialogue'.[44]

This dialogue is, of course, not a simple teaching procedure. For Paul VI, it was the kind of dialogue that should take place between a doctor and his patient. In his address given at the closure of the final Session on 7 December 1965, he called it the charity of the good Samaritan for the wounded man.[45] His address to the United Nations on 4 October 1965 ended with an appeal to *metanoia*. (The New Testament word appears in the original Italian text.) This aspect of Paul VI's thought was certainly developed later, on the day devoted to *Ecclesiam Suam*. Here I would simply point to the parallel between this thought and that of John Paul II in his Encyclical *Redemptor hominis*, according to which Christ is for and in every man and man is the 'way of the Church' – which is, of course, very close to my own subject.

In the thought of Paul VI, dialogue implies that we receive from the other and reach a deeper level because of the other.[46] At the Council, this idea is found underlying the whole of *Unitatis redintegratio* (Ecumenism). It is also expressed, in my opinion in a rather restricted way, in *Gaudium et Spes* 44: 'The Church knows how richly she has profited by the history and development of humanity.' In this debt, the Constitution is conscious of the activity of the Spirit (see 26, 4; 38, 1). The relationship between the Church and humankind and the world is understood as being historical or at least that is what has been suggested.[47] Vatican I proclaimed the transcendence of God, avoiding all compromise with pantheism. Vatican II, on the other hand, showed that a historical plan resulting from the missions of the Word and the Spirit is carried out in the relationships between nature and the supernatural or creation and salvation. It therefore showed that God was, in that respect, in the world.

The idea that God's work takes place in the history or development of the world resulted, after the Council, in the emergence of a new type of pastor in the Church. The Council of Trent resulted in a new type of bishop, who was no longer a lord, but a pastor. Vatican II produced a type of bishop who was no longer content simply to preside over a Church with its sacral activities and its purely confessional works. As the 1971 Synod and John Paul II said after the Council, the post-conciliar type of bishop regarded development and liberation as part of the task of evangelization. A pilgrim Church was being built up.

Societas inaequalis, hierarchica

This concept was not rejected by Paul VI, the Council or the post-conciliar Church. On the contrary, they reaffirmed it. They did not, however, regard it as of first importance or as the door by which one had to enter ecclesiology. Of first importance was the sacramentally based Christian being committed to the mission of communicating Jesus Christ. The most significant indication of that is the order of Chapters II (The People of God) and III (the hierarchical structure) of *Lumen Gentium*, the result of a vote in the Council. According to my diary, Paul VI was not in favour of the order that was eventually agreed. He attached great importance to the mission of the Twelve as distinct from the general and less clearly defined mission of the whole People of God. A note that he sent to the Commission concerned with Missions shows how significant this was for him. An attempt was made to satisfy him at the beginning of *Ad Gentes divinitus* 5.

One of the most fruitful ideas that emerged from the Council was, of course, that of the People of God or the 'messianic people'.[48] It has sometimes been misunderstood, especially in the sense of restricting it to believers at the 'base' and not applying it also to the ministers and pastors of the Church. Despite this error of interpretation, however, it continues to be a true and very fruitful affirmation – one of the most fruitful made during the entire Council.

What is the situation since Vatican II with regard to the almost obsessive dominance of the Roman pontiff in classical ecclesiology? Neither the Council nor the work done after the Council have succeeded in reducing the authority of the Pope. The crisis in his *magisterium* has come from other sources, including the partial non-acceptance of *Humanae Vitae*. In Chapter III of *Lumen Gentium* alone, there are no less than sixteen references to the union of the bishops in subordination to Peter's successor. The Council did, however, renew the episcopate in its form of co-responsibility in the conferences of bishops with its sessions that had been called 'councils' in the early Church and in the Middle Ages.

The Council also reopened the chapter on the conciliar or synodical life of the Church. It did not deal with it as a simple datum, but rewrote it, including many new developments in ecclesiology. This represents a real synthesis incorporating a spiritual and not simply a juridical principle of unity and a diversity that has fundamentally to do with persons and ethnic realities. It also represents a movement away from an ecclesiology concerned simply with the universal Church and the expansion of one Church – the Church of Rome – throughout the world and forgetful of the reality of the local Churches; in other words, an ecclesiology orientated towards a uniform universality which is pragmatically subdivided into dioceses.[49] The principle of collegiality is based on a recognition of the reality of local Churches. That recognition was initiated by the Council. Karl Rahner even believed that it was the most fundamentally new and the most promising contribution made by the Council. Since its introduction, this theological insight has continued to make progress and to reach greater depths.

The structures by which the *Ecclesia* is represented and expresses itself began to be formed. They consist basically of synods of bishops, national synods, councils of priests and pastoral councils. In his conference given in 1962 to the University of the Sacred Heart in Milan on the study of the Councils and the life of the Church, Cardinal Montini quoted Newman's famous article on the need to consult the faithful in the matter of doctrine. The question of making those Churches that had until recently been missionary Churches fully indigenous was asked, but the problem was not solved. I was personally very impressed by this statement made in the address, which I quote freely: Saint Paul did not found missions. He founded Churches. That means that they should not be transplanted. They should come to life and grow indigenously . . . What is the situation with regard to Africa, Asia and Oceania? The widespread – perhaps too widespread – abandonment of Latin is a cultural datum and it is difficult to foresee its consequences. It may result in a diversification of the liturgy and greater creativity. Above all, it will mean a new and more widespread participation on the part of communities. What we share with many others – and in particular with our Orthodox friends – is the conviction that this new practice in the Church should be based on a very deep theology of the Tri-unity of God and on a Pneumatology. What a perspective of excellent work this opens up!

A CHANGE IN THE CHURCH'S VIEW AND LIFE ON THE BASIS OF A CHANGE IN OUR VIEW OF THE TEMPORAL OR THE WORLD

In January 1963, Cardinal Montini told young priests:

At the Council, *the Church is looking for itself*. It is trying, with great trust and with a great effort, to define itself more precisely and to understand what it is. After twenty centuries of history, the Church seems to be submerged by profane civilization and to be absent from the contemporary world. It is therefore experiencing the need to be recollected and to purify and recover itself so as to be able to set off on its own path again with great energy . . . While it is undertaking the task of defining itself in this way, *the Church is also looking for the world* and trying to come into contact with that society . . . How should that contact be established? By engaging in dialogue with the world, interpreting the needs of the society in which it is working and observing the defects, the necessities, the sufferings and the hopes and aspirations that exist in men's hearts.[50]

These ideas form a link between the two terms used in the discourse of 5 December 1962, *Ecclesia ad intra – Ecclesia ad extra*, and anticipate the link that was to be developed in *Ecclesiam Suam*: dialogue, love and care for the wounds inflicted on humankind. In other words, it was recognized that the Church could understand itself only in its relationship with the world – not with an abstract world, but with the real historical world.

One of the most damaging deficiencies in the training of clergy in the nineteenth century was a lack of historical understanding and openness in the historical sense. This fault even persisted into the early part of the present century. I have documented this question quite thoroughly. The phenomenon had to do with a poor knowledge of Scripture and an exclusively conceptual or juridical presentation of the Church.

There was also – for the same reasons – a lack of eschatological insight. There was at that time certainly a *De ultimis rebus*, but this teaching about the 'last things' was no more than a study of what existed after this life, in other words, of death, purgatory, heaven and hell.[51] Eschatological understanding is quite different. It is being conscious of the fact that everything on this earth is involved in a movement, that it is a history moving towards an end and acquiring from that datum its stimulus and its meaning as a movement or as history.

One of the greatest deficiencies of classical religion has therefore been its failure to inspire the world as such with hope. The hope that it provided as part of the 'last things' was individual. It was not cosmic, social or historical. There is an almost complete absence of documentation on this aspect of hope produced by the Roman *magisterium*. A clear example of this lack can be found in the Encyclical *Quas primas*, instituting the feast of Christ the King (11 December 1925). The liturgy of this feast, on the other hand, is not defective in this way, because it contains many excellent biblical texts! Several of the Fathers of the Second Vatican Council criticized the schema *De Ecclesia*, which was debated during the Second Session of the Council (1963), even after it had been drafted, for lacking this eschatological sense.[52] Mgr László, for example, said: 'The Church cannot be thought of

143

in any other way than as the eschatological People of God, on pilgrimage through time and proclaiming the death and resurrection of the Lord until he comes again' [Cf. 1 Cor. 11:26].

The result of this absence of eschatological insight was a religion without the world. The counterpart of this was of course a world without religion. Other deficiencies can be verified with reference to the enormous – and extremely useful! – *Dictionnaire de Théologie Catholique*, published in fifteen volumes containing 41,338 columns between 1903 and 1950. In many cases, this great dictionary has either no article at all or else a quite insufficient entry.

> *Profession*: there is one article, entitled 'Profession of faith'. *Trade*: nothing. *Work*: nothing. *Profane*: nothing. *Family*: nothing. *Fatherhood*: nothing. *Motherhood*: nothing. *Woman*: nothing. *Love*: a third of a column, divided into Love of God: see Charity/Love of neighbour: see Charity/Self-respect (*Amour-propre*): a few lines referring the reader to Ambition/Pure love: see Charity. But there is nothing in the dictionary on human love as such. *Friendship*: nothing. *Happiness:* a third of a column, referring the reader back to the article on Beatitude. *Life*: an article on eternal life. *Body*: one article, but on the glorified body. *Sex*: nothing. *Pleasure*: nothing. *Joy*: nothing. *Suffering*: nothing. *Sickness*: an article beginning with the words: 'Under this heading we include various cases of exemption from the law applicable to certain sick persons because of their bad state of health'. *Evil*: 25 columns. *Economy*: nothing. *Politics*: nothing. *Power*: a long article of 103 columns (four times as many as for Evil) on 'the power of the Pope in the temporal order'!
>
> *Technique* or *technology*: nothing. *Science*: a long article subdivided into four parts: Sacred science, Science (= Knowledge) of God, Science of the angels and the separated souls and Science of Christ. But on what we now know as science, there is nothing. *Art*: a long article on primitive Christian art. *Beauty*: nothing. *Value*: nothing. *Person*: one line: see Hypostasis. *History*: nothing. *Earth*: nothing. *World*: nothing. *Lay* and Laity: nothing apart from an article on Laicism, which is stigmatized as a heresy![53]

Vatican II, on the other hand, as revealed especially in *Lumen Gentium*, had a very different view. It was resolutely based on the history of salvation and eschatology. This was, moreover, not simply because the Council has assimilated all that was best in biblical, theological and patristic studies during the preceding thirty years, but because it was above all a pastoral Council. It was doctrinal too, of course, but was concerned with teaching only in a pastoral perspective. It was also led by pastors, men who could not be content simply to repeat merely speculative arguments expressing a pure 'in itself'. They spoke of a Church that was actively involved with and committed to the world and to the history of men. They were convinced that it was only by joining that world and that history that Christianity could ever become a dynamic event.[54] It would be tedious to try to summarize and assess the eschatological statements made in *Lumen Gentium*,[55] but it will help to make clear what I have to say about the renewal of ecclesiology resulting from a new approach to the world if I quote part of *Lumen Gentium* 48, which opens Chapter VII of the Constitution, *De indole eschatologica Ecclesiae peregrinantis* ('The Eschatological Nature of the Pilgrim Church').

> The Church, to which we are all called in Christ Jesus and in which we acquire sanctity through the grace of God, will attain her full perfection only in the glory of heaven. Then will come the time of the restoration of all things (Acts 3:21). Then the human race as well as the entire world, which is intimately related to man and achieves its purpose through him, will be perfectly re-established in Christ (cf. Eph. 1:10; Col. 1:20; 2 Pet. 3:10–13).
>
> Christ, having been lifted up from the earth, is drawing all men to himself (Jn. 12:32, Greek text). Rising from the dead (cf. Rom. 6:9), he sent his life-giving Spirit upon his disciples and through this Spirit established his body, the Church, as the universal sacrament of salvation . . . The promised restoration which we are awaiting has already begun in Christ, is carried forward in the mission of the Holy Spirit and through him continues in the Church. There we learn through faith the meaning too of our temporal life, as we perform, with the hope of good things to come, the task committed to us in this world by the Father and work out our salvation (cf. Phil. 2:12).
>
> The final age of the world has already come upon us (cf. 1 Cor. 10:11). The renovation of the world has been irrevocably decreed and in this age is already anticipated in some real way . . . However, until there is a new heaven and a new earth where justice dwells (cf. 2 Pet. 3:13), the pilgrim Church in her sacraments and institutions, which pertain to this present time, takes on the appearance of this passing world. She herself dwells among creatures who groan and travail in pain until now and await the revelation of the sons of God (cf. Rom. 8:19–22).

I have cited this text because it summarizes the Church's new view of the temporal and the spiritual or its view of itself living and working in the world. Let me explain what I mean by this.

We no longer try to resolve the problem of the two powers which has passed through so many vicissitudes and yet remained dominant for fifteen centuries. This attempt to define the Church ended with a view of the type of the Church comparable to that of the secular state and a conception of the Church based on juridical and social categories similar to those of the state. The preparatory schema included a chapter in this vein – Chapter IX – in which the thesis of so-called indirect power of the 'Church' was based on the idea of the temporal city, because of the subordination of the ends. The text was amply documented with references to the Popes, from Benedict XIV to John XXIII. But it was criticized at the Council[56] because it only spoke of the Church's rights, whereas a true perspective can only be acquired by examining the Church's task to evangelize, a task which clearly presupposes freedom. Traces of this classical position can still be found in *Gaudium et Spes* 76, but that is all. The Council had, as I have already said, a very different view of the Church. The temporal and the spiritual were not seen or defined in terms of power.

For the Second Vatican Council, the temporal was the whole of man's work in time. It includes all the efforts made by men to order the world and their life together in a human way. This attempt to establish human order in time is discussed, for example, in *Pacem in terris* (1983) and *Populorum progressio* (1967). It embraces all those realities about which the *Dictionnaire de Théologie Catholique* has nothing to say. The temporal has cosmic dimensions, yet it is marked by the historicity, complexity and sequence of historical achievements. John XXIII, and Paul VI in *Octogesima adveniens* (1971), both distinguished these aspects from the ideologies which may have given rise to them.

In the same way, the spiritual as related to the temporal also cannot be defined as a juridical power. It is the leaven that is working for the kingdom of God and for eschatology. That leaven begins with the Spirit of Jesus Christ, acting either directly and freely or as mediated by the 'sacrament of salvation' which is the Church as the People of God, the 'messianic people' that forms part of the world of men. *Gaudium et Spes* speaks of 'the People of God and the human race in whose midst it lives rendering service to each other' (sec. 11, 3; cf sec. 40, 2 and, of course, sec. 1).

The Church, then, is in the world. It moves forward in history. The world is also included in the plan of salvation. The source of that plan is the death and resurrection of Jesus Christ. The end is the eschatological kingdom. It is proclaimed on this earth by the Church, which is its sacrament. The temporal does not have to be subjected to the Church, but it has to be referred to eschatology, which is the promise of its fulfilment.

The Church and the world cannot be identified with each other, but their unity at the end of time means that in a sense they share the same history. This unity also implies that the active principle should be the same and that principle is Christ: 'The same God is Saviour and Creator, Lord of human history as well as of salvation history'.[57] As in *Lumen Gentium* and the entire thought of Paul VI, everything is clearly contained within the mystery of Christ.

In the case of man, the Council was convinced of the non-extrinsic character of grace in its relationship with nature. The texts clearly reflect the influence of the writings of Maurice Blondel, Henri de Lubac and Karl Rahner. The same applies to the Council's attitude towards 'human history and salvation history' – man is seen as both individual and social. The action of the Church takes place through man, who is the subject of both time and eternity. All these themes were greatly valued by Paul VI. They appear in his address to the Council at the closure of the Fourth Session and also in *Ecclesiam Suam*, in which man is presented as restless and hurt, but full of aspirations and possibilities and the Church as offering him the model and the power of Jesus Christ. The man Jesus Christ mediates between the Church and the world.

Since the pontificate of Leo XIII and Pius XII, the Popes have frequently spoken of the dignity of the human person. There is a clear connection between these earlier Popes' way of thinking and the Council's Declaration on Religious Freedom which Paul VI valued so highly.[58] In *Gaudium et Spes*, that dignity takes the form of man on the one hand made in the image of God and called to sonship, but on the other as a sinner and destined to bodily death.

The danger or the limitation of these considerations is that man is seen simply as an individual and as existing outside time. Christians influenced to a greater or lesser extent by Marxism have often expressed this criticism. This is a relatively new way of thinking that was, if I am not mistaken, not followed either by the Council or by Paul VI. The historical and social dimensions of the conciliar documents will have to be carefully considered. A synthesis will have to be made of the first chapter of the first part of *Gaudium et Spes* (sec. 12–22) and the section on the 'signs of the times' (sec. 4ff.), the whole course of that Pastoral Constitution, the encyclical *Populorum progressio*, the text of the 1971 Synod of Bishops, Medellín (1968), Puebla (1979) and the declarations made by John Paul II in Mexico, Africa and Brazil. The statement that 'man is the way' by which the Church goes forward in time, which is repeated three times in *Redemptor hominis* (1979), will have to be seen in its historical and social perspective.

This task will take us into an area in which various historical realities are inevitably encountered and in which it is quite inadequate simply to deduce from principles. This historical concept was known to Paul VI at least through his friend Jacques Maritain's *Humanisme intégrale*. In their reports made in the ante-preparatory period, several (Argentinian) bishops had asked for this text to be condemned and those who insisted on the truth in itself also wanted this.[59] But since then we have had, in 1971, Paul VI's own

Octogesima adveniens, which is (in my opinion) the model of a new way of exercising the pastoral *magisterium*. This has been followed by the work of Lebret, Vincent Cosmao, Leonardo Boff, Joseph Comblin and Gustavo Gutiérrez.

This synthesis will be made in tears and in the blood shed by Mgr Oscar Romero and many others. A Church of the people is being reborn and it promises to be both serious and lasting because it has its martyrs. It is no longer, as it did in the past, claiming priestly power in the sphere of political power. It is trying to let the Gospel, as experienced in the lives of Christians, be effective and influential. How should I define the new form that this Church takes? I would say that it is that of the Gospel lived in the realities of human lives on earth or their 'temporal' experience. It is in that life that the Gospel is spread and is able to act in souls.

How fundamentally right it was to place an open Gospel on the coffin of Paul VI when it was lowered into the earth. Its pages were turned by the wind! This reborn Church is not the only form that a Pilgrim Church can take. The requests made by African and Asian Christians that their Churches should be really indigenous are also authentic requests made by a Pilgrim Church. That pilgrim way has been open in principle since the Son of God became man and sent us, from the Father, the Spirit who makes us proclaim God's glory in every human language.

NOTES

1. There are ninety-three quotations from the documents of previous Councils in the texts of Vatican II, twenty-one of them from Trent and twenty-four from Vatican I. There are also no less than 201 quotations from or references to ninety-two of Pius XII's acts. See E. Innocenti, 'Le citazioni pontificie nei documenti conciliari', *Concretezza* (16 July 1966), 6–10.
2. Discourse pronounced on 8 December 1969, DC 67, No 1554 (10 January 1970), 10ff. *DC = La Documentation Catholique.*
3. *Acta Synodalia Sacrosancti Concilii Oecumenici Vaticani II*, Volumen I, Periodus prima, Pars IV; *Congregationes generales* XXXI–XXXVI (Vatican, 1971), 292.
4. Sec. 8 of *Lumen Gentium* corresponds almost exactly to these sections 6 and 7, but the same data are seen (and formulated) in it in a different perspective. It is quite instructive to make a comparison between the two texts.
5. A. Acerbi, *Due ecclesiologie. Ecclesiologia giuridica ed ecclesiologia di communione nella 'Lumen Gentium' (Nuovi Saggi Teologici)* (Bologna, 1975). In a note, Acerbi provides the following details: The schema contains 309 references to pontifical documents out of a total of 460 references in all, as against 168 references to Scripture and thirty-six to the Fathers. The author adds: 'A merely numerical comparison, however, does not do justice to the real relationship between the different sources. The biblical and patristic texts are clearly subordinate to the magisterial texts.'
6. Pars II: *De intima constitutione Ecclesiae, Proemium* (2 ed, 1903), 280 (3 ed, 1909), 272.

7. E. Przywara, 'Corpus Christi mysticum. Eine Bilanz', ZAM 15 (1940), 197–215.
8. De Ecclesia Christi: Tractatus apologetico-dogmaticus (Rome, 1940), 104f. It was common for authors writing at this time to take a purely philosophical definition as their point of departure. This text, written by Tarquini, Iuris ecclesiastici publici Institutiones (1960) (19 ed, 1904), 3, quoted by Acerbi, op cit, 18, is typical: 'Concerning the power of the Church, which is deduced from its nature, we will take the following course in investigating the power arising from that source. First, study aside and abstracting from the Church, we can see from natural law which and how great will be the powers belonging to any complete society in virtue of its nature. Secondly, having considered the nature of the Church, we will demonstrate that it is a complete society. When these two have been set forth, the power of the Church itself arising from that source will become evident of itself through sheer logic.'
9. See, for example, ST Ia IIae, q. 9, a. 3; q. 90, a. 3, ad 3. The study by A. Müller, 'Il concetto della Chiesa come Societas perfecta in S. Tommaso e l'idea moderna della sovranità', RISS 97 (1923), 193–204, is unsatisfactory. See also M. Useros Carretero, 'Statuta Ecclesiae' y 'Sacramenta Ecclesiae' en la Ecclesiología de S. Tomás (Rome, 1962), 104–9.
10. T. M. Parker, 'The Medieval Origin of the Idea of the Church as a "Societas perfecta" ', Miscellanea Historiae ecclesiasticae (Stockholm Congress, August 1960/Louvain, 1961), 23–31.
11. Controv. I: De Summo Pontifice, lib V, c 7: 'Respublica ecclesiastica debet esse perfecta et sibi sufficiens in ordine ad suum finem.'
12. S. Fogliano, 'Il compito apologetico del Ius Publicum Ecclesiasticum', Sal. 5 (1945), 49–80; idem, 'La tesi fondamentale del Ius Publicum Ecclesiasticum', Sal. 6 (1946), 67–135; H. Müllejans, Publicus und Privatus im Römischen Recht und im älteren kanonischen Recht unter besonderer Berücksichtigung der Unterscheidung Jus publicum und Jus privatum (Munich, 1961); A. de la Hera and C. Munier, 'Le Droit public ecclésiastique à travers ses définitions', RDC 14 (1964), 32–63; C. Munier, 'Eglise et Droit canon du XVIe siècle à Vatican I', REDC 19 (1964), 589–617.
13. C. Constantin, 'Constitution civile du Clergé'. DThC II, col. 1562.
14. A conflict for the diocese of Posen-Gnesen. For what followed, see K. Walf, 'Die katholische Kirche – eine "societas perfecta"?', ThQ 157 (1977), 107–18. See also Roland Minnerath, 'Le droit de l'Eglise à la liberté du Syllabus à Vatican II', Le Point théologique 39 (Paris, 1983).
15. Mansi 51, 539ff; ADSCR (Collectio Lacensis) VII, 570ff.
16. Pius X, Compendio della dottrina cristiana (for the province of Rome) (1905), I, c X, 1, p. 119 (quoted by Sohm). Benedict XV, Constitution Providentissima Mater Ecclesia, promulgating the Codex Iuris Canonici of 1971. Pius XI, Encyclical Divini illius magistri (30 December 1929), AAS 22 (1930), 53/DS 3685.
17. F. Solieri (2 ed, 1921)/M. Conte a Coronata (1924)/A. Ottaviani (1958).
18. L. Bendix (1895), etc. See also A. Rouco-Varela, 'Die katholische Reaktion auf das "Kirchenrecht I" Rudolf Sohms', 'Ius Sacrum'. Festgabe K. Mörsdorf (Schöningh, 1969), 15–52.
19. Quoted by A. Grillmeier SJ, ThPh 45 (1970), 344, N. 55.
20. Mansi 51, 543. Translated by J. Maritain at the end of his edition of H. Clérissac, Le Mystère de L'Eglise. The chapter ends with a statement about the societas perfecta.
21. Letter, Exortae in ista, addressed to the Brazilian bishops (29 April 1876)/Acta Pii IX, VII, 213f.
22. Letter to Cardinal Guibert (17 June 1885): 'The Church of God, which the divine

149

Author moulded in such a way that, drawing a distinction of persons, he absolutely ordained that some should teach and others learn, and that there should be a flock and a shepherd, and that among the shepherds one should be the chief and the greatest Shepherd of all . . .' See the *Lettres apostoliques de Léon XIII* (Paris), VII, 62. The whole of one letter deals with this subject, namely *Lettre à l'archevêque de Tours* (17 December 1888)/*Acta* III, 183–6.

23. Encyclical *Vehementer nos* (11 February 1906): 'Scripture declares and the doctrine handed down by the Fathers confirms that the Church is the mystical body of Christ, administered by the authority of shepherds and teachers; i.e. a society of human beings in which some are above others with full and complete powers of ruling, teaching and judging. This society is therefore unequal in its power and nature . . . and its ranks are so distinct from each other that there resides only in the hierarchy the right and authority to move and direct their fellow members to the proposed end of that society; but it is the duty of the multitude to allow itself to be governed, and they should obediently follow the lead of the rulers.'

24. Möhler, *ThQ* (1823), 487, quoted in my 'Bulletin d'Ecclésiologie (1939–1946)', *RSPhTh* 31 (1947), 77–96. For the theme of the Church as a hierarchical society in current teaching, see E. Germain, 'A travers les catéchismes des cent cinquante dernières années', *RDCCIF* 71 (1971), 107–31.

25. See n. 3 above.

26. Acerbi, *op cit* (sec. 5), 107f.

27. *Symposium theologicum de Ecclesia Christi Patribus Concilii Vaticani II reverenter oblatum* (Rome, Lateran, 1962). The texts form Instalment III of the review *Divinitas* 6 (1962), 461–585, but this is without Cardinal Ottaviani's introduction. Ecumenism is dealt with by Cardinal Siri. What the Council had to say about this subject is quite different.

28. *op cit* (sec. 3), 293.

29. 'Il mistero della chiesa nella luce di S. Ambrogio', *Osservatore Romano* (10–11 December 1962), 6. It is worth noting here that, in an address that he gave on 16 August 1960 on 'The Councils in the Life of the Church', Mgr Montini quoted this passage from the article on the Vatican (Council) by I. Brugerette and E. Amann in the *DThC* XV, 2, col. 2583 (1950): 'The problem of how to reconcile the divine rights of the episcopate with the divine rights of the Pope was unfortunately never debated (see the article 'Primauté', *DThC* III, col. 247ff). Just as the applications of practical living have to be regulated, so too does this question have to be asked by a theology of the Church that aims to be balanced. Will it be asked at a second Vatican Council? That will only be known in the future.' This address has been published in French in Cardinal J.-B. Montini, *L'Eglise et les Conciles*, with a Preface by P. Veuillot (Paris, 1965), 119–37. In it, Mgr Montini speaks explicitly of collegiality. See also *ibid*, sec. 42 of the Pastoral Letter of Lent 1962, 165.

30. Cyprian, *De orat Dom*, 23 (*PL* 4, 553/Hartel, 285). In a note in *Lumen Gentium*, 4, there are references to Augustine and John Damascene. To these could be added Epiphanius.

31. E. Lanne, 'Hommage à Paul VI. En mémorial d'action de grâce', *Irénikon* 51 (1978), 299–311. The breve can be found in the *Tomos Agapis*, 176 (Rome and Istanbul, 1971), 386–92.

32. A. Ganoczy, 'Ministère, épiscopat, primauté', *Istina* 14 (1969), 99–136, writes on p. 111: 'The word *potestas* occurs very frequently in the Constitution *Pastor aeternus* of 1870, as do such terms as *auctoritas, iurisdictio, principatus* and *regimen*, whereas the term *ministerium* or *diaconia* is not used at all. In the Constitution *Lumen Gentium* of 1964, on the other hand, the latter is the dominant idea. There are also other striking new ideas:

the explicitly pastoral orientation and the mainly missionary emphasis (*Lumen Gentium* 17, 25, 27), the insistence on the ministry of the Word (*LG* 11, 17, 23, 24, 25), and on the variety of both charismatic and institutional ministries in the People of God (*LG* 12, 13, 32) and finally the explicit affirmation of episcopal collegiality.' I would point out here that, although the term *potestas* appears 89 times in the documents of Vatican II, it relates (in the singular) to God or the People of God in forty-five cases. There is not a single reference to the *potestas ordinis* or the *potestas iurisdictionis*. This is all the more striking in that these terms were frequently used not only in the texts of Vatican I, but also in the preparatory schema of *Lumen Gentium*. It is, moreover, clear from their ante-preparatory reports that the bishops and the theological faculties also wanted these ideas and their relationships to be clarified.

33. R. Aubert, M. Guéret and P. Tombeur, *Concilium Vaticanum I. Concordance, Index, Liste. de fréquence, Tables comparatives* (*Informatique et étude de textes* IX) (Louvain, 1977), 202–39. See also my review of this work in *RSPhTh* 62 (1978), 61–4.

34. The Council: *Lumen Gentium* 6 and 8 ('purify'); *Unitas redintegratio* 4 and 6 ('reform'). Paul VI: the collection cited above, n. 29, pp. 100, 132, 159, 168, 214; *Ecclesiam suam*, *AAS* 56 (1964), 628–30; Audience held on 7 May 1969, *DC* (1969), 506.

35. See *Lumen Gentium* 27; Decree *Christus Dominus* 8 and 16.

36. See the Declaration *Dignitatis humanae personae* 13 and the Constitution *Gaudium et Spes* 42, 5, etc.

37. See, for example, the documents, many of them consistorial allocutions, to which the Syllabus refers. They can be found in the original Latin and accompanied by a French translation in *Recueil des Allocutions consistoriales, Encycliques et autres Lettres apostoliques...*, *citées dans l'encyclique et le Syllabus du 8 décembre 1864* (Paris, 1865). See also my book *Eglise catholique et France moderne* (Paris, 1978), 31–7.

38. The section of *Ecclesiam suam* devoted to dialogue (sec. 52ff) begins in this way.

39. See the preface, dated 23 August 1954, to Mgr Veuillot's collection, *Le Prêtre*.

40. Nos. 55 and 56, *AAS* 56 (1964), 627 and 628, quoted in the Decree *Presbyterorum Ordinis*, 3.

41. Sec. 78, *AAS, op cit,* 646ff.

42. *DC* (1964), 1222.

43. *Lumen Gentium* 1. See my book, *Un peuple messianique* (Paris 1975).

44. Decree *Ad Gentes divinitus* 11; Declaration *Nostra aetate* 2, 3.

45. One text in this discourse – 'we also have the cult of man' – has been scurrilously wrongly used by certain people in order to accuse Paul VI of false teaching. See H. de Lubac, ' "Le culte de l'homme": En réparation à Paul VI', *Petite Catéchèse sur Nature et Grâce* (Paris, 1980), 181–200; ET *A brief catechesis on nature and grace* (San Francisco, 1984), Appendix D, 261–90 [Ed.] The image of the doctor lovingly attending to his patient or that of the good Samaritan were frequently used by Paul VI when he addressed newly ordained priests. See, for example, his addresses given on 6 June 1955 and on Wednesday and Maundy Thursday 1971 and his allocution of 31 December 1975. See also Daniel-Ange, *Paul VI: Un regard prophétique, I. Un amour qui se donne* (Paris & Fribourg, 1979).

46. This aspect, which is not very explicit in the text, is present in the intention of *Ecclesiam suam*. See J. Guitton, *Paul VI secret* (Paris, 1979), 53.

47. C.J. Pinto de Oliveira, 'L'Esprit agit dans l'histoire. La totalisation hégélienne de l'histoire confrontée avec les perspectives du Concile de Vatican II', L. Rümpf et al, *Hegel et la théologie contemporaine: L'absolu dans l'histoire?* (Neuchâtel and Paris, 1977), 54–73.

48. The term *populus messianicus*, which occurs twice in *Lumen Gentium*, 9, is my own. I

used it in response to a wish expressed by Mgr Marty. It appeared at least once in *Gaudium et Spes*, but was removed from the final document, I was told, to prevent apparently separating the People of God from the whole of mankind.

49. See my study 'De la communion des Eglises à une ecclésiologie de l'Eglise universelle', Y. Congar and B. D. Dupuy, ed, *L'Episcopat et l'Eglise universelle (Unam Sanctam 39)* (Paris 1962), 227–60. See also J. M. R. Tillard, 'La jurisdiction de l'évêque de Rome', *Irénikon* 51 (1978), 358–73, 509–20, and especially 509ff.

50. Cardinal Montini, *Discorsi al Clero 1957–1963* (Milan, 1963), 78–80, quoted by M. D. Chenu, *Peuple de Dieu dans le monde* (Paris, 1966), 12, n. 1. The italics in this quotation are by Fr Chenu.

51. This is obvious in the manuals and in the article on eschatology in *DThC* V (1913), col 1913. This article, which hardly fills a single column, was written by Mangenot.

52. This criticism was expressed for example by Mgr Ziadé, the Maronite Archbishop of Beirut as well as by Mgr László, the Bishop of Eisenstadt in Austria. See Y. Congar, H. Küng and D. O'Hanlon, eds., *Discours du Concile Vatican II* (Paris, 1964), pp, 41 and 52 [quotation from ET, *Council speeches of Vatican II* (Sheed & Ward Stagbook 1964), 29. Ed.] respectively. See also *Acta synodalia* II. Periodus secunda. Pars III, p. 213, for Ziadé (22 October 1963) and *ibid.*, p. 498, for László (15 November 1963). See also Cardinal König, *op cit* (see below, n. 56).

53. *Union catholique des Scientifiques français, Bulletin* 92 (June 1966), 11f. See also above, n. 51.

54. See E. Schillebeeckx, *L'Eglise du Christ et l'homme d'aujourd'hui selon Vatican II* (Le Puy and Lyons, 1965), 146ff.

55. This has been done briefly on pp. 522–4 of the remarkable study by G. Martelet, 'L'Eglise et le temporal: Vers une nouvelle conception' in Ed G. Baraúna, *L'Eglise de Vatican II (Unam Sanctam 51b)* (Paris, 1966), 517–39. This study throws considerable light on what follows in my chapter.

56. It was criticized from the first day, 1 December 1962, by Cardinals König [Vienna], Alfrink [Utrecht] and Ritter [St Louis] and on 3 December by Cardinal Döpfner [Munich] and Mgr Huyghe [Arras]. See *op cit*, n. 3, pp 133, 135, 137, 185, 197.

57. *Gaudium et Spes*, 41, 2; cf 42, 2.

58. See J. Courtney-Murray SJ, 'Vers une intelligence du développement de la doctrine de l'Eglise sur la liberté religieuse', in Edd J. Hamer OP and Y. Congar OP, *La liberté religieuse (Unam Sanctam 60)* (Paris, 1967), 111–47.

59. A. Acerbi, *op cit* (see 5), 145, n. 122.

PART THREE

THE COUNCIL'S OBSERVERS

9

OBSERVERS AND GUESTS
OF THE COUNCIL

JOHN R. H. MOORMAN

After the Council had been going for six weeks, Professor Oscar Cullmann of Basel University, in a press interview, reported that all Observers received all Council texts, were able to attend all General Congregations, were able to make their views known to the Secretariat for Promoting Christian Unity each week, and enjoyed contact with the Fathers and their periti. He remarked: 'I am more and more amazed every morning at the way we really form a part of the Council.'

At the Second Session, Dr Kristen Skydsgaard of the Lutheran World Federation expressed the Observers' gratitude at being present again. Expressing reassurance that the new Pope, Paul VI, had no illusions about the length of the road to reunion, he went on to hope that light shed by a historical theology – nourished by the Bible and the teaching of the Fathers – would shine more and more strongly in the work of the Council. He noticed a new ecumenical spirit becoming manifest: 'We find ourselves meeting together at the beginning of a road whose end only God knows.'

Later on, Archpriest Vitaly Borovoy of the Russian Orthodox Church spoke of the Holy Spirit working upon the Churches, 'calling us to unity and helping us to understand its necessity and urgency'. He said: 'We are always ready to help our Roman Catholic brothers in anything which may contribute to harmony and unity among all Christians, so that with a single tongue and a single heart we may together glorify the most Holy Spirit.'

The Bishop of Ripon, John Moorman (now over eighty years old) led the Anglican Observers, and they were the first to accept the Secretariat's invitation, coming from Cardinal Augustin Bea. At the end, after the Joint Service at St Paul's (the 'English basilica') on 4 December 1965, it was he who replied to the Holy Father for all Observers and Guests: 'Now, with the entry of the Roman Catholic Church into this field, we realise that ... the whole Christian world is engaged in the search for that unity for which Our Blessed Lord prayed.' On return, John Moorman wrote Vatican Observed: an Anglican view of Vatican II *(DLT 1967). He went on to be the Anglican Co-Chairman, Anglican/Roman Catholic Preparatory Commission, and then to be for its full twelve years a member of the Anglican-Roman Catholic International Commission (ARCIC I).*

It was in February 1962 that the Archbishop of Canterbury wrote to me to say that he had been invited, as leader of the Anglican Communion, to send three observers to the Second Vatican Council, and that he wished me to be their leader. The other two who were invited were Dr Grant of New York and Harold de Sousa from Colombo in Sri Lanka. Of course I accepted this invitation and, as a result, attended all four sessions of the Council, though

155

with other assistants. These were Americans and coloured people to show that the Anglican Communion was not just the same as the Church of England but extended over all the world. We also had with us Canon Bernard Pawley, who had been sent to Rome as representative of the Archbishops of Canterbury and York about a year before and remained during the sessions of the Council. The next few months I learned all that I could about the Church of Rome and the coming council from Hans Küng's admirable book, *The Council and Reunion* and Pawley's reports to the Archbishops.

What was the purpose of the Council? John XXIII was not really what we should call an ecumenist. He was brought up in a narrow circle of Church people, and entered a minor seminary at the age of eleven, though later on he went as a papal emissary to Bulgaria, Constantinople and Paris. But he seems then to have learned very little about the people among whom he worked. When at Constantinople he wrote in his diary of the remnant of Christians there 'lost in a weltering mass of Jews, Muslims and Orthodox', as if the Orthodox were scarcely Christians at all.[1] His idea in calling the Council was to reform the Church, to bring it up to date (*aggiornamento*) so that those outside would say how glorious it was and return to the fold. 'We cherish the hope for your return' he wrote in his 1959 encyclical *Ad Petri Cathedram*, and 'when we lovingly invite you into the Unity of the Church, we are inviting you not to the home of a stranger, but to your own, your Father's house' as if the only hope of Christian reunion was for all other Churches to give up their respective doctrines and go back to Rome, and he spoke of 'union with this Apostolic see'. He called us the 'separated brethren' in spite of the fact that all Christians were separated from each other, including Roman Catholics. But though Vatican II was a council of reform, it turned out to be in the end a council of ecumenism, so bringing Rome into the Ecumenical Movement where it had never been before. John set up the Secretariat for Promoting Christian Unity in 1960, and invited Observers to the Council, and saw to it that we were treated royally. We were given the best seats in the Basilica of St Peter, and at all other functions. We were received by the Pope who told us that he had had comfort from seeing us there. Perhaps we should bring our Churches back to union with Rome, back to our father's house.

On arriving in Rome I found myself among a number of distinguished scholars from all over the world – Professor Skydsgaard from Denmark, Professor Schlink from Germany, Dr Harold Roberts, a Methodist from England, Professor Outler, also a Methodist from Texas, Professor Cullmann from Basel and Paris, Lukas Vischer from the World Council of

Churches headquarters in Switzerland, and many others. There were also the Eastern representatives, from the Coptic, Armenian, Ethiopian and Syrian Churches, though no one came from the Eastern Orthodox Churches who felt unable to agree to send anyone, though two Russians arrived on the second day of the Council and one or two others drifted there as the Council proceeded. There were about forty of us, Observers and Guests of the Council, a number which increased in time to about eighty. We sat in what we called the 'Observers' Box' [in the tribune of St Longinus] in the Basilica, next to the Presidents and Moderators, and therefore in a position from which we could see all that happened. We were guarded here by Monsignor [Jean-François] Arrighi, of the Secretariat for Unity, who kept any episcopal intruders out. We also had interpreters who translated the Latin for us, since we found it difficult, with our schoolboy Latin, to understand all that was said, especially by Spanish, Japanese, German and other speakers, all spoken very quickly and with widely different accents. In the second and succeeding years we were given a summary, in our own language, of the previous day's speeches, which made it less necessary to listen, and which enabled us to walk in the aisles of the Basilica, to meet many people, and to drink a cup of coffee at what was known to the English as the 'Bar Jonah'. We attended most regularly every day of the Council, and discussed among ourselves what the Fathers were saying and how the original *Schemata* were being improved and altered in many ways.

We also had a weekly meeting of Observers when someone, probably one of the *periti* came, and talked to us, in English or French, about the subject then under discussion, and we had the opportunity of asking questions. These were when we most understood the topic being discussed.

The first subject to be debated by the Council was the Liturgy, a subject in which we were deeply interested. This is true especially of the Anglican Observers since we had reformed the Liturgy in 1549 whereas the more Protestant Churches had cleared away the old rite altogether and substituted a new form of worship, far more unconventional than the old. The *schema* which was to be debated concerned not only the theological basis of worship and the Eucharist, but the other sacraments, the Divine Office, the Liturgical Year, Church furnishing, Church music and Church art. Many of the Council Fathers agreed with us that the old Tridentine Mass would not really meet the needs of the present day. It had long since ceased to be an act of general worship in which the People of God could meet together and offer their praise and thanksgiving to God and receive his inestimable gifts, and had become much more of a sacrifice offered to God by the priest on behalf of the people. Inaudible and unintelligible, the priest had become more and more separated from his people, who were left to make their own devotions, with the help of their rosaries, since they could neither hear 'the blessed mutter of the Mass', or, if they could hear it, were unable to understand what was being said. They knew, of course, what was happening, and were able to recognize parts of the service by the position and movements of the priest. The great moment in the service was no longer, as it had been in early time, the giving of the consecrated bread and wine to the worshippers, but the devotion of the Host when the bells rang and everyone knelt down and worshipped it. By the later Middle Ages, in England, at any rate, lay people normally made their communion only once a year, the priest being the only communicant at the Mass; and, in recent times, a habit has grown up of people coming to church to receive the reserved Sacrament from the tabernacle, quite apart from any celebration of the Mass.

All this sort of thing the Anglicans did away with in the sixteenth century, when the Eucharist was made a much more corporate affair. The Prayer Book does this by demanding that there should be no celebration unless there were at least some to communicate with the celebrant. The custom has now grown up that, in most parish churches, instead of an early service attended by only a few, the Parish Communion is held at a convenient hour when all can attend, and all the confirmed members of the congregation communicate, while the children are brought up to the rail to receive a blessing.

Moreover, those who communicate have always, in Anglican worship, received the Sacrament in both kinds, the Bread and the Wine. This is based on our Lord's own words: '*Drink* ye all of this' and 'Unless you eat the flesh of the Son of Man and *drink* his blood, you have no life in you' (John 6:53). This was the practice in the early Church and down to the thirteenth century when, with the doctrine of transubstantiation being proclaimed, the chalice was more and more withheld from the laity for safety's sake, and the doctrine of concomitance grew up, which declared that both the Body and the Blood of Christ are wholly present in either species of the Sacrament. This withholding of the chalice from the people was one of the great divides in Eucharistic worship between Rome and the rest of the Christian world, and was discussed at some length at the Council of Trent. So the *schema* on the Liturgy began by saying 'This sacred Council, desiring to augment the Christian life among the faithful day by day, to adapt those ecclesiastical institutions in so far as they have become unsatisfactory through various changes, (and) to foster whatever may lead to a union in the Churches of the separated brethren' makes certain changes. This was, undoubtedly, regarded as a serious step forward, as were also those passages which said that the Eucharist should become a corporate action in which all could participate, that it should be said sometimes not in Latin but in the language of the people, that it laid greater emphasis on the use of the Bible and of preaching, and that it adopted the principle of communion in both kinds, though this was to be limited to a very few special occasions, such as a wedding or an ordination.

The Constitution on the Liturgy, when it came out seemed, to the Observers, excellent in principle, but rather cautious in practice. In principle it declared that 'Christ is always present in his Church, especially in her liturgical celebrations', but priests must 'ensure that the faithful take part knowingly, actively and fruitfully' in the Eucharist, that there must always be a 'full and active participation by all the people' by way of 'acclamations, responses, psalmody, antiphons', and says that 'the ministry of preaching is to be fulfilled with exactitude and fidelity'and that the faithful should not be there as 'strangers or silent spectators'. But in practice the document is cautious. It retains the Latin Mass, though allowing the vernacular to be used in certain circumstances, and it reserves communion in both kinds 'in cases to be determined by the Apostolic See'.

If the faithful are to be active participants in the Eucharist, then it is essential that it should be in the vernacular. It is all right for bishops and priests, and the better educated of the laity, to take part in a Latin Mass. But what of the uneducated in Ireland, in China and Central Africa or in South America? What possibility have they of understanding the service when read in a totally unknown tongue, or of knowing what the priest is saying on their behalf? During the last twenty years, since the promulgation of the Constitution, the Church has gone a great deal further. Nowadays it is quite normal for the Mass to be said entirely in the language of the people. As Cardinal Cushing [Boston] said to me: 'A man prays best in the language he learned at his mother's knee.' It is also fairly common for communion to be given to the laity in both kinds, so being true to our Lord's specific commandments.

To the Anglican Observers this was especially interesting, and a real drawing together of the two Churches. It is now difficult to distinguish between a Roman Catholic Mass and an Anglican Eucharist, except that Anglicans do not pray for the Pope. Anyone entering a church would have great difficulty in knowing which of the two Churches was celebrating. The altars look identical, the priests wear the same vestments, and they say almost the same words and preach a sermon. This is surely a great advance towards unity. Moreover, the Anglican-Roman Catholic International

Commission [ARCIC I, Windsor 1971] has shown that both Churches believe in the Eucharist as the sacrifice of Christ, as 'a means through which the atoning work of Christ on the cross is proclaimed and made effective in the life of the Church', and also believe that 'communion with Christ in the Eucharist presupposed his true presence, effectually signified by the bread and wine which, in this mystery, become his body and blood'. Agreeing on the nature of the Eucharist, and celebrating almost identical rites has brought the two Communions much closer together than they have been in the last 450 years since the breach with Rome, and must, therefore, represent a real step forward in the ecumenical sphere.

Another step forward was made in the Dogmatic Constitution of the Church. Here again Observers were anxious to see what the Council made of this. Hitherto the Church had always, to Roman Catholics, meant simply the Church of Rome in communion with the Pope as its leader on earth. Everyone outside that Church was a heretic or a schismatic, and must be brought back. Pius XI in *Mortalium Animos* (1928) declared that the Church of Rome was the body of Christ and 'whosoever is not united with the body is no member of it, neither is he in Communion with Christ its head', thereby declaring that all non-Catholics, including those members of the ancient Oriental Churches, were also non-Christians, out of communion with Christ. Then Pius XII, in *Humani generis* (1950) had declared that 'the Mystical Body of Christ and the Catholic Church, in communion with Rome, are one and the same thing', and in *Mystici Corporis* (1943) had gone so far as to plead with all who were not members of this great Church 'to yield their free consent to the inner stirrings of God's grace and strive to extricate themselves from a state in which they cannot be secure of their own eternal salvation... With open arms we await them, not as strangers, but as those who are coming to their own father's house'. John XXIII in *Ad Petri Cathedram* (1959) repeated this aspiration about non-Catholics 'coming home' to the true fold, misquoting our Lord's words about there being 'one fold and one shepherd', though in fact what Christ said was 'one *flock* and one shepherd', which is quite a different thing and has been put right in the latest edition of the Vulgate where the word *grex* (flock) is used and not the word *ovile* (fold). A flock can be divided into many folds.

The Dogmatic Constitution on the Church adopts quite a different line from these papal utterances. First it announced that 'the Church is a kind of sacrament or sign of intimate union with God, and of the unity of all mankind', and that 'by communicating his Spirit to his brothers, called together from *all* people, Christ made them mystically into his own body', and 'God has gathered together as one *all* those who in faith look upon Jesus as the author of salvation and the source of unity and peace, and has established *them* as the Church', so completely reversing the statements made by Pius XI and Pius XII. This is a most important statement. It is in line with the Anglican assertion that the Church is 'the blessed company of all faithful people', and (in the *XXXIX Articles*) that it is 'a congregation of faithful men in which the pure Word of God is preached and the Sacraments be duly administered'.

But the document *Lumen Gentium* still leaves open the question of the infallibility of the Pope, which has always been a stumbling-block to non-Catholics. It does, in fact, say that in the matter of the 'sacred primacy of the Roman Pontiff and of his infallible teaching authority' the Council remains firm. But it goes on to speak of the apostolic college which existed in order to shepherd the Church under Peter as its head. The bishops now formed this apostolic college, who 'together with its head, the Roman Pontiff, and never without its head . . . is the subject of supreme and full power over the universal Church'. This idea of collegiality occupied a good deal of the Council's time and thought, and was particularly interesting to the Observers. These all felt offended by the Infallibility Decree of 1870, and found it very difficult to be at one with a Church which held it. But gradually we came to see that infallibility did not mean quite what it was commonly supposed to mean,[2] and that Vatican II had introduced and supported the idea of collegiality of the Pope always acting in consultation with the bishops. As the Report of the Anglican-Roman Catholic International Commission said that 'a primate exercises his ministry not in isolation but in collegial association with his brother bishops', so liberating the Pope from the sole responsibility afforded to him in Vatican I.

Dr Outler of Texas (see below p. 170) speaks of the 'truly pastoral tone and ecumenical spirit' of the Constitution on the Church, and says that 'there is a very real sense in which *De Ecclesia* has reopened the way to serious and fruitful discussion of Christian unity after four centuries of closure'. This discussion is now taking place. The Roman Catholic Church is holding it with various Churches – Oriental, Anglican and Protestant. The talks with Anglicanism were inspired by Archbishop Ramsey's visit to Pope Paul VI almost immediately after the Council ended [24 March 1966], and the start of 'serious dialogue' undertaken by the Preparatory Commission and then by the Anglican-Roman Catholic International Commission. This, after thirteen years, produced joint fully agreed statements on the Eucharist, the Ministry, and Authority in the Church, and made what would be regarded as the extraordinary avowal that 'the only see which makes any claim to universal primacy, and which has exercised and still exercises *episcopé* is the see of Rome, the city where Peter and Paul died. It seems appropriate that, in any future union, a universal primacy such as has been described should be held by that see'. This is a remarkable step forward in Anglican-Roman Catholic relations. Hitherto, in all discussions, the primacy of the Pope has been the chief difficulty to be overcome. Now it has been agreed upon by a very mixed Commission, and needs only to be accepted by the Anglican Communion as a whole, which should be done by the next Lambeth Conference in 1988.

But naturally the *schema* which interested the Observers most was that on Ecumenism. In the First Session, the Council had to discuss a document 'On the unity of the Church: that all may be one'; but it soon appeared that this was not about Christian unity nor concerned that all should be one. It was, in fact, no more than a draft, drawn up not by the Secretariat for Promoting Christian Unity, as one would have supposed, but by the Preparatory Commission set to deal with the Oriental Churches with a view to defining the relations between the Uniat Churches, which are in communion with Rome, and the Orthodox and non-Chalcedonian Churches, which are not. It had nothing to do with the Churches of the West, which was a disappointment to most of the Observers who represented these Churches. So, on the vote taken, 2,068 of the Fathers voted against it, and only 36 in its favour; and a new *schema* was prepared, this time by Cardinal Bea's Secretariat for Promoting Christian Unity.

The new *schema* was very different from the old one, and of much greater interest to the Observers. In the first part it declares that all the people of the New Covenant 'comprise the Church', and that 'men who believe in Christ and have been properly baptized are brought into a certain, though imperfect, communion with the Catholic Church', which is very different from what had been said by Pius XI in 1928 and Pius XII in 1943 and 1950 when the sole thought was of returning to their father's house. We are now all engaged together on the pilgrimage towards Christ and Eternal Life. The Ecumenical Movement, which had hitherto been all but banned to Catholics, was now welcomed as one of the means whereby unity of all Christians would be achieved, and the Council expressed its gratitude that the Catholic Church was growing daily in ecumenical work. It went on to say that 'we beg pardon of God and of our separated brethren, just as we forgive those who trespass against us', so echoing the words which Paul VI had said in his introductory address to the Council when he said that 'if we are in any way to blame for that separation, we humbly beg God's forgiveness and ask pardon too of our brethren who feel themselves to have been injured by us'. As for belief, there is of course a difference in certain matters between the belief as held by the Catholic Church and the belief of other Christian communities separated from them. But, says the Council, there exists a 'hierarchy of truths', so differentiating between the common faith of all who call themselves Christians and the lesser differences which separate them.[3]

Then, to the surprise and joy of the Anglican Observers, the Council declared that among many communions separated from the Roman see, yet in which 'Catholic traditions and institutions continue to exist, the Anglican Communion occupies a special place'. It is odd that the Council included this sentence, for many of the bishops would have only the vaguest idea as to what the Anglican Communion was, since it scarcely exists in many of those parts of the world from which they came. The Eastern Churches are mentioned *en masse*, but the Anglican Communion is the only Western Church referred to in the sixteen decrees of the Council. This must, I think, have been due to the conversations which the Anglican Observers had had with the bishops and with members of the Secretariat for Christian Unity which drew up the *schema*. It led to the Archbishop of Canterbury, Dr Michael Ramsey, visiting the Pope in 1966 and the setting up of the Commission to discuss the differences between the two Churches, and which led to the unanimous report, finally published in 1982, which included the Common Declarations of 1966 and 1977 together with the Malta Report of 1968 which stated that 'there remain fundamental theological and moral questions between us' and set out the three primary subjects for dialogue – the Eucharist, the Ministry and Authority.

The decree on Ecumenism marked the entry of Rome into the Ecumenical Movement, with enormous prospects ahead. Hitherto, since the Modern Ecumenical Movement started with the Edinburgh Conference in 1910, the Roman Church had remained aloof and took no part in its proceedings. They regarded themselves as holding the only kind of unity which existed, and simply invited others to give up their cherished beliefs and practices, and enter into the one and only fold of Christ. All this has now been swept away, with astonishing results, especially with Anglicans. Dialogue has taken, and is taking, place. Sharing of churches and joint missions goes on. Preaching at each other's services is now quite common. We now meet each other and discuss matters of importance to both sides. There are, it is true, signs of hardening of hearts against all this, and a danger of slipping back into the old ways of intolerance and suspicion. But Vatican II stands firm as a rock, and can always be referred to.

Other texts which interested the Observers very much were the

Declaration on Religious Freedom, the Pastoral Constitution on the Church in the Modern World, and the Dogmatic Constitution on Divine Revelation.

In preparing the draft on Religious Freedom the Secretariat for Promoting Christian Unity did consult some of the Observers as they were known to have considered the question for a long time, and to have produced some thoughts on the subject. It was the most controversial document of the whole Council because it raised the question of the development of doctrine, which was strongly opposed. But Paul VI declared that it was 'one of the major texts of the Council'.

It speaks a lot about the dignity of the human person and his rights to exercise his religion, and hold fast to the truth as he sees it, in the society in which he lives. This is an obvious reference to the state of things in Russia, and other countries of the Warsaw pact, where religion of any kind is condemned, and to Nazi Germany, where religion was defined by the Government. It talks about the Church (meaning, of course, the Church of Rome) and its right to proclaim the truth as she sees it, but it says that no one is to be 'restrained from acting in accordance with his own beliefs', which is something the Observers had to notice for it expresses the right of the non-Catholic to hold and to teach what he believes to be true. Moreover, it says that parents have the right to decide the kind of religious education that their children are to receive. It talks about 'the Church and other religious communities', and is, on the whole, addressed to all men of goodwill. The whole thing is really a battle for the Truth, and is therefore Protestant as well as Catholic.

The Pastoral Constitution on the Church in the Modern World was not one of the decrees prepared in advance by the Committees, but was suggested, on the floor of the Synod, by Cardinal Suenens in 1962. It deals with all the problems now facing mankind, and is addressed not only to Catholics but to mankind as a whole, the People of God, the entire human family. Consequently it is the least Roman of all the decrees, and could almost have been written by the Observers. It is just what all Christians have been saying for some time, about Sin, the Conscience, Atheism and Agnosticism, Marriage, Family Planning, Labour relations, and War. There are several references to 'our Christian brothers' or 'the other Christian Churches', which shows how conscious the Council was of the so-called 'separated brethren' represented there by the company of Observers. To us, it was inevitably of interest and importance, laying down a Christian approach to all these problems, but it is not typical of the other decrees, most of which were addressed only to Catholics.

The Dogmatic Constitution on the Divine Revelation had a stormy passage through the Council, and interested the Observers considerably. When the first draft was given to us it was called *De duplici fonte Revelationis* (or the Double Source of Revelation) composed of the Bible and Tradition as of equal authority for the doctrine and teaching of the Church. 'Tradition' said the text 'preserved in the Church in continuous succession by the Holy Spirit, contains all those matters of faith and morals which the Apostles received either from the lips of Christ or at the suggestion of the Holy Spirit, and which they passed on as it were from hand to hand, so that they might be transmitted by the teaching of the Church'.

This was a Tridentine recognition of Tradition, more or less repeated by the first Vatican Council, and believed by many Catholics. But Anglicans and Protestants objected very strongly to it as it reduced the authority of the Bible as the sole source of revelation. So they quoted St Augustine who said: 'In those things which are plainly laid down in Scripture, all things are found which embrace faith and morals'. So the Anglican ordinand is asked to reply to the question put to him by the bishop: 'Are you persuaded that the Holy Scriptures contain sufficiently all doctrine required of necessity for eternal salvation through faith in Jesus Christ?' Of course there must be Tradition in the life of the Church. To begin with, a whole generation of Christians had grown up before any part of the New Testament was written at all. But the problem is that, whereas the Bible is open to all, Tradition is a kind of secret source of information, the true nature of which has never been revealed. Are we to suppose that the Roman Catholic Church has access to a separate supply of divine truth which is not accessible to other Christians? This was the Church *docens*, pronouncing the truth, to the Church *discens*, forbidding every lay member of the Church to find out things for himself.

But there was more to come. The draft decree went on to deal with the inerrancy of the Scriptures, which were all written at the inspiration of the Holy Spirit, and therefore to be taken as absolutely free from error. This was a shocking thing to say, taking no account whatever of what was happening in the world of biblical scholarship, and an Observer, a good scholar, said to me: 'If they pass this, they will make themselves the laughing-stock of the academic world'. But they did not pass it. Cardinal Liénart [Lille] sank it by saying: 'What is said here of inspiration and inerrancy is at once offensive to our separated brethren in Christ, and harmful to the proper liberty required in any scientific procedure', while Bishop de Smedt of Bruges said that this *schema* was against all that the Church was doing with the other Churches, and, if it were passed, 'we shall be responsible for causing Vatican II to destroy a great, an immense hope'. After some rather strange voting about whether or not to carry on the debate, the Pope himself intervened and declared that a new *schema* would be prepared with Cardinals Ottaviani and Bea as joint presidents.

When the *schema* came back to the Council two years later it had been considerably changed. It now laid great emphasis on the study of the Bible, and introduced what the Observer, Oscar Cullmann, called 'this marvellous phrase' which says that 'in the Holy Scriptures the Father, who is in heaven, constantly meets his children, and speaks with them'. It encouraged the clergy and the laity to indulge in regular and diligent Bible-reading, and called for the co-operation of non-Catholics in providing translations into the vernacular. Bishop (then Abbot)[4] Butler OSB said: 'Let us not be afraid of scholarly and historical truth. Let us not be afraid that one truth may tell against another truth. Let us not be afraid that our scholars may be lacking in loyalty to the Church and to traditional doctrine... What we want is not the childish comfort which comes from averting our gaze from the truth, but a truly critical scholarship which will enable us to enter into dialogue with non-Catholic scholars.' So the *schema* said that 'the books of Scripture must be acknowledged as teaching firmly, faithfully and without error the truth which God wanted to put into the sacred writings for the sake of our salvation', and that 'God speaks in sacred Scripture through men in human fashion'.

Cardinal (then Father) Jan Willebrands of SPCU, on saying good-bye to me at the end of the First Session, asked if I would be returning in the following year. 'I hope you will' he said. 'The presence of the Observers here is very important. You have no idea how much they are influencing the work of the Council.'

This influence was in three ways. First of all, we were some kind of check on what was being said by the Fathers of the Council. Every bishop who stood up to speak knew that, in the tribune of St Longinus, was a group of intelligent and critical people, their pens poised to take down what was said. Members of the Council, therefore, tended to be very sensitive to what other Christians were thinking, and did their best to avoid saying foolish things which would cause offence. If one of the Fathers said something which was likely to cause a flutter among the Observers, he was often rebuked by a later speaker. Our presence made the Council more than just a domestic affair, concerned with nothing more than the Roman Catholic Church. It was much more than that. It was a real turning-point in Church history, a sign that the Roman Catholic Church was emerging from its 'closed citadel' (as Fr Yves Congar called it) and taking some interest in what the rest of the Christian world was thinking and saying. Not all the

Fathers were aware of this. They were so bound to the Church which they knew that they had little knowledge of, and no interest in, the rest of Christendom. But some were very keen that a new era in Church relations would come out of the Council, and that the Roman Catholic Church would now enter into the Ecumenical Movement.

This meant that, secondly, the Observers made it possible for the Council Fathers to discover what the rest of the Christian world was thinking about the subjects which they were debating. Often a chance encounter in the coffee-bar, or in some other part of St Peter's, or indeed outside it, led to an enquiry of what we thought about Family Planning, or the gift of the chalice to the lay communicant, or the place of the laity in the Church's worship and government, or some other subject.

Thirdly, although the Observers were unable to speak in the Council, it was sometimes possible to get a friendly bishop to speak on their behalf. For example, at one of the weekly Observers' meetings, Professor Skydsgaard criticized the *schema* on the Church for lacking a sense of the judgement of God upon the Church. He pointed out that throughout the Bible the people of God are always represented as in need of God's forgiveness. The 'wrath of God', he said, was emphasized over and over again in the Scriptures. What was true of past centuries was also true of this. But, he said, this sense of man's treachery and God's forgiveness was wholly lacking in the *schema*, which he described as a 'pale document'. A few days later, as I was going into St Peter's, one of the Observers said to me: 'You remember Skydsgaard's speech at the meeting the other day. Well, you're going to hear it again this morning. One of the Cardinals, who heard of it, was so impressed that he is going to make the same points today': which, sure enough, he did. In the same way, some of the things said about the Anglican Communion in the debate on Ecumenism were undoubtedly the result of the conversations which some of the Anglican Observers had had with members of the Council.

But perhaps the thing which did most to draw us together was that we worshipped together every morning. Each morning began with a Mass in St Peter's at a nave altar close to where the Observers sat. In the early days some of the Observers felt that they could not attend this service. Bred in Protestant ways of worship, they had always thought the Roman Mass corrupt, unspiritual and even, perhaps, hypocritical; and consequently they stopped away. But gradually this criticism dwindled. The Mass itself became much less hardened and old-fashioned, and much more congregational. Consequently, though some of them began by sitting rigidly in their chairs, gradually they began to follow the service in their books, to stand for the Gospel, to bow their heads at the Elevation of the Host, and so on. Some of us, of course, whose ways of worship were not dissimilar from those of the Roman Catholic Church, felt more at home from the start, and could, without twinges of conscience, play a full part in the daily worship with as much concentration as the Council Fathers themselves.

Common prayer, intercommunion or *communicatio in sacris*, has always been regarded as a rather distant goal; but, before the Council ended, we had all joined in a great act of worship in which the Observers had been invited to play their part. This took place in the Church of St Paul's-without-the-Walls in December 1965. In this vast basilica were assembled the Holy Father, about fifty cardinals, a large number of bishops and the whole group of Observers. Here we sang together a psalm, read two lessons, sang (in English) 'Now thank we all our God', heard an excellent sermon by Pope Paul (in French),[5] had a number of prayers said by a Roman Catholic and by Canon Maan of the Old Catholic Church, and ended with the *Magnificat*. Nothing of this kind had ever been done before, and by no means all the Council Fathers approved of it. After all, if, for many years, you have been teaching the faithful that it is a sin to worship with schismatics, it is rather disconcerting if the Holy Father invites you to do this very thing. On the other hand Cardinal Döpfner of Munich told me afterwards that he had found this service the most impressive moment in the whole of the Council.

The joint service, which was entirely Pope Paul's own idea, was followed by an audience for the Observers at which we were able to express our thanks for all that had been done for us, and the Pope presented each one of us with a bell, an instrument, he said, which is designed for the purpose of calling people together.

But if the Observers were exercising some influence on the Council, one has a right to ask what sort of influence the Council had on us. This is a more difficult thing to assess; but there is no doubt that most of the Observers – especially those who spent some considerable time at the Council – came away from it with a much more favourable attitude towards the Roman Catholic Church than they had had before it all began. Of course, some came to Rome in a very critical, if not hostile, mood. As one Observer remarked rather cynically: 'It is, of course, more pleasant to feel the warmth of fraternal embrace rather than the acrid heat of inquisitorial flames – but the purpose is the same.' Anglicans had been taught to believe that 'the Church of Rome hath erred', and that 'General Councils may err, and sometimes have erred, even in things pertaining to God' (*XXXIX Articles*, Nos 19 and 21), while Presbyterians are still tied to the belief, expressed by the Westminster Confession that 'the Pope of Rome . . . is that Antichrist, that man of sin and son of perdition, that exalteth himself in the Church against Christ and all that is called God', though many devout Presbyterians would regard this is rather out of date, especially after what John XXIII and Paul VI had done.

But even those most critical of the Church of Rome were to some extent mollified, mainly because they saw the Catholic Church adopting a progressive and humanitarian attitude to the problems of present-day Christology and the nature and function of the Church.

Someone said to me as I set out for Rome: 'Hitherto you have written books about Church history, now you will see Church history being made under your eyes': this was true. Vatican II was a real turning point in the history of the Christian Church. Till then people had looked on the Ecumenical Movement as a great movement, yet without Rome being concerned with it. Roman Catholics had been forbidden to take part in joint gatherings like the World Council of Churches [until New Delhi, 1961]. They were The Church, and everyone outside it was invited to come in and be saved. But all this has changed. Rome is now part of ecumenism, and is working towards that unity for which Christ prayed. It will take a long time. Four hundred years, or nine hundred years of separation have left their marks on both sides, and there has been much bitterness and persecution in the past. But now we look to the future, and see all Christians desiring to grow together and become one.

NOTES

1. Cf John Moorman, D.D. ' "His name was John": some reflections on the *Journal of a soul'*, *Heythrop Journal* VI (1965), 399–411 [Ed.].
2. Cf ARCIC I, *The Final Report* (CTS/SPCK 1982), 91–8 = Windsor 1981 Statement, Authority in the Church II, sec. 23–33, 'Infallibility'. Bishop Moorman was a signatory to this document, as a member of the International Commission [Ed.].
3. Cf *Council speeches of Vatican II* (S&W 1964), 125f; Cardinal Jan Willebrands, 'A variety of *typoi* within the communion of the Church', SPCU *Information Service*, July 1970, 11–14; Yves Congar OP, 'On the *Hierarchia Veritatum*', Edd. D. Neiman & M. Schatkin, *The Heritage of the early Church* (Pont Oriental Inst 1973), 409–20; Karl Rahner SJ, 'Paying due heed to the hierarchy of truths', *Theological Investigations* 14 (DLT 1976), 37–40. [Ed.].
4. Abbot President of the English Benedictine Congregation. Presidents of the sixteen Congregations and other Superior Generals of Congregations of Religions were present at the Council with full voting rights. [Ed.].
5. English translation: *One in Christ* 1966.2, 162–4; *Vatican Observed*, 207–10. Paul VI said to the Observers: 'Your departure will leave a loneliness around us which we knew nothing of before the Council but which now saddens us; we would like to see you with us always'. Bishop Moorman's reply, 211–3. [Ed.].

169

10

'STRANGERS WITHIN THE GATES': AN OBSERVER'S MEMORIES

ALBERT C. OUTLER

Customarily the Fathers in the Aula began their speeches: Eminentissimi patres vosque fratres Observatores. *It is related of one rather nervous bishop that he began:* Eminentissimi Observatores! *The Observers and Guests were prominently placed in the* confessio; *and to them many of the speeches were undisguisedly addressed.*

For all the courtesy and kindness shown on 'both sides', a residual critical suspicion remained among several of the Observers, some of whom were wont to put a minimalist interpretation upon what others willingly maximalized. And they were not always wrong to keep their critical guard in place. A case in point is the interpretation of subsistit in *as to the Church's location (Lumen Gentium, sec. 8), which can be viewed either inclusively or exclusively. A recent Instruction from the Congregation for the Doctrine of the Faith criticizing the Brazilian theologian, Fr Leonardo Boff's 'relativising concept of the [Roman Catholic] Church', rejected his reading and went on to say that ecclesiological pluralism 'is exactly the contrary' to the authentic meaning of the Council's text, since 'the Council had chosen* subsistit *exactly in order to make clear that the one sole "subsistence" of the true Church exists [in the Roman Catholic Church], whereas outside her visible structure only* elementa ecclesiae *exist' – which, as some Observers had warned, recalls that such a reversal of interpretations is exegetically possible. Most of the Observers were not so sceptical, fondly acknowledging* subsistere *as an explicit acknowledgement of the Church of Christ in other Churches, notably in Orthodoxy. Were they right?*

The author, now in his late seventies, was a Methodist delegate to the Third World Conference on Faith & Order, the great 1952 Lund Conference; and to the Fourth at Montreal in 1963. He was a delegate to the World Council of Churches third Assembly at New Delhi in 1961 (the first to which the Church of Rome sent their own Observers). He was at all four Sessions of the Council, then becoming a member of the Academic Council of the Ecumenical Institute (Tantur) during 1966–78. He has been President of the American Theological Society, the American Society of Church History, and the Catholic Historical Association. Of his thirteen honorary degrees, three are from Roman Catholic universities: Notre Dame, Loyola (New Orleans) and Catholic University of America. His books include The Christian tradition and the unity we seek *(1957); and* Methodist Observer at Vatican II *(1967). He is Professor of Theology Emeritus at Southern Methodist University.*

The news from Rome, in early 1959, of a projected 'ecumenical council' was exciting – but uninvolving. It was exciting because everything in Rome beyond its daily round catches the world's attention, and an 'ecumenical council' would certainly do that. Later, we would learn that even the Roman Curia had been startled, and some of them alarmed, by so unexpected a challenge to a *stabilitas* that ran back at least to Pope Pius IX (1846–78). Even so, such an event would scarcely concern us 'non-Catholics', since we already knew where we stood in Rome's eyes. Our status had long since been defined by Pius XI in one of the few papal encyclicals that we knew very well, *Mortalium Animos*:

> Thus, Venerable Brethren, it is clear why this Apostolic See has never allowed its subjects to take part in the assemblies of non-Catholics. There is but one way in which the unity of Christians may be fostered and that is by furthering the return to the one true Church of Christ of those who are separated from it. For it is from that one true Church that they have fallen away in the past.
>
> ... Let them come, not with any ... hope that [the one true Church] will cast aside the integrity of its faith and tolerate their errors, but prepared to submit themselves to its teaching and government ...

Other conditions of the 'submission' of 'non-Catholics' included our repudiation of all distinctions between 'fundamental' and 'non-fundamental' articles [of faith]'. It was further stipulated that

> all true followers of Christ will, therefore, believe the dogma of the Immaculate Conception of the Mother of God with the same faith as they believe the mystery of the August Trinity, and the infallibility of the Roman Pontiff (in the sense defined by the Oecumenical Vatican Council) with the same faith as they believe the Incarnation of our Lord ...

Accordingly, we were not surprised when Pius XII had declined the invitation from the World Council of Churches to send 'observers' to its inaugural Assembly in Amsterdam in 1948 or to its second Assembly in Evanston (1954). His encyclical, *Humani Generis* (1950), with its wide-ranging condemnations of 'modern tendencies' in contemporary philosophy and theology, had bolstered our impression of a Church immovable (in our old phrase, 'unreformed and irreformable'). Many of us had been greatly interested by the accounts of the earlier 'Malines Conversations' (between Cardinal Mercier and Lord Halifax, 1921–25). Our impression, however, was that they had not been taken seriously in Rome. Later, we learned of the guarded concessions of the Holy Office monitum, *Ecclesia Catholica* (1950), which allowed Catholics and non-Catholics to 'meet together as equals' (*par cum pari*), so that the Catholics might 'set forth the teachings of their faith as their own view'. This was something like the role of the Orthodox in the World Council of Churches (where they had long served as gracious tutors of *the* true faith of which they, too, were sole proprietors). The effects of this concession were immediately fruitful, as when Fr George Tavard, AA was able to act as unofficial consultant to a Faith & Order Study Commission on 'Tradition and Traditions' (1953–63); or, again, when Fr Gustave Weigel SJ and Fr John Sheerin CSP could participate in the first North American Conference on Faith & Order in Oberlin in 1957 – to our great profit.

We were, of course, aware of a small group of Catholic mavericks (as they seemed to us) who had been venturing beyond the boundaries of 'Denzinger theology' – men like the Jesuits John Courtney Murray and Karl Rahner, the Dominican Yves-Marie Congar and others, including an able young German professor named Joseph Ratzinger! For all their talent and boldness, however, it was clear enough that they had been safely marginalized by the Holy Office.

It is still worth remembering this sense of unbridgeable distance between Catholics and non-Catholics, if only to underscore Vatican II's chief achievement: to alter the ecumenical climate in the Christian world, from mutual indifference to mutual recognition, from forced toleration to cordial co-existence, from wariness to love and trust, from *Mortalium Animos* (1928) to *Pacem in Terris* (1963). To this day, none of us knows precisely the terms of Christian unity, or the prescribed steps by which separated Christians ('Catholics' and 'non-Catholics') may hope to move towards more complete communion in Christ. But we do know that now, in almost every country in the world, a multitude of mutually acknowledged Christians have come to various experiences of *koinonia* and cooperation that were inconceivable when the Council was first announced. We had long known the conventional 'way to Rome', and had thus far declined it, for conscience's sake. Even the Eastern Orthodox Christians, who also believed the doctrine of the Immaculate Conception, could not accept Pius IX's pronouncement of it as a dogma. And none of us was prepared to rank the dogma of papal infallibility on the same level as our faith in 'the Incarnation of our Lord'.

Thus, when out of the blue, a Secretariat for Promoting Christian Unity was set up and invitations were sent to the various 'confessional families' to appoint observers to the Council, a startled wonderment began to grow as to what all this might portend. Some of these observers were to be delegated by their official Church bodies: The Ecumenical Patriarchate of Constantinople, the Russian Orthodox Church, the Coptic Orthodox Church, the Syrian Orthodox Church, the Apostolic Armenian Church, the Assyrian Catholicate, the Old Catholic Church, the Anglican Communion, the Lutheran World Federation, the World Presbyterian Alliance, the Evangelical Lutheran Church of Germany, the World Methodist Council, the International Congregational Council, the Friends World Committee, the World Convention of the Churches of Christ, the International Association for Liberal Christianity, the Church of South India and the World Council of Churches. Provisions were made for 'substitutes' to fill the chairs of the principals when absent. In addition, a number of ecumenical notables were invited as 'special guests of the Secretariat' – most notably Dr Oscar Cullmann (of Basel and Paris), Rev David Du Plessis (a Pentecostal), and both the prior and subprior of the Taizé Community.

It was as motley a group of 'non-Catholics' as ever had been assembled. We were often referred to as 'the observers corps' – an obvious misnomer. Actually, we were a mélange, not only with widely different backgrounds but with differing concerns and differing degrees of wariness. We were not organized, and our traditions had had widely different dealings with Rome. It was the supernatural charity of our hosts in the Secretariat that gathered and held us together, and not even then without a certain careful distancing of some groups within 'the corps' from others. Moreover, our expectations of the Council differed almost categorically. There were 'Hussites' among us, who remembered Constance and feared another Roman 'trap'. More numerous were the 'skeptics', who simply doubted the Council's intention to crack the *status quo* by much. Still more numerous were the 'realists' whose highest hopes envisaged a somewhat more cordial co-existence with Rome, without much change on either side. Finally, there were the 'visionaries', who had come to see the Council itself as a sort of miracle in its own right, and who found it, therefore, credible to hope for something more. We were a distinct minority.

On the Council's eve (11 October 1962) all expectations were still on the modest side. The Roman Synod that had served as the Council's 'test run' had lasted barely a week (January 1962), and seemed an ill-omen for any prospect of drastic change in the Council proper. We had come from the ends of the earth to see a glittering spectacle, but most of us had also read the 'ante-preparatory' documents, finding no new horizons being opened up. Roman gossip had it that the Council's 'management' hoped to get all necessary business over and done with by St Catherine's Day (25 November). Nobody that I knew was prepared for what actually happened.

Three things, above all, exceeded our highest hopes. The first was the shining vision of Pope John XXIII's opening allocution, with his rebuke of his own 'prophets of doom' and his eloquent plea for an *aggiornamento* in Catholic self-understanding. That, in turn, must have given heart to the handful of far-visioned reformers who moved alertly to encourage the Council to seize the initiative and to establish its own autonomy, (with

173

unexpected help from the missionary bishops and from a large fraction of the bishops from North America). Finally, we were literally overwhelmed by the warmth and breadth of Catholic hospitality to us 'strangers within their gates'! This came not only from our hosts in the Secretariat, but from everyone in Vatican City, from the Swiss Guard to the Vatican Infirmary to the Pope himself. Such cordiality was so genuine and so unexceptionable that it compelled our gratitude – then and still.

Once the Council was under way, under its own self-chosen leadership, those of us who were Church historians began to realize what a unique lesson we were having in historiography. Here we were, with ring-side seats at an epochal event, with access to the conciliar documents as they progressed from draft to draft; we were provided with translations of and commentaries on the debates.[1] We were able to verify that this was the most efficiently recorded event of this magnitude in the whole of Church history: the secretaries' desks were directly below our chairs in the tribune of St Longinus and we soon learned that Archbishop John Krol [Philadelphia] would never let them 'shut up shop' until each day's records were in order and deposited in the Vatican archives.

But as we read the newspapers, attended the news conferences, listened to the pundits – and as we exchanged impressions among ourselves! – we began to realize more clearly than before the inherent discrepancy between great occasions observed and great occasions reported at second or third hand. The Council observed was an organic process, uneven and groping, replete with drama, of course (and humour), but unfolding in a complex dialectic, aimed at authentic consensus, in an atmosphere of solemnity and spiritual seriousness. The Council reported (even by the 'instant historians' who knew so much more about 'backstage affairs' than we) was more like an ecclesiastical soccer-cup match – with more interest in the antagonists ('progressives', 'immobilists') than in the substance of the texts that were being so painstakingly debated in St Peter's and in the commissions. It was a sobering lesson in hermeneutics, for if Vatican II was inadequately communicated by its contemporary historians (whose accounts may come some day to be listed 'primary source material') where are we in the matter of all our confident generalizations about Nicaea, Chalcedon – or Trent?

Even more crucial, in ecumenical terms, is the question as to how the conciliar texts were to be read and understood by succeeding generations, when the principals and the 'eye-witnesses' would have passed from the scene and when the tacit assumptions about intended meanings, so nearly 'self-evident' at the time, would have been forgotten? Already, what seemed then to be 'progressive developments' to so many (including the

174

immobilists) may now be read with more conservative overtones. What seemed to us as minor concessions in the interest of the widest possible consensus now appear to some as 'proofs' that Vatican II changed little or nothing, after all. There may be no way of avoiding such hermeneutical transformations. But they should be remembered, so as to temper all claims to absolute certitude about '*the* literal meaning' of this ambiguous passage or that.

As Observers, we were interested in all the issues before the Council, but chiefly as they were related to Pope John's great vision for the Council: a new flowering of spiritual life and energy within the Roman Catholic Church which would in turn strengthen her Christian witness in 'the modern world' (*mundus huius temporis*) even as it enhanced her winsomeness and hospitality to 'those who are cut off from the Apostolic See' (as in Pope John's first encyclical, *Ad Petri Cathedram*). Most of all, however, we wanted to see whether or not the rigid stand of *Mortalium Animos* might be altered – and if so, with what conceivable consequences. We knew the landmarks of *piononismo*: the Marian dogmas, the *Syllabus of Errors, Pastor Aeternus,* the *Index*, the anti-modernist encyclical and oath, *Pascendi Gregis* and the *Antistitum*. They stood as forbidding sentinels, guarding an 'orthodoxy' that exceeded any sort of 'catholic Christianity' prescribed by Holy Scripture, Holy Tradition or the 'Nicene' Creed. What, then, was conceivable in the place of the old double-or-nothing approach to the 'non-Catholics' (including the Orthodox, and the Anglicans, and at least some Protestants who understand themselves as 'catholics' in some sense or other)?

As the Council unfolded, from its impasse in the First Session to its decisive breakthroughs in Session Two and Three, we saw many of the old walls of separation dismantled from the Roman side. It was a curious process. In the early drafts of the constitution *Dei Verbum* on 'revelation', the two-source theory of Trent was put forward as if it could be taken for granted. We then saw this altered towards an emphasis on the primacy of Scripture. With this, as far as we were concerned, one of the principal issues in the sixteenth-century tragedies had been quietly deflated. The early essays in ecclesiology were so triumphalist that they tended to chill further dialogue. But as we saw the 'draft constitution' originally entitled *De Ecclesia* grow into *Lumen Gentium,* with its old mystical vision (different from the ecclesiology of *Mystici Corporis Christi*) and its new vision of episcopal collegiality, we saw a new ecumenical frontier opened up.

Thus, in its final text, after a profound and elevated description of the Church in Christ (sec. 8), the text would affirm that 'this Church *subsists in*

175

the Catholic Church . . . although many elements of sanctification and truth can be found outside her visible structure'. The implication that this distinction (between 'exists in' and 'subsists in') allowed for an ecclesiology of degrees was made explicit by Bishop André Charue (Namur) in his *Relatio* on the penultimate draft of *Unitatis Redintegratio*, where (sec. 3) it is also said that the fullness of Christian unity 'subsists in the Catholic Church'. The usage appears a third time to the same effect in the proem of *Dignitatis Humani* ('this one true religion *subsists in* the Catholic and Apostolic Church') – where the context makes no sense if all that is meant is that *no* degree of 'this one true religion' exists anywhere else other than in the Roman Catholic Church.

The issue here, of course, is whether the way to Christian unity was still where it was in 1928 or whether a notion of 'convergence' somewhere and somehow in the future was emerging – as Rahner and Fries have suggested.[2] This same prospect has been explored still further by Fr Avery Dulles SJ, in his [unpublished] 1985 Wattson Lecture at the Catholic University of America. In 1965, this idea of 'convergence' seemed quite credible at the Council, among the observers, the Secretariat for Promoting Christian Unity and most of the Fathers of the Council with whom I discussed the matter. Two decades later, it has not only been denied but repudiated – in such things as a signed editorial in *L'Osservatore Romano*[3] and also in the recent 'Statement of Notification' from the Congregation for the Doctrine of the Faith to Fr Leonardo Boff.[4] Shades of Cardinal Ottaviani! Shades of Professor Edmund Schlink, murmuring 'What did I tell you?'[5]

The first drafts of *De Ecumenismo* sought to explain the distinctive 'principles of *Catholic* ecumenism', along with descriptions of Protestantism that were friendly enough but woefully inadequate. We dutifully complained of such infelicities and then were delighted, in the next draft, to find an alteration in it to 'Catholic *principles* of ecumenism' (much more than a hair's splitting). The Secretariat also challenged us to help them with their descriptions of us, and when we found some of our suggestions taken up in the final draft, we were so flattered that we were not much offended when Pope Paul felt it necessary, for the sake of some tender consciences, to amend them. Our proposal had read: 'At the prompting of the Holy Spirit, they [the Protestants] *find* God in the Holy Scriptures, as he speaks to them in Christ'. Pope Paul had altered it to read more tentatively, 'Invoking the Holy Spirit, they *seek* God in these sacred Scriptures, as he speaks to them in Christ' (sec. 22). With Mt. 7:7 in mind, we thought we saw a way in which 'seek' and 'find' could be reconciled!

By the end of the Council, it seemed self-evident (to the 'progressives' among the Catholics and to the visionaries among the observers) that the least these texts could mean was a massive ecumenical re-orientation of the Roman Catholic Church towards some sort of concept of reciprocal reconciliations between Rome and other Churches, in place of the older prescriptions for unilateral return. Our realists kept reminding us of the residual ambiguities in *Unitatis Redintegratio* and how they might be interpreted in the older sense. Others, like Professor Cullmann, stressed the distance the Council had moved beyond the ante-preparatory documents.

None of us could recollect anything of this magnitude since the futile exercises of the great sixteenth-century conciliators (Contarini, Gropper, Bucer, Melanchthon – The Conference of Ratisbon [1541], and all that). We were intrigued when the Pope and Council commissioned the return to the Orthodox of the silver reliquary, said to contain the skull of St Andrew, that had been brought to the West in the wake of the Fall of Constantinople (1453). On their return from Patras, one of the members of the Roman delegation told me of their cordial and grateful reception by the Orthodox – and then the added query from their hosts, 'what about the *body*?' (long since encrypted in the cathedral of Amalfi!). This gesture had then been followed by a notable meeting between Pope Paul and Patriarch Athenagoras in Jerusalem and Bethlehem. Finally, there came what seemed to us a real climax: the mutual lifting of the muddled excommunications of 1054, 'by Pope Paul VI and Patriarch Athenagoras *with his Synod*' (7 December 1965). On that occasion, the two great churchmen spoke of their 'shared hopes for reconciliation', and of their mutual commitment 'to the goal of full communion in the faith, fraternal accord and sacramental life which existed among them during the first millenium of the Church's life'. Since it was common knowledge that reunion with Constantinople was Rome's top ecumenical priority, some of us thought that this goal was now in sight, if not in reach. Twenty years later, negotiations still continue, but at a snail's pace. Nor will it quicken if the current interpretation of *subsistere* by the Congregation for the Doctrine of Faith is left to stand.

On the eve of the Council's closure (6 December 1965) an unprecedented service of shared worship with the observers was held in the basilica of St Paul's-without-the-Walls. It was attended by the Pope and many bishops, with a half-dozen Observers (Orthodox, Old Catholic and Protestant) assisting with lections and prayers, and with the entire assembly joining together in Johann Crüger's *Nun Danket Alle Gott*. When staff members from the Secretariat for Promoting Christian Unity arrived at St Paul's two hours before the ceremony to check the arrangements, they found a towering papal throne on the podium, and were barely able to persuade the

Benedictine monks to change this to something more modest – by invoking Pope Paul's express desire 'to be seated in the midst'. Some of the immobilists were scandalized; the Pope shrugged them off.

In our euphoria, what we heard most clearly were the Pope's ecumenical *affirmations:* his hope that 'the problem of our separation can be resolved – not today, certainly, but tomorrow; slowly, gradually, honestly and generously'. We also heard his *caution* that

> there is still a long way to go to reach full and authentic communion – many prayers to be made to the Father of Lights, many vigils to keep. May we at least, however, at the end of the Council record this victory: we have begun to love each other once more . . .

Some of us were not as attentive to his *reservations:* his emphasis on the Council's care to safeguard the full deposit of the Christian faith, his assumption that none of us would really wish for unity on any other terms. 'The Catholic Church has never failed in her careful custody of "the trust" (cf 1 Tim. 6:20) which it has carried with it from the beginnings.' Nor did we grasp the full import of the striking parable with which he closed his allocution. It has not often been cited, and may be worth repeating, especially now in retrospect:

> Many years ago, we were told of a charming and symbolic episode from the life of one of the great Oriental [sic!] thinkers of modern times, and we tell it to you as we remember it.
>
> It seems that it was [Vladimir] Solovieff. At one time, while staying in a monastery, he had been having a spiritual conversation with a pious monk. Finally, wishing to return to his cell, he went out into the corridor on which the doors of the other cells opened, all alike and all closed. In the dark, he was not able to identify the door of the cell which had been assigned to him. On the other hand, he felt it impossible to return to the cell of the monk he had just left and he did not want to disturb anyone else during the rigorous monastic silence of the night. Thus the philosopher resigned himself to pass the night walking slowly up and down the corridor, suddenly become mysterious and inhospitable, absorbed in his thoughts. The night was long and dreary but at last it passed, and with the first light of dawn the tired philosopher easily recognized the door to his cell which he had passed time and time again. And he remarked: 'It is often thus with those who search for truth. They pass right by without seeing it until a ray of sunlight of divine wisdom makes easy and happy the consoling revelation.'
>
> The truth is near. Beloved brothers, may this ray of divine light allow us all to recognize the blessed door.
>
> This is our hope. And now let us all pray together at the tomb of St Paul.[6]

Were there intimations here as to our prospective ecumenical situation once the hospitable doors of the Council were closed? And had he expected the Orthodox, and some of the rest of us – despite our exaltation in so high a moment – not to recall how Solovieff, under a cloud in his own Church, had converted to Rome? What more was implied in this simple story than a cordial counsel to patience?

In any case, the Council's closure did not dampen the ecumenical enthusiasm that it had generated. Responding to an initiative from the Observers, earlier on, the Pope commissioned an 'Ecumenical Institute for Advanced Theological Studies' (established at Tantur, between Jerusalem and Bethlehem) where Orthodox, Roman Catholics, Protestants – and 'non-Chalcedonians'! – could feel 'at home together' (it was the only such place in the world).[7] The Secretariat for Promoting Christian Unity launched a massive, complicated programme of 'bilateral dialogues' with various 'confessional families' (Anglican, Lutheran, Reformed, Methodist and the like) and these have continued with great profit, both to the participants and to their respective Churches. Fresh ventures in cooperation were undertaken between the Vatican and the World Council of Churches; Karl Barth (no visionary!) paid what he himself called a belated *ad limina* visit to Paul VI. Pope Paul paid an official visit to Geneva. An eminent Catholic historian, Mgr John Tracy Ellis, was elected president of The American Church History Society; a Protestant, myself indeed, was elected president of the American Catholic Historical Association. The University of Notre Dame sponsored an international theological conference under the rubric 'Vatican II: An Inter-faith Appraisal' (1966) (with a host of Council Fathers and *periti* [including Karl Rahner], plus Orthodox, Anglican, Protestant theologians – along with two eminent rabbis: Marc Tannenbaum and Abraham Heschel). All over the world, old silences were broken; 'separated Christians' found themselves in animated converse. There was a veritable outburst of Christian cordiality in an exciting new atmosphere. We began to think the unthinkable: the darkness was lightening towards a dawn.

The decade was not out, however, before this momentum seemed on the wane, in the upper echelons of the Churches and the World Council of Churches. An obvious 'cause' for this was a renewed preoccupation within the denominations with their own internal problems. Since 1968 at least, Rome has had a succession of upheavals within its own ranks.[8] Orthodoxy continued to be concerned not only with its own integrity but also with survival in many countries of the world. Many Protestant denominations were engrossed with new ventures in 'reunions' within their [confessional] families. Given such 'distractions', the urge to bridge old lines of cleavage had abated; ecumenical priorities were downscaled – sometimes deliberately, more often by default. The World Council of Churches shifted its priorities from 'unity' to the equally urgent causes of Christian social action (peace and justice, poverty and homelessness, human rights), as if there were just enough energy and commitment to promote one or the other but not both.

Another paradoxical 'explanation' for this ecumenical deceleration can be found in the passage, within a single generation, from a theological climate dominated more by a sense of the classical Christian heritage, to new doctrinal weather patterns. Historically, the ecumenical enterprise had focused on the doctrinal barriers that had divided Christians and on the possibilities of a consensus that might surmount them. The 'new generation' of theologians profess to be more deeply scandalized by injustice than by disunity (as if they had been forced to such a choice!). There is, of course, a sense in which 'liberation theologies', 'ethnic theologies', 'feminist theologies', 'pacifist theologies', are 'ecumenical'; their stake in denominational particularities is typically minimal. There is, however, another sense in which they undermine the ecumenical cause in its traditional forms. They ignore the fact that Christians united for justice while separated from each other at their Lord's Table send the wrong message out to a skeptical world.

Even so, the experience of Christian fellowship has continued to grow and spread, even if more quietly than before, *at the grass roots*. It is as if Christians of all sorts and conditions were still inspirited by the heart of the decree, *Unitatis Redintegratio*:

> 7. ... There can be no ecumenism worthy of the name without a change of heart. For it is from a newness of attitudes, from self-denial and unstinted love, that yearnings for unity take their rise and grow toward maturity. We should therefore pray to the Divine Spirit for the grace to be genuinely self-denying, humble, gentle in the service of others ... Thus, in humble prayer, we beg the pardon of God and of our separated brethren, just as we forgive them who have trespassed against us ...
>
> 8. This change of heart and holiness of life, along with public and private prayer for the unity of Christians should be regarded as the soul of the whole ecumenical movement, and can rightly be called 'spiritual ecumenism' ... In certain special circumstances, such as in prayer services for unity and during ecumenical gatherings, *it is allowable, indeed desirable, that Catholics should join in prayer with their separated brethren* ... (italics added)
>
> As for common worship (*communicatio in sacris*), however, it may not be regarded as an indiscriminate means for the restoration of unity among

Christians. Such worship depends chiefly on two principles: it should signify the unity of the Church, and it should provide a sharing in the means of grace. The fact that it should signify unity generally rules out such worship. *Yet the gaining of a needed grace sometimes commends it.* (italics added)

This was and remains a charter for ecumenical change that may still be appealed to (particularly in its intended sense) as normative Catholic teaching. Along with other leadings of the Holy Spirit to the same end, a bountiful harvest of 'new attitudes' between Catholics and 'non-Catholics' has been harvested already and is still ripening. All over the world, Christians who had lived apart have come to sense themselves as 'members one of another in the Body of Christ'. The denominations, as such, may or may not be much nearer than before to organic union. But who will deny that the People of God are more nearly joined than before in faith, hope and love?

The quest for 'oneness in Christ' goes forward still, in many countries, on many levels, with or without official sanctions. The 'Faith & Order Commission' of the World Council of Churches has made notable progress in its struggles for doctrinal consensus, as in its now familiar pamphlet on *Baptism, Eucharist, Ministry* (received with such enthusiasm by the Vancouver Assembly of 1983 and even more widely among the Churches). The progress achieved in the 'Bilaterals' is slowly being shared within the theological community (itself now 'ecumenical', almost as if by definition). Roman and Anglican relations are greatly improved; their ARCIC agreements are now being set on a firmer footing by a commission authorized jointly by Pope John Paul II and the Archbishop of Canterbury, in Canterbury (its affectionate nickname – Ben-ARCIC!). A chair in Ecumenics has been established at The Catholic University of America in honour of a late *Anglican* ecumenist.

Amidst all this, a painful and profound confusion has arisen among 'separated brothers and sisters in Christ' who are eager to pass beyond the old limits still enforced by their leaders. It has to do, of course, with the vexed question of 'intercommunion'. Many of us, aware of 'the rules', have prayed through hundreds of masses without offering ourselves for communion, even when invited – not on our own principles but out of respect for what we are taught about Roman sensibilities. It has invariably been edifying, since there is not a line in the eucharistic liturgy that we cannot affirm unfeignedly. It is also painful, and ambiguous. Other 'non-Catholics' receive communion from Roman priests (with their tacit consent), as if it were some sort of 'private eucharistic hospitality'. I know of Roman Catholics communing with Protestants and appealing for their permission (doubtfully, one thinks) to the Ecumenical Directory issued by the Secretariat for Promoting Christian Unity. Such confusions may go with the ferments of the times. Who would turn the clock back? But who will set it forward?

It is not easy, any more, to know whether the way of wisdom towards the ecumenical future is one of holy patience or holy impatience. The warrants for authentic Christian unity and its relevance in a world in agony and for the Churches in confusion, are clearer now than they have been at any time since the *Exsurge Domine* of 1520. The rejection of the Roman papacy by the Orthodox is less adamant than any time since 1054 (or 1204!). More Protestants would accept the papacy as a visible symbol and effectual agency of Christian unity than ever before (though not in the formula of Vatican I – *ex sese non autem ex consensu ecclesiae*; [as in Ed Peter J. McCord, *A Pope For All Christians*, (Paulist Press NY 1976)]). Nearer to the heart of the matter, more Protestants than since the sixteenth century are prepared to embrace some credible doctrine of the real presence of Jesus Christ in the Eucharist (wrought by the supernatural agency of the Holy Spirit), along with a lively sense of our own participation in Christ in *his* Supper ('that we may evermore dwell in him and he in us').

Is it then still permitted, at this distance from Vatican II, to hope and pray for further miracles that will ease the pain of separation on the part of Christians who are nearer to each other than ever before but are still denied the oneness that God has willed, that is still prerequisite to the Gospel's full effectiveness? Is there not good reason for a holy impatience that the 'hungry sheep look up and are not [led]'? Christians who partook of the wondrous outpourings of Christian charity at Vatican II, and who still remember what seemed its manifest intentions, cannot easily believe that their experiences were illusory.

The ambiguities of Paul VI's parable about Solovieff continue to haunt us. The question will not lie down as to whether it is our pride, our courtesy or our conscience that keeps us in our darkened corridor. Surely, the Pope was trying to reassure us that the long night of Christian disunity was not forever, that our tediums and bewilderments – of being so near to where we yearn to be and yet still so far – would fade with the dawning light. But that was a full twenty years ago.

Meanwhile, the quest for a unity worthy of the name goes on. Is a continuation of our more amiable co-existence ('spiritual ecumenism') the best that we should hope for? Are the divided Churches to be left to proceed along their separate ways until the dawn finally breaks and Providence opens 'the blessed door'? If this is our prospect, when will the tides of ecumenical hope begin to rise again, and the old sense of urgency be renewed?

NOTES

1. The Observers sat, many bewildered at the latinity; but were then put at their ease by instant translation from host-members of the SPCU who, often with speech texts to hand, spoke out in any of four languages: as to English, three such translators were the American Jesuit Fr Gustave Weigel (who died during the Council), Fr Gerard Corr O.S.M. (now Prior of the Servites at Begbroke, Oxon) and Mgr Francis Davis (retired to Eynsham Abbey, Oxon). These hosts were given a full set of documents, as though they were bishops, and expected to keep the Observers abreast of daily developments. [Ed.].

2. Heinrich Fries & Karl Rahner, *Unity of the Churches: an actual possibility* (Paulist Press, NY 1985). Rahner's posthumous work was promptly dismissed by Cardinal Ratzinger as a 'case of theological acrobatics'; and by Fr Daniel Ols O.P. as a grave misunderstanding of Catholic ecclesiology.

3. Mid-March 1985. Cf *The Christian Century*, 13 Mar 1985, 264 for excerpts from Fr Ols' editorial: 'The Church of Christ *exists in* [*esse*] the Catholic Church and the fulness of grace and truth are the patrimony of the Catholic Church, so that she alone possesses the complete means for salvation.' Note the reversion from *subsistit in* to the *est* passed over by the Council. (Is this a sign of returning to *Mortalium Animos?*)

4. A newly prominent Brazilian theologian whose book, *Church: Charism & power* (Crossroads NY 1984) and other essays in liberation theology have brought him into conflict with the Congregation for the Doctrine of the Faith. Cf SCDF 'Instruction' to him, *Origins* XIV.42 (4 April 1985), 683ff.

5. Professor of Ecumenics at Heidelberg, and the most prominent Lutheran Observer. His appraisal of the Council was always cautious. His book, *After the Council* (Fortress Press, Philadelphia 1968) is full of warnings against false hope. Cf his minimalist views on the *est/subsistit in* change, 87f, 245f; perhaps he was right – in the light of the SCDF Instruction – to be cautious.

6. *The Council Daybook,* III, 354.

7. The Institute's agenda included private and corporate study, lectures, seminars and conferences. Daily worship was in the charge of Benedictine monks seconded from Montserrat. On special occasions, *cum permissu*, there was intercommunion.

8. E.g. the furore set off by the encyclical *Humanae Vitae* (1968); the challenges from 'liberation theologies'; the controversy over the Dutch Church; the Küng and Schillebeeckx affairs; 'traditionalist' dismay over the vernacular Mass; searching questions over celibacy, women priests, 'inclusive language'; turmoils within the Society of Jesus; etc. Cf such hyperventilated accounts of this period as in Peter Hebblethwaite, *The Runaway Church* (Collins 1975) or Garry Wills, *Bare ruined choirs* (Doubleday NY 1972).

PART FOUR

THE COUNCIL AT WORK

11

THE LITURGY CONSTITUTION: *SACROSANCTUM CONCILIUM*

JOSEPH CARDINAL CORDEIRO

On 4 December 1963 Paul VI, 'Bishop of the Catholic Church', and the 'Venerable Fathers' put their signatures to the first Constitution of the Council, 'in approving, decreeing and establishing these things in the Holy Spirit' (to be) 'published to God's glory'. The Sacrosanctum Concilium *of the title is Vatican II itself, which had begun its deliberations surprisingly not upon a document* de Ecclesia *(establishing the* locus *of liturgy and all else) but upon its professed goal 'to intensify the daily growth of Catholics in Christian living; to make more responsive to the requirements of our time those Church observances which are open to adaptation; to mature whatever can contribute to the unity of all who believe in Christ; and to strengthen those aspects of the Church which can summon all of mankind into her embrace.' So the Church's liturgy was to be renewed and fostered.*

The Constitution was quickly followed by Paul VI's Motu Proprio Sacram Liturgiam *and an Instruction on its proper implementation; and then a spate of liturgical legislation or guidance of which the most famous was the Pope's Apostolic Constitution* Missale Romanum *(3 April 1969) which ushered in the* Missa Normativa *or 'new Mass', 1970 replacing 1570. Gradually the universal Church made its considerable changes over two decades of steady evolution. What was the effect far from Rome, especially in missionary situations? This chapter, an address given in Rome in October 1984, offers some insights.*

Joseph Cordeiro was born in Bombay in January 1918. He was educated in Karachi, at Bombay University and Oxford. He was ordained priest 1946 and called to episcopacy in the last year of Pius XII at the very young age of forty. He attended the Synod of Bishops, finding himself appointed to the Council of the Secretary-General. He has also served with the Sacred Congregation for Religious and the Secretariat for Non-Christians. As Cardinal Archbishop of Karachi, he is President of the Pakistan Episcopal Conference.

In celebrating the twentieth anniversary of the Council Document on the Renewal of the Liturgy let us gaze across these two decades and seek to assess what has come about in the entire Church across six continents. Surely none of the Council Fathers could have guessed the size and shape of things to come. A Reformation scholar and Vatican Council II Observer, Professor Jaroslav Pelikan, thus expressed himself in his response at the time: that the Document can be translated into action 'still remains to be seen'. Clearly he registered a mood of doubt and minimal expectancy.

Obviously in such a vast and unwieldy body of people as the Catholic

Church, change and development are bound to be uneven and hetero-geneous, even within the same country, diocese or parish. But if we alight on some random spot where the Document has been taken seriously and pick for example an average or even unlettered Catholic; let him see on a video tape his own comings and goings and doings at a Sunday Mass of the early 1960s; then expose him to a corresponding video tape of the way he fits into the Sunday celebration of today, he would probably be startled out of his wits. Without realizing it, without keeping tag of the intervening stages, he finds that he has been through a revolution in his mode of worship.

I would dare to say, however, that in a mission country like mine, the revolution has been more readily accepted, and that despite the rather con-ventional attitude of the other religions around us. I remember asking a Muslim friend of mine what he would think if we introduced Urdu into the liturgy, especially at Mass. He could not agree. He looked at Latin as the Arabic in the Koran, and would not dream of a change. But the revolution has come to stay.

Why is this so? On reflection we discover that there are many reasons, some stronger and more far-reaching, for the profound impact of the document.

The most important is that it touches life

The Document deals with worship which of its very nature touches life, springs from life, and flows into the rough and tumble of life. Life and worship are so inseparable and intimately connected that freshness and newness in the mode of worship was bound to send ripples into the lives of the faithful. Many pronouncements of the official Church might leave the man in the street untouched and distant; but when it came to the way he prayed and sang and bowed his head in the house of God, it touched him to the quick, even when in some cases he threw up his hands in protest against change.

It would be unfair to history if it were not recorded that sometimes liturgical excesses and exaggerations went well beyond the limits of fidelity to the Document. By making the celebrations very commonplace the great damage done was that the sense of mystery, *mysterium*, was shattered. What happens in such cases is that perhaps unintentionally but inevitably the reality of the Eucharistic event weakens. Instead of celebrating God, the community celebrates itself. 'The community celebrates its own happy, pious feelings. Pharisaism is near!', suggested Hans Urs von Balthasar.

On the whole, however, I am convinced that the liturgical renewal has brought man to worship God in gratitude. In worship he also finds some kind of cushioning against the thorns and the shocks; he hopes to carry therefrom the inner reserves he needs to meet the mounting pressures of existence, or as the Document has succinctly put it, consciously or unconsciously, worship works out to be 'the summit and source of Christian living'.

The Relaxing Church

At this point you may well raise the question: Wasn't this true before? Isn't this close link between life and worship true of the Church in any age? Wasn't it true of the long stretch from the Council of Trent to Vatican II? Why then do we harp so strongly on this theme as though it belonged to our time – or to the Church of our time? Let us face this question in all honesty.

At the time of the Council of Trent the Church was reeling under the shock of the Reformation and consequent break-up of Christendom. The cyclone all around was threatening to blow away not only the roof and odd bits of furniture, but the most precious treasures of the household as well. The Church lived in a state of siege – desperately trying to repel the attacks of the enemy – the over-turning of ancient values, the flouting of authority, and a centrifugal chaos. This state of tension and insecurity and the concern to 'hold on' is reflected in the worship of the time: the clinging to Latin (which fewer and fewer people understood), the stress on centralizing (the priest and the altar boy made the Mass; the people came in almost as a kind of after-thought to 'hear' the Mass), the vast distance and separation between aisle and sanctuary; the worship of a church in tension. As against this, the Document shows us the Church not merely at worship, but *relaxing* at worship, relaxing to be herself as church, regardless of all else.

It is this posture of relaxation I believe that endows the Document with a quiet drive and inner resilience that will take many more decades fully to be actualized. Meanwhile, I pick out three aspects of life in the Church which I think have been largely inspired by the Document.

A Sense of Community

The layman now enters the church building not as a second-class citizen, but as a living member of that primary category that God first called to the work of salvation, viz. the People of God here gathered to celebrate the

New Covenant in the victory of Jesus' death and resurrection – and called to do so 'knowingly, actively, fruitfully'. It is this experience of group participation that has engendered among Christians the sense of community and community relationships, which was such a marked feature of the Church in the Acts of the Apostles. This sense of community is in most cases still inchoative and hesitant at the big parish level – but it has blossomed impressively in many parishes and dioceses throughout the world, in small communities at prayer, and in particular in movements like the Focolari, the Neo-Catechumenate and the Charismatic communities. In this day and age, community worship has come to the rescue of the beleaguered Christian none too soon. It is increasingly realized that the individual Christian, or even the individual family cannot maintain its foothold against the secularizing onslaught of the Mass Media geared to Big Business. It is in the relaxed and reassuring atmosphere of the Sunday liturgy that Christians can find their feet again via the openly expressed solidarity of the Body of Christ.

The Presence of the Lord

But I believe the *pièce de résistance* of the Constitution is the recognition of the Risen Lord's Presence at the heart of the entire ritual. The relaxed posture of the Church shines clearest as she leads her members in the deep absorption of encountering that Presence . . . Jesus present in the praying assembly, Jesus present in the word of Scripture proclaimed aloud, Jesus present in the exercise of the priesthood, and Jesus present in the sacramental species as the Bread of life. These progressive encounters call for deep inner responses which enable the faithful to experience the trans-forming power of the Spirit as happened at the first Pentecost.

Scripture and Ecumenism

Lastly let me comment on the decisive Paragraph 24 of the Document where Scripture is restored to its rightful place not only in the liturgy but in the extra-liturgical life of Catholics. Scripture is forthrightly acknowledged (a refreshing stance again of the relaxing Church) as the fountain and inspiration of so many liturgical elements: the Readings and homily, the psalms and hymns, the prayers, the very actions and gestures derive their meaning from Scripture. But the heart-warming sentence comes at the end, 'to promote that warm and living love for the Scripture' among the faithful. Perhaps no single utterance of Vatican Council II has been greeted with such thunderous approval as 'this warm and living love of the Scripture', to replace the former wariness (if not fear) of opening the Bible. As the Renewal Movements and communities can testify, the Bible (in this age of widespread literacy) is barely given a fair chance in our lives if the Scripture experience of the average Catholic is restricted to a mere 'hearing of the Word' on a Sunday. Many Catholics have felt the need of drinking daily from this fountain through reflection, prayer and sharing within the group or family circle. Accordingly our Bible-thirsty Catholics have lapped up these biblical handbooks and aids, brochures, illustrations, maps and encyclopedias (not to mention the Bible itself) which have the advantage of being readily available, attractive, and suited to the poor man's pocket. This is a good example of the ecumenical outreach of the Document.

While we rejoice in and celebrate the positive achievements of the Document, it is important to think of the future. I sincerely believe that there are some aspects of *Sacrosanctum Concilium* which have hitherto been somewhat neglected and are only now beginning to receive attention. In the short time allotted to me I dwell on a few of my own choice.

One such touches the Eucharist

Personally, since my Ordination [in 1946] I have considered the Mass a daily privilege and a responsibility to be with Christ in the ministry of his saving Passion. But the last twenty years have shown the Mass to dominate the horizon in a paramount fashion, almost disproportionately so, to the neglect of lesser elements in the liturgy . . . the Divine Office, Benediction, Vigils before the Blessed Sacrament, the other sacraments and sacramentals. It does not add to the glory of the sun to have its satellites permanently eclipsed. Besides in the exclusive emphasis on the Mass there is a danger that crops up repeatedly in the history of religion. The unreflecting public can become so absorbed in the pursuit of the one thing considered necessary, that they tend to make a fetish of it, and thereby lose sight of the transcendence of God who acts sovereignly in so many ways, whose Spirit blows where he wills.

New Liturgies and New Cultures

Perhaps the most astonishing liturgical development of the future will be the flowering of indigenous liturgies in the far-flung local Churches, drawing their sap, vigour and variety from all that is best in native cultures, the seed of which has been so quietly and unobtrusively sown in Paragraph

191

37 of the Constitution. To fill in any details of such a kaleidoscopic picture is at the moment impossible. But it will surely be one of colossal and bewildering variety. The facing of such an issue, with so many unknown complexities and tensions still hidden beneath the horizon, clearly shows the relaxing church at her imposing best.

Repent and Believe

The Synod of Bishops in 1983 spoke of the close relationship between the Eucharist and Reconciliation. It is my opinion that while we have emphasized the Eucharist, we have not sufficiently emphasized the need for reconciliation. Yet the Christian coming hotfoot from the world to celebrate the liturgy finds himself impeded. If he would immerse himself in the atmosphere of relaxation, he needs to rid himself of the great enemy of true relaxation and peace, namely sin and its satellites, depression, anxiety, fear. The Document's insistence 'to believers also the Church must ever preach repentance and faith', and the rite of forgiveness at the very threshold of the Mass, brings this about with a new kind of effectiveness. A people ever conscious of failing and falling has no hesitancy in being led forward into the deeper dimensions of worship.

Sacred Music

While making an exception for some mission countries, in many ways the development of music in the post-conciliar years has been disappointing on the larger scale. This is unfortunate; for as the Constitution so clearly underlines 'the musical tradition of the Church is a treasure of immeasurable value, greater than that of any other art; because music is intimately linked with the liturgical action, winningly expresses prayerfulness, promotes solidarity and enriches sacred rites with heightened solemnity'. In the earlier days there was much experimentation of all kinds, psalmody, pop, rock, operatic, etc.; the more conservative tended to pour old wine into new wineskins or lift Latin thought and sentiment into a modern idiom. Often the results have been dull, melodramatic or bizarre. On a more general plane much can be learned from the development in the secular field through television and video tapes, e.g. the use of background music to foster the right emotions. This practice has found its way into many worship situations. But mere art and expertise are not enough; what serves to stimulate and entertain need not stir to faith, praise and repentance.

It is to be hoped that music and psalmody, fostered through prayer and discernment, nourished by a relationship to the Lord and expressed in a rendering of native genius appropriate to true worship, will eventually find their way into life in the Church.

All said and done, the liturgy, while being 'a thing of beauty', must prepare itself for the future. We must recognize that we are living in an age of rapid change, technological, sociological and value-wise. The age we are passing through does not seem to be a mere transition to another stage of new constants. On the contrary, the indications are that the present speed of change carries with it an in-built acceleration. Apart from the gathering speed, the nature of such change will be further diversified and augmented by the migration of people across the planet in different directions, not to mention their reaching out to the stars.

In such a world the Church must prepare its members for the future, so that they may ride the crest of change without future shock. It would be wise to recall here the words of *Sacrosanctum Concilium*: 'For the liturgy is made up of unchangeable elements divinely instituted, and elements subject to change. The latter not only may but ought to be changed with the passing of time if features have by chance crept in which are less harmonious with the intimate nature of the liturgy, or if existing elements have grown less functional.'

It would be too venturesome for me to spell out how this preparation should be done, but I would like to conclude with two thoughts. The first is that we will require the courage to continue to pursue liturgical renewal with responsible creativity. Responsible creativity must be constantly encouraged.

> The celebrant and the people will need to have the responsibility to celebrate the paschal mystery as they are now experiencing and living it as a community, never as a community in isolation, but in the Church as a part of the whole Christ. Thus, parameters will be established both by the nature of the paschal mystery and its liturgical Eucharistic celebration and by the nature of the community as of the Church. Liturgical norms should make these clear and at the same time make clear how they flow from the very nature of reality. Within these parameters freedom should prevail so that the community can properly and responsibly celebrate its own immediate experience of these realities. A careful study of the Apostolic Constitution of Paul VI and other relevant documents is also called for. Without a thorough knowledge of the general instruction it is impossible for the priest to understand the conciliar reform. (B. Pennington, *The Eucharist Yesterday and Today*.)

Secondly, it is my sincere conviction that if the liturgy does not bring about a true and full conversion in our lives, then there is a lot more to be done. Above all, the evangelizing force of our lives will have been greatly reduced.

In spite of all its achievements in the past twenty years, and all the resounding successes that *Sacrosanctum Concilium* has gained, humbly I feel that the dichotomy in our lives still remains; there still remains much of that separation between liturgy and life. In short, the process of interiorization as the result of the liturgy has yet a long way to go. I see the need for this interiorization all the more, living in a mission country where the *external* force of non-Christian religions is so great.

The world may be changing fast, but its people are also coming closer together. If we are to be saved as one people, as Vatican Council II says, then the liturgy of the future will have to urge us more and more to live a life in close union with Christ in God.

12

COMMUNICATING WITH THE WORLD: THE DECREE *INTER MIRIFICA*

WALTHER KAMPE

On 5 June 1960 a Secretariat for the Instruments of Social Communication was established, one of ten commissions and two secretariats set up to prosper the Council. Its President was the Rector of the North American College, Rome; and with him were four other American bishops and one from the UK. They provided a draft document for the Fathers in August 1962.

The schema was considered in Aula on 23 November 1962 – as a relaxation to the Fathers after their toil on the Liturgy and Revelation. It was to be passed without argument, after introduction by Archbishop Stourm of Sens; but he painted such a daunting picture of the powers of the press, periodicals, films and broadcasting that the Fathers felt compelled to admonish the faithful to make responsible use of these vast media. Cardinal Wyszynski exhorted the Church to aspire to a human culture wider than mere Catholicism. Others called for more emphasis on the role of the laity in media, since they had the qualification and the experience. The Decree, with that on Liturgy, was the first to be promulgated (on 4 December 1963). It was subsequently judged to take little account of the insight into the nature of the Church and her relationship with the world which the Council later reached. Considering the present state of discussion among intellectuals and communicators, it is judged as almost 'pre-conciliar'.

Walther Kampe, Bishop of Limburg is over seventy-five. After studies at Frankfurt and Munich he was ordained at Limburg in 1934 (the year of the Barmen Declaration). During the Nazi era he was chaplain to the German community in Rumania. He spent two years of internment in the USSR, returning in 1947 to a curacy in Frankfurt. During the thirty-two years of 1952 to 1984 he was Auxiliary Bishop of Limburg with special duties as to public relations for the German Bishops' Conference. He was also President of the German Pax Christi. Of his half dozen books, before the Council he published Mirroring the time *(Frankfurt 1961); during it, two volumes of* The Council as recorded in the press *(Würzburg 1963); after it, with Martin Niemöller,* Young Christians wonder about the Church *(Munich 1968).*

PUBLIC RELATIONS FOR VATICAN II

In June 1962 I had the privilege of a private audience with Pope John XXIII to submit a number of ideas in reference to the briefing of the world's press during the forthcoming Ecumenical Council. I had been encouraged in this approach by that great champion of conciliarism, Cardinal Bea; I had also discussed the matter beforehand with Cardinal Frings of Cologne and

Cardinal König of Vienna, and with their recommendation gained the support of the Episcopal Conferences of Germany and Austria.

Together with Professor J. B. Hirschmann SJ I had developed a plan to supplement the work of the official Vatican press office by a series of press centres run in each of the main languages under the aegis of the respective Episcopal Conference. The idea was that professional journalists could not be expected to have the necessary theological training themselves to analyse the complex issues under discussion, but if more fully briefed by experts could by in-depth coverage of the Council win a high degree of public interest in its proceedings.

His Holiness approved the plan, and it was in fact an undoubted success. The German press centre was set up in the main house of the Salvatorians in the Via della Conciliazione, very close to St Peter's Square. There a press conference was held every Wednesday evening, attended not only by newsmen, but also by many others interested in the Council, those working in Rome and others merely passing through. Each week one of the Council Fathers or Theologians expounded on the current subject of debate in the Council; this was always followed by a lively discussion. And after each session of the Council the then president of the German Episcopal Conference, Cardinal Frings, gave a reception in the Hotel Columbus for German speaking journalists.

Alongside the official events there were also numerous informal contacts with journalists, observers and guests of the Council. Of particular value and importance were the links thus established with the many Protestant visitors. A good example of the outreach to professional media men was the group visit by the heads of all the West German radio stations. They stayed several days, attended a sitting of the Council, heard a talk by Cardinal Josef Ratzinger (then a young professor), and were received in audience by Pope Paul VI.

By these means we ensured that the Second Vatican Council attracted a degree of public attention rarely given to Church affairs. After only a few sessions my collection of the more important press notices and articles (*Das Konzil im Spiegel der Presse*, Würzburg 1963/64) ran to two volumes. A certain number of errors and misinterpretations in press reporting was inevitable, but in general it can be said that the German media made every effort to present a fair and accurate picture of what took place at the Council to a wide section of the public.

The English, French, Spanish and Dutch press centres were equally successful. Liaison between the different centres ensured fruitful cooperation; and all relations with the media were coordinated by the conciliar press office, which issued a communiqué in all the principal languages after each sitting. With the conciliar press office there were representatives for each of the main languages, for German Professor Fittkau, who did sterling service in promoting interest for the Council and its work among the press corps.

THE CHURCH AND THE MEDIA

While all this liaison work with the world press was taking place behind the scenes more or less as a matter of course, it was perhaps more surprising that use of the media became itself a subject of conciliar debate. From the 23rd to the 26th of November 1962 the Council discussed the 'means of social communication', and a year later issued the Decree *Inter Mirifica* (4 December 1963), a document much criticized for its inevitably somewhat provisional character. But the mere fact that the Council had dealt with the matter at all shows the importance of the media in our time; and the Council Fathers themselves were well aware that the topic needed more work to be done on it. They therefore asked that an office for all means of social communication be established to draw up a Pastoral Instruction to give practical effect to their deliberations. Pope Paul VI accordingly set up the Pontifical Commission for the Instruments of Social Communication by means of the Motu Proprio *In Fructibus Multis* (2 April 1964); and this body published the Pastoral Instruction *Communio et Progressio* (29 January 1971). This latter document, prepared with the aid of internationally recognized experts, fulfils all the requirements left unsatisfied by the original Decree.

The two conciliar documents, *Inter Mirifica* and *Communio et Progressio*, need to be taken together as a whole. In both we read that information and the exchange of information (communication) are indispensable to modern society, and therefore to the Church as well. Because society is structured round large, and in many cases international, organizations which depend on the exchange of information, communications technology is an essential feature of our modern world. We are ever more dependent not on our own, immediate perceptions of reality, but on the observations of others. Experience shows the very real danger of manipulation by misrepresentation of reality whenever the means of communication are concentrated in too few hands, whether a monopoly is held by a political group or commercial interests. The Church must therefore speak out in defence of inalienable rights to freedom of information and equal access to the means of communication.

Modern communications technology thus represents a great danger to human freedom. But it also presents a wonderful opportunity to spread the Church's message to the farthest corner of the globe. Providence has given us the means to develop a truly catholic, world Church. What would the Pope's visits abroad and his addresses be, if they were not broadcast on radio and television? Saint Paul exploited the medium of the letter to spread the Gospel; now, just as at the time of the Reformation and Counter-Reformation the newly developed art of printing lent itself to the rapid transmission of ideas, the electronic revolution gives the Church a golden opportunity to make her voice heard throughout the world.

Behind the Council's concern with the media, however, lay a more fundamental problem, the subject in fact of the whole Council: *aggiornamento* – neither a superficial conformity to modern trends of thought, nor a 'sell-out' as some have later thought. Pope John XXIII had recognized deep-rooted changes in a society transformed by the Enlightenment, the development of empirical science, and technological progress. He knew that these outward changes had been accompanied by a spiritual revolution, which had dispensed with much of the old common heritage of European thought, and that the Church was ill-prepared to meet the challenge of these new circumstances. He was also well aware that in spite of the preliminary work done in response to the call of his predecessor, Pope Pius XII, it would take the combined efforts of the whole Church to adapt itself to the modern world: the task of updating the Church was beyond the competence of the papacy alone, and so John XXIII convened the Ecumenical Council to assist him.

The events of 1968, shortly after the close of the Council, showed how right John XXIII had been in his assessment of the situation facing the Church. Student revolts heralded an era of cultural revolution in the industrialized world, which saw a drop in Church membership comparable indeed to the losses incurred during the Reformation, the French Revolution or the rise of Marxism-Leninism. The rejection of received morality and belief was particularly striking among the younger generation.

Faced with such a crisis the Church had two options: to retreat in on itself, or to open itself up in dialogue with the new society. Two main schools of thought developed within the Church to advocate one or other of these options, and both parties are characterized by very different assessments of the value of Vatican II. The traditionalist school of thought considers the Council to have been the one great mistake of judgement made by a good, but old man; not even Paul VI could undo the damage begun. The ranks of the Church had been so weakened by the confusion and

loss of confidence wrought by the Council that they were unable to with-
stand the onslaught of anti-religious thought in the modern world; the
Council was thus no more than an embarrassing error of judgement and an
episode in Church history to be forgotten as soon as possible – the sooner
the restoration of the post-Tridentine status quo, the better.

The other, more progressive school of thought holds that the only thing
wrong with Vatican II was that it was fifty years too late: the Church
should have adapted itself in the first half of this century instead of committing itself to the hopeless task of combating modernism by means of strict
discipline. In many cases the conciliar reforms had come too late, but there
was no turning back now. The only way out of the Church's difficulties
was forward, along the path of continuing reform and modernization
indicated by the Council.

With reference to the specific question of the Church's use of the media,
there are again two options. One is to recognize the Church's task to bring
the good news of Christ to all men, including those who have become
estranged. She must therefore adapt her means of communication to the
times. If the Church is not to fulfil her missionary nature and purpose then
of course she has no need of modern communications technology; a few
tracts and religious pamphlets will suffice to strengthen the faith of those
who already belong, and in that case the Council might have spared itself
the trouble of producing a Decree, and the Church might have saved itself
the development of public discussion within her ranks as recommended by
Pope Pius XII. But this would have been to deny the Church her catholicity
and to reduce her to the level of a mere sect protected from the contamina-
ting influence of the modern world by being almost completely cut off from
it. It becomes clear when we consider the particularities of the Church in
relation to the mass media that the option of isolationism is not a viable
alternative for the Church after all, if she is to remain true to her nature.

This is not to say that the Church has not on occasion made mistakes in
the development of its use of mass media. Many ventures in the field of
newspapers, radio and television have failed, largely due to inadequate
planning and preparation: lack of finance, staff shortages, lack of support
from the ranks of the Church, and from project leaders a lack of determination to overcome the inevitable difficulties faced by any commercial undertaking. Naturally Church initiatives have also encountered a certain amount
of opposition peculiar to them from more hostile groups in society.
Sometimes the concentration has been on diversification to reach a broader,
non-Catholic public at the expense of providing a Catholic press for the
benefit of those who are already Church members. But these setbacks do

not invalidate the general principle that the Church should be expanding her media outreach.

If it is agreed that the Church is bound by her office to use the media to broadcast her message of salvation to society, we must also ask whether the Church should support society's own use of communications to promote understanding and cooperation between men. Her attitude towards the secular use of communications will be determined by her view of culture in general. If in Johannine terms we see the world as the realm of evil, it follows that the Church's relations with society must be determined by a wish to protect her members from intimate contact with that world. For too long the Church has in fact taken such a view of secular society. But the view expressed by Vatican II, most notably in its Pastoral Constitution on the Church in the Modern World, *Gaudium et Spes*, is very different. It sets out from the premise that there is a 'mystery of human history' (sec. 40), an interpenetration of things earthly and heavenly, and a reflection of the divine glory on to the whole of creation. This entails a positive attitude on the part of the Church towards human activity and achievement, a view repeatedly stressed by the present Pope, John Paul II. The Decree *Inter Mirifica* on the Means of Social Communication should be read in this context, although indeed it was produced two sessions (two years) before the composition of *Gaudium et Spes*, and therefore falls short of the maturity of outlook expressed in that late and great classic. Quite properly, the Pastoral Instruction *Communio et Progressio* of 1971 explicitly links the two documents.

The Council has often been accused of an unrealistic optimism in its view of the world, and it is certainly true that there is a great difference between the attitude of hope prevalent in the sixties and the underlying deep anxiety of the eighties. The Council did not ignore the effects of sin, but saw in them a calling to share 'the joy and hope, the grief and anguish of the men of our time' (*Gaudium et Spes* sec. 1) and a challenge to counter and overcome the suffering of man separated from God.

Twenty years on, there are signs of renewed interest in spirituality both within and outside the Church. This is particularly welcome since it counteracts the effects of a possible over-concentration on the Church's social outreach; but equally it is important that the balance does not now move too far towards spirituality at the expense of continuing to evangelize and engage with an increasingly hi-tech society using its own hi-tech means of communication.

The missionary situation facing the Church is thus continually changing over the decades, but it is also possible to discern a broader pattern of change over the centuries. In the first millennium the Church had to fight for her very existence in a hostile, pagan society that was also deeply religious and a great influence on the piety of the early Christians. The second millennium has been characterized by the situation of those Churches in Europe and America which found themselves almost subsumed under the state authorities of their respective nations. Characteristics of the third millennium can already be observed in our own time: the Church coexisting in a pluralist society alongside a multitude of other faiths, ideologies and philosophies of life, all competing on a global scale for the hearts and minds of men, and no single one (with the partial exception of the anachronistic phenomenon of Marxism-Leninism in the eastern bloc) able to achieve a monopoly within a state. Any of these faiths may choose to withdraw from missionary outreach, and it may survive such a retreat into isolationism, but only at the cost of self-mutilation.

CONCLUSION

As the Church approaches her mission in the third millennium after Christ, the aims and methods of social communication are of the greatest theological and pastoral importance. The Church exists to communicate. In the latter part of the twentieth century the technology of mass communication has proliferated dramatically. The Second Vatican Council paid particular and close attention to all the means of social communication. It might therefore reasonably be expected that the Church would in the twenty years after the Council have taken great care to update its use of the media to spread its message of salvation across the world. Yet, despite the present Pope's own skill in media presentation, the Church as a whole is still found seriously wanting in this area of its work. Indeed her influence and presence in public life has actually declined. In the case of the Decree on the Means of Social Communication, then, the post-conciliar Church has failed lamentably to put into practice the Council's teaching and recommendations; and I would suggest that the correction of this shortcoming should soon be given a new priority in planning for the Church's future.

13

PRAYING TOGETHER:
COMMUNICATIO IN SACRIS IN THE
DECREE ON ECUMENISM

GEORGE H. TAVARD AA

When at the Stoll Theatre in May 1941 Archbishop William Temple and Cardinal Arthur Hinsley chose to pray the Our Father in ecumenical brotherhood, they were regarded as having gone beyond the bounds of suitable sharing. When even the Korean veterans wanted to bury their dead together after combat together in defence of the principles of the United Nations Charter, they found that they had to pray separately. By degrees, with pain and with patience, the Churches of Christendom have been able to come together in worship and supplication, if not yet in sacramental co-operation. Intercommunion does occur privately, even on public occasions; but it publicly awaits a closer relationship of Churches, as a sign of achievement rather than as a sign that furthers achievement.

On this matter the foremost essay in English before the Council came from Fr Maurice Bévenot SJ of the Secretariat for Promoting Christian Unity (in Christian unity; a Catholic view, Sheed & Ward 1962, 114–39); though it soon became a period piece. He wrote hearteningly: 'What is new and unprecedented is not the existence of heresies, nor the effort to recall heretics by argument or persuasion, but the common admission that friendly relations do not involve any surrender of principle.' The Anglican/Roman Catholic Malta Report of January 1968 echoed this in its section 18: 'The question of accepting some measure of sacramental intercommunion apart from full visible unity is being raised on every side. In the minds of many Christians no issue is today more urgent. We cannot ignore this, but equally we cannot sanction changes touching the very heart of Christian life, eucharistic communion, without being certain that such changes would be truly Christian...'

Educated at Caen and Lyon, Georges Tavard worked for Documentation Catholique. From 1959 he has been an ecumenical theologian in America. Since 1970 he has been Professor of Theology at the Methodist Theological School in Ohio. His writings before the Council include Holy writ or holy Church: the crisis of the Protestant Reformation *(Harper 1959); and* Two centuries of ecumenism *(Indiana 1960). The Council over, he wrote* The pilgrim Church *(Burns & Oates 1967). Most recently he has written* Justification: an ecumenical study *(Paulist Press 1983). With the subject of this chapter he was directly involved at the Council.*

The purpose of this paper is to survey the history of the writing and official interpretation of the text of Vatican II on prayer in common or *communicatio in sacris* (Decree *Unitatis redintegratio*, sec. 8). The survey will be made with the help of unpublished material which is still in my hands and which I shared as a council *peritus* directly involved in writing this text. I will draw to some extent on personal remembrance, but I will refer to other persons by name only where such an identification already belongs to the public domain. Such a survey should help to understand the scope of the decree. It should also assist in assessing the evolution of thought on the point in question since the Vatican Council, and, if necessary, to judge the current demands for some sort of 'intercommunion' and the widespread and still generally unauthorized practice of receiving and giving communion indiscriminately.

This study should also suggest that there is an inside history of the texts of Vatican II that is still to be written. It would seem urgent to investigate this history before all the bishops and *periti* of the council have passed away.

The code of Canon Law of 1917 included the following canon 1258:

1. It is not licit for the faithful actively to assist, that is, to take part in, 'sacred functions' of non-catholics.

2. May be tolerated a passive or purely material presence, for reason of civil office or of honour, for a grave motivation, which in case of doubt must be approved by the bishop, at funerals, nuptials, or similar solemnities of non-catholics, provided that there is no danger of perversion or scandal.[1]

This canon was itself extended and protected by other canons, which applied similar principles to *communicatio* with excommunicated Catholics (canon 2259: 2261, # 2–3), and by others which foresaw penalties for delinquents. According to canon 2316, anyone who 'communicates *in divinis* with heretics against the prescription of canon 1258' is automatically suspect of heresy. While this is not the proper place for a study of the origin, meaning, and intent of these canons, one may note the discrepancy between canon 1258, which speaks of 'non-catholics', and canon 2816, which speaks of 'heretics', and the apparent assumption of canon 2316 that the non-catholics of canon 1258 are heretics. This naturally raises the question whether the non-catholics of canon 1258 included both Western Protestants and Eastern Orthodox, and also whether for purposes of common prayer, non-catholics were always considered heretics in the formal or material sense of the term.

It is fair to note that the application of these canons was never uniform. In fact, some *communicatio in sacris* with Orthodox Christians has always been practised in countries like Lebanon or Syria. Acceptance of Orthodox faithful at the sacrament of reconciliation has never been unusual in areas with many Orthodox. In regard to the churches of the Reformation, however, the practice has always been stricter. Nonetheless, in some parts of Western

Europe, the notion of 'merely passive assistance' was taken broadly, as implying simply non-reception of communion; in others, such as Ireland or England 'merely passive assistance' was taken to mean that one must not take part even in congregational singing. There was in fact a debate, in England, shortly after the Second World War, on whether it was permissible to recite the Lord's Prayer together with other Christians, and even if it was licit to receive the blessing imparted by a bishop of the Church of England. This debate was illustrated by a lengthy exchange of letters in the columns of the London *Times* at the end of the forties.

In the work of the Secretariat for Christian Unity, the question of *communicatio in sacris* was raised for the first time during the session of 14–15 November 1960, the first plenary meeting of the Secretariat after its creation by John XXIII. A limited number of participants (members and consultants) had been invited to submit written remarks and suggestions to be taken as bases for discussion of the work of the Secretariat. Two of these raised the question of prayer in common; one of them envisaged also *communicatio in sacris* properly so called.

The first suggestion, to judge from its contents, comes from England:

> It would perhaps be useful and in keeping with charity to enlarge the application of the moral principle expressed by Moldin in these words: 'Thus a Catholic may licitly recite the Lord's prayer or other prayers together with a Protestant, for in this action there is no profession of a false religion: a private worship in which nothing false is contained is not heretical' (Moldin: *Theologia Moralis*, II, 1926 ed., p. 38b). One should perhaps examine whether Catholics could pray more frequently with non-Catholics for the public good or for a private good, provided that, (a) the prayers be approved by the Church, (b) they take place outside a Protestant church, without the participation of a non-Catholic minister and without Protestant sacred rites. In England, non-Catholics commonly resent the fact that Catholics are never willing to pray in any circumstances with non-Catholics, even outside a church.[2]

As one can see, the suggestion is simply to allow the common recitation of the Lord's Prayer and other prayers approved by the Church, on the basis of the opinion of a somewhat conservative moral theologian. In terms of probabilism, this was an appeal to extrinsic probability in favour of shared prayer. This suggestion went no further.

The other allusion to the problem of canon 1258 is part of a longer and more theological document. I believe it originated in Belgium. The reference to our question runs as follows:

That, where possible, there be encouraged common prayers for unity, for peace, for other common necessities. That, for instance, common endeavours with the World Council of Churches be continued for the promotion of common prayers on the occasion of international political events. That common meetings for extra-liturgical praying or singing be promoted. Hence one should better see and declare when, on occasion, some *communicatio in sacris* may be authorized.[3]

Compared to the proposal from England, this is relatively advanced: the suggestion is not just for sharing the Lord's Prayer, but for frequent praying in common for causes of general interest to humankind. Further, a revision of canon 1258 is explicitly suggested, with the proposal for deeper study of the cases when some *communicatio in sacris* could be possible. In these two texts one may sense the ambiguity of the concept of *communicatio in sacris* as it was understood before Vatican II: does it include only sharing sacraments and official liturgies (strict interpretation, the only one, I believe, that could be defended canonically) or does it extend to prayer in general (broad interpretation)? The English text takes the broad interpretation for granted, and wants to change the law. The Belgian text assumes the strict interpretation, but also considers that the law can and ought to be changed.

At this meeting the projected task of the Secretariat was divided among ten subcommissions. Two of these could properly have envisioned an alteration of the law and the practice regarding prayer in common and sacramental sharing between Catholics and other Christians: the sixth subcommission, entrusted with liturgical questions, and the eighth, charged with a study of the octave of prayer for Christian unity and the forms under which it was in use in different places (the Wattson and the Couturier forms).

The subcommission on liturgical questions (VI) finished its work first. As its recommendations were to be passed on to the conciliar commission for liturgy rather than directly to the council, its report had to be finished early enough to be considered by the commission for liturgy.

The first draft of the report was drawn up by the Archbishop of Rouen, Cardinal Martin, mostly on the basis of a preliminary draft authored by myself. It is dated 13 January 1961. It contains the following passage:

8 – *Communicatio in sacris*

Le principe qui interdit la 'communicatio in sacris' pourrait être sauvegardé tout en en assouplissant l'application. Les chrétiens séparés les mieux disposés trouvent difficile à concevoir que les catholiques refusent de prier avec eux.

On ne peut évidemment pas admettre une participation active à une célébration de la Cène où l'Eglise ne reconnaît pas la présence réelle du Christ. Mais là où l'Eglise reconnaît cette présence réelle (chez les Orthodoxes), il serait souhaitable que les catholiques puissent, pour des raisons proportionnellement graves, prendre part aux cérémonies liturgiques.

Avec les chrétiens séparés d'Occident (Anglicans, Luthériens, Protestants) il serait bon de permettre une participation, pour des raisons graves et 'absque scandalo', aux réunions de prières non eucharistiques, quand les prières utilisées ne contiennent pas d'hérésie explicite.[4]

This text was debated at the plenary session of the Secretariat of February 1961 at Rocca di Papa. Worth noting is the remark of Mgr H. Francis Davis, from England:

Est-ce que l'on pourrait ajouter: Même pour des raisons moins graves on pourrait permettre, 'remoto scandalo', en dehors du temple protestant, et en dehors des services officiels ou liturgiques protestants, des prières communes entre catholiques et protestants? Par exemple, s'il y a un instituteur catholique dans une école d'état où l'on permet des prières publiques, est-ce que l'on ne donne pas plus de scandale si on ne permet pas à l'instituteur de commencer la journée par une prière commune avec les élèves?[5]

Following this session, the report of the subcommission was rewritten in the light of the discussion. The statement on *communicatio in sacris*, dated 21 February 1961, was not modified in this revision. It was put into Latin, and came out in the following form:

(G) *COMMUNICATIO IN SACRIS*

The principle which prohibits *communicatio in sacris* could be retained so that its application be flexible. For separated Christians, even with the best dispositions, do not easily understand that Catholics will not pray with them.

It is obvious that actual participation in some celebration of the Supper in which the Church does not recognize the real presence of Christ cannot be permitted; but where the Church recognizes this real presence, that is, among the Orthodox, it would be desirable that Catholics, under conditions to be determined, could somehow participate in liturgical ceremonies. With Western separated Christians, that is, Anglicans and Protestants, it would be good if some participation were allowed, for valid reasons and without scandal, in non-eucharistic services, when the prayers contain no explicit heresy, especially when these services take place outside a religious building.

Votum IX

That the law by which *communicatio in sacris* is forbidden be softened, so that the separated Christians may pray together when the ceremonies and prayers contain nothing that contradicts the Catholic faith.[6]

The final version of the recommendation was presented to the Secretariat at its session of 15–18 April 1961. While the introductory explanation remained intact, the *votum* was slightly expanded:

That the notion of *communicatio in sacris* be clarified, so that, without scandal and with the approbation of the Ordinary, the Catholic faithful and separated brethren may pray together, at least outside sacred ceremonies, provided that, in these common exercises, nothing be done or said which contradicts the Catholic faith.[7]

As endorsed by the members of the Secretariat before the end of this same session, the *votum* was identical, with a grammatical change in the last clause, which was also shortened: '. . . may pray together, when in the meeting nothing is done or said which contradicts the Catholic faith'.[8] In this form the recommendation was passed on, along with others, to the Liturgical Commission. All were in fact incorporated in the conciliar decree on the Liturgy, except the one on *communicatio in sacris*. One may presume that the Liturgical Commission considered this particular question to be outside its own competence. But the early concern of the Secretariat about the problem was to bear fruit later.

Subcommission VIII, dealing with the question of the 'octave of prayer for Christian unity', did not broach the question of joint prayer with other Christians, and still less that of *communicatio in sacris*. Yet the problem surfaced unexpectedly in subcommission III. Originally created to examine the relative merits of individual conversion versus organic reunion and, for reasons that are not clear to me, to look at the 'restoration of the diaconate' from an ecumenical angle, this subcommission had its mandate enlarged to include *de oecumenismo catholico et de opere conversionum*. Understood in a broad sense, this mandate, which became effective with the second plenary meeting of the Secretariat (February 1961), could include a general treatment of the ecumenical movement. A subcommission IX was to look more specifically at what was called 'the central ecumenical question', namely the World Council of Churches and its relation to Catholic ecumenism. As yet, there was no intention of composing a conciliar decree *de motione oecumenica*.

At the plenary session of 26–31 August 1961, which took place at Bühl, Germany, a long report *De oecumenismo catholico* was presented by the theologians of subcommission III (chairman Thils, from Belgium; Mgr Thijssen, from the Netherlands; and Mgr Davis, from England). The idea was to provide a document with a theoretical section on 'the ecumenicity of the Church', and a practical-pastoral section dealing directly with the ecumenical movement and its practice by Catholics. Whether this would be promulgated by the council or be left for the Secretariat for Unity to publish it later was not clear, nor, for that matter, was it certain that the Secretariat itself would survive the Council. The practical section of the report included a long passage on prayer, under the title, *Activité de prière et de culte*. This is too long to reproduce here. The text distinguished between four kinds of prayer: (1) 'religious and prayerful silence'; (2) 'general prayers which do not reflect specific dogmas' (curiously enough, the Lord's Prayer was placed in this category); (3) a more organized prayer led by 'pastors or spiritual leaders', which, however, is not official worship; and (4) 'cultic, liturgical, confessional prayer'. The text noted the desire of fervent Christians in many Churches to be able to pray together, at least with the first three sorts of prayer. It then broached the question of 'participation in an official cult', this being taken as amounting to *communicatio in sacris*. After a reference to canon 1258, #2, it noted a recent canonical interpretation of the difference between material and formal participation: material participation simply corresponds to the fact of participating; formal participation refers also to the motive, when this is precisely to take part in the official liturgical worship of a given Church. The text then asked: *Ne serait-il pas possible d'élargir la portée du canon 1258, #2, en faveur de tous les fidèles amenés à participer à des activités oecuméniques, ou du moins à des groupes bien déterminés dans des activités plus limitées?*[9]

After remarking that this was a delicate question which should have different solutions in regard to the Orthodox and to the Churches of the Reformation, the text continued: *Un degré de progrès paraît possible et devrait être accompli.*[10] The text then asked for a broad permissiveness in relation to 'unofficial religious ceremonies', to 'religious silence', and to 'general prayers'. It further asked that the people of the Church be truly encouraged to pray with others, in order 'publicly to lament their lack of unity and to sing their praise of Christ as Lord and Saviour'.

At the plenary session of 27 November–2 December 1961, sub-commission III proposed a number of *vota* as the epitome of its longer report. *Votum* VI ran as follows:

> That common meetings be organized, to which the Catholic and Protestant faithful would be invited, in order, not to hold theological discussions, but to increase the desire to union and to promote prayers for unity. For all can and should pray. Let sincere non-Catholics and Catholics set an example of faith and trust in the power of prayer before God. Let such meetings begin with the common recitation of the *Pater Noster* and of other prayers approved by the Church. Let them take place outside churches, in order to avoid all suspicion that this is *communicatio in sacris*.[11]

After discussion, this was expanded into three complementary *vota*:

Votum sextum:

That the faithful be exhorted to pray and to make sacrifices for this goal of unity. For all can and must pray for whatever they should wish to have. Let sincere Catholics and non-Catholics set an example of faith and trust in the power of prayer before God.

Votum sextum bis:

Identical with the first part of the original *votum*, down to 'prayers for unity'.

Votum septimum:

That, as regards unity in prayers, the law of *communicatio in sacris* be understood more broadly for ecumenical gatherings. That, scandal being removed, above all through the instruction of the faithful, all prayers and non-sacramental acts of worship that are not led by the minister of a separated community, be approved for all ecumenical gatherings.[12]

At this same meeting of November 1961, the original number of sub-commissions was increased to fifteen. Subcommission XIV was to 'prepare a directory on Catholic ecumenism', which could provide the substance of a conciliar decree, were this to become necessary, or be issued after the council. As a basis for the work of this sub-commission, an outline entitled, *Directorii oecumenici prima delineatio*, had been prepared and was presented to the Secretariat with explanations and elaboration. Under Part II, #2, c, the outline had:

c. *Oratio et cultus*:
   1) *factum et momentum de spiritu 'religioso'*
   2) *preces approbatae: Pater, Psalmi, etc...*
   3) *de 'Hebdomada pro unitate' ejusque sensu...*
   4) *de ceremoniis plus minusve liturgicis...*
   5) *de communicatione in sacris...*

In order to appreciate these early orientations of the Secretariat for Unity towards a revision of the law concerning *communicationem in sacris*, one should remember that, at the very same time, the Theological Commission for the council was working at its projected constitution *de Ecclesia*. In this, a chapter was foreseen that would examine 'ecumenism' (ch. XI). In this chapter, as it was eventually distributed to the fathers and *periti* of the council, a sec. 54 was entitled, *de communione in sacris liturgicis*. This was a long section of nearly three pages (p. 83–85 in the edition of 1962). The chief effect of it, had it been approved by the council, would have been to reinforce a strict interpretation of canon 1258. The heart of this passage was contained in the statement: 'The same inviolable doctrine on the unity of the Church generally forbids an active assistance of Catholics in the sacred rites of separated communities.'[13] The text, however, ended on a short paragraph which was due to have an influence on the corresponding section of the eventual decree on ecumenism: 'By no means is it licit to consider true *communicatio in sacris* as a means to be used universally which could lead to a renewed unity of all Christians in the one Church of Christ . . .'[14]

When the council opened on 11 October 1962, the Secretariat for Unity had therefore in hand, not a *schema*, since there was no talk yet of a decree on ecumenism, but several *vota* relating to 'ecumenism' and to 'the Church's ecumenicity'. It also had partial drafts or outlines on (1) prayer for unity, (2) the Word of God, (3) religious liberty. None of them referred to common prayer or *communicatio in sacris*. The concern of the Secretariat, at that moment, was more basic: it was to attempt to insert an ecumenical note into the work of the Council. There was as yet no way of foreseeing how far the bishops would be willing to go along this line. The task done by the preliminary Theological Commission scarcely permitted any optimism in regard to the ecumenical dimension of the council. But the picture changed dramatically as soon as it became clear that there was widespread dissatisfaction with the work of the Theological Commission, especially with its *schema De Ecclesia*. The implications of this were drawn by the council itself, on 1 December 1962, when it decided, by a vote of 2083 to 36, that the Secretariat for Unity should prepare a document which would incorporate elements from the *schema* on 'the Unity of the Church'[15] prepared by the Commission for the Oriental Churches, elements from the last chapter, 'On ecumenism', of the rejected *schema* on the Church, and an expanded version of the *vota* already prepared by the Secretariat.

In keeping with this resolution, the Secretariat formed several sub-commissions, made of *periti* and bishops, to work along the proposed lines. The first version of the new document, the decree on ecumenism, was distributed to the Council fathers in May 1963.

This first version of the decree included, in Chapter II, sec. 7, a passage on prayer under the subtitle, *De oratione unanimi*, which was drawn largely in the spirit of abbé Couturier. It encouraged prayer in common with 'separated brethren', but it made no effort to overcome the hurdle of *communicatio in sacris*. It even explicitly excluded participation 'in an official cult' and ended with the complaint: 'However, these links, alas, flourish only in part and imperfectly, and furthermore it is not licit to celebrate together the sacred mysteries of the eucharist'.[16]

As this second chapter was debated at the council on 25, 26 and 27 November 1963, a number of bishops asked for a positive statement on the possibility of some shared liturgical participation among separated

Christians, especially, but not exclusively, in relation to the Orthodox. Patriarch Maximos and the Melchite synod, the episcopal conference of Argentina, bishops in Italy and in France, especially in the regions of Bordeaux and Avignon-Marseilles, the Japanese Cardinal Matsuo Doi, and several other bishops asked for an up-dating of the law on *communicatio in sacris*. Several of these and a few others wanted also to eliminate the negative reference to 'official cult'. Some urged that a distinction be made as to what is possible in sharing prayer and worship with Orthodox and with Protestants.

In keeping with these debates and the recommendations made in writing to the Secretariat, Chapter II was re-written and, along with it, the section on prayer. This became sec. 8. Of the last three lines (the above cited complaint), only the word *Attamen* was retained. The text continued with a sentence borrowed, with some modifications, from sec. 54 of the initial *schema* 'On the Church' already quoted: 'it is not licit to consider *communicatio in sacris* as a means to be used universally (soon to be changed to *indiscriminatim*, then to *indiscretim*, "indiscretely") to restore Christian unity'.[17]

For the rest of the passage, which provides the theological basis for a limited liturgical and sacramental sharing, I may rely on my remembrance of the events. In February 1964 (the exact date escapes me), meeting at the residence of Bishop Willebrands on Monte Mario, five *periti* were given the task of rewriting sec. 7 (now become sec. 8). Besides Michalon as the original author of sec. 7, there were Gregory Baum, Jerome Hamer, Emmanuel Lanne and myself. Hamer chaired the meeting. At some point in our discussion of the issue, prior to writing anything on *communicatio in sacris*, one of us stated, approximately: 'The idea is simple; the problem is how to express it properly. There are two principles involved. The liturgy is an expression of unity. But it is also a means of grace. As an expression of unity, it presupposes oneness. As a means of grace, it brings it about.' Just then, word came that this person had a telephone call. While he was gone, I wrote a couple of Latin sentences formulating what he had said in French, the most common language of this small group. When he returned from the telephone, I read my sentences aloud. A few words were changed in it. And this became the statement of the decree on ecumenism concerning *communicatio in sacris*.

This new version was approved by the Secretariat at its session of Ariccia (25 February to 7 March 1964). Along with the whole of Chapter II of the proposed decree on ecumenism, it was introduced formally to the Council by Bishop Helmsing of Kansas City, Missouri, on 6 October 1964. Bishop

Helmsing's *relatio* had in fact, at his own request, been composed by myself. As I remember, only one word in it was taken out when it was discussed by the Secretariat before its approval as the official *relatio* for Chapter II. The relevant passage throws light on the intended meaning of sec. 8:

> III. To promote this conversion of the heart it is most useful, and even necessary, to pray for unity; this must be encouraged everywhere, even in fraternal association with Orthodox and Protestant Christians. To this purpose very many Fathers have asked that the Decree on Ecumenism propose some positive principle regarding *communicatio in sacris*, so that, with the approbation of episcopal authority, that is, of the Ordinary or of the Episcopal Conference, all Christians may join in common prayers, even liturgical, at least at certain times. Since circumstances differ widely in different regions, such a principle should be general enough, so that the bishops may decide individual cases and prudently instruct the faithful. This principle, which consists, so to say, of two dialectical parts, is found in sec. 8. Prayer in common and the general principle regarding *communicatio in sacris* will be the subject of vote 3 in our chapter.[18]

On 6 October 1964, this number 8 was approved by the Council with the following vote: *Placet* – 1872; *non-placet* – 292; *null* – 2. On 7 October the chapter as a whole was approved: *Placet* – 1573; *non-placet* – 32; *null* – 5; *placet juxta modum* – 564.[19]

The next step had to do with sorting out the numerous amendments that were proposed, in and out of the sessions, by many bishops. I was assigned the task of studying those that affected sec. 8, of classifying them, presenting them to the full Secretariat, and making recommendations about them. My *synopsis modorum circa numerum 8*, dated 20 October 1964, spreads over three thickly typed pages. There were in fact over seven hundred requests, many of which cancelled one another out. At this stage, only amendments that conformed to the sense of the text could be accepted, since the text itself had been endorsed by the previous votes. As a result of this rule, only the last sentence was modified. The new version specified more carefully which 'episcopal authority' was competent: it was the authority of the Ordinary, unless other decisions had already been made by episcopal conferences for their region or by the Holy See. A summary of these amendments with the responses of the Secretariat takes two and a half pages in *Modi . . . examinati. Caput II: De oecumenismi exercitio* (Typis polyglottis Vaticanis, 1964, pp. 7–9).

In this form, the passage on shared prayer was returned to the Council along with the rest of Chapter II. It was approved with this chapter in its new form on 11 November 1964: *placet* – 2021; *non-placet* – 85; *null* – 3.

Finally, the entire decree was approved on 20 November: *placet* – 2054; *non-placet* 64; *placet juxta modum* – 6 (invalid, since at this stage no amendments were acceptable); *null* – 5.[20]

As it seems to me, the history of the decree on ecumenism and of its sec. 8 throws light on the intent of the text and accordingly on the meaning of the council's position concerning common liturgical worship in an ecumenical context. The mind of the framers of the decree went through several stages. First, it was widely felt that the law excluding all *communicatio in sacris*, as embodied in canon 1258, could not possibly be altered. All concessions in favour of joint prayer would have to exclude official liturgical acts of cult; and prayer led by a minister was equated by some to an official act of cult. Second, the suggestion was made that some steps could be taken in the direction of more common worship, even of an official or liturgical kind; yet it was not clear whether the Secretariat itself, given its function in the preparation of the council, would have the authority to make the necessary proposals. At some stage along the way, some were prepared to admit a fairly wide practice of common prayer, but not if this was led by a Protestant minister (leader of prayer). Third, as it became apparent that the Secretariat would have responsibility for a full-sized decree on ecumenism, the Secretariat was still reluctant to propose a radical alteration of the relevant canon. Yet there also existed, both in the Secretariat and in the council at large, a current of opinion that favoured such a step. Fourth, at the request of bishops, the Secretariat introduced consideration of *communicatio in sacris* in its sec. 8.

The sense of this expression was clarified in response to requests 'for more precision'. *Communicatio in sacris* designates directly 'participation in sacraments', and indirectly 'participation in worship and prayer'. Further, rather than simply state a law, the Secretariat established a theological principle, namely that of the double aspect of worship, as expressive of unity and as channel of divine grace. Relating this principle to the situation of disunity, it concluded that, as expressive of unity, worship chiefly (*plerumque*) forbids joint participation; yet, as channel of grace, it sometimes (*quandoque*) recommends it. These two aspects of the ecumenical scene were called, in Bishop Helmsing's *relatio*, 'dialectical'. I understand by this expression that the two aspects cannot be really isolated from each other. A dialectical relationship implies that each side relates intimately to the other in creative tension. This is the key to the adverb, *indiscretim*, which is used at the beginning of the passage. *Indiscretim* is not the equivalent of the word, *universally*, which preceded in the first redaction of the text. In fact, the

213

different terms used in the successive forms of the decree clearly indicate the mind of the Secretariat for Unity in proposing the relevant passage to the Council: from *universaliter* to *indiscriminatim* to *indiscretim*. I do not find the adverb *indiscriminatim* in the dictionaries. It is a made up word with the connotation of 'discrimination/non-discrimination', and it therefore refers to personal subjective judgement, as when one is advised to combat racial discrimination. *Indiscretim* I find in the dictionaries, at least in the better form, *indiscrete*. It refers to an objective non-separation and, by extension, to an 'inseparability'. Accordingly, *indiscretim* does not mean that *communicatio in sacris* may be practised, not indiscriminately but discriminately or with discretion; it means that the two aspects of communion (means of grace, and expression of unity) cannot be separated. *Indiscretim* means 'indiscretely' in the sense of 'indiscontinuously', rather than 'indiscreetly' in the sense of something needing to be done 'with discrimination'.

Common sacramental worship cannot be used indiscriminately to further Christian unity, because its two aspects cannot be separated. One of them, however, may, in certain circumstances, prevail and have priority over the other. Should one follow – the more frequent case according to the text – the principle of abstention, because the unity to be expressed in worship does not yet truly exist? Or – the less frequent case – can common worship, being a channel of grace, be practised as such by specific persons in specific circumstances? One should look carefully, intelligently, at the circumstances of time, place, and persons before reaching a conclusion. But in this case the person who will make the decision needs to be qualified to make it. This is why the text refers, in keeping with the present structure of authority in the Catholic Church, to the three levels of episcopal authority, namely the ordinary, the episcopal conference, and the bishop of Rome.

In the years which followed the Council, the Secretariat for Unity issued a series of instructions which confirmed its understanding of sec. 8 of the decree. On 14 May 1967, the first part of its 'Directory' was published under the title, *Ad totam ecclesiam*. On 7 January 1970, a 'declaration' composed in French, *Dans ces derniers temps*, spoke directly to the problem of the growing practice of unauthorized 'intercommunication' (to use a very misleading, yet widely accepted, term). On 1 June 1972, an instruction, *In quibus rerum circumstantiis* again spoke explicitly of the growing problem of widespread intercommunion. And once more, on 17 October 1973, it was felt necessary to issue a clarification of *In quibus* . . . ; this was in Italian, *Dopo la pubblicazione* . . .

The doctrine of these documents is constant: 'There is *communicatio in sacris* when anyone takes part in the liturgical worship or in the sacraments of another Church or ecclesial community' (*Ad totam* . . . , sec. 30).[21] A distinction is made between this liturgical participation and *communicatio in spiritualibus*, a phrase which is used 'to cover all prayer offered in common, common use of sacred places and objects . . .' (sec. 29). While 'Christians should be able to share that spiritual heritage they have in common, in a manner and to a degree permissible and appropriate in their present divided state' (sec. 25), this should be done only when 'a certain reciprocity' is possible (sec. 27). The principle of reciprocity rules out 'intercommunion', at least with Churches and communities whose orders and eucharist are not recognized by the Catholic Church:

> sec. 55. Celebration of the sacraments is an action of the celebrating community, carried out within the community, signifying the oneness of faith, worship and life of the community. Where this unity of sacramental faith is deficient, the participation of separated brethren with Catholics, especially in the sacraments of the eucharist, penance, and anointing of the sick, is forbidden. Nevertheless, since the sacraments are both signs of unity and sources of grace, the Church can for adequate reasons allow access to those sacraments to a separated brother . . . A Catholic in similar circumstances may not ask for these sacraments except from a minister who has been validly ordained.[22]

The circumstances in question are danger of death and urgent need, along with the absence of a minister of the person's communion; there should also be a faith 'in harmony with that of the Church'.

If this seems more restrictive than sec. 8 of the decree on ecumenism, the interpretation provided in the next document, *In quibus* . . . enlarges the perspective: 'Sec. 55 of the Directory allows fairly wide discretionary power to the episcopal authority in judging whether the necessary conditions are present for these exceptional cases.'[23] It also allows them to judge whether other cases, unforeseen in the text, are also proper exceptions: 'Christians may find themselves in grave spiritual necessity and with no chance of recourse to their own communion.' These points are repeated in *Dopo la pubblicazione*, where the 'basic principles' are formulated once more:

> a) There is an indissoluble link between the mystery of the Church and the mystery of the eucharist, or between ecclesial and eucharistic communion . . .
> b) The eucharist is for the baptized a spiritual food . . . [24]

Again it is specified that 'it is the local ordinary's responsibility to examine these exceptional cases and make concrete decisions' (sec. 6).[25]

Through all these documents the Secretariat for unity did not vary from the principles set out in sec. 8 of the decree on ecumenism. 'Exceptional circumstances' are left to the judgement of the ordinary as long as the principle of the decree is respected. But the Secretariat has never admitted a practice of 'intercommunion' that would be justifiable only for ecumenical reasons. This idea, which had been broached early in the Secretariat's discussion of such matters, was never accepted. Ecumenical groups (whether ecumenical dialogues or retreats or specific meetings of the Cursillo movement, Marriage Encounters, or 'charismatic' or other gatherings) should not become elite groups in the Church with a special dispensation in regard to liturgical worship and the reception of the sacraments.

It has not been my purpose in this paper to discuss whether a celebrating priest may never give communion to a Protestant Christian by way of exception. The principles set out by the Vatican Council and reaffirmed by the Secretariat for Unity deal with general cases. Exceptional cases are left by law to the discretion of the Ordinaries. Further exceptions may be admitted only in keeping with general principles of law, or moral theology, of liturgical principles and rules, and of the discipline of the sacraments.

The perspective opened by the Secretariat for Unity and Vatican Council II on *communicatio in sacris* has now been embodied in the new Code of canon law.

On the one hand, the ministers of the eucharist may licitly give communion only to Catholics, and Catholics may licitly ask for communion only from Catholic ministers (canon 844 # 1). On the other, 'whoever is baptized and is not prohibited by law (*jure*) can and must be admitted to holy communion' (canon 912).[26] The contradiction between these two canons reflects the paradoxical situation of divided Christianity. Between these two principles there lies a grey zone of exception. In danger of death, and when according to the judgement of the diocesan bishop or the episcopal conference there is another grave necessity, 'the sacrament may be given licitly to other Christians who are not in full communion with the Catholic Church, if they have no access to their own ministers, they ask for it of their own accord, and provided they share the Catholic faith toward the same sacraments and they are properly disposed' (canon 844, # 5).

With these new canons the difficult journey from canon 1258 of the code of 1917 has temporarily ended. It may resume again, if ever the principle embodied in canon 912 becomes theologically more important than the principles which lie behind the legal restrictions of canon 844. Then the proper question will be: Is the *lex* of canon 844, # 1, truly identical with the *jus* of canon 912? Whatever answer may be given to this question it will have to be framed within the principles of the decree on Ecumenism, n. 8: the two aspects of the sacraments, as expressions of ecclesial unity and as means of grace for the individual faithful, are dialectically related.

NOTES

1. Canon 1258: #1. *Haud licitum est fidelibus quovismodo active assistere seu partem habere in sacris acatholicorum.*
   #2. *Tolerari potest presentia passiva seu mere materialis, civilis officii vel honoris causa, ob gravem rationem ab Episcopo in casu dubii probandam, in acatholicorum funeribus, nuptiis similibusque solemniis, dummodo perversionis et scandali periculum absit.*

2. *Esset forse utile et caritati consonum applicationem extendere principii moralis his verbis a Moldin expressi: 'Sic licite catholicus cum protestante simul orationem dominicam vel alias preces recitare potest, quia in hac actione non continetur professio falsae religionis: privatus enim cultus, in quo nihil falsi continetur, non est haereticus' (Moldin, Theol. Moralis, II, ed. 1926, 38b). Consulendum forsitan catholicos frequentius cum acatholicis preces communes pro bono publico vel privato fundere, dummodo, a) preces sint ab Ecclesia approbatae; et, b) extra templum protestanticum et exclusis ministro acatholico et ritibus sacris protestantibus fiant. In Anglia acatholici communiter aegre ferunt catholicos nunquam et in nullis circumstantiis cum acatholicis, etiam extra templum, orare velle.*

   (Unpublished material). Where I give no reference, the text will come from unpublished material in Xeroxed form. The translations will be mine. In principle, the Latin text will be in the note, even when it is the original text. I will include the French text in the body of the article when it is the original.

3. *Ubicumque sit possibile, foveantur communes preces pro unitate, pro pace, pro ceteris necessitatibus communis. Continuentur v. gr. communes labores cum Consilio Universali Ecclesiarum in promovendis precibus communibus occasione eventuum politicorum internationalium. Promoveantur conventus communes extra-liturgici precandi vel cantandi causa. Exinde profundius videri ac declarari deberet in quantum in casu aliqua concedi posset 'communicatio in sacris'.*

4. 'The principle which forbids *communicatio in sacris* could be kept while its application is made more flexible. Separated Christians with the best dispositions find it difficult to conceive that Catholics refuse to pray with them. One can obviously not permit an active participation in the Supper where the Church does not recognize this real presence. But where the Church recognizes this real presence (among the Orthodox), it would be desirable that Catholics could, for proportionally grave reasons, take part in liturgical ceremonies.

   With the separated Christians of the West (Anglicans, Lutherans, Protestants), it would be good to permit a participation, for grave reasons and without scandal, in non-eucharistic prayer meetings, when the prayers that are used do not contain explicit heresy.'

5. 'Would it be possible to add: Even for less grave reasons one could permit, without scandal, outside a Protestant church and outside official or liturgical Protestant services, common prayers among Catholics and Protestants? For instance, if there is a Catholic teacher in a state school in which public prayers are allowed, does one not give more scandal by not allowing the teacher to start the day with a common prayer with the pupils?'

6. *Principium quo prohibetur communicatio in sacris retineri possit ita ut illius applicatio mitigetur.*

Etenim Christiani separati, quamvis optime dispositi, non facile intelligunt Catholicos cum ipsis orare nolle.

Ut patet, nullo modo admitti potest participatio actuosa celebrationi cuidam coenae in qua Ecclesia Christi praesentiam realem non agnoscit, sed ubi Ecclesia illam praesentiam realem agnoscit, nempe apud Orthodoxos, optandum esset ut Catholici, conditionibus quidem determinandis, caeremoniis liturgicis quodammodo participare possint.

Cum Christianis separatis occidentalibus, Anglicanis scilicet et Protestantibus, bonum esset ut participatio quaedam permittatur, validis quidem rationibus et remoto scandalo, ad functiones non eucharisticas, quando preces nullam explicitam haeresim continent, praesertim cum functiones illae extra aedificia religiosa haberentur.

VOTUM IX:

 Ut mitigetur lex qua vetatur communicatio in sacris, ita ut Christiani separati simul orare queant cum caeremonia et orationes nihil habent quod fidei catholicae contradicat.

7. *Ut elucidetur notio 'communicationis in sacris', ita ut, remoto scandalo et approbante Ordinario loci, fideles catholici et fratres separati, saltem extra sacra, simul orare queant, dummodo in illis communibus exercitiis, nihil fiat vel dicatur quod fidei catholicae contradicat.*
8. *. . . simul orare queant, cum in coetu nihil fit vel dicitur quod fidei catholicae contradicat.*
9. 'Would it not be possible to widen the scope of Canon 1258, # 2, in favour of all the faithful who may be led to take part in ecumenical activities, or at least for well defined groups that are engaged in more limited activities?'
10. 'A degree of progress seems possible and should be achieved.'
11. *Coetus communes proponantur ad quos fideles catholici et protestantes invitentur, in finem, non discussiones theologicas habendi, sed spem unionis excitandi, et adorationes pro unitate exhortandi. Orare enim omnes possunt et debent. Homines sinceri acatholici et catholici dent exemplum fidei et confidentiae in potestatem orationis apud Deum. Hujusmodi coetus incipiant communi recitatione PATER NOSTER et aliarum precum ab Ecclesia approbatarum. Habentur extra ecclesias, ita ut suspicio communicationis in sacris evitetur.*
12. *Votum sextum:*
 Adhortentur fideles ad orationes et sacrificia in hunc finem unitatis. Orare enim omnes possunt et debent pro omni re quam cupire tenentur. Homines enim sinceri catholici et acatholici exemplum dent fidei et confidentiae in potestatem orationis apud Deum.
 Votum sextum bis:
 [Identical with the first part of the original *votum: coetus communes . . . exhortandi.*]
 Votum septimum:
 Quod ad unitatem in precibus attinet, lex communicationis in sacris in conventibus oecumenicis latius intelligatur. Excluso praesertim per fidelium instructionem scandalo, omnes preces et cultus non sacramentales quae non a duce communitatis separatae dirigantur in omni conventu oecumenico approbantur.
13. *Eadem inviolabilis de unitate Ecclesiae doctrina assistentiam quoque activam catholicorum in sacris ritibus sejunctarum communitatum generatim prohibet (Schemata constitutionum et decretorum de quibus disceptabitur in Concilii sessionibus. Series secunda: De Ecclesia et de B. Maria Virgine.* Vatican City: Typis polyglottis, 1962, n. 53, p. 84).
14. *Minime ergo veram communicationem in sacris considerare licet veluti medium universaliter adhibendum quod ad unitatem omnium christianorum in unica Ecclesia Christi restituendam conducere valeat . . . (Schemata constitutionum et decretorum de quibus disceptabitur in Concilii sessionibus. Series secunda: De Ecclesia et de B. Maria Virgine.* Vatican City: Typis polyglottis, 1962, n. 53, p. 85).
15. Text in *Schemata . . . Series prima,* p. 250–268.
16. *Attamen nexus isti, pro dolor, solummodo ex parte ac imperfecte vigent, ac propterea Eucharistiae*

sacra mysteria in unum simul celebrare non licet (Schemata...: Schema decreti De Oecumenismo, 1963, p. 16).

17. ... *communicationem in sacris non licet velut medium universaliter* (soon changed to: *indiscriminatim*, then to *indiscretim*) *adhibendum ad christianam unitatem restaurandam (Schemata Decreti De Oecumenismo*, 1964, p. 15).

18. III. *Ad hanc conversionem cordis promovendam valde utilis est, immo et necessaria, oratio pro unitate, quam oportet ubique suscitare et, rerum adiunctis consideratis, etiam in fraterna consociatione cum Christianis Orthodoxis et Protestantibus. Ideo permulti Patres postulaverunt ut Decretum de Oecumenismo aliquod positivum principium proponat circa communicationem in sacris, ita ut, judicio auctoritatis episcopalis, id est, sive Ordinarii loci, sive Conferentiae Episcopalis, omnes Christiani possint in communibus, etiam liturgicis, orationibus saltem ad tempus coadunari. Quia rerum adiuncta valde differunt in diversis regionibus, tale principium debet esse sat generale ita ut Episcopi possint de singulis casibus iudicare et Christifideles instruere secundum prudentiam. Hoc principium, ex duabus – ut ita dicam – dialecticis partibus constans, in ultima paragrapho numeri 8 invenitur. – De oratione unanimi et de generali principio circa communicationem in sacris fiet votatio III nostri capitis. (Relatio super schema emendatum decreti De Oecumenismo*, 1964, p. 8–9).

19. *Acta synodalia S. Concilii Oecumenici Vaticani Secundi*, vol. III, p. VII, Vatican City: Typis polyglottis, 1975, p. 412–413.

20. *loc cit.*, p. 451 (11 November); vol. III, p. VIII, 1976, p. 636–637 (20 November).

21. Austin P. Flannery (ed.), *The Documents of Vatican II*, New York: Pillar Books, 1975, p. 493; following references, pp. 493; 492; 493.

22. *loc cit.*, p. 499.

23. *loc cit.*, p. 558–559.

24. *loc cit.*, p. 560.

25. *loc cit.*, p. 561.

26. Cf. *Code of Canon Law: Latin-English Edition*, Washington, D.C.: Canon Law Society, 1983, p. 319 (can. 844 # 1); p. 341 (can. 912) (my translation). A full study of the question in the new code should include consideration of canons 908 (which forbids concelebration with priests or ministers of Churches that are not in full communion with the Catholic Church) and 1365 (which specifies that persons who are guilty of forbidden *communicatio in sacris* should receive a suitable penalty).

14

CHRISTIANS AND JEWS:
A NEW VISION

JOHANNES CARDINAL WILLEBRANDS

When in November 1960 the Secretariat for Promoting Christian Unity (SPCU) members and consultors met for the first time, the President, Cardinal Augustin Bea SJ told them they were to undertake 'the question of treating the Jews not on its own initiative, but at the express command of Pope John XXIII'. He added that, foreseeing difficulties, the Pope requested that even the fact of initial discussion and drafting be treated sub secreto.

What emerged on 28 October 1965 was the Declaration on the Relation of the Church to Non-Christian Religions,[1] in which for the first time in history a General Council acknowledged the search for the absolute by non-Christian races and peoples, and honoured the truth and holiness in other religions as the work of the one living God. It was the first time also that the Church had publicly recognized the universal presence of grace and its activity in the many religions of mankind, giving glory to God especially for his enduring faithfulness towards his chosen people, the Jews.

This chapter originated as the 1985 Cardinal Bea[2] Memorial Lecture, delivered at Westminster Cathedral by his Secretary and successor at SPCU, who had himself worked on this Declaration from the outset. Notes have been added by the Editor (A.J.S.)

Johannes Gerard Maria Willebrands was born in 1909 and was brought up in Bovenkerspel in the Netherlands. Called to the priesthood, he studied philosophy and theology at the major seminary of Warmond, Holland. Ordained in 1934, he went on to graduate studies at the Angelicum in Rome, receiving a doctorate with a dissertation on 'The illative sense in the thought of John Henry Newman', a furrow fairly well ploughed since then at doctoral level, but pioneer in those days. For the three years till the War, he returned to be chaplain/curate to the Begijnhof church in Amsterdam.

In 1940 Willebrands became Professor of Philosophy at Warmond, and in 1945 director of the seminary. The following year he was appointed President of the St Willibrord Association, a society to promote ecumenical work in the Netherlands.

In 1951 he organized 'The Catholic Conference for Ecumenical Questions' (CCEQ), a group of Catholic theologians, mainly from Europe, which met almost annually to discuss trends. From the outset it maintained relations with the World Council of Churches and especially with its Faith & Order Commission, even before the Vatican Council had traced the outlines of ecumenical initiatives. Of this, Père Congar made due comment: 'I have often marvelled at the ways of God. When John XXIII created the Secretariat for Promoting Christian Unity on 5 June 1960 and made Cardinal Bea its President, the latter chose as secretary Mgr Jan G. M. Willebrands who had no difficulty in finding numerous collaborators among the members of the CCEQ which (since 1951) has continued to lead a free and independent existence. At the moment when the Holy See emerged from semi-absenteeism in ecumenical matters, it found the ground tilled and sown with thickset and high grown grain.'[3]

220

Mgr Willebrands at once established a mass of official and unofficial contacts with other Christian communities and with such international organisations as the WCC. During the course of the Council he was responsible for receiving the non-Catholic Observers and for drafting documents leading to the Decree on Ecumenism, the Declarations on Religious Freedom and on the Relation of the Church to Non-Christian Religions; and to a substantial part of the Constitution on Divine Revelation. And so on 28 June 1964 Willebrands was consecrated a bishop by Paul VI; and when Cardinal Bea died in November 1968, he naturally succeeded him, being created a Cardinal Deacon at the next consistory in April 1969, as President of the Secretariat for Promoting Christian Unity. When he became Primate of Holland and Archbishop of Utrecht in December 1975, and a Cardinal Priest, it was Paul VI's express wish that, though he could not give his full time to Rome, he should remain President of SPCU. In December 1983, Cardinal Willebrands did resume his duties in Rome on a full time basis, having given eight years to the leadership of the Church in Holland.

The year 1985 happens to be the twentieth anniversary of the Vatican Council's Declaration *Nostra Aetate* on the Church's relationship with Non-Christian religions. Conciliar documents come, in the last analysis, from the Holy Spirit and – as Pope John Paul II has told representatives of the Jewish community in Venezuela[4] – from the Divine Wisdom. Once promulgated, they belong to the whole Church. That being so, it should in no way diminish the importance of the role of persons chosen by Providence to be instruments of the Wisdom and the Spirit of God.

In the present case, it was Cardinal Augustin Bea, the first President of the Secretariat for Promoting Christian Unity who was such a person. He was in fact not only the mind behind, but the heart within, the hand upon the text of this Conciliar Declaration we commemorate. I am happy to witness to this remarkable link between the person and the work, hoping that this link will never fade from the memory of the Church. This brings me to the heart of my subject; and its presentation should, I believe, include three different dimensions, so to speak:

a reference to the past, to the work of the Council itself;
a reference to the immediate past, what is being done since the Council;
a reference to the future, what remains to be done.

WHAT WAS DONE AT THE COUNCIL

I do not think it my task here to narrate history for the sake of history itself. The history of how the Declaration *Nostra aetate* came about should by now be well known. It has been told, among others, by Cardinal Bea himself in the commentary he wrote on that document.[5]

What I would like to do here is to highlight some points, historical and theological, which I believe have a bearing on the unique importance of the

Conciliar Declaration and the impact it has already had and should still have in the Church.

The first point is the fact that 'the Jewish question' was ever given a place on the Council's agenda and despite some (as they are now called) technical incidents,[6] was kept there. That this is an absolute *unicum* should not be obscured by the fact that we now have the Declaration, and have gone a long way towards putting it into practice. Some Councils, it is true, have had Jews and Judaism written into their agendas, mostly in a negative light. Such is the case of the Fourth Lateran Council (1215), which however had its positive side. The Council, in fact, specifically forbids forced baptism of the Jews.[7]

Never before has a systematic, positive, comprehensive, careful and daring presentation of Jews and Judaism been made in the Church by a Pope or a Council. This should not be lost sight of.

There were indeed difficulties and crises. Could it have been otherwise? The remarkable thing would have been if there had been none or if, on the other hand, the difficulties had not been overcome. The former would have meant that there was no problem with the Jews and Judaism; the latter, that the Church was not mature enough for a document like *Nostra Aetate*. One and the other supposition have proved to be wrong.

The great merit of John XXIII,[8] as the visionary or prophet he was, is to have taken before God the fateful decision of including the Jewish question in the Council's agenda. And a still greater merit is to have kept it there when it had been suppressed. In each of these historical steps, the man called to implement the first decision and the man behind the second was, needless to say, Cardinal Bea. To the Pope and the Cardinal we therefore owe the conception (so to speak) of the document; as we owe to Pope John's successor in St Peter's office, Pope Paul VI, and always to the same Cardinal, the nurturing and the growing process – a painful growing process indeed – of that small embryo.

The difficulties in the way of the document were mainly of two sorts. This is enlightening, because they somehow forecast the shape of the things to come.

Some were *theological* difficulties: how to express the role of the Jewish people in relation to the Church; how to deal with difficult biblical texts which at first sight might seem intractable for a positive presentation of Judaism; what to do with the intervention of some Jews in the death of Jesus on the Cross, and the accusation of deicide?

Others were *political* difficulties. It may seem unexpected that a *conciliar* document, on a *religious* subject, should raise *political* problems. But this is only another instance of the sometimes inextricable interrelation between different realms of the reality we live in. It is also an example of the different, and even at times divergent, ways in which a selfsame text can be read under different lights. However that may be, Cardinal Bea and myself, as his close collaborator, literally went out of our way to make it crystal clear to all and sundry that the text now called *Nostra aetate* is religious in its inspiration, religious in its concern, and religious in its orientation.

It was Cardinal Bea's task and his privilege to introduce to the Council Fathers the four successive stages of the document on the Jews, from first to last; something which he did not do for *Unitatis Redintegratio* (the Decree on Ecumenism) even at the stage when *Nostra aetate* was to be a chapter of that Decree.

In those four presentations, the text of which has been available in English for many years, the Cardinal faced and solved the theological, historical and even political difficulties just mentioned, at least to the extent that these last impinged upon the meaning and the wording of the text. It would perhaps not be a waste of time to go over them again even today, so as to establish a clear idea of what exactly is the weight of each and all of the sentences of *Nostra aetate* in its final draft, and their carefully balanced structure.

The Cardinal's presentation obviously convinced the Conciliar Fathers, as the successive votations demonstrate. The last and decisive one, on 28 October, was positive beyond all expectation: only 250 negative votes against 1763 votes in favour and 10 abstentions.[9]

Who could have foreseen such a vote at the start of the long gestation, five years earlier? It is important to note that the Church, through her bishops, was united on the question of how to relate to the Jews and Judaism, not torn apart by it. And this has been, and remains, the solid guarantee of the changed, renewed attitude towards Jews and Judaism in the Catholic Church. It is like a house built upon a rock – nothing can tear it down. More than one comment on *Nostra aetate* at this time, or even more recently, has taken this insufficiently into account. Regrettably so, I must say.

Let me underline what I believe are the very real, indeed quite revolutionary, contributions of *Nostra aetate*, as finally promulgated, to a new theological vision of Jews and Judaism and the corresponding new pastoral attitude towards both.

The Church, in the Council, 'remembers' her 'spiritual links with Abraham's stock'. There is, therefore, nothing less than a spiritual link, lying deep in the Church's mystery, which creates a kind of family relationship between the people of Israel ('Abraham's stock') and the Church. This link can be forgotten or obscured. It has again been brought to the living memory of the Church by the Council, to remain there. On this living memory the whole edifice of Christian-Jewish relations is built and it receives therefrom its permanent solidity.

Out of this theological affirmation all the rest flows, theologically and pastorally. It is, I am convinced, rather obvious that the Council did not intend to make explicit in the few pages of *Nostra aetate* all the possible theological and pastoral implications. This is the work the Church has to do, and in fact has already done, and of which stock is taken in this twentieth anniversary celebration.

That the Council itself was aware of some of these implications is clear from the first sentence of *Lumen Gentium*, sec. 16, the dogmatic Constitution on the Church, frequently overlooked in this connection, although it is extremely important.

The perspective is a different one here. The central subject is the People of God and the point to be made here is how other peoples are connected with this people. The first one is 'that people' (*populus ille*), who received the gifts and privileges from God, whence Christ came forth according to the flesh, who 'remains dear (to God) because of the fathers', his gifts and his calling being 'without repentance'. In this way, the *ethnic* reality of Israel is identified and described *theologically* with a series of quotations from the New Testament. The ring of this passage is unmistakable: it affirms the ongoing reality of Israel as a people, mysteriously chosen by God, and as such related to the Church. Or shall we put it the other way round: the Church related to Israel, Israel being what it is? Both perspectives are complementary. If *Lumen Gentium* has chosen the former, *Nostra aetate* has chosen the latter. Both should be kept in mind.

Nostra aetate has also faced two of the major problems, which have vitiated our relations with Judaism for centuries and were part and parcel of what Jules Isaac called *The teaching of contempt*.[10] Such a teaching was never perhaps so systematic as his title would seem to imply, but there is no doubt that both these points were the main support of it.

These two problems can be formulated as follows: The Jews were guilty of killing Christ and have since remained so. Therefore they bear upon themselves a kind of original sin with its corresponding condemnation, be it to eternal pilgrimage across the world and outside the land of Israel, or else to God's equally eternal disgrace, malediction and reprobation. Or worse still, to all these put together.

Said like this, it sounds impossible and unspeakable. However, accusations of 'deicide' and of being 'damned Jews' have said, sometimes even still say, nothing less.

Both these errors have been rejected by the Council. The Jews are not all of them, either in that time or since, guilty of killing Christ, whatever the role of the 'leaders of the Jews and their followers' in the Passion. Rather, this careful phrasing excludes the people as such from this guilt.

And it should not be taught in the Church that the Jews are, again as such, subject to God's malediction and reprobation, as if such were the right meaning of Holy Scripture. Therefore, even when faced with difficult or obscure texts in the New Testament (like 1 Thess. 2:15), the Christian, the theologian and the pastor, knows now how to interpret such texts and read them in a light more consonant with the whole message of the entire Bible, Old and New Testament.

In such a perspective, anti-semitism is well nigh impossible. If it is 'deplored' and not 'condemned' outright, as in the 1974 *Guidelines*,[11] this is only a way of expressing a consequence of the very harsh premises just exposed. One 'deplores' that such forthright, official interpretation of Catholic teaching has not yet seeped down to all concerned, nor is it heeded by those outside the Catholic fold (or indeed the Christian fold). But anti-semitic actions of any kind are and have been condemned, because of our common 'patrimony'. By one brother being hit, the other one is necessarily hit at the same time. And if one brother is killed, the other one (according to Genesis 4) is responsible for the killing.

These, then, are some of the highlights of *Nostra aetate*.

THE PERIOD AFTER THE COUNCIL

The Council was barely over when different and important initiatives sprang up all over the place to translate into the daily practice of the Church what had been officially promulgated in *Lumen Gentium* and *Nostra aetate*. This happened, I am sure, because the conscience of the Church had been deeply affected by the wording of the document, but even more so by the fact of its existence. It also happened because the other interested party, the Jews, or those many who are most interested in the attitude of the Church towards them, rightly realized that now was an opportunity for them to take the necessary initiative.

It would be tedious to review the very many documents, decisions and actions uttered in these last twenty years. That history has still to be written. However, those interested may at least follow the highlights in

225

several publications in various languages, which gather together the main documents (mostly official) published since, although none is exactly up-to-date.[12] Whenever such a publication comes out, it is always one document behind. Granted, documents are not all. But they are extremely important, nay decisive. Decisions and actions, on the other hand, cannot be catalogued in books. They are mostly arguments for the media; and in these what is wrong or distorted finds its place much more easily than what is right.

Let me refer here briefly to at least some of the more important decisions taken by the Holy See for the implementation of *Nostra aetate*. Already in 1966, the Secretariat for Promoting Christian Unity, whose responsibility it was to follow and promote the implementation, called a Dutch Bible professor, Dr Cornelius Rijk, to take care of this entirely new task. To have somebody in the Roman Curia concerned with relations with Judaism was an absolute novelty. Professor Rijk, under Cardinal Bea's direction, had to find his own way in a field not yet tilled – or tilled the wrong way. (The Sisters of Sion know well what such beginnings meant.)

A first need to be met was the preparation and publication of an official document for the application of the Conciliar Declaration, as foreseen by the rules of the Council itself. This document was finally drafted in 1974, under the title '*Guidelines*'.[13] Since it was made public at the beginning of 1975, we can well say that we are now celebrating its tenth anniversary.

The preparatory work took many years, again because the field was so new; the related experiences were not that many; and, last but not least, because it was addressed to the whole Catholic Church and therefore had to consider many different situations. All considered it is a remarkable piece of work and I am sure it has already done and will continue to do a lot of good. Some Episcopal Conferences (like the NCCB in the USA) have produced similar documents when ours had been published. Others followed suit, as most recently the Brazilian Episcopal Conference.[14] And the Vatican '*Guidelines*' could profit from those published before, as also from Cardinal Bea's commentary on *Nostra aetate*, published first in Italian and translated afterward into various languages.[15]

But even before the '*Guidelines*' were made public, our Jewish friends had approached the Holy See and proposed that we start an official dialogue group with the Jewish community, so as to have a regular occasion for meeting and together facing many different issues, some of which had lain between us for centuries. Those who approached us came from a new Jewish body, created for that purpose, the International Jewish Committee on Interreligious Consultations (IJCIC), which at that time brought together five major Jewish organizations, some of them worldwide. The

Holy See accepted their proposal and the so-called *International Liaison Committee* was born in 1971.

It has met twelve times since, in various places (including Jerusalem and Rome, Toledo and Madrid, Regensburg in Western Germany). It is composed of official representatives on each side, the Catholic one including always at least two bishops. It has studied many and difficult, even conflicting, questions, like Mission and Proselytism; Faith, People and Land; Violence in the present world; Religious freedom; and, for two sessions, 'The Image of Jews and Judaism in Catholic Education' and 'The Image of Christianity in Jewish Education' – an ongoing subject of common concern. The agenda has not yet been exhausted nor will it soon be exhausted.

Similar Liaison Groups or Committees have sprung since, nationally and internationally, especially among international Church bodies, such as the World Council of Churches, the Lutheran World Federation, the Church of England, and even the Orthodox Churches. What has now become normal and does not provoke headlines anymore, was quite unexpected in 1971, and the fatefulness of the decision then taken by the two related bodies, the Holy See and IJCIC, for the first time in history, must not be lost sight of. Indeed, it should always be a source of inspiration and a continuing frame of reference for the International Liaison Committee in the tasks it is still called to do.

Again in 1974, an important date for Catholic-Jewish relations at the level of the Holy See, the *Commission for religious relations with the Jews* (CRRJ) was created, linked to, but distinct from, the Secretariat for Promoting Christian Unity. This is obviously another revealing fact. It means, of course, that things had got to a certain stage of maturity, in which a person and an office in the Secretariat were not enough, not only because of the amount of material work, but much more because of the ever growing and self asserting importance of the matter to be dealt with, namely, relations with Judaism. These relations, from the point of view of the Holy See, had gone beyond infancy and even adolescence and had entered adulthood. Fr Rijk had by that time left the Secretariat. Fr Pierre-Marie de Contenson OP had taken his place and thus became the first Secretary of the Commission. In that capacity he signed, along with me, the *Guidelines*, a permanent witness to his commitment in body and soul to Jewish-Christian relations in the Church.[16]

I am thoroughly convinced that the Commission has proved to be a remarkable instrument in relations with Jews and Judaism at large, whether organized or not, friendly or unfriendly, approving or disapproving – but mostly, of course, approving and friendly. It has also proved to be necessary for relating with the Episcopates around the world, and with religious Orders, theological Faculties, parish priests and faithful men and women. And last but not least, it has found its place and become a necessary instance, for matters Jewish inside the Roman Curia, again in itself a remarkable achievement with manysided projections and results.

Let me now refer to the Pope himself. It can be said, very truly, that whatever has been done in the Holy See for the implementation of *Nostra aetate* comes from the Pope, whether it be the creation of the Commission for relations with the Jews, or the inauguration of the international Liaison Committee or the publication of the *Guidelines*. But if anyone imagines that these are mostly administrative acts and that the Pope would not necessarily be concerned with such matters, he need only to look at the example personally set by the Popes to dispel this idea.

Paul VI expressed his feelings about relations with Judaism when he received the International Liaison Committee on the occasion of their meeting in Rome on 10 January 1975.[17] This text is worth reading even now, ten years afterwards. At a different level, however not less significant, it was Paul VI who first started the series of audiences to Israeli governmental leaders (Mrs Golda Meir was the first) which has continued till the present day. And, last but not least, he was the first Pope in many centuries to set foot in the Holy Land and the Holy City of Jerusalem.[18]

As to Pope John Paul II, his list of audiences to Jewish leaders, organizations, rabbis and ordinary men and women, is simply endless.[19] It must be said that the Pope's house is wide open to the Jewish people at large, no less than it is open to Catholics and other Christians. And many times these audiences are marked by important speeches which in some way make the point about the state of Jewish-Christian relations, the road we have travelled and the road still ahead. While journeying outside Rome, the Pope frequently meets Jewish representatives, from Germany to Spain, from Canada to Venezuela and Peru from Brazil (twice) to the USA and in England. On such occasions the Pope's speech sometimes expresses his thoughts on some aspects of our relations, or calls the local community to foster its relations with their Jewish neighbours, or energetically condemns anti-semitism. One such speech, the one delivered in Mainz (Germany) on 17 November 1980, could be read as a blueprint of the path dialogue with the Jews should follow.[20] But sometimes it is the Jews present who use the occasion to express to the Pope their wishes and desires, or their chief concerns in our mutual relations.

I have just mentioned anti-semitism. It will perhaps not be amiss to recall here the many times, during these last years, when the Holy See, mostly on behalf of the Pope, has strongly reacted against anti-semitic acts of violence, which sadly continue to endanger the peaceful existence of Jews in not a few places, even including Rome. It remains to be seen, however, whether Pope John Paul did not do more against anti-semitism and for the promotion of Jewish-Catholic relations in his own diocese of Rome, when he met with the Chief Rabbi of Rome, Professor Toaff, in the parish church of San Carlo ai Catinari, in February 1981, than when he made his strong condemnation of the attack against the Synagogue of Rome on 10 October 1982. However that may be, soon afterwards, in 1983, the diocese of Rome published its remarkable 'Guidelines for relations with Judaism', short but substantial and to the point.

I shall close this second section by stating something which, I believe, well illustrates what we have achieved throughout these twenty years. I think we have achieved two main results, one on the Jewish side, the other on our own. On the Catholic side, notwithstanding all that remains to be done (of this I am well aware as we shall see below), at least this is true: those who chose to ignore *Nostra aetate* and subsequent actions and documents, including the example of the Pope, are put in the situation of having to explain their attitudes, theological or pastoral. In other words, an attitude which repeats ancient stereotypes or prejudices, not to say one that is aggressive against Jews and Judaism, does not anymore have a right to legitimate existence in the Church. It may be there, and it may still be frequent in some places, but it has been put onto the defensive. It is not taken for granted, as it was – I fear – twenty years ago.

On the Jewish side, I would only say this: I believe a certain amount of trust has been generated, or at the very least an awareness of the right Jews have to be heard and paid heed to, as such, in the Catholic Church. This means that some, if not all, barriers have been torn down. And it means also, on our side (because both go hand in hand), that we in the Church, have become, or are becoming, aware of our historical and our theological responsibilities towards our elder brother, grounded in the link the Council spoke about.

WHAT REMAINS TO BE DONE

Jewish-Christian relations are an unending affair, as are love and brotherhood, but also (regrettably) hatred and enmity. The main point is to change the fundamental orientation, from hatred to love, from enmity to brotherhood. It is not a question only of deploying documents, or of particular actions, however highly placed those who act happen to be. It is a question of people, men and women of flesh and blood. Still more, it is a question of hearts.

Once the foundations had been laid in the Conciliar Declaration and the following documents, then the work had to be undertaken of helping people to change, those who were adults twenty years ago, those who have since become such, those who are still to come: and this all around the world, the Catholic Church becoming more and more true to her name, a universal reality. Now people have their agendas, their priorities, their day to day concerns, their cultural and historical inheritance. It is in the midst of all this that we have to go on planting the seed of a new Catholic vision of the Jewish people: in the midst indeed of a very diversified, always renewed, Catholic universal community. This is – I believe – no more, no less, the task that confronts us. It has taken around two thousand years to arrive at *Nostra aetate*. It cannot be expected that everything will be undone, magically, in twenty years, especially when it is a question of people facing people.

In this situation, the immediate task seems to be twofold – one part mainly on the Catholic side, the other mostly together with our Jewish brethren.

On our side we could be asked to put our own house in order, namely, to set aside prejudices and to have them replaced by new ideas, in accordance with what is now the official teaching of the Church. This is certainly necessary, and this is why Catholic-Jewish relations have to place so much weight on education, whether formal or informal, elementary or advanced, secular or religious, whether through catechetics, preaching, theology or public and private deeds. A lot has been done, including the correction of manuals and curricula; but a lot remains to be done.

Let me point out one thing among others, but something extremely important, which remains to be done in this particular field. It is fairly easy to dispel prejudices and correct stereotypes, respectfully perhaps but strongly: it is quite another matter to instil new ideas. To this end, a certain amount of systematizing is needed (or, as the Germans say, *Thematies-ierung*). The Conciliar Declaration and subsequent documents have made the main points. Now a certain theological organizing of such points is needed, in themselves, and in relation to other subjects of Catholic teaching and study, like, for instance, exegesis of the Bible. The Jewish question being so central to that teaching, it is certainly not surprising that a long and deep effort of reflection is required, to be translated thereafter into manuals, curricula and day to day school experience. If it is to be at all useful and permanent, this huge work has to be done with most careful attention to, and inspiration from, the true sources of Catholic doctrine. Adventurous theories and extravagant hypothesis are of no help here: indeed they are counter-productive.

I must say, and I am happy to do so, that a certain amount of work is being done in this entirely new field. But it is no secret how enormous and momentous is the task still to be done. It is a question of elaborating a new systematic Christian view, or rather theology, of Judaism, nothing less. And I would like, in this connection, to call upon theologians, Bible scholars and other dogmaticians to respond to this urgent challenge.[21]

Simultaneously, but I dare say at a faster pace, the revision of textbooks, manuals and similar, should continue. Here the office for Catholic education could be of much help, in collaboration with the Commission or offices for Catholic-Jewish relations (CJJR), wherever they exist. And I express here the hope that they become still more numerous than they are now. This last development would help bishops, bishops' conferences and parish priests to keep the Jewish communities in their own areas in their minds, where these exist, and also not to forget them in areas where there are no Jews. It will also give more credibility to our reaction against anti-semitic phenomena, wherever they crop up.

While it is almost universally acknowledged now that present anti-semitic attacks have nothing to do with religious prejudices, it is, however, always our own responsibility to condemn them strongly, following the Pope's example and that of many bishops everywhere. Therefore we need to have ready at hand the instruments to know, assess and react to what is going on. In this connection Jewish sensibilities should be respected and cared for, although they may not enter into our normal perspectives. I shall name only two here: the recent past history of Jewish suffering during the Nazi persecution, and the Jews' commitment and concern for the land of Israel; this concern is political or secular, but also, for many, it is religious. It belongs, I believe, to an exercise of Christian charity towards one's own brother, with whom we are seeking reconciliation for offences which are very real, not to gloss over this dimension even slightly. To carry the memory of many million deaths is a terrible burden; to have a place under the sun to live in peace and security, with due respect for the rights of others, is a form of hope. Here we have two important points of reference in Catholics' day to day relation to the Jews.

It is at this daily level of common living that relations among people of different religions or cultural backgrounds are really placed. We are all con-vinced, of course, that documents, decisions and deeds at the highest levels of Catholicism, and whatever may be a corresponding level of Judaism, are not only significant but absolutely necessary. A large part of this chapter has been dedicated to making and evaluating this point. But we are equally convinced, or should be, that the real challenge before us is to have those historic acts translated into daily practice and lived out in the lives of human beings. It is readily admitted that a certain amount of divergence between theory or belief, and behaviour is alas the common plight of all religious faiths. It is not, however, an excuse to allow matters to remain as they are.

On the Catholic side, with which I am now mainly concerned, I believe there are two main directions to be followed to bridge the gap between belief or official teaching, and daily practice, always presupposing what I have said about education and its requirements. The first direction has proved successful in ecumenical relationships, relations namely between Christian Churches and communities. It is sometimes called 'growing together', but what it really means is that people from different religious backgrounds, in the present case Jews and Christians, who in many places happen to live together, study and work together (ghettos leave only a sad memory), should meet as such. That is to say, they should meet as Jews and Christians, and try to confront together, on the basis of what they have in common, as religious men and women, the challenges and issues forming the texture of life in the present world. This implies in its turn that people are religiously committed and that some kind of religious grass roots organizations, like parishes and synagogues or students groups, or whatever, can serve as meeting places and also as irradiating centres. This is already being done in several places with good results. I earnestly hope this will develop elsewhere, and indeed everywhere. Of course the responsibility for this devolves in the first place upon the parish priest and the local rabbi; but also at another level, upon the Chief Rabbi and the local Ordinary, or again upon some kind of national Jewish organization and the Episcopal Conference. Each town, province, region or country has to find its own solution, according to local circumstances, which vary greatly from place to place. And we still have to find some other kind of solution, along other lines, for places where there are no Jewish communities, and likewise for Israel, where the Jews form a vast majority. Yet, I am convinced that this is a very important way to avoid replacing prejudice and enmity with mutual indifference and mere co-existence, or what is worse, with another, colder, form of the ancient discriminating practices.

Secondly, it is the normal presupposition for collaboration, common action, or, if we wish to use a Christian expression, common witness. Christians and Jews share many religious convictions, of which not only

Conciliar and other documents have made us aware, but even more so the situation of the present world, where God is absent, human dignity is baffled and oppressed and hope for the Kingdom to come is in danger of becoming an empty word – or an opiate. At different levels of society, whether it be in the case of a local catastrophe, or of some persecuted minority, or still, in a larger perspective, when large sections of the population of a continent languish with famine, or refugees are trying to find for themselves at least a shelter and a bed, Jews and Christians, right across the board, are called in the name of their common biblical heritage, to stand up and do something together – separately of course if it proves useful, but mainly together. And this not only because joint resources become more abundant and more easily organized, but in the first place because we both believe in the God of Abraham, Isaac and Jacob, and of Jesus, and in man his creature and his image. Help and assistance then becomes an act of faith; and therefore in the face of the world, but also in the presence of God and his angels, a witness to that faith. We all know that this road is already being followed in many places. Let us try to begin following it ourselves, if we have not yet done so.

I am not blind to the issues such a decision will raise, or has already raised. The main such issue also becomes, once the twenty years of first encounters have elapsed, one of the major challenges we have to face – perhaps the greatest. It thus becomes also a significant part of our task for the future. I refer to the asymmetry between our Catholic and Jewish communities or, better still, between Church and Judaism. The Church is a Church, a worldwide religious community orientated mainly to the glory of God and the ministry of salvation of those called to her bosom. It has, as such, no particular ethnic or cultural identity; every man and woman from any background should feel at home with her. Judaism is a very different matter. While defined by some as an instrument of redemption, it is at the same time, and almost in the same breath, a people with a definite ethnicity, a culture, with an intrinsic reference to a land and a State. These differences should by now be obvious, but it is an open question whether we are on each side well enough aware of all the implications thereof. It means, at the very least, that agendas do not always coincide, priorities are not necessarily the same and concerns can go very different ways.

Now, if with all this asymmetry we have arrived where we are in our mutual relations, we must gratefully acknowledge that the hand of the Lord is upon us and that we have been abundantly blessed by him. If the lessons of the past twenty years have taught us, painfully at times, to become more conscious of the differences and the identity proper to each side, it would seem that the task ahead of us must be that of finding ways and means to live together, grow together and witness together, in the respect – and even more positively, the appreciation – of such differences.

Catholics are wont to stress the 'religious' side of our relationship, as the official title of the Holy See Commission reads, because notwithstanding all political implications and perhaps even entanglements, we are first and foremost a Church, a God-orientated community in and through Christ. Jews sometimes stress the political dimensions of their people, because they are one, and no people exists in this world without some form of political identity. Now, if we were not linked as we are, and as Pope John Paul II once said 'at the level of our religious identity', it would be well nigh impossible to establish between us a real religious relationship, namely a brotherhood, given the differences that separate us.[22]

But the fact is that we are linked and there is no way of denying or obscuring this fact, as we Christians have learned to our loss. So, I believe the challenge lying before us in the years ahead in a world becoming more akin to a desert than to a living place, is to make the most of that link, which is God-given, whatever our differences and divergences. We are divinely called to this and I fear that if we do not live up to this call we will be faced with severe judgement before the Lord of history. This, I readily grant, may imply for many Catholics, if not all, a real, deep conversion of the heart, as Ezekiel prophesied in the sixth century B.C., a conversion indeed made manifest in contrition of many sins committed against the Jewish people.[23]

It is not for me to say what the same decision would imply on the Jewish side. However, I am sure that, whatever that may be, there is only one way to bring us together again, as sons and daughters of Abraham, distinct yet related, asking and receiving forgiveness, reconciled at last. And this is the Spirit of God coming upon us (as in Ezekiel's vision), in a way creating us anew; for it is only the God of Israel and Jesus, in whom we believe, that can pull down all barriers and draw hearts and minds together.

NOTES

1. *Nostra Aetate*: 'In this age of ours, when men are drawing more closely together . . .', AAS 58 (1966), 740–4 with English Translation SPCU; Walter M. Abbott SJ, *The documents of Vatican II* (Geoffrey Chapman 1966), 660–8; Austin Flannery OP, *Vatican Council II: the conciliar and post-conciliar documents* (Fowler Wright 1975/1981), 738–42; CTS booklet Do 360 (1966). Section 4–5 only, Thomas F. Stransky CSP & John B. Sheerin CSP, *Doing the truth in charity*: Ecumenical Documents I (Paulist Press 1982), 340f. Cf. Herbert Vorgrimler, *Commentary on the documents of Vatican II* (Herder &

Herder/Burns & Oates 1968), III, 1–154, this section by Mgr John M. Oesterreicher = a consulting member of SPCU. Cf. *Idem, The rediscovery of Judaism: a re-examination of the Conciliar statement on the Jews* (1971).

2. Augustin Bea SJ (1881–1968), from Swabia. In 1924 he was appointed to the Pontifical Biblical Institute in Rome, of which he became the Rector (1930–49). For thirteen years he was confessor to Pius XII. In 1959 he was made a Cardinal, and the following year founder President of SPCU.

3. *Dialogue*, 41.

4. On 28 January 1985.

5. A. Bea SJ, 'The Church and the non-Christian religions', *The Month* (Jan 1966), 10–20, reprinted in *The way to unity after the Council* (Geoffrey Chapman 1967); *The Church and the Jewish people* (1966).

6. Oesterreicher *op cit* 41ff, 'The "Wardi Affair" – the first setback', etc.

7. Philip Hughes, *The Church in crisis* (Burns & Oates 1961), XII. The Fourth General Council of the Lateran, 183–92 esp 190. Christians were protected against Jewish money-lending rapacity; Jews were to wear distinctive dress, so that no Christian might unknowingly marry them; during Passiontide they were put under house curfew; no Jews were to be elected to public office, lest they held authority over a Christian.

8. Oesterreicher *op cit* 4–8, 'The initiatives of John XXIII'. See Excursus below.

9. Oesterreicher *op cit* 128f records these figures; but adds: 'On 28 October, the day of the promulgation, another solemn vote was taken. 2312 bishops voted for, 88 against the Declaration and three votes were invalid.'

10. Jules Isaac, *L'Enseignement du mépris*. His appeal to John XXIII in the summer of 1960 was reproduced in *Du redressement nécessaire de l'enseignement Chrétien concernant Israel* (1960).

11. *Guidelines and suggestions for implementing the Conciliar Nostra Aetate (N.4) Declaration*, AAS 67 (1975), 73–9. It was issued by CRRJ on 1 December 1974, text in French. ET by SPCU in Stransky & Sheerin, 342–7; Flannery *op cit* 743–9.

12. The Cardinal cites instances: 'Stepping stones for Jewish-Christian relations', and 'Le Chiese cristiane e L'Ebraismo'.

13. See note 11 above.

14. In November 1983.

15. See note 5 above.

16. Fr Rijk and Fr Contenson both died soon afterwards, untimely deaths.

17. AAS 67 (1975), 95–7 in French. ET, Stransky & Sheerin 347f. Dr Gerhard Riegner, Secretary General of the World Jewish Congress, first addressed the Pope, saying that the Jews 'are happy that Christians have been invited to learn by what essential traits the Jews define themselves in the light of their own religious experience. We hope that this effort will lead to a greater appreciation of the essential significance that peoplehood and land hold in the Jewish faith.'

18. 4–6 January 1964, Amman-Nazareth-Mount of Olives. Cf. Oesterreicher *op cit* 56–9. Paul VI was 'the first to dare to speak of peace on both sides of the Israel-Arab border'.

19. Stransky & Sheerin 348ff.

20. AAS 73 (1981), 78–82; Stransky & Sheerin 357f, ET Stransky. Pope John Paul began: 'If Christians must consider themselves brothers and sisters of all men and women, and behave accordingly, this holy obligation is all the more binding when they find themselves before members of the Jewish people!'

21. The Cardinal himself responded in the Oxford Union on 13 March 1985 with a lecture, 'Is Christianity anti-semitic?', ms 1–17. He looked at both Testaments and at the

235

Fathers, and at inherited modern prejudices. He pointed out that the decree of the Congregation of the Holy Office, AAS 20 (1928), 104 explicitly condemned anti-semitism; and that in September 1938 Piux XI had said to Belgian journalists that 'we are all, spiritually, semites'. Christianity is absolutely not anti-semitic.

22. AAS 71 (1979), 435–8; Stransky & Sheerin 350–2. This was a speech addressed to the representatives of episcopal Conferences and other experts in Jewish-Christian relations, Rome, 12 March 1979.

23. Ezekiel 36:26f: 'I will give you a new heart and put a new spirit within you; I will take the heart of stone from your body and give you a heart of flesh.'

Excursus on Angelo Roncalli/John XXIII & The Jews:
He began the Second War as Apostolic Visitor in Istanbul by helping Polish Jews on their way to Israel. During the course of the War he was said to have 'helped 24,000 Jews with clothes, money and documents' (evidence of Franz von Papen, German ambassador to Turkey). At his coronation Mass in 1959, the new Pope preached: 'Through the events and circumstances of his life, (he) is like the son of Jacob who, meeting with his brothers, burst into tears and said "I am Joseph your brother".' In his first encyclical some months later he repeated that telling phrase. When on 17 October 1960 he gave audience to 130 Jews from USA, he told them the story about Joseph recognizing his brothers, and went on: 'I am your brother. Certainly there is a difference between those who admit only the Old Testament as their guide, and those who add the New Testament as the supreme law and guide. But the distinction does not abolish the brotherhood that comes from a common origin. We are all sons of the same father. We come from the Father, and must return to the Father': Peter Hebblethwaite, *John XXIII, Pope of the Council* (Geoffrey Chapman 1984), 186–8, 192–6, 295–7, 333–4.

15

'TOIL IN THE LORD':
THE LAITY IN VATICAN II

DEREK J.H. WORLOCK

One's mind goes back to an essay of Newman's, 'On consulting the faithful in matters of doctrine', more read today than when it first came out, thanks to a good and timely edition by John Coulson (Geoffrey Chapman 1961). He is to be thanked also for an ecumenical symposium during the Council, Theology & the university (DLT 1964), which included a valuable section, 'An educated laity – problems and opportunities' (p. 25–104).

The Laity Decree, Apostolicam Actuositatem, had a long history – indeed five years of gestation. By the end of the First Session of the Council more than half of its original draft had been either excised or taken over by other decrees such as that on the Church in the world, the Church's missionary activity or its ecumenical activity. It became clear that the laity is involved in the whole mission of Christ in and with his Church. The drafters found no precedent, there being as yet no official teaching on the lay apostolate nor even a theology of the laity. When Lumen Gentium, the Constitution on the Church, put forward a fresh theology of the People of God, its implication for the laity urgently needed to be spelled out. A growing educated laity, more responsible and more active in a Church served less by priests and religious, required a document of guidance; for, as the Decree states, 'modern conditions demand that the (lay) apostolic activity be more intense and broader'.

Ordained from St Edmund's College, Ware in 1944, Derek Worlock was private secretary to successive Archbishops of Westminster (Cardinals Bernard Griffin, William Godfrey and John Carmel Heenan) during the twenty years of 1945–64. As such, he played a considerable part in organizing or orchestrating the responses of English prelacy; and his testimony to this is the collection he edited, English bishops at the Council (1965). He attended all Sessions as a peritus, and the last in his own right as Bishop of Portsmouth. During 1967–76, as a result of his conciliar interest, he was a Consultor to the Council of the Laity; and from 1977 he has been a member of the Pontifical Laity Council and Committee for the Family. Now Archbishop of Liverpool, he was chairman of the National Pastoral Council, Liverpool 1980; and helped to draft the episcopal response, The Easter People (St Paul Publications 1980).

The feast of the Immaculate Conception, 8 December 1965, was one of those bright but cool days in Rome which justify holding a religious ceremony in the open air and enable participants to risk sun-stroke and pneumonia simultaneously. With less hair on my head than that with which I had processed into St Peter's for the opening of the Council just over three years earlier, I was fortified by the instruction that for the first time in my life I must wear a skull-cap: but not yet an episcopal ring.

Although I had been named a bishop six weeks earlier, I had to wait another fortnight for what in those days was still called 'consecration'.

THE CHARTER ON THE CHURCH

So we assembled before the basilica which had been our Council Chamber and various messages to the world were boldly proclaimed before we, Fathers of the Council, should return to our people with the glad tidings of renewal. At the concluding assembly in St Peter's the previous day we had been given a clear mandate by Pope Paul VI. Everything was to hinge on the new insights into the nature of the Church which had been drawn together in our source document, the Dogmatic Constitution *Lumen Gentium*. Its various applications were to be found in what must be regarded as subsidiary decrees. But the manner of our approach to a still largely unsuspecting world was now set forth in the Pastoral Constitution, *Gaudium et Spes*.

'This Council can be summed up in its ultimate religious meaning' Pope Paul had said at the session on 7 December 'as nothing other than a pressing and friendly invitation to mankind of today to rediscover in fraternal love the God "to turn away from Whom is to fall, to turn to Whom is to rise again, to remain in Whom is to be secure, to return to Whom is to be born again, in Whom to dwell is to live".'

If it had not been for the pressing proximity of my new duties, the recollection of all we had been through since that shock announcement of 25 January 1959 might have been overwhelming. As in any long conference there had been moments of crisis and times when elation followed hard-won achievements. At that stage it was quite impossible to foresee what reception our glad tidings would receive. Already the terms 'progressive' and 'conservative' were being bandied about all too easily. A number of us, perhaps understanding better than some the far-reaching effects of what had happened, settled for being described as 'radical'. Even if we had not yet heard about the 'grass roots', we appreciated that there was something quite fundamental which had to be achieved in relationships and in the so-called 'structures of dialogue' in a renewed Church.

Between-session conferences in England had given evidence of a new breed of Catholic proclaiming confidently that we had moved towards the age of the laity, if not actually the Church of the laity. We were told that the pendulum was swinging. Our insistence that in fact we had moved into the age of the Church tended to fall flat: for one reason or another very few had yet appreciated the full implications of *Lumen Gentium*, with its insistence on one mission, a variety of ministries, and an equality of dignity.

All this would be within a hierarchical structure in which decision-making was to be shared, whilst the actual taking of those decisions must continue to rest with those who held particular responsibilities in virtue of their office.

Nearly six years had passed since Pope John XXIII had taken us all by surprise by announcing his intention to summon an ecumenical Council. The very term had led to fiendish questioning by the Press. At the time all I could remember from eleven years in a seminary was the assurance of my lecturers that in light of what had been decided at Vatican I there would never be a need for a further Council. Now, as had been pointed out during the long debates leading to *Lumen Gentium*, infallibility had been given its setting. Peter had been placed amongst the apostles. The head had been placed upon the shoulders. Just how much *we* must shoulder was not, on that brisk sunny December morning in Rome, entirely clear.

The very word 'ecumenical' had caused some confusion at first. Many journalists had clearly linked the word with certain initiatives already evident, designed to improve contact and perhaps relationships between Christians. As the so-called 'official Roman Catholic spokesman' at Arch-bishop's House, Westminster, my instructions were to emphasize that an ecumenical council was a general council of the Church. The adjective indicated its extent and constituency rather than the subject of its concern. Yet as the reign of John XXIII progressed, it was evident that the promotion of Christian Unity would be high on the list of the matters to be studied.

The Preparatory Commissions were comprehensive in their coverage but predominantly juridical and canonical in membership. Not surprisingly therefore the initial documentation, all strictly *riservata*, dealt primarily with matters causing concern at headquarters and about which rulings would be sought. Even if it was not likely to produce theological definition, the Council was expected to produce enough of these rulings to still what was coming to be known as a 'questioning' Church.

The first sign of any other kind of approach occurred when the Central Preparatory Commission started somewhat belatedly to meet in Rome. All the various commission drafts were submitted to it with the intention of securing a co-ordination of agenda and the expected rubber stamp of approval. But the Curialists had other ideas both about the extent of the material to be offered and the manner of its treatment. The non-Curialists, on the other hand, revealed themselves as having a different set of priorities and of approaches.

A year before the Council officially opened, battle was joined and but for

Pope John's determination to see the Council started in his rapidly failing lifetime, this preliminary struggle could have continued for the rest of the decade. The Curia evidently decided to shake off the outsiders by convening almost impossible monthly meetings. The outsiders hung on with remarkable tenacity and with the encouragement of the ailing Pope. The result was that the initial documentation for the Council was for the most part ill-prepared, unsifted and disordered. Many of the drafts were also of considerable length. Had they been submitted to conciliar procedures in the form they reached the Fathers, the whole process could have been prolonged beyond the financial and physical resources of the Church.

THE DECREE ON THE APOSTOLATE OF THE LAITY

The Council's Decree on the Apostolate of the Laity, *Apostolicam Actuositatem*, was no exception. When eventually it was approved by the Fathers on 18 November 1965, it was hailed as the fruit of some five years of work. True enough, the Preparatory Commission for the Apostolate of the Laity had held its first session in November 1960, but the development of the teaching it contained had over a much longer period reflected each new insight into ecclesiology. This is best appreciated in the context of *Lumen Gentium* which lifted the concept of the lay person out of the negative status of 'non-priest' and set him positively amongst the faithful People of God, sharing fully in the salvific mission of the Church.

It is often suggested that the apostolate of the laity came to be recognized formally in the time of Pius XI when various lay organizations and structures came into being. But even with the development of 'Catholic Action', almost all lay activity worth its salt had to be carried out by direct mandate from the bishop or bishops and within rigidly structured diocesan frameworks. In its manner of acting the Church often reflects contemporary secular structures and we should not forget the highly organized and disciplined forms of national socialism prevalent at the time. With Pope Pius XII, especially in the post-war years, the laity moved forward to the position where they were recognized as 'auxiliaries of the hierarchy'. But that was as far as it went.

Against that background the Preparatory Commission was charged by the Central Commission to develop certain topics which had been suggested by the initial inquiry amongst the episcopal delegates: (i) the Apostolate of the Laity, its nature and extent, its relation with the hierarchy and development in accord with contemporary needs; (ii) Catholic Action – again its nature, extent, relation with the hierarchy and its difference from other groupings;

and (iii) Societies: the adaptation of their activities according to contemporary needs and aims, with special reference to charitable works and social action.

This is not the place to write the history of the eventual text of the Decree on the Apostolate of the Laity.[1] The fact that it was overwhelmingly passed by the Fathers of the Council on 18 November 1965, with 2,340 affirmative, and only six negative votes, is a tribute to the guidance of the Holy Spirit, the perseverance of the Commission and possibly the exhaustion of the Fathers. It cannot disguise the fact that quite apart from the amendments of the final submission, the text went through a number of almost total re-writes. The original draft went before the Central Commission in the summer of 1962. It was in four parts, consisting of some 131 pages and no less than 272 articles. The emasculation which followed was due not so much to views about content as the insistence of the Presidency of the Council and the Co-ordinating Commission that, like most other schemata, it be cut drastically in length. Not without reason had Cardinal Cushing returned to Boston after a few weeks in Council, saying 'I give it two hundred years'.

The demands produced laughable school-boy tactics. The schema must be one booklet: then it must have no chapters: then it must be no more than twelve pages. So the revised text was produced in the smallest type on the largest pages. A reprieve was allowed by Cardinal Cicognani: the text could be divided up for readability. Immediately five chapters were restored, with five sub-commissions employed in the constant work of revision. But even these restraints were not the real problem. Once the Council really got under way, it was clear that the Decree on the Lay Apostolate could not be written until the Fathers had prepared, debated and settled on the chapter in *Lumen Gentium* dealing with the role of the laity in the Church. Nor was it possible to write much about the secularity of the vocation of the laity until it had been decided what form the famous *Schema XIII*, as it was called, (later *Gaudium et Spes* or the Church in the World Today) should take.

By this time the Commission had grown to a Cardinal President, two Vice-Presidents and twenty-eight members (including Bishop John E. Petit of Menevia), and a galaxy of *periti* (about twenty strong), including such stalwarts as Mgr Joseph Cardijn and Père Jean Daniélou SJ. To this body was added a number of lay auditors and eventually auditresses (*sic*). Over the years we came to know each other very well and were used to working between debates and between sessions in groups of four or five. Each had his own particular speciality and occasionally hobby-horses. Often the more effective with the pen were the more silent in the plenary meetings. These plenary meetings were usually held in large rooms and halls not built for acoustics and frequently had to be abandoned in chaos. The President had little knowledge of the role of a chairman. When work pressed, a certain skill developed in speeding up the abandonment of the meeting so that the *periti* might retire to get on with their work of drafting and revision.

After some twenty years, the six chapter headings of the eventual decree bring memories of battles lost and won. The first chapter dealt with the 'Calling of lay people to the Apostolate'. It underlines the truth that, at least with laity, it is easier to describe what they do than what they are. Above all we were striving to get away from the 'non-priest' designation. We wanted to advance beyond the description of 'Catholic Action' as 'the participation of the laity in the apostolate of the hierarchy'. So a point of great importance, reflecting *Lumen Gentium*, is made. There is a unity of mission in the Church, but a diversity or plurality of ministries. As Père Congar OP has insisted: 'We rejoice at this return to the idea of ministries, in the plural, in contrast to the usage which for so long has reserved this term for the ministry of the priest alone. Laymen must be able to exercise true ministry in the Church, if their apostolic service is to have any kind of stability and is to be recognized in the Christian community.'

The two main forms of lay apostolate are distinguished: 'both within the Church and in the secular order'. There is the outright proclamation of Jesus Christ and his way of salvation, and there is the exercise of Christian influence on secular things to order them according to God's laws. This responsibility of the lay person flows from his baptism and confirmation. Yet this simple statement was a tremendous challenge to the clericalism of old. I remember how, as the Council years passed, there was a growing antipathy towards the term 'lay apostolate'. Surely it was enough that they were laity, the auditors argued in the Commission, adding that they could find no reference to 'priestly apostles'.

It was reaction against the idea that the lay person had to make do in a second-class way with what was thought best for the clergy that led to the emphasis placed upon a spirituality suited to the apostolate of the laity. Not that it is a particularly well-developed article in the Decree. Some of us insisted that the spirituality of the laity was not different in kind from the spirituality of the clergy but must be expressed in a way relevant to the responsibilities of lay people in the secular sphere. Others wished to stress the union of laity with Christ through the scriptures and the liturgy. What resulted was no more than an outline, though emphasis is placed upon the spiritual formation of those engaged in the work of the lay associations and family movements in the Church.

The second chapter of the Decree, dealing with 'The goals to be achieved', presents the work of redemption as being directed to the salvation of God's people as individuals, men and women, and directed also to the renewal of the whole secular order. Again we see the balance between the laity's inalienable role of sharing in the work of sanctifying and evangelizing on the one hand, and of their specific task of trying to renew the secular order on the other. The treatment of this latter point clearly has to be accepted as no more than an introduction to the second part of the Pastoral Constitution *Gaudium et Spes*, on the writing of which many of us were engaged at that same time. One of the difficulties we encountered was the need to underline the special responsibility of the laity in the secular order without seeming to absolve or exclude clergy and religious from their responsibilities as citizens. The notion of sharing but with different ministries, which was the heart of *Lumen Gentium*, was not at that stage sufficiently developed.

To some extent there was the same problem in article 8 'On works of charity as the hallmark of Christian apostolate'. It was of great importance to show the shared responsibility of all Christians to meet the charitable and social needs of the deprived. At the same time the laity had increasingly a special technological expertise to offer in this field. It seemed almost impossible to adhere to the main thesis of *Lumen Gentium* without obscuring to some degree the Constitution's individual chapters. It was a tension often apparent amongst the *periti*, each of whom seemed to have a particular line to advance. Indeed, much remained unsatisfactory until the post-conciliar Papal documents took some of this rather inconclusive treatment in the Lay Apostolate Decree to its logical next stage, if not conclusion.

Chapter three of the Decree provided the opportunity for some of this thinking to be given more specialized treatment. The 'Various Areas for apostolic Action' chosen for special mention are the family, youth, the social environment, the nation and the international community. This looks innocent enough but it was to prove increasingly a threat to the specialized work of the Catholic lay organizations which had always played a considerable part in the apostolic formation of their members. Now the pendulum was swinging back towards the parish as the basic structure, not just for worship and community but also for the expression of the viewpoint and apostolic activity of lay persons. In the commission it was argued that all talk of working effectively on inter-parochial, inter-diocesan, national and international levels was futile unless it was related to the real problems of parishioners; these must be dealt with in the parish life and liturgy. At the same time it was recognized that the increasing mobility of people was a real challenge to parish commitment and to the ability of parish clergy adequately to form their people for today's apostolate.

In retrospect it seems clear that inadequate attention was paid in this chapter to the formative role of the lay organizations. The family apostolate is stressed. The Cardijn line of the mission of like to like is shown with regard to young people, described as 'the first and immediate apostles to other youth, exercising an apostolate of their own among themselves, with some consideration of the social environment of the place where they live' (art 12). Yet the magnitude of the task is shown when the Decree speaks of the apostolate as the 'effort to touch with the Christian spirit the attitudes, morals, laws and community structures in which one lives'. The parish may well be the scene in which consciousness of what needs to be done may exist. Yet if the secular order is to be renewed, the base from which the effort is to be launched must be more widespread. The formation needed must frequently be more profound and even specialized than can be given in and by the local community.

Some appreciation of this is shown in the article dealing with the national and the international order. The mutual support of Catholics engaged in this difficult and demanding work is of great importance, but it is interesting also to note the welcome given to co-operation with all men of good will. I seem to recall the impact which Pope Paul VI's visit to the United Nations (4 October 1965) had made upon us. Yet our text seems timid when it acknowledges that 'Catholics with political abilities' should not *avoid* public office. There was still fear of political involvement in the minds of many of the Fathers. Some redress was had when in *Gaudium et Spes* we managed to secure positive praise for those 'who devote themselves to the service of the State' and for those Christians who 'fight for justice' and socio-economic development. As already mentioned, this decree on the Lay Apostolate must be read in conjunction with *Lumen Gentium*, especially chapter 4, and with *Gaudium et Spes* (the Constitution on the Church in the World Today), especially chapters 4 and 5 of part II.

To return to the Lay Apostolate Decree, chapter 4 deals at some length with 'Various types of Apostolate'. Underlying it all was the hard-waged war about Catholic Action as an almost exclusive mandatory form of authorized lay activity within the Church. The difficulty has been there from the start. Indeed it has been with most European countries since the 1930s when the highly-structured organization which suited some Latin countries was commended, if not nearly imposed, by the Church authority in Rome and rapidly came into conflict with individual lay organizations, national and international. In the early texts for the future decree of the

Council strenuous efforts had to be made to challenge the exclusive commendation of 'Catholic Action' as *the* form of organized apostolate. In the final text 'Catholic Action' was commended as 'worthy of special recognition', but it was mentioned amongst 'these and similar institutions' which had 'a rather close relation to the hierarchy' (art 20).

At stake was the issue of a mandate required of those acting officially in the name of the Church and the freedom and right of lay people to 'form organisations, manage them and join them, provided they maintain the proper relationship with ecclesiastical authority' (art 19). Once again the phrase 'the co-operation of lay people in the apostolate of the hierarchy' found its way into the text. This was despite efforts to refer back to *Lumen Gentium* and its clear reference to laity in their own way sharing in the priestly, prophetic and kingly functions of Christ (art 31).

Those putting forward the 'participative' consideration argued for 'lay people and bishops as associates in the work of Christ'. But in the end it was felt necessary to make clear that the renewal of lay associations and indeed of Catholic Action itself could only take place in 'obedient self-determination'. The years since the Council have shown how difficult that phrase has proved. This has been especially difficult at international level, where official recognition has depended upon conditions which have not always appeared to take adequate regard of the rights and aspirations of the laity concerned. Equally, in their attempts to break new ground in renewal, lay associations have not always exhibited the responsibility and willingness to consult, let alone submit, to achieve the recognition and formal approbation they have sought.

This delicate matter of relationships and dialogue was further dealt with in the fifth chapter 'On maintaining proper relations'. The relationships between laity, religious and clergy flow, according to *Lumen Gentium*, from the bond of baptism, from confirmation and holy orders. Yet to be effective they have to be formalized in some manner by what came to be called 'structures of dialogue'. Without communication, it was argued, collegiality and co-responsibility would become subject to personality or chance opportunity.

So far as the bishops were concerned, the Decree emphasized the importance of their 'promoting the apostolate of lay people' and of providing them with the spiritual principles and aids needed to be effective witnesses in the secular sphere. There were many opportunities for lay initiative but again it is stressed that 'no undertaking should claim the word "Catholic" for its title without the permission of legitimate ecclesiastical authority' (art 24). Once more we find expressed the requirements of specific 'mandate' though it is mentioned that lay people must be able to retain freedom to act on their own initiative.

Behind this constant balance lies the long drawn out struggle between those pressing for a clear juridical basis for apostolic activity and those anxious to present true lay responsibility for Christian mission. Some sort of compromise was reached by the assertion of 'the duty of the Church's hierarchy to teach and provide an authentic explanation of the moral principles to be applied in the secular order'. This does not disguise the underlying issue of shared responsibilities within an hierarchical structure. The nice distinction between decision-making (to be shared by all) and decision-taking (to be exercised in virtue of office) had not yet been made. The contrast between genuine consultation and prior information was already being mentioned.

The following article 25 was however more satisfactory for the lay experts and the lay organization priests. For here is set out clearly the priest's responsibility to call the laity to the apostolate, to ensure their adequate formation for their task and to help to sustain them in their often lonely mission. But there was demand for an indication of the more formal structures needed to ensure for the laity a known means for playing their part by 'diocesan councils, which through the co-operation of clergy and religious with lay people, can assist in the apostolic work of the Church'. This was needed for evangelizing, sanctifying and for charitable and social works. By the time the implementing *motu proprio Ecclesiae Sanctae* had emerged in August 1966, it had become 'that the life and activity of the people of God may be brought into greater conformity with the gospel'. If that seems a little abstract, the new Code of Canon Law states that in each diocese a Pastoral Council is to be set up 'to study and weigh those matters which concern the pastoral work of the diocese and to propose practical conclusions concerning them' (canon 511).

A vital if finicky point arose with regard to such consultation at international level. Even if there is strictly no national Church, dioceses in a nation could collaborate in sharing responsibility. There was (and still is) the problem of how laity effectively share responsibility for the apostolate at the international level. More precisely how were the laity to share in the work of the Holy See? There were many pressing for an assurance that each Roman Congregation would have a suitable proportion of lay members, resident and/or consultative *ad hoc*. In the end it became possible merely to insist that the Holy See should establish 'a secretariat to promote and serve the apostolate of lay people'. The day was saved by the use of the words *'apud Sanctam Sedem'*. This left unresolved the issue of whether

246

membership of such a body would be formally part of the Curia, with membership chosen by the Holy See, or be in some way a sort of mid-way body, accepted by the Holy See but with membership chosen by international Catholic organizations, etc.

Subsequently there was another interesting play on words when in 1967 Pope Paul VI, who was sensitive to these issues, decided on a provisional Concilium de Laicis (*about* the Laity) and not *pro* Laicis (*for* the Laity) desired by some. Pope Paul described us as his 'listening-post in the world' and we were to listen also to the Holy See in matters concerning the laity. But it was not all plain sailing. There were many early problems, especially about the traditional Curial oath of secrecy which the members refused to take.

The first provisional Laity Council, with a five year term, had all lay members and episcopal, religious and lay consultors. The second had a membership and consultorship of bishops, laity and priests. By the time the body was formalized in 1977 it had become a Pontifical Council for the Laity (*pro* Laicis). But by then the title was no longer of much consequence. What was important was that it be given and accepted as possessing an integral role in the life of the Curia – even to the extent that it has a Presidency of three Cardinals, with priest and lay officials in a permanent office in Rome, and with predominantly lay membership, male and female, drawn from all over the world. All this flowed from the battle of '*apud*', as we knew it.

The sixth and final chapter of the Council's Decree dealt with the important issue of formation for the apostolate. None doubted its need. The stress was now that it had a distinctive character related to the needs of lay life and a spirituality proper to it. There must be formation in a living faith and with a rich spiritual foundation. But this formation must also be doctrinal. Pope John's encyclical, *Mater et Magistra* (1961), had taught us that social justice was part of the Church's doctrine and not an optional interest for those that way inclined. Clearly also the laity must be helped to achieve a lay and if necessary professional competence, so that, without establishing a Church of the elite, apostolic lay persons could be effective in their secular role in life.

Before the final exhortation, this chapter finishes with a rag-bag of interests when everything was included, from the training of small children within a family to the 'intelligent use of secular things', public welfare and – a final litany, as each *peritus* fought for the inclusion of his interest to prove he was there – 'seminars, conventions, retreats, days of recollection, conferences, books and lectures' (art 32).

The final exhortation was, in accordance with orders from above, threaded with scriptural quotation, urging on the full collaboration of all concerned. It is understandable if, at the end of so many years of work, the members of the Commission drafted for the Fathers of the Council a plea to the laity to respond to the Lord's call that they 'show themselves to be his fellow-workers, devoting themselves fully at all times to the Lord's work, realising that this toil in the Lord can never be in vain (cf 1 Cor 15:58)' (art 33). At the worst times we had wondered!

A LAYMAN'S WITNESS

Piecemeal though this reminiscent analysis may seem in retrospect, nevertheless it was possible for Patrick Keegan, the former YCW International President and the English auditor at the Second Vatican Council, to write of the Decree of the Lay Apostolate as 'an epoch-making document in the history of the Church. For the first time the apostolic activity of the laity is the object of a conciliar decree. The decree consecrates all the achievements of the lay apostolate in the previous forty years; it also ratifies most solemnly the task of the layman in the Church, the people of God.'[2]

The Decree must be read in conjunction with the great charter of the Council, *Lumen Gentium*, Keegan asserts, and also with the Declaration *Dignitatis Humanae* on Religious Liberty and *Gaudium et Spes*. He quotes Père Congar as saying: 'These documents are a full and frank recognition of the lay nature of present society. The Church does not cease to teach with authority but she enters into dialogue with mankind and ascribes to lay people the specific and proper task of witnessing in the secular order and renewing that order.'

It is moving to read Patrick Keegan when he writes: 'All of us who have been involved in the lay apostolate over the years feel indebted to the priests who have sustained us spiritually in our commitment to our work in the modern world.' I for one will never forget the morning during the third session of the Council when Patrick was chosen to address the Fathers in St Peter's in the name of the laity. It was allegedly the first time a lay voice had been heard in a General Council of the Church since the days of the Emperor Constantine in A.D. 325. It was certainly one of the high spots in my recollections of Vatican II. In retrospect I remember working with him on his text the night before almost more than the historic moment when, in shiny new shoes, he made his way across the perilous marble floor of St Peter's to give witness to the lay person's role in the Church of the renewal.

His '*Venerabiles Patres*' was an appreciated nod to the official language of the Church; then he moved to his mother-tongue: 'The Lay Apostolate cannot be an isolated entity in the Church. It reaches its fulness in close collaboration with all the other members of the Church. By its very nature it demands a constant and regular exchange between the Hierarchy and the laity. It is for us as lay people to bring to our pastors our experience of the needs of the world in which we live, and to seek from them guidance in our endeavour to respond to these needs. In simple terms, there must be the "family dialogue" of which our Holy Father, Pope Paul, has spoken so frequently and emphasised in his recent Letter *Ecclesiam Suam*' [6 August 1964]. It was an historic and applauded moment; sadly not repeated when his mentor, by then Cardinal Josef Cardijn and almost totally deaf, read an unaccustomed Latin text in a debate and failed to hear the moderator's bell to warn him that he had over-run his allotted time.

A happier memory comes from the days when Cardijn served with us as a *peritus* on the Lay Apostolate Commission. He used to sit with us at the experts' table, smiling contentedly till we gave him the sign to intervene with a speech we had come to know irreverently as 'the old one-two'. Came the day when it was announced that he had been made a Cardinal; and when he turned up for a Commission meeting that afternoon, clad in his old black cardigan over his cassock, we took him to the Commission President's table and sat him next to Cardinal Cento. Without his hearing-aids, he beamed down at us through his rimless glasses. Work continued but at last we enlivened things by signalling that the time had come to make his intervention. He took from his pocket his two ear-pieces, set them in place, rose to his feet and, without obvious reference to the matters under discussion, delivered an enthusiastic address on the mission of like to like and the importance of the role of working youth in their own *milieu*. By that stage in the Council we knew it almost by heart but we cheered him on until exhausted he sat down in his chair. After a short breather, he removed his hearing-aids, replaced them carefully in a little box which he pocketed, and took his departure. There was much rejoicing in Rome that evening. He may have grown old but this chapter would not have been written without him.

THE DECREE IN PRACTICE

Reminiscences can provide background information to help understanding. But how has the lay person – itself a change in terminology from the layman – fared in the past twenty years? It was *The Tablet's* Rome correspondent who described the layman emerging from the Second Vatican Council as a 'kind of bowler-hatted monk'. It was not the happiest of designations: the monk presumably because he was to be interested and involved in worship, and the bowler-hat to reflect his commitment as a Christian in the world, but not, one hopes, his enforced retirement or withdrawal from the scene. But insofar as society itself has changed greatly in that time, so has the role of the laity where it has focused on their secular priorities. Even though there was this great release in the Council, we shall not find the answer to today's problems merely by basing our stand on the decree of 1965. But if we are going to learn from what has happened, we must look at two points: first, has it been made possible for people to share in the life of the Church at local level? Second, have we so strangled ourselves with structure-for-structure's-sake that we have forgotten the object of the exercise, the shedding of the light of the Gospel on the world in which we live?

'Through their baptism and confirmation *all* are commissioned to that apostolate by the Lord himself' we are told in the Constitution on the Church (art 33). To be practical we know that we cannot even succeed in bringing all people to baptism; but nowadays we are anxious not to be lost in the numbers' game. We know that not all baptized Christians are willing to be drawn into the direct work of the Church – whether this is judged to lie in 'churchy' matters or in the secular order. Though in some respects numbers have fallen, we find reasonable consolation in the manner and degree of the commitment of the many committed laity today, who have found their way more fully into the life and mission of the Church.

People are often critical of structure-for-structure's-sake and even of 'structure' itself nowadays. But without some structure, how in practice can we ensure for all the faithful (or more realistically, any of the faithful who are willing) the opportunity to enter into the apostolic life of the Church in their parish or in their diocese? There needs to be enough structure to ensure that the way of collaboration is open to all and that the endeavours of priests and laymen can be co-ordinated and directed for the effective fulfilment of the evangelizing task given by the Lord to his people.

The responsibilities and rights of the laity are well set out in art 37 of the Constitution of the Church: 'Every layman should reveal to his sacred pastor his needs and desires with that freedom and confidence which befits a son of God and a brother in Christ. An individual layman, by reason of the knowledge, competence, or outstanding ability which he may enjoy, is permitted and sometimes even obliged to express his opinion on things which concern the good of the Church. When occasions arise, let this be done through the agencies set up by the Church for this purpose.'

In practice, what has happened? There have been some notable experiments at various levels and experiences will differ. But if I may generalize, the sad thing is that quite often long years have been given to the turgid task of preparing constitutions, orders of procedure, etc which have sometimes hamstrung apostolic endeavour. At the same time consultation with the laity is often thought to refer only to matters of finance and administration: almost as if these were the only spheres of non-clerical super-competence and interest. This is as wrong as it would be to tell a priest that he has no competence to express his interest and concern in anything outside his church-building; in, for example, an industrial dispute, which is throwing half his parishioners out of work. In such a situation, priest and laity must consult and work together. Structures of dialogue, with all their growing pains, have been tried at every level. The two principal lessons learned are that, first, the most successful are those which truly reflect the whole Church, with all ministries represented; and second, their value is in proportion to the accountability and truly representative character of their membership. It is not just that the individual must answer for what he or she says: there must be subsidiary structures to refer the recommendations or decisions, and there must be an openness on the part of those bearing greater responsibilities to listen and take good account of what is being said.

It was inevitable that at first many of these Councils and similar consultative bodies concerned themselves with the inner workings and problems of the Church. Not until they began to look out to the Church's life and mission did they show real signs of health and hope. In his Apostolic Exhortation *Evangelii Nuntiandi*, Evangelization in the Modern World (8 December 1975), Pope Paul calls our attention to words from the declaration issued from the 1974 Synod: 'We wish to confirm once more that the task of evangelizing all people constitutes the essential mission of the Church.' He says that it is a task which the state of present-day society makes urgent but it has always been there. 'The Church', he says, 'is born of the evangelizing activity of Jesus and the twelve.' That particular Synod of Bishops was for many the turning point after some of the confusion of ministries in the late 1960s and early 1970s. It gave new direction to the missionary concern of the Church, new expression to the notion of co-responsibility. Identity crises tended to fade before the Pope's insistence that for all the Church the first means of evangelizing must be 'the witness of fidelity to the Lord Jesus – the witness of poverty and detachment, of freedom in the face of the powers of this world: in short, the witness of sanctity'.

Today we have to recognize that the laity's task is the work of evangelization. This is not just playing with words: 'The whole Church is missionary and the work of evangelization is a basic duty of the People of

God.' Pope Paul provides this reminder with a quotation from the Second Vatican Council's Decree on the Church's Missionary Activity. The Pope says quite clearly that evangelization is for no one an individual and isolated act; 'it is one that is deeply ecclesial'. The individual acts not in virtue of a mission which he attributes to himself or by a personal inspiration but in union with the mission of the Church and in her name. As we examine the structures which have been established, we must ask ourselves whether they relate to the following words of the Pope: 'If each individual evangelizes in the name of the Church, no evangelizer is the absolute master of his evangelizing action, with discretionary power to carry it out in accordance with individualistic criteria and perspectives; he acts in communion with the Church and her pastors.'

The ever-present danger of the lay person's over-involvement in 'churchy' things to the neglect of his mission in the secular world is dealt with specifically by Pope Paul in this all important Apostolic Exhortation: 'The primary and immediate task of lay people is not to establish and develop the ecclesial community – this is the specific role of the pastors – but to put to use every Christian and evangelical possibility latent but already present and active in the affairs of the world.' He goes on to list the laity's responsibilities in the field of politics, economics, the world of culture, science and arts, international life and mass media. He mentions their particular concern with the family, the education of children, professional work and quite simply suffering. Then he uses a designation which for me marks the real progress of the past fifty years. No longer does he speak of 'lay auxiliaries of the hierarchy' or even of 'lay apostles'. He refers to the need and role of 'Gospel-inspired lay people'. In that phrase is encapsulated so much of what we strove for in the corridors of the Council.

No one would want to pretend that it is the end of the process, that there is no further development to come. But it will be important, whilst stressing that one mission of the Church, not to confuse the distinct if complementary ministries. Pope John Paul II has himself pointed to the danger of attempts at 'the clericalisation of the laity' and 'the laicisation of the clergy' (*Address to Swiss Bishops*, 15 June 1984). The evangelizing and sanctifying role of the lay person is clear but must not obscure the secularity of the lay vocation.

In his response to the suggestion that the next Synod of Bishops (now in 1987) be devoted to the laity, the Pope made plain that the subject should be 'Vocation and Mission of the Laity in the Church and in the World'.[3] Addressing the Council of the General Secretariat of the Synod in May 1984 he said: 'The mission of the laity, as an integral part of the salvific mission of the entire people of God is of fundamental importance for the life of the Church and for the service which the Church herself is called to render to the world of humanity and of temporal realities.'

Nowadays, against a background debate of 'religion and politics', the issue is raised again. Have some of the parish and diocesan structures had the effect of devaluing the lay organizations which have such an important part to play in the formation of lay persons for their effective role in the Church, and even more in public life? If the pendulum tended to swing that way after the Council – and none can deny the fall-off in membership of lay apostolic organizations – has it now begun to swing back? There is evidence of increased membership: it is too early to assess whether this will lead to the more effective witness of the Christian in today's society.

One of the main flaws in society today is the polarization of views and of manners of commitment. Some of this is reflected in the Church. Yet evidently it is not an 'either . . . or' situation. There is room for variety of approach and of ministry. The structures of dialogue need the experience of lay persons well formed by lay associations. But the world needs them too, and they will be more effective in the secular sphere for their contact with, even membership of, the consultative structures of the Church.

Developments will be related to changing needs in the society in which we live. In the Western world at least the ministers of the Church, clerical and lay, must somehow penetrate a society which is either blinded by its affluence or starved by its poverty. They must reach out and affirm amongst floundering but good and generous people a faith in Christ of which in many cases they are almost unaware. They must be close enough to the secularism of the age that their witness may be visible and audible. They will need each other's help and collaboration. An interesting feature of recent years has been the increase in the number of spiritual movements for the laity (though not always exclusively so). This says much for the spiritual searching of our times. But it must not be to the exclusion of those lay associations, even mass-movements, needed to penetrate the world of industry and politics – all those spheres of activity outlined by Pope Paul in *Evangelii Nuntiandi*. This is a most important point to which the 1987 Synod must give its attention. The various ministries in the Church need one another. We discovered one another in a marvellous manner in Vatican II. The method of our collaboration and partnership has still to be perfected.

A REMEMBRANCE

In this connection I may be allowed one last reminiscence from Council days. In October 1965, during the final session of the Council, I learned that I had been nominated a bishop. I was of course in Rome on the day of this announcement. When as usual that afternoon I went to the Vatican to work with the Commission preparing the final stages of *Gaudium et Spes*, the word was just getting around. At 6 p.m. there was the customary fifteen minutes' break and we moved outside our great meeting hall for what the Latinists called *pausa coco-cola*. Various of my colleagues came to greet me and ease my embarrassment, when suddenly I saw a flustered and blinking Cardinal Ottaviani, our President, before me. He dragged me aside and asked anxiously if the news were really public yet. I was seized with terror and had visions of the dungeons of the Holy Office until I remembered and told him that I had seen the announcement in the *Osservatore Romano*. He turned on his heel and went straight back into the hall and strenuously rang the hand-bell on the President's table.

Some sixty or more of us trooped back inside and there to my astonishment this Proto-Deacon of the Church, charged with announcing to the world the election of Popes, solemnly proclaimed amidst great amusement: '*Annuntio vobis gaudium magnum. Habemus pontificem...*' When at last laughter had subsided we sat down and tried to continue our work. But at that moment the doors burst open and Patrick Keegan, also a lay member of the Commission but for some reason absent from that meeting, dashed into the room and, having just heard the news, came to claim me, if not acclaim me. I bowed to the Proto-Deacon, gathered up my papers and left the hall. Then in the corridors of the Vatican to the astonishment of the onlooking guards, Patrick and I hugged one another, not in pride but in sheer excitement at what lay ahead of us, layman and bishop, together. That was twenty years ago. Much has still to be done.

NOTES

1. Cf. Ed. Herbert Vorgrimler, *Commentary on the documents of Vatican II* III (1969), 273–404 (text editor, Ferdinand Klostermann). [Ed.]
2. Foreword to *Laymen*, published by Catholic Action Federations, Chicago, 1966.
3. Cf. Synod consultation document. *Ex Ecclesiae Coetibus* (CTS Do 563 1985). [Ed.]

16

DE CURA ANIMARUM:
A VOICE FOR THE PRIESTHOOD

BRIAN CHARLES FOLEY

The title reminds us not only that some schemata *died before reaching the record book, but that others lost their names and became progressively absorbed into others now household words. The souls that are ever to be cared for remain, but their* schema *took its journey elsewhere:* De Cura Animarum *was never tabled.*

Instead a bare list of propositions was tabled at the Third Session (1964), in an endeavour to keep the Council's agenda manageable, no time being granted at first for the Care of Souls. That schema *became absorbed more into* Christus Dominus *(especially sec. 30–35) on the bishops' pastoral office than into* Presbyterorum Ordinis *on the ministry and life of priests; it was enmeshed with another such* schema *on 'Diocesan government' (both discussed in their details in H. Vorgrimler, Commentary on the documents III. 165–87). The other* schema *that grew out of the Care of Souls equally had its developing fortune: its title was changed from* De Clericis *to* De Sacerdotibus, *from* De Vita et Ministerio sacerdotali *to its almost final* De Presbyterorum Ministerio et Vita. *We are reminded that the corpus of the Council's* acta *had a long and jostling journey to make, quite unforeseeable at the outset.*

Educated at Ushaw College, then the English College and Gregorian University in Rome, the author (who is now over seventy-five) was a priest for twenty-five years in southern English parishes before being a bishop for almost as long in the diocese of Lancaster. In June 1985 he handed over his episcopal task and immediately wrote this chapter. He is well known among scholars of English recusant history, his papers being sought after at post-Reformation conferences.

My most vivid memories of the Second Vatican Council are of the debates and discussions leading up to the Decree *Presbyterorum Ordinis* on the ministerial priesthood.

The English and Welsh Bishops met invariably each afternoon from 4 p.m. to 6 p.m. in the Library of the English College to take part in discussions with their *Periti* and others such as those Bishops serving on Commissions. It was generally as a result of these discussions that interventions by a Bishop would be made in the Aula. Having listened to the experts and those with special knowledge, Bishops would raise issues which they felt should be ventilated. Thus it was that after an announcement from Archbishop Felici, the General Secretary, had been made one morning to the effect that the Schema *De Cura Animarum* (issued on 22 April 1963) was to be withdrawn for lack of time, I spoke of my regret at this step. Other Bishops immediately agreed and it was suggested that I should prepare a draft for a speech to be given on the 'care of souls' whenever an occasion should occur. This I did and outlined to the Bishops a day or so later what I had in mind to say. Archbishop Heenan had spoken to me of this in the meantime; he said he thought the matter of importance and that a contribution on 'the care of souls' was one that we could and should make. The difficulty was where in the Agenda, which now had nothing on the priesthood, such an intervention could be made. After further discussions I was advised that, since on the withdrawal of *De Cura Animarum* it had been promised that something on the priesthood would be incorporated in the Decree on Bishops, I might be able to get my intervention accepted during the debate on the Schema for Bishops. Accordingly I began to put it together.

I had left parish work only three months earlier and since my first days as a priest visiting families in their homes in accordance with our synodal law[1] I had become persuaded that to fulfil the principle of the priestly apostolate – 'I know mine and mine know Me' – it was vital to encourage the priest to visit his flock.

In order, too, to prepare for the Council I had been reading the debates which had taken place at Trent on 'General Discipline' under the title *De Reformatione*.[2] These debates of Trent were dominated by the oratory of the Ven. Archbishop Bartholomew de Martyribus, of Braga, a Portuguese Dominican, who told the Fathers of Trent that he had spent half of his twenty-two years as Bishop in the saddle, 'visiting, visiting, visiting'! He appeared at Trent as a kind of John the Baptist, crying out with the words of Ezekiel: 'Woe to the shepherds of Israel . . . I will require my flock at their hands!'[3] The Archbishop carried with him a notebook into which he had written for his own inspiration passages from St Gregory the Great's *Regula Pastoralis*, St Bernard's *De Consideratione*, from the *Confessions* and other writings of St Augustine, and of others of the Fathers. He showed this to the young Cardinal Borromeo, who was completely fascinated and moved by him. St Charles had the little book printed and presented it to the Fathers of Trent under the title of *Stimulus Pastorum*.[4]

I had also chanced upon a book in a Roman second-hand shop entitled *La Cura delle Anime nelle Grandi Città*. This had been presented to the University of Vienna as a doctoral thesis by a Dr Enrico Swoboda some years before. In it the author comes to the conclusion that where tridentine legislation on '*operosa residentia*' and '*visitatio*' and '*associatio*' had been implemented, and personal contact between priest and people maintained (as in England and Germany, he says) there had been less falling away from the practice of religion whereas in other places where there had been little 'care for souls' exercised personally the losses had been great. The author concludes by saying the evidence showed the necessity of ideally there being one priest in a parish who would be the '*rex instrumentorum*' in touch personally with every member of his flock.

I was full of these matters and tended, I fear, to minimize the importance of liturgical, ecumenical, and other issues which were taking up all the debating time. I worked away on an intervention with the encouragement especially of Archbishop Heenan and others who wanted an English voice to be raised regarding the priesthood. Finally, I outlined to the Bishops one afternoon what I proposed to say and then the following morning handed the text in to Archbishop Veuillot, one of the Secretaries. He scrutinized it and asked when I hoped to give it and then said that, of course, it would rest with the Moderators whether it was accepted. He seemed rather dubious altogether as to its suitability. For some time I heard nothing.

The debate on 'The Role of Bishops' eventually came on and when we arrived at St Peter's on 18 September 1964, to my surprise and alarm I found my name down on the list of speakers. I hastily extracted my speech from my case, and following a further exhortation as to brevity from the General Secretary proceeded to cut out some passages, especially those which cited our own local synodal law and practice. That morning the German Cardinal Frings and the Dutch Cardinal Alfrink, using their prerogative of intervening at will, each spoke *extra ordinem* on the *De Ecclesia* document though the debate on that had been adjourned.

When the debate on 'The Role of Bishops' started it was opened by Cardinal Richaud of France. He was concerned over difficulties of jurisdiction and wanted a greater role for Archbishops who should be called in more often to help in disputes. Next spoke the Irish Dominican Cardinal Browne from the Curia who *inter alia* wanted not preaching to be called the *praecipuum munus* among the Bishop's tasks but rather 'worship and sanctification of his flock'; he spoke of the priestly tasks of assisting the dying and hearing confessions. Seven other Bishops (from Italy, China, Canary Islands and an Irish Jesuit, Bishop Corboy from a new Diocese in Zambia) spoke also on various topics. Altogether thirty-one spoke during this stage of the debate on 'The Role of Bishops'. I found myself called tenth and spoke as follows:

Venerable Brothers,

I wish to speak briefly on the 'care of souls'. The purpose of the Council is a pastoral one. It is concerned with restoring religious practice to 'de-christianised' parts of the world and with bringing the gospel to those who have not received it. Now, this object will not be achieved principally by a new liturgy or by new scriptural and doctrinal insights but rather by a truly pastoral aspostolate. This is shown by the history of the Church and by present experience.

There was in former days, as can be seen from certain writings, an intense pastoral apostolate through the intimate contact of priests with their flock. We read of the splendour of such pastoral life, for instance, in such works as the Italian book *I Promessi Sposi*, where the figures of Padre Cristofero and Cardinal Federigo and other priests are shown. These were truly great priests who spent their lives like their Master *conversando cum hominibus*. Where there exists close contact between priest and people there is to be found a vigorous religious practice, where it is absent the churches are empty. Our divine Lord by word and example inculcated the need for this. Yet today it seems to be becoming taken for granted that a personal apostolate is no longer possible or desirable for the priest in a parish.

In July of this year there appeared in *L'Osservatore Romano* an article giving an account of a priest in a parish who was said to have visited six hundred homes in his parish in a single year. This was spoken of as something unheard of and even heroic. A book was written about it in which the priest concerned was said to have brought many back to the Church, made converts and comforted many lonely souls. Surely this is an extraordinary state of affairs. Is it not the strict duty of *all* priests working in parishes regularly and systematically every year to visit each family in his parish and render a *status animarum* to the bishop? How else can he perform his apostolate? How can it be said of him that 'I know mine and mine know me'?

As I was speaking I noticed the four Moderators conferring. Then Cardinal Döpfner, the presiding Moderator of the day, sounded the gong. He explained: '*Tu bene loqueris, Pater, sed non ad rem. Agitur nunc de munere episcoporum non parochorum*'. I had anticipated that I might not be able to proceed and said that I would hastily bring my intervention to a conclusion. I was allowed to continue and finished by saying:

I propose that either there should be prepared a new Schema *De Cura Animarum* or that some part of this Schema '*De Pastorali Munere Episcoporum*' should include these matters. I propose also that there should be a discussion on certain modern difficulties facing the priestly apostolate such as how to exercise the apostolate in large cities or urban areas. I would like to hear a debate as to why religious practice is high in certain places and low in others... DIXI

Among the Bishops who followed more immediately three (Proano of

Ecuador, Ruiz of Mexico and Himmer of Tournai) seemed to depart from their script to stress that in their opinion the knowledge of one's flock demanded by the Gospel was a 'general rather than an individual one'. (One used the term 'sociological'.) They, of course, were speaking strictly on the Schema which was concerned, as the Moderators had pointed out, with Bishops and not priests. It was interesting that when eventually the Decree of Bishops was voted on it stipulated that the Bishop should know personally 'the *principal* members of his diocese', which clearly is all that is possible for the Bishop. I was surrounded by Italian Bishops who received me back with fulsome praises for my words while indicating that they thoroughly disagreed with the sentiments. *Tanto forte è la carità!*

No sooner had I sat down than emissaries, usually young seminarians, began to arrive with messages. Cardinal König sent thanking me and asking if I could call at his place, and whether I knew of St Clement Hofbauer and asking for a number of copies of the full text which I would have given. Cardinal Browne, describing himself as 'only a curial man', sent to say he 'much appreciated' what I was trying to say. The Australian Hierarchy wanted texts, as did several others from the English-speaking world.

It might be well, before mentioning my second intervention, to give a synopsis of the complex developments which led to the eventual adoption of a full Schema on the priesthood. This is what occurred. Towards the end of the First Session in 1962 Pope John had become alarmed at the slow progress the Council was making. It seems extraordinary now but it was said that he had expected the Council to be completely finished by the end of that year and had not envisaged originally even a Second Session. At the Pope's instance it was announced shortly before the First Session ended that some Schemata would have to be amalgamated and others dropped. It became known that discussion of the priesthood would have to go.

When the Bishops arrived for the Second Session in 1963 we learned that the Schema *De Cura Animarum* (issued between the First and Second Sessions in early 1963) had been withdrawn for lack of time. So there was nothing at all on the agenda relating to the priesthood when the Second Session opened on 29 September 1963. This Second Session was to be dominated by the important document on the Church. All through the debates on that, the embarrassment of the Bishops that nothing was to be said on the priesthood became more and more evident. Soon this disquiet began to make the Presidents very anxious and they decided hastily that before the end of the Second Session a *Nuntius* or Message should be sent to the priests of the world. On Friday, 29 November 1963, therefore, Archbishop Felici, the General Secretary, announced that the text for this was being circularized that day. Then, to the general astonishment, he said that he was instructed to state that any amendments from the Fathers to this would have to be in the Secretariat Office by the following day, a Saturday and therefore a *dies non*, when there would be no General Congregation. In spite of this we heard that a great number of highly critical amendments had been proposed. Many of the Bishops had asked that the *Nuntius* should not be sent at all. Rumour had it that it had been compiled by Cardinal Richaud advised by Archbishop Marty and other French Bishops. Many Fathers thought that it was vague and they wanted something more inspiring and practical; they felt, too, it lacked the dimension of the 'care of souls'. Accordingly, the Presidents, because of the clear opposition to the Message, felt it would be better not to proceed with it and nothing further was done concerning discussion of the priesthood during the rest of the Second Session of 1963.

When the Third Session opened on 14 September 1964, the Fathers were presented with a document on the priesthood containing twelve Propositions. The debate on this did not begin until 13 October, the day when the hundredth General Congregation took place. Archbishop Marty of Rheims[5] was the Relator. He stressed the great industry and care with which this list of Propositions had been prepared. He regretted the lack of a full Schema on the priestly life and ministry but stated that much of what such a Schema would have contained would, he hoped, be found either in these Propositions or elsewhere.

Cardinal Meyer, Archbishop of Chicago, was the first speaker. He immediately launched a vehement attack on the Propositions. He demanded a full discussion of the ministerial priest's work in the modern world and resented anything that emphasized mainly duties and obligations. The Fathers were continually being told that '*plausus vetantur*' but this opening speech met with loud and prolonged applause. He had voiced the disquiet felt by most of the Bishops. He was followed by Bishop Theas of Lourdes, who used to say that he knew more Bishops, their aspirations and anxieties, than any other because of his weekly hospitality to Bishops at the Residence in Lourdes. He spoke equally scathingly of the Propositions; he declared that the saying 'nothing without the Bishop' was true also for the priest. Nothing can be done without the clergy. There followed an attack on these Propositions as violent and sustained as any during the Council. Whole Hierarchies through their spokesmen repudiated them. Archbishop Gomes of Goiânia, speaking as he said on behalf of more than a hundred Brazilian bishops, said: 'this text, even in its revised form . . . is almost an insult to our priests'. One after another, Cardinals rose to exercise their right of intervening without notice and one by one spoke out against the adoption of the Propositions.[6]

The Moderators hastily consulted the body of Presidents and called for a 'standing' vote as to whether the debate should be closed. Most unusually over half the Fathers remained seated. Upon this, Archbishop Marty, the Relator, asked 'on behalf of the Commission that the Propositions should be dropped'. He offered in the name of the Commission to draft another *Message to Priests* if that should be thought desirable. When a vote was later taken, however, on Monday, 19 October, an overwhelming majority voted for a new and full Schema on the 'Ministry and Life of the Priest'.

Very soon the Fathers learnt that the Holy Father and the Presidents had ordered that such a Schema should be prepared and time be made for its discussion. As it was, the Schema *Presbyterorum Ordinis* was the last of all to be debated. This was at the very end of the Fourth Session in December, 1965. It was due to the insistence of the Bishops that a full schema had emerged.

When it came to the debate so great was the number of Hierarchies wishing to field speakers, and Cardinals wishing to intervene, as well as individual Bishops, that it was decided to hold General Congregations on Saturdays. The debate on the Schema, now called *De Ministerio et Vita Presbyterorum*, began on 14 October 1965, Cardinal Lercaro of Bologna being presiding Moderator. Archbishop Marty was again the Relator. It was known that the Schema was heavily influenced by the French. The Relator was generously thanked by most of the speakers and in spite of many criticisms no one wanted the Schema to be rejected, except the Maronite Cardinal who claimed that it ignored the needs of the Eastern clergy. Cardinal Ruffini wished the words of the title to be reversed since the priestly *life* was even more important than his *ministry*. A number of Spanish Bishops and Cardinals, all of whom praised the Schema in general, wanted more stress on 'sacerdotal sanctity'. Cardinal Léger of Canada almost alone was more condemnatory than otherwise of the Schema; he doubted whether this Schema would help the priest of today, a view shared by a good number of the Bishops. Every now and then the Moderator, or the General Secretary, would intervene with anguish to say that there were yet many speakers and many *modi*, or amendments, on texts such as that for Religious Liberty and Revelation which also had to be debated. Speakers were asked to cut short their interventions and not to be repetitive. One of the problems was that so many Cardinals, who had the right to intervene without notice, were rising in their places continually as they heard something on which they felt they must comment. Cardinal Döpfner

(Munich) intervened to say that he noticed the 'tone' of the Schema was rather sentimental. He thought priests would be amused to learn that they were the 'precious spiritual crown of the Bishop'. Cardinal Suenens was satisfied with the text on the whole but thought the insistence on discipline and obedience overdone. Bishop Charue of Namur, whose book on 'Diocesan Clergy' had recently been published, aroused special interest, though his book had not been everywhere well received. It was almost certainly due to his intervention that a new note was struck in the final Decree, which stresses that the sanctification of the *ministerial* priest, as distinct from the *religious* priest derives rather from his active work in the apostolate than from religious exercises (such as mental prayer and spiritual reading). It was striking how Bishops from English-speaking backgrounds, one after another, made *practical* suggestions. Bishop Lever, for instance, an Auxiliary of San Antonio, USA, spoke up for *curates* who, he said, in large dioceses made up more than half the number of priests and 'did much more than half the work'. He wanted them to have juridical status and rights. Cardinal Roy of Canada defended the *parish* as an essential unit in the Church's structure. Cardinal Sheehan of Baltimore wanted the priest to be seen not as a kind of appendage to the Bishop, as he thought the Schema tended to suggest. The debate showed no sign of ending and the Presidents, in order to clear up business on amendments on other documents, felt compelled to force an adjournment. Some hoped the Holy Father would prolong the Council or at any rate lengthen this Fourth Session, but Pope Paul made it clear that this could not be done. All was to finish by 8 December.

Since numbers of Fathers were still due to speak and they and groups were invoking the right to do so provided they were sponsored by seventy Bishops, time was found for further debate a few days later. This, however, was conceded by the Presidents on condition that only those who had seventy signatures would be permitted to speak. These were at once given the name of 'The Septuagints'. I had sent in my script quite a while ago but as I had not such sponsorship and did not like to solicit names, I took it for granted with some relief that my second attempt to intervene, which our Bishops had encouraged, would not now be possible.

The resumed debate began on 25 October. The first of 'The Septuagints' was Bishop Arrieta of Costa Rica who sought help for countries of South America and other areas where there were few priests. He suggested international seminaries, an idea that found its way into a Council Document. He appealed to Religious not to make it a condition of sending priests to an area that they should be given its jurisdiction. One Spanish Bishop, speaking for two hundred others, spoke of the need for 'spiritual direction for diocesan priests', a thing St Ignatius had always wanted, it was said.

The last day of the debate, 26 October came on. To my confusion and dismay when I sat down in my place I found that not only was I down to speak but was the first due to be called after the Mass and Secretary's notices. As stated, I had ceased to expect to be called not having, as far as I knew, seventy sponsors. I can only think that Cardinal Heenan, as he now was, who was so anxious that an English voice should be heard in this debate on the priesthood, had told those that were arranging the speakers that there were in fact at least seventy anxious to hear me! The Australians had been in touch through their Bishop Muldoon, and perhaps others too. At all events, here I was due to speak. I hastily searched my briefcase to see if I had my copy of the intervention and found a rather crumpled copy. I was very conscious of the continual appeals for brevity and so cut out little passages here and there. The Secretary's notices were unusually protracted but *tandem aliquando* I was called upon to speak. Save for a few omissions here and there, as stated, this is what I said:

Venerable Brothers,

. . . *Concerning the Ministry of the Priest*, though the schema in this part has much which is praiseworthy, it seems to me to be wanting in one important aspect.

For the schema in this first part, speaking of the ministry of the priest, remains almost completely silent upon the priestly *apostolate of the care of souls*. Indeed, it speaks as if priestly administration consisted solely in the offering of the sacrifice of the Mass, in the giving of the sacraments and in preaching. This is surely a grave defect in itself, but it is especially unfortunate since throughout the whole of the Council scarcely anything has been said concerning the care of souls. It is true that the matter was briefly touched upon in the schema *De Pastorali Episcoporum Munere in Ecclesia*, but nothing positive or really useful or in any way commensurate with the importance of the subject has appeared in any schema.

This contrasts unfavourably with the Council of Trent which, in three long sessions (XX, XXI and XXIV), discussed this important matter and laid down certain precise and detailed rules for the priestly exercise of the care of souls. Because of lack of time neither the First nor the Second Vatican Council has treated of the priestly apostolate. It was a great pity that the schema *De Cura Animarum* should have been withdrawn from our discussions without even a *Declaration* or *Letter to the Clergy* being substituted to take its place. I greatly fear lest the liturgical and other reforms enacted by the Council will remain without effect as a result. Unless in this last schema, where it could be so suitably inserted and for which it was promised, something useful upon the priest's care of souls is inserted, those reforms may well not find fruition. I wish, therefore, to propose the following:

1. I propose that it be clearly stated in the first part of the schema that a most important part of the duties of a priest consists in the care of souls exercised through personal contact.

2. I propose that a section be added to this first part in which certain of the more striking texts from holy scripture illustrating the priestly apostolate should be inserted. Such texts as the following might be set down from many such: 'Be diligent to know the countenance of thy cattle and consider thy own flock' (Prov. 27:23).

'For three years I ceased not with tears to admonish every one of you' (Acts 20:31).

'. . . the shepherd of the sheep calleth his own sheep by name' (Jn. 10:3).

'Go ye . . . to the lost sheep of the house of Israel' (Matt. 10:6).

3. I propose also that there should be quoted some sayings from some of the classic writings of the saints and Councils and theologians upon this subject. For example, let there be cited something from the *Regula Pastoralis* of St Gregory the Great, which many have called the basis of all subsequent pastoral writing. There could be quoted the Decrees of St Charles Borromeo and his Provincial Councils of Milan, the Decrees of the Council of Trent and of Diocesan Councils. There are the letters of St Francis de Sales, the regulations of St Joseph Hoffman, the directions of St Alphonsus de Liguori, who wrote to the Clergy of Naples that 'the care of souls is the first of all tasks of the priest'. And there is the beautiful *Exhortation to the Clergy* of St Pius X. Let these or other pastoral writings be quoted.

4. I propose that something should be said in this First Part of the Schema specifically upon the exercise of the apostolate *in great cities and towns*. The increase in the number and size of great cities has been one of the great phenomena of this last century. There are now nations where more than three quarters of the population dwell in large towns or suburbs. This is a development which inevitably has had a serious effect upon the care of souls. It has always been recognized that to exercise the apostolate in large urban areas is far more difficult than in less populous districts. St Charles Borromeo convened his first Council of Milan in 1565, as he himself says, precisely to find a remedy to the falling away from religion in the great city of Milan and to the difficulties which his priests were experiencing in exercising their apostolate in that great city. Everyone will recall his famous chapter in the Decree of that Council which was called *De Visitatione (Pastorali)*. In that chapter it was enacted – and I quote the words used – 'the priest of a parish is to have a book in which he is to set down the Christian and surnames of all his people' with details of their state. The Decree then goes on to say that '(priestly) visitation is wholly necessary and is the principal means of the salvation of souls'. Other matters connected with the apostolate in the cities are dealt with in that chapter such as the size of parishes and the numbers of faithful in them, various methods of contacting them and so on. The Council of Trent in its

Decrees made similar legislation. If this Saint and that Council considered it so necessary to make rulings in the matter of the care of souls in those distant days when urban conditions were much less difficult than they are today, how much more should not this Council address similar instructions to our priests to help them in their care of souls.

5. Lastly, I propose that if in the schema the priestly care of souls cannot be included, some *Declaration* or *Letter* or *Directory on the Care of Souls* be prepared to be addressed to the clergy of the Catholic world. It could take the form which other conciliar Declarations, such as that on Religious Liberty, have taken. It could contain a brief analysis of present conditions especially in great cities, together with suggestions and regulations as to how the priestly apostolate can be exercised in them. In this way the gap left by the withdrawal of the Schema *De Cura Animarum* could at least be partly filled. To this end, I have left in writing some suggestions with the Secretariat.

I would like to conclude with one last observation. More than once we have heard it stated in this Aula that the Church has lost the working classes and it has been suggested that this is because of the incompatibility between modern industrial conditions and religious practice. We are here to bear testimony to the faith and practice and morals of our own countries. I do not, therefore, apologize for telling you, Venerable Brothers, that the Catholic Church in England has not lost the working classes. Indeed, it is commonly referred to as the 'Church of the working classes'. Our churches all over the country are filled often every hour with great congregations mostly comprised of working men and women. In 1861 a census was taken in London which gave a percentage of only some 4 per cent of the total population as Catholics. Today in some parts the figure would be somewhere between 15 and 20 per cent. The reason for this advance is not to be sought only in immigration. The chief reason is this: that the Westminster Synod of 1858, following the rulings of the Council of Trent, enacted – and I quote its words – 'priests are to fulfil their pastoral duty with solicitude, visiting the whole of their districts'. That Synod arranged that a special set of priests' 'visiting books' should be printed in which the parochial clergy were to set down the names and addresses of all their people and the number of visits which they paid to them; it was suggested that the visits should be monthly. The gradual increase in the number of Catholics and their steadfastness in the great city of London is mainly to be ascribed to the fact that for more than a century the priests have faithfully carried out this pastoral visitation. Where the priest enters, infidelity cannot gain admittance.

I, therefore, ask that an inspiring call should go forth from this Council, and be enshrined either in this last schema or in a separate Declaration, urging that priests go to their people and thus bear fruit which will remain and which will allow them to appropriate to themselves the words of Our Divine Lord: 'Of those whom thou gavest me I have lost none except the son of perdition' (Jn. 17:12).

265

As I made my way back to my seat a neighbouring Bishop said audibly '*Nolite transire de domu in domum*'. My Italian neighbours again welcomed me back to my place with many felicitations, but felt in conscience bound to tell me that they hoped such revolutionary ideas would not find their way into the final text; they thought their priests would be deeply shocked by them.

Cardinal Heenan himself, who was so anxious that English voices should be heard in this debate on the priesthood, also intervened himself, being one of the last speakers at the Council. He spoke warmly of his thankfulness that a full Decree on the priesthood had found a place at the Council. He had thought my own intervention had gone too much into details and made a point of saying in his speech that 'because the actual practice of the pastoral care of souls varies inevitably according to local conditions', it would be best for the Decree to suggest 'only general lines'. He was, however, he said, very glad that the need for a true '*cura animarum*' had been stressed in addition to liturgical and other ministerial duties of the priest.

In the Aula, as he spoke, Mr Frank Duffy, the Founder of the Legion of Mary (of which the Cardinal had at one time been National Director) sat listening to the debate. The Cardinal spoke admiringly of the Legion as a perfect model for the lay apostolate especially as its rules insisted on all being done 'with and under the priest'. Among other things the Cardinal mentioned the need for priests to 'associate together' (another tridentine idea). He said priests should be mutually hospitable and take their recreation together, mentioning the salutary nature of a day's clerical golf. Before the end, just to make quite sure he was not misunderstood, he declared: 'I *do* believe that regular visitation of his families is a vital part of the priestly ministry.' Lastly, he asked that Religious Orders should assist in the pastoral field even if sometimes this might seem to conflict with their Rule. This he said in his customary direct and arresting manner and, as he wrote himself later, 'these remarks of mine were interpreted by the journalists as being an attack on cloistered clerics'.

The Decree *Presbyterorum Ordinis* was approved and promulgated on 7 December 1965, the day before the Council closed. Some time later two *Directories*, one for Bishops and one for priests, which had been requested, were sent to the Fathers. Subsequently, at a Low Week Meeting, the Bishops' Conference of England and Wales discussed the desirability of a local *Directory* for our own priests to assist them to embrace the recommendations of the priestly Decree and I was asked to prepare a section of this to be devoted to 'the care of souls'. This was done and circulated to the Conference. The many great tasks which the Conference had to undertake following the Council caused the idea of this local *Directory* to be shelved. It was thought that in any case before long there would have to be a Provincial and Diocesan Synods and these would cover such matters.

The scene has changed since the Vatican Council ended. Now there are less priests than in the decades before the Council – a time which was so rich in vocations and ordinations. Priests' administrative tasks have increased. Meetings of all kinds have multiplied. There is an ever-changing situation in society. It is less easy today to be confident in offering suggestions as to the priestly care of souls. Whatever the reason, the kind of priestly visitation advocated at Trent and once so common amongst us has declined. A layman speaking lately at a large gathering in the North of England spoke nostalgically of the days when 'our families harboured priests at the risk of everything. Now', he said, 'we should like to see those days again when we had priests visiting our homes.'

Some years after the Council I was taking part in the Plenarium meetings of the Congregation of Propaganda Fide. Cardinal Döpfner was one of the participants. I had known him distantly as a student attending the same theology lectures in the thirties and he came up to me, recognizing me. He did not recall the Council incident of his 'gonging' me during my first speech. He stoutly defended his stopping those who were not speaking to their brief. On the other hand, he accepted that the English Bishops were right to try to break into the Decree on Bishops to raise something on the priesthood as, at that time, it seemed likely that the priesthood would not find a place at all on the Council agenda. I reminded him, which he did not seem to remember, that when the *De Cura Animarum* document was withdrawn, a promise had been given by the Presidents that the priesthood would at least find some mention in the Decree on 'the Role of Bishops'.

Finally, reference should perhaps be made to one incident which took place while the debate on the priestly document was taking place, since it led to much misunderstanding and misinterpretation. Since it belongs to that debate on the priesthood document it seems right to include it.

Archbishop Roberts, SJ, had made it known that he wished to intervene and those who were asked gladly gave him their signatures; he easily obtained the seventy names needed. When he submitted his text to the Secretaries it was seen to be on the subject of Conscience and not on the priesthood or seminaries which were still under discussion. Since the closure on the Religious Freedom document had already some time ago been applied, the Moderators felt unable to allow this intervention except as something *scripto exhibitum*.[7] Journalists alleged that the Archbishop had been deprived of his right to speak because his views were not acceptable to

267

the Moderators. This was not so. Subsequently the Archbishop gave the intervention at one of the *'conferenze paraconciliari'* (or 'fringe meetings', as we should call them today). In it he is said to have set out his position on the place of conscience and to have objected to what had been said in the document relating to *presumptio juris*.[8]

All the Bishops felt a sense of relief that a Decree on the priesthood had finally found a place among the conciliar documents. Individual Bishops will have liked to have added some item and to have had others omitted. The mention of the 'Priest Worker' movement, for which the French had pressed, was not well received. A writer in the *Tablet*[9] wrote that: 'The decree on the priesthood failed to face up to the indispensable importance of pastoral visiting.'

For myself I welcomed the fact that *Presbyterorum Ordinis* had found a place among the conciliar documents. I felt it to be rather weak and not as practical as I should have wished. It seems to me to add little to the papal encyclicals of Popes Pius X, XI and XII. I remembered the splendid tridentine enactments on *operosa residentia* and *visitatio* and *associatio* and *disciplina generalis*. I thought of the Archbishop of Braga's tremendous interventions and of his hurrying home to set in being provincial and diocesan synods within a year of the ending of Trent. I recalled how St Charles Borromeo had added to Trent's injunctions as to priests knowing their people by instituting the practice of the annual rendering of a *status animarum*. He stipulated that this had to be made every Lent by parish priests *per se et non per alium* and was to be obtained by a personal visit to each family of his flock. This practice was soon copied by other diocesan Bishops and found its way into the long-awaited *Ritus Romanus* of 1614 (Trent's last document) and so entered into the universal law of the Church; and, when our newly restored Hierarchy held their Westminster Synods, it got incorporated into our English and Welsh legislation.

The Church of Vatican II addressed herself to her priests and people by exhortations and recommendations rather than by edicts. Doubtless this is more suited to the times. The Council, too, did not have to deal with such great evils as 'non-residence' and rampant corruption in high places.[10]

NOTES

1. *Westminster Synods, I-IV*.
2. Cf. *Acta Genuina Concilii Tridentini*, by Theiner, Sess. XXI-XXIV with its enactments as to the placing everywhere of a *'perpetuum peculiarumque parochum qui eas cognoscere valeat'*. Mgr L. McReavy of Ushaw, one of the *Periti*, informed me that it was not until the *Super Universam* decree of Leo XII in 1824 that new parishes were ever set up with

more than one priest. This was so that there might be personal fatherly contact between pastor and people. It was initially allowed for new parishes in Rome itself because of the density of population.

3. *Ezekiel 34:2.*
4. The Portuguese Bishops were asked by Pope Paul VI to re-print this book and the Holy Father presented a copy to all the Bishops of the Council before we left in 1965.
5. Later Cardinal Archbishop of Paris.
6. For the full account of this and all Council debates the *Acta Concilii Vaticani Secundi,* now available with an Index, should be consulted.
7. A document *scripto exhibitum* was one either not submitted to be spoken or not spoken for lack of time. They are recognized as conciliar documents and are printed in full in the *Acta Concilii Vaticani II.*
8. Cf Henri Fesquet *Le Journal du Concile,* Italian edn, Milan, 1967, 949f.
9. *The Tablet, 22 January 1966.*
10. Cf such books as Gerard Strauss *Manifestations of Discontent in Germany on the Eve of the Reformation,* Indiana Univ Press, 1971.

17

AD GENTES:
A MISSIONARY BISHOP REMEMBERS

DONAL LAMONT O. CARM

The great central Dogmatic Constitution, Lumen Gentium *on the Church, begins: 'Christ is the light of all nations'. The Decree on the Church's missionary activity begins: 'To all nations has the Church been divinely sent . . .' The two mirror one another in many more ways: both embody the missionary dynamic, that the Church is the great sacrament of unity for all mankind, even those as yet beyond it. The Decree* Ad Gentes *consciously opened perspectives to those who are non-believers. The work of preaching the gospel for the first time and building up the Body of Christ to its fullness the Fathers called 'the greatest and holiest work of the Church'. The Decree went on to state: 'The whole Church is missionary'. Missionary work is the task of the whole People of God, as a fundamental duty. No other Council has ever insisted this so strongly.*

Educated at Terenure College (the Dublin Carmelites), where he is now retired at the age of seventy-five; at University College, Dublin and the Carmelite International College in Rome, the author became in 1946 the first superior of the Carmelite mission to Rhodesia (now Zimbabwe). There he became Prefect Apostolic (1953), then Bishop (1957) of Umtali; he became President of the Rhodesian Bishops' Conference in 1970 and represented it at the 1969, 1971 and 1974 Rome Synods. During 1976–80 he was a constant critic of the government's racial policies and was sentenced to ten years of prison with labour and stripped of his citizenship. Reinstated, he retired in November 1981 to be succeeded by an African priest.

This essay comes in response to an urgent request from the Editor, who wrote: 'May I please ask you to tell your story about the Mission Decree *Ad Gentes*?' I had practically nothing at all to do with the preparation of *Ad Gentes*, and so I asked myself, 'Why call on me to write about it?' And yet, I probably had a tiny little bit to do with the very existence of the Council document. Even in the most memorable events of human history there has been room for the hitherto insignificant fly which got into the ointment, for the mote which was in the other fellow's eye, and even for the straw that broke the camel's back. Perhaps that was the sort of role I played.

Memory is less reliable twenty years after the event and source material where I am at the moment is not readily at hand, so I propose to tell my story quite simply, just as I recall it. It will be a human-interest story, different probably from the rest of this book but it may be useful in showing how the Holy Spirit in surprising but in completely simple ways uses very human means to achieve His purposes.

I came from Africa to the First Session of the Second Vatican Council not really knowing what was likely to happen or how the great assembly would function. Very probably I was not the only bishop from what were known as 'the missions', or indeed from the developed Western world who arrived like men from rural areas coming into a big city for the first time and being overwhelmed by all one saw there. In some ways I was better off than many. I had been a student in Rome from 1933 till 1938. I knew the city and I knew some Italian. I knew a little bit about the central administration at Vatican City. Possibly most valuable of all, I had done all my Roman studies through Latin and I was still reasonably familiar with that language and capable of using it for Church purposes.

Before coming to the Council of course, we bishops received the preparatory documents and had studied them as well as the daily demands of our newly established mission dioceses, our limited resource material and the quality of our own priestly formation permitted. But for most of us, that was all the preparation we had.

On the opening day of the Council we were thrilled by the splendour of it. There were at least two thousand bishops in the great procession, walking four deep in best copes and white-starched mitres, and as we turned around occasionally to see if there was ever going to be an end to the flow coming out of the Vatican we got a glimpse of the old Pope, carried shoulder high in the Sedia Gestatoria, tilting slightly and precariously from side to side, in time with the measured step of his white-gloved and well-tailored bearers. The whole scene was breath-taking. We had never seen anything like it. It was majestic, magnificent. We had not yet been taught to see it as triumphalistic! It was simply taking up again where the First Vatican Council had been interrupted. The portly figure of the great Pope John and his advanced age fitted perfectly into the picture and seemed to confirm the historical continuity.

Within a few days after the opening ceremonies had been suitably accomplished the machinery of the Council slipped into gear and the real work began. The daily opening Mass, the long and beautiful invocation 'Adsumus quaesumus Domine', the indescribable sense of history evoked by the setting of the basilica, stamped and sealed the assembly as an indisputably spiritual one; and yet there was clearly present a strong, human and down-to-earth managerial group well in command of the proceedings. The rumour spread that we would be finished with all the Council business in quick style and be back home for Christmas.

Meanwhile we daily became familiar with procedure, finding the Latin easier and able to identify the different accents of those who had the temerity to submit an intervention and speak in the Aula. The magisterial presence and voice of the General Secretary Felici and his totally brilliant and easy competence with Latin were enough to chasten the ambitions of any mere missionary bishop who might dream of having recorded in his obituary notice that he had spoken at the Vatican Council.

In practice most bishops from missionary dioceses were happy enough to leave the actual interventions in the Aula to one among them chosen for the task, after they had agreed on the matter to be submitted and had the Latin text shaped and polished by some official or non-official *peritus*. The *periti* were legion and were everywhere. At the same time the bishops themselves through daily study of the growing mass of documents, by meetings in committees or at social functions were sand-papering one another into awareness of the issues evolving and preparedness for participation when the moments of decision would arrive.

About this time in the early weeks of the Council there were heard in the Aula new and commanding voices of some bishops and non-Curial cardinals – mostly from Europe, challenging the procedures of the central administration of the Council. It began to appear that perhaps the Council might last somewhat longer than had been anticipated and that its business was not going to be completely finished, wrapped up and safely stowed before Christmas, before too many new-fangled ideas could be promoted and spread abroad.

Meanwhile something very important for me had happened. Shortly after the Council had got under way the Secretary General announced that elections were to be held to fill up places in the Preparatory Commissions of those who had become incapacitated or who had died in the interim. Members of these groups were to be chosen from among the assembled Council Fathers.

I shall never understand how my name came to be proposed as a candidate for the newly created Secretariat for the Promotion of Christian Unity, but it was, and after the ballot papers were counted I was declared to be elected with almost 1000 votes. I do not know how this came about but I rather suspect that not knowing that I was Irish, and seeing the name 'Lamont', the French speaking bishops of the Council thought I was one of them and loyally supported me. I say that I *suspect* that something like that happened. I have no way of knowing; but if it did, it just goes to show how the Holy Spirit presiding over the Council could turn errors to good advantage – to my advantage at any rate.

However unqualified I felt as an ordinary member of the Council I felt immeasurably more unqualified and out of my depth among the gifted and dedicated men who worked with Cardinal Bea in his Secretariat. [During 1962–75 he was a member of the Secretariat for Promoting Christian Unity. Ed.] As everyone now realizes this was a most influential, sensitive and newly established body in the Church, with wide-ranging interests but specifically orientated towards the aims of the Ecumenical Council. Simply to be a member of the Secretariat, to attend the regular and hard-working meetings, to have one's mind sharpened and enlarged by the subjects discussed with such brilliant men as Bea, Willebrands, de Smedt, Congar, Duprey, Pavan, Courtney Murray, Barnabas Aherne and others was an education *sans pareil*, a formation for life and for this Council in particular. Who could associate with such men without something rubbing off?

As a result of all this I grew in my understanding of the Council and of the way its work was being organized. I began to become aware of the wheels within wheels, which made things go forward smoothly or slowed them down discreetly and which could put the machine into reverse or even bring it to a halt if it were so desired. However, I became absorbed in the work of the Unity Secretariat and so separated from the other mission bishops by living in our own Carmelite College, that I lost touch with what was going on behind the scenes, in the preparation of a Council document on the subject of the missionary work of the Church.

It was about this time that I attended a meeting of the English-speaking bishops of Southern Africa and came to realize that the official organization of the Council did not intend to produce a comprehensive Schema on the work of the missions at all. Instead, after considering many attempts to prepare a suitable document, it had been decided that an elaborate statement on the subject was not really necessary, because in fact, although perhaps summarily, the essential matters concerning the mission apostolate of the Church were already incorporated in other Council documents which were awaiting approbation. Duplication was to be avoided and time was short. It would be sufficient, (so 'they' believed) to compress into a number of concise and weighty Propositions all that this ecumenical Council had to say on the subject. In this way the discussion could be brought authoritatively and expeditiously to a close. I was dumbfounded and could scarcely believe my ears.

Remember, we were already in our Third Session and away from our dioceses and the end of the Council was not yet in sight. To compound difficulties, the old Pope had died and had been followed by Pope Paul VI, who newly at the helm, was grimly holding on to the task bequeathed him of directing the Council to a fitting conclusion. It was a daunting task. Powerful new and prophetic voices were now being heard at official meetings of Commissions and were increasingly influential in moulding opinions in the Aula. The Pope wished to hear these opinions and at the same time he had to handle diplomatically the old guard and the curial officials who in large measure controlled the proceedings. Many of them had worked for years in the Curia and were known to him personally. He had his hands full.

Back at the meeting of the bishops of Southern Africa when I heard that we were to get no full Mission document but were to be asked instead to approve a series of Propositions, I spoke up and protested. Others present had spoken before me with great vehemence and even with bitterness. We were resolved not to be fobbed off with such a substitute, but to reject it and to make our feelings known in the Aula. We also agreed to join with all the other mission bishops of whatever provenance and to approach some of the now acknowledged 'big guns' of the Council, people like Cardinals Bea and Suenens and get them to speak on our behalf as well, demanding a proper document worthy of the occasion.

In my protest at our meeting I had referred scathingly to the Propositions, as the 'dry bones' of Ezekiel's prophecy. Leaving the hall, someone (I think Archbishop, now Cardinal, McCann of Cape Town) said: 'Why don't you prepare an intervention and speak in the Aula and repeat what you have just said here?' I replied that other people had already agreed to speak and that that should be enough. 'No', he replied, 'the stronger our protest the better. Get something ready. The more objections the merrier!'

Encouraged by this advice and furious that the work of the Missions should seem to have been worthy of such scant consideration, I went back to our College and sat down to compose my intervention, realizing that I would have only a tight ten minutes to speak in the Aula if by any stroke of good fortune I were to be called at all from among the great number of those who wished to be heard.

Obviously the 'big guns' whom we hoped to enlist on our side would provide the most powerful opening assault. They would be heard attentively and their arguments would not lightly be set aside. These friends of our cause could sway the undecided. On the other hand, once our selected speakers of established reputation were seen to reject the Propositions and to demand a proper Mission Decree, there would certainly arise influential, experienced and astute conservatives who had the ear of the Council Secretariat and would demand to be heard too and would oppose any change.

Realizing that all the weighty and coercive arguments would already have been delivered by previous speakers I prepared my brief intervention confining myself almost entirely to the dry bones analogy. As I wrote, the concept showed that it permitted of further development and quite soon amusing ideas for the speech began to appear to me and seemed happily to fall into place. On the other hand I realized that my proposed intervention, (like Ezekiel's bones themselves), lacked weight; it was not 'meaty' enough; it might even appear skittish and be rejected out of hand. However, I handed to the General Secretary the summary of what I wished to say in the Aula. It was simply this: the propositions were like dry bones and should be rejected. An Italian Carmelite colleague polished up my own hesitant Latin text and I waited for the opening of the Mission debate and for the possibility that my name might be among those chosen to speak. It was like having a ticket in a lottery and waiting for the luck of the draw.

In the first week of November while the theme of the Church in the modern world was being discussed in the Aula, the proceedings were suddenly interrupted and we were informed that the debate on Mission activity would be introduced next day. When we assembled full of expectancy on that Friday morning (6 November 1964) we were given the surprising news that the Holy Father would be present and would personally preside. It was the first time since the Council of Trent that a Pope had done so. This time he was taking his place at the head of the table of the Council Presidents and so manifesting the principle of collegiality with his fellow bishops.

It was also appropriate for the subject to be discussed that the thoughts of the assembly should be turned to the missionary world by the celebration of the long and impressive Liturgy of the Ethiopian rite.

The ordinary work of the day then began with the Secretary General of the Council Archbishop Felici reading out the names of those who had been chosen to speak. Five cardinals and fourteen bishops were to be heard. My name was among them, down towards the end. I was shattered. How could I rise in the presence of the Holy Father and speak what I had written with such irony? I could not change it. My summary had been accepted by the Council authority and I had to stick to it. I would not be permitted to vary my argument. I was ruined.

When Pope Paul himself began to speak introducing the mission theme, we strained to hear. He spoke briefly, not longer than the ten minutes permitted the other bishops. But to our amazement he seemed to approve of the Propositions. He thought that 'the document contained many things worthy of praise'; it emphasized that 'the whole Church not just parts of it was obliged to be missionary'; it clearly established that 'the missionary apostolate was the most excellent of all in importance and efficacy'. The more we heard the more we shuddered in disbelief. This was simply an approval and a preparation for a final vote in favour of the wretched Propositions which the missionary bishops had agreed were totally unacceptable. The Holy Father's words sounded almost like a directive: 'We believe, therefore that the text will be easily approved by you even after having noted the necessity of final improvements.'

When he sat down I am sure he received a generous round of applause but I cannot remember. My mind was topsy turvy. We all admired and loved Pope Paul and sympathized with the awesome burden of responsibility he carried. Anyone who had ever known him and spoken to him in private recognized how much he consumed one with deep concern as he listened. How had he formed this strange idea about the Propositions, so much at variance with the opinions of the bishops in the front line? Who was behind this unimaginative and old-fashioned view of the present day pagan world now unbelievably accessible and with untold readiness for the Gospel? Pope Paul of all people, with his long experience at the Secretariat of State; who had travelled widely in the Third World (he had even come to Rhodesia to visit his own Milanese people constructing the Kariba Dam), how could he have come to believe that the mission activity of the universal Church could ever be summarized and satisfied with what to us were thirteen lifeless platitudes culled from some worm-cankered textbook on Missiology? Who was behind all this?

The answer seemed to be found in the next speaker who went to the microphone when the Pope had finished. This was Cardinal G. P. Agagianian, Prefect of the Sacred Congregation of the Propagation of the Faith and the one to whom all missionary bishops were most immediately responsible. Speaking as President of the conciliar commission on the missionary apostolate he delivered his official report on the disputed document, thanked the Holy Father for his presence in the Aula and finally announced that the Pope would shortly make a practical gesture of his concern for the missionary world by visiting India. This brought immediate applause, more sustained than before. When that was over the Pope then rose and walked out of the Aula, greeting all as he left and reserving a particular and affectionate acknowledgement of the presence among us of the big, emaciated and craggy-looking Archbishop Josyf Slipyi of the Ukrainian rite who had been released from long imprisonment by the Soviet regime the year before.

As soon as the Holy Father left and the normal day's proceedings began again, the first of the speakers to the subject was called to the microphone.

In my place I sat with my typed intervention and began to consider how I might change it before I was called. I would have to alter and modify what I had written so as not to appear to contradict the Holy Father in public or in any other way to show him disrespect. When I took out my pen and began to amend the script my hand shook. I turned to the bishop sitting on my left, Bishop Olivotti, Auxiliary of Venice (I think it was) hoping that as I might dictate the changes he would write them in for me. He was helpful but it wouldn't work. There were things of greater importance to be done, voices to be heard in the Aula as the 'big guns' began to be called to the microphone and commanded attention. Cardinal Léger of Montreal was speaking in our favour, so was Cardinal Doi of Tokyo and the tall and regal Cardinal Laurean Rugambwa of Tanzania was speaking up for Africa. The list was coming closer to my name. I watched the clock as the minutes dragged on. Then thankfully there was a pause in between the speeches while votes on earlier documents were distributed and collated. If this kept up, time might run out before I was called. I might be saved by the bell. I was. The closure was announced just as I was soon to be summoned to speak. Never were my prayers so opportunely answered.

Thankful beyond measure for my last minute reprieve, I returned to my College and straight away set about solving the problem of adhering in principle to the outline of the intervention already submitted to the General Secretary, and how not to appear brazenly and publicly to contradict the Pope himself at an ecumenical Council. I would probably be called to speak next day. The manner of my presentation would be important if I were to influence the minds of those Council Fathers who did not see eye to eye with the mission bishops. A spoonful of honey rather than a barrel full of vinegar was the only thing that might work. Fortunately, the good will shown us by Pope Paul's choosing the mission debate to break with tradition and appear in the Aula would help. I could refer to that in my intervention and no one could reasonably object that I was departing from the outline which I had submitted to the Secretary General and about which I had been given permission to address the assembly.

Next morning, Saturday 7 November, Cardinal Julius Döpfner of Munich presided in the Aula and opened the working session by announcing the day's list of speakers. My name was among them, seventh on the list. It was a good omen. Seven is my lucky number – so superstitious are we bishops! It was the one hundred and seventeenth session of Vatican II; it was the seventh of November. Although I had not known all this until long afterwards, it looks a propitious omen.

It is an ordeal to be called to the microphone in the great Roman basilica and to address the Church in Council. Fortunately the address system was excellent and the acoustics remarkably good. My voice sounded strange to me as I spoke the traditional opening words: *'Venerabiles Patres'*. After that, with my text shaking in my hand, the words came easily. The first paragraph straight away rejected the Propositions: *'Episcopi aliquid aliud expectabant; non nudas et simplices propositiones, sed Schema doctrina et propositis plenum capax generandi in missionariis vires apostolatu dignas.'* There was a slight ripple of applause. The missionary bishops at least were listening and were with me.

It was the moment to say something favourable about the Propositions. After all, the Holy Father had not totally rejected them. They had a lot to offer but they were not perfect. They could be improved. They were at least the props on which something useful could be mounted. Here the image of an electricity system with great pylons holding up cables or wires suggested itself. The analogy appealed to the audience who were already listening and found amusing and easy to understand, simple Latin words for things like 'infrastructure', 'pylons', 'electric wires' which like the Propositions were good in themselves but of little use if the wires were not connected or the motor not yet switched on. One sensed a sort of background reaction from the assembly as they heard: *'Propositiones utiles sunt, necessariae sunt, sed non sufficiunt. Aequiparari possunt infrastructurae systematis electricae quae comprehendit columnas, lucifera fila et alia adjumenta technica, cum motore tamen nondum conjuncta vel a motore nondum excitata.'* All this was of course spoken with grave emphasis and with the Latin pronunciation used by old theology professors known in Rome thirty years earlier.

Now it was time to turn to the opposition and soften them up, offering generous acknowledgement of the Holy Father's appearing in the Aula the previous day, sitting among us as the chief missionary. This I declared was a consolation far beyond our expectations and deserved our unqualified gratitude. The applause greeting these words spoken with warm affection, came at once loud and sustained from all parts of the basilica. The initial tension eased. The asembly at once was noticeably relaxed. The bishops were listening. In the language of the theatre, it was 'a warm house'.

Speaking at the microphone was relatively easy from that moment on, and it required no particular courage to declare that the unfortunate Propositions had even failed to satisfy the Holy Father. They should be rejected. They were lifeless and simply resembled the sunbaked bones that lay strewn along the valley of the prophet Ezekiel's vision (cf. Ezekiel 37:1–10). Calling them *Ossa sicca!* and articulating the words with sibilant and emphatic *disprezzo*, the phrase had an immediate impact and brought more laughter from the assembly. It was the most natural thing in the world to follow this up with the powerful rhetoric of Ezekiel himself, addressing it to the Council Fathers: '*Putasne vivent ossa ista?*' They replied at once in a babble of accents: '*Non! Non!*' followed by general laughter. It was the high moment of the morning. People were enjoying the session – so was I!

On other days there had been enthusiastic applause for great speeches made by acknowledged orators like Cardinal Suenens or Bishop de Smedt. This was something different – no profound theological insight had been enunciated, no new and fundamental programme of action proposed, no strange Pentecostal hush had come down upon the assembly. In fact just the very opposite. Man's innate sense of humour seemed to have been touched, and hard cerebral attitudes melted. The Holy Spirit acts that way. Thoroughly mature and integrated men cannot remain too serious for too long. The Council began to be a happy place.

The opportune moment had come to hammer home our rejection of the wretched Propositions. They would have to go. 'Have these Propositions inspired any of you Venerable Fathers to make new sacrifices on behalf of the missions? If they have not moved you, how can you expect them to have any impact on the religious Orders and Missionary Congregations of men? – or, what probably is much more important, on any Mother General of a Congregation of Sisters?' The Fathers assembled took the point and chuckled their agreement.

'Would these Propositions reverberate to the far corners of the pagan world and change it?', I challenged. No! They would no more do that than would my voice fill this vast basilica without the aid of this microphone – which I was tapping. We missionary bishops were completely frustrated by these thirteen dry bones. We had come from all over the world to the Council looking for the Pentecostal fire which the late lamented Pope John XXIII had asked for. What did we get in the Propositions? – 'This penny candle! – *haec candela*!' We had asked for modern weapons to conquer the world for Christ in this critical age: We were being offered instead bows and arrows – '*arcus et sagittae*'. As in the Gospel story we asked for bread and we were given, I would not say a stone, but these thirteen cold sentences extracted from some antiquated tract on missiology!

Time was running out on me. This cheeky intervention might easily be switched off by the Cardinal President if he became irritated, and I could be left there standing like a fool before the Council and speaking to a dead microphone. However, my luck held out for me: I survived. I had a right to my full ten minutes and I had not exceeded the limit. There was just time to appeal to the bishops again, using that magnificent invocation which Ezekiel addressed to the bones in the valley: 'Come from the four winds, breath; breathe on these dead; let them live . . . and the breath entered them; they came to life again and stood up on their feet, a great, an immense army!' (vv. 9, 10). It was, if I may say so myself, a great moment when I pronounced the final '*haec spes mea, ecce labor noster*', then stopped with the customary curt '*Dixi*' and went back to my place.

All around me bishops moved to allow me to return to my seat. I heard applause from the Aula and cries of 'Bravo! Bravo!' but as I sat down I also heard the dull gravelly accent of the President, Cardinal Döpfner, calling for order in the Aula and for silence so that the next speaker could begin. I recognized that he was telling the bishops that he did not wish to listen to any more demonstrations of the art of oratory. It was fair comment I suppose, but in spite of the reprimand I would not have missed the experience for anything.

At the end of the morning's business I was delighted that I had done everything I could to prevent the Propositions being foisted on us. Outside the basilica many of the bishops had come over and warmly congratulated me. The 'dry bones' motif seemed to have made a particular impression on them and smiling broadly and with great good humour they were already making jokes on the theme quoting from the Psalmist: '*Exultabunt ossa humiliata*!'

For me however, the most memorable comment came from a friend, the late Bishop Petit of Menevia. He came over to me as we made our way through the crowd of bishops leaving the basilica and greeted me with undisguised pleasure saying: 'Splendid my friend! Marvellous! The last of the great Irish orators!' I purred with pleasure. I could not have asked for a finer compliment. But then he straight away properly and completely punctured my self-esteem by adding: 'But of course, you didn't really *say* anything, did you?' He was perfectly correct. I had not really said anything; but whatever I did say had worked.

When the debate on the missions opened on the following Monday the Propositions were in effect rejected. After that morning the subject was dropped and it was decided that although it would involve increased labour and therefore the prolongation of the Council into the following year, a totally new and comprehensive document on the missionary activity of the Church should be prepared and presented to the Council in time for what was hoped would be the final session.

That Fourth and final Session of Vatican II opened formally on 14 September 1965. Soon we began to recognize that the vast and laborious endeavours of the past years were really now showing concrete and positive results. The Constitution on the Liturgy and the Decree on Communications Media had been solemnly promulgated by Pope Paul in 1963 at the end of the Second Session. The great Constitution on the Church and the Decrees on Ecumenism and on the Eastern Churches had been similarly approved at the close of the Public Congregation of November 1964. Other important Council documents were already debated and completed and were now only awaiting the formal public vote in the Aula. Things had really made headway.

The new document on the missions had still some way to go and had yet to be debated. The Propositions of the previous year, the old dry bones had been quietly interred and a promising, new, and vibrant work on the Church's missionary apostolate was now in the hands of the Council Fathers. Full of enthusiasm for this new Decree, I prepared an intervention and hoped to be allowed to speak again at the Council. Many other bishops had in this final session come to me and urged me to do so, and to ensure that the new document would be approved.

The matter was introduced to the Council on 7 October 1965 by Cardinal Agagianian who was followed by the Superior General of the Divine Word Fathers, a prominent member of the Commission for the Missions. This man, Father J. Schütte, described in considerable detail the format and content of the future *Ad Gentes* and noted that it had been completely rewritten out of concern for the hundreds of Council Fathers who had been so disappointed by the previous Propositions. In further elucidating the substance of the document he mentioned something which was soon to have a very personal and decisive factor in my own missionary career. This was that genuine preaching of the Gospel should never leave itself open to the accusation that it was in any way chauvinistic or concerned with imperialistic ambitions.

The debate proceeded and continued the following day with interventions in favour of the new document delivered by such authorities as Cardinals Frings, Journet, Alfrink and even on 11 October by the formidable Cardinal Ruffini of Palermo. There were others too, mostly missionary bishops who were showering their praise on the new work. There was still no sign of my own name on the list of those who would be called to speak. I began to think of someone in the centre of organization saying to himself: 'Who will rid me of this troublesome prelate?' but I was in actual fact not greatly worried. The new Decree was sure to go through.

Other bishops seemed to have the same thought that I might be prevented from speaking again in the Aula, and they spoke to me about it. I told them not to do anything. I might be called when the debate continued. However, they insisted and a deputation of missionary bishops came to me and persuaded me that I should insist (if I were *not* called in the ordinary way) on my right to be heard in Council when I had the support of at least seventy Council Fathers. They said: 'If you who so notoriously condemned the old Propositions can now be heard in the Aula, to approve of the new Schema we will be sure to get lots of support.'

At the assembly on 12 October, the debate on the missions continued, seventeen speakers being heard with most of them in favour of the new document. Then suddenly as if bored with the monotonous and repetitive approval, a closure was called on the discussion and authority sought for this action by a standing vote. This action, intended to speed up the proceedings was later sanctioned by a written paper vote.

The assembly then took up other business; matters concerning other subjects which had to be voted and approved. The work went on for some time and then suddenly to my surprise I heard my name called by the Cardinal President of the day and I was introduced by his saying I was to speak in the name of at least seventy other Council Fathers.

The speech which I then delivered had a great deal more substance to it than my 'dry bones' effort of the previous year. It was quietly received but with some applause at the end. Apart from the enthusiastic support I gave the new Schema the only thing commentators remembered from the intervention was a simple Latin sentence which seemed to justify all the work of the Council and summarize in pithy fashion the purpose of the Decree *Ad Gentes*. It read: '*Nulla gens tam fera est ut Christi Evangelii capax non sit, neque tam culta ut Evangelio non indigeat,*' – 'No people are so primitive as to be unfit for the Gospel; none are so civilized as not to need it.' It is worth remembering. *Ad Gentes* received a final vote of: *Placet* 2,394; *Non Placet* 5; Nulla 0.

18

THE RIGHT TO RELIGIOUS FREEDOM: THE SIGNIFICANCE OF *DIGNITATIS HUMANAE*

FRANZ CARDINAL KÖNIG

Of the three Declarations (on Christian Education, on non-Christian Religions and on Religious Freedom), this was the last and at the time the most debated. It has been so well absorbed (some say ignored) since then, that it rests to be quoted – where the Declaration Nostra Aetate *has recently come into greater prominence particularly in regard to relations between Jews and Christians (sec. 4; cf.* The common bond: Christians & Jews, *June 1985). This Declaration arose as part of* De Ecclesia *Chapter IX, which dealt with the conduct of the State towards religion. In a Catholic State, citizens belonging to other religions – dicitur – do not have the right not to be prevented from professing (these other) religions, though for the common good the State should tolerate their profession. In a non-Catholic State, it is the duty of the State to follow the natural law, leaving Catholics wholly free to profess their own religion and the Church free to accomplish its mission. To that view the Fathers and periti were distinctly opposed: so the subject was simply removed from the* schema De Ecclesia *(which is no solution!). Inevitably it surfaced later on.*

Late in the Second Session the Secretariat for Promoting Christian Unity presented the Fathers with the first of five draft texts (six in all) that became the subject of 120 speeches and 600 written interventions, to which should be added consultations with the Observers. Beginning as Chapter V of the Decree on Ecumenism, moving to an appendix to that, it then became an independent document. It remains an ethical, a political and a theological doctrine intertwined; a late acknowledgement by the Church of what has long been enshrined in constitutional law.

The connection between the Cardinal Archbishop of Vienna and the United States, home of the initiation of this Declaration, goes back to 1959 when he was made a Doctor of Laws by the University of Notre Dame, Indiana. In 1964 he was given honorary doctorates by four colleges in America, and notably by the Catholic University of America, Washington DC. In 1966 he was made a member of the American Academy of Arts & Sciences. So, as the Declaration was being fashioned in Rome, he was finding favour in the United States.

Franz König was born in 1905 and was brought up in Rabenstein, Lower Austria. Called to the priesthood, he studied philosophy and theology at the Gregorian University, Rome; going on to doctoral studies in ancient Persian religion and language at the Pontifical Biblical Institute in Rome. Ordained in 1933, he returned to his home diocese of St Pölten, where in 1938 he was made a cathedral canon. From then on, after two semesters at Lille for social studies, he spent his time until the end of the War on oriental and legal studies at the University of Vienna, as well as working with the young and with prisoners of war.

In 1945 Franz König became professor of religion at Krems-on-Donau; he was appointed to the Catholic Faculty of Theology at Vienna and the following year he published a study, The Old

Testament & the ancient oriental religions. *By 1948 König had become Professor of Ethics and Moral Theology at Salzburg; during that period his main contribution was to the three-volume edition of* Christus und die Religionen de Erde *(Vienna 1951, 3 ed 1961), a massive study of world religions.*

In 1952, Franz König was appointed Bishop and in 1956 Pius XII appointed him to succeed Cardinal Innitzer (1932–55) as Archbishop of Vienna. At the first Consistory of John XXIII he was made a Cardinal Priest.

At the planning stage of the Council, Cardinal König was appointed to the Central Preparatory Commission, and was then elected to the Theological Commission. In 1961 he became the first Cardinal to pay a visit to Patriarch Athenagoras in Constantinople; and two years later the first to visit Cardinal Mindszenty, Primate of Hungary, since 1956 seeking refuge in the American Embassy, Budapest (until he was able to fly to Rome in 1971). In 1964, König was present at the Eucharistic Congress in Bombay, where, characteristically, he went on to hold discussions with prominent experts on Hinduism, Parseeism and Islam in India.

In the summer of 1965 a third Vatican Secretariat was created, the Secretariat for Non-Believers; and of this he became the President until June 1980.

At the Second Vatican Council the Catholic Church took a decisive step forward in its transition from defensiveness, characterized by apologetic, to a much more positive and outgoing attitude towards the world and mankind, characterized by the will to engage in discussion and collaboration. Fear and mistrust of secular society were dispelled by renewed appeal to Christian hope. The Dogmatic Constitution on the Church, *Lumen Gentium*, for example, refers to the all-embracing love of God who 'wills all men to be saved' (cf. 1 Tim. 2:4). The plan of salvation includes Moslems, who, acknowledging the Creator, 'profess to hold the faith of Abraham, and together with us adore the one . . . God'. His will to save also extends to 'those who in shadows and images seek the unknown God'. (sec. 16. Cf. sec. 22, 41; Declaration on the Relation of the Church to Non-Christian Religions, *Nostra Aetate*, sec. 1, 2.)

This readiness to enter into dialogue can also be seen in the Declaration on Religious Freedom, *Dignitatis Humanae*, although this document is intended primarily as a defence of human rights in general, and religious freedom in particular, against the attentions of Marxist-Leninist régimes. The final text emerged only after much deliberation, and its significance in the life of the Church and the world is only now beginning to be fully recognized.

The Declaration on Religious Freedom is in fact one of the most important documents to have come out of the Second Vatican Council, although, unfortunately, still one of the least well known. It is also one of the shortest, some fifteen pages out of the four hundred produced by the Council. Of the sixteen Vatican II documents only the Declaration on the Relation of the Church to Non-Christian Religions (five pages in paperback edition: Flannery, *Vatican Council II*, from which the English quotations are taken) is shorter. The significance of the Declaration on Religious Freedom lies not only in its explanation of the Catholic Church's position on this question, but also in its (much needed) clarification of the meaning of the term 'religious freedom', and its effect on subsequent developments in areas such as ecumenism, the Helsinki Conference on European Security and Cooperation and the resulting 'Helsinki Accord', the Vatican's 'Ostpolitik', relations with other dictatorial régimes, and Pope John Paul II's concern with human rights.

The sixth schema (draft) was finally accepted by the Council on 7 December 1965 by 2308 votes to only 70 against, and promulgated by Pope Paul VI the same day under the title of its opening words, '*Dignitatis humanae*'. It also bore a long sub-title; 'On the Right of the Person and Communities to Social and Civil Liberty in Religious Matters.'

The genesis of the final text had been a long and difficult process. Indeed when preparations were being made for the Council before the autumn of 1963 religious freedom was not one of the many topics suggested for the Council's consideration. It appeared on the agenda only as chapter five of the schema on ecumenism drafted by the Secretariat for the Promotion of Unity of Christians. This body under the chairmanship of Cardinal Bea had only recently been appointed by Pope John XXIII. A leading figure on this new commission was Bishop Emile de Smedt of Bruges, who was later to be the foremost speaker on the subject of religious freedom in the Council debates.

The general public took a great interest in these debates, and the world media joined in the discussion; although the acclaim which greeted the document's final acceptance was not always matched by a perfect understanding of its theological content. The document's progress through the Council may also have been overshadowed by the equally fraught passage of the Declaration on the Relation of the Church to Non-Christian Religions, which in its final paragraph anticipates our text: 'the Church reproves, as foreign to the mind of Christ, any discrimination against people or any harassment of them on the basis of their race, colour, condition in life or religion' (sec. 5).

The difficulties in drafting an acceptable text were partly political as well as theological. For centuries Catholics had enjoyed privileges of religious expression, while denying equal rights of freedom of religious practice to confessional minorities, in those countries such as Spain, Italy or South American countries where Catholicism was the state religion. A similar situation in reverse existed in those countries of northern Europe where Catholics formed a disadvantaged minority. This institutionalized inequality was probably all that remained of the '*cuius regio, eius religio*' principle behind the religious settlements of Europe after the Reformation and Counter-Reformation (notably the Augsburg settlement of 1555 and the Peace of Westphalia 1648). In the sixteenth and seventeenth centuries it had meant that the religion of a state and all its citizens was determined by that of its ruler. In the eighteenth and nineteenth centuries the tenet was more liberally intepreted, and tempered by tolerance: the state religion of a country was that of the majority of its citizens; and minority confessions were tolerated in the public interest.

The theological difficulties confronting the Council were even more severe. Some of the Council Fathers insisted that Error does not have the same inalienable rights as Truth. In this they were still influenced by the views expressed all too clearly in March 1953 by Cardinal Ottaviani. As Prefect of the Sacred Congregation for the Evangelisation of Peoples he had explained the Church's position: only he who is in possession of truth has a right to freedom of practice and expression of his religion: only the Catholic religion is in possession of the truth, all other religions, including non-Catholic Christian confessions, containing elements of error; therefore only the Catholic Church and her corporate members have a right to religious freedom. Other faiths are entitled to tolerance and understanding, because it is to be assumed that these beliefs are held sincerely. The state is obliged to acknowledge God and accord him fitting (i.e. Catholic) worship, (although it was recognized that this was a practical possibility only in countries with a Catholic majority). Where Catholicism is a minority religion the state should recognize Catholic believers' rights to religious freedom on the basis of natural law.

Cardinal Ottaviani had meant to emphasize that no barriers should be placed in the way of disseminating truth, but his words caused a furore in many countries, and the Pope himself, Pius XII, had expressed his unease. Nevertheless a small number of Council Fathers continued to be influenced by his opinion. Others objected that the early schemata favoured religious indifferentism, that the document placed the civil authorities in a neutral, or even antagonistic position vis-à-vis religion, and that it contradicted Church teaching on a number of points. It is hardly surprising, therefore, that agreement on a final text cost so much time and effort. At one point a Council Father was moved to comment, 'Thus ended a debate that was perhaps the most violent ever to have taken place in the Aula. It had been rich in dramatic moments, reflecting the love of truth and pastoral concerns as well as the interests of the various milieux in which the fathers have to exercise their apostolate' (Art. 'Vatican II' *LThK* Vol II, 708; tr. H. Graef, art. 'Declaration on Religious Freedom', P. Pavan, *Commentary on the Documents of Vatican II* Vol IV, 57).

The document that finally emerged from this controversy represents a major advance in Church thinking on religious freedom. The key-note is heard in the very first paragraph: 'This demand for freedom in human society is concerned chiefly with man's spiritual values, and especially with what concerns the free practice of religion in society. This Vatican Council pays careful attention to these spiritual aspirations and, with a view to declaring to what extent they are in accord with the truth and justice, searches the sacred tradition and teaching of the Church, from which it draws forth new things that are always in accord with the old.'

The main text begins with a bold statement: 'The Vatican Council declares that the human person has a right to religious freedom.' This freedom is then defined as immunity from coercion by individuals, social groups or any human power (sec. 2). From the context it is clear that this right applies to all men and women irrespective of language, race or creed.

In matters of religion no one may be forced to act contrary to his beliefs, or be restrained from acting according to his beliefs in public or in private, alone or in association with others.

Religious freedom is also connected with the rights of parents, for they have a right to choose a religious education for their children 'in accordance with their own religious beliefs' (sec. 5). This right should be respected by government authorities. It is violated if children are forced to attend classes that are not in accord with their parents' beliefs, or if parents directly or indirectly have unjust burdens laid upon them because of their exercise of this right. This freedom of choice in education applies not only to Catholics, but is a right common to all parents.

This right to religious freedom which the Catholic Church claims on its own behalf and for all people and faiths should be recognized by civil authorities and guaranteed by law. All religious groups are entitled to legal protection: 'It is certain . . . that men of the present day want to profess their religion freely in private and in public. Indeed it is a fact that religious freedom has already been declared a civil right in most constitutions and has been given solemn recognition in international documents' (sec. 15).

When applied correctly the right to religious freedom is an important contribution to international peace and understanding, for it is a fact that nations are becoming increasingly interdependent. Closer links are formed between different cultures and faiths, and awareness of the individual's responsibility is growing. The peaceful harmony of such contacts is promoted by safeguarding freedom of religious expression.

Religious liberty must, however, be curbed where the rights of others or the common good are endangered. The state and society have a right to protect themselves against any misuse of the right to religious freedom, which would use religion as a pretext to encroach on other rights. Government authorities should assess such situations by objective criteria 'for the effective protection of the rights of all citizens and for peaceful settlement of conflicts of rights' (sec. 7). The civil authorities' role to intervene in the interests of law and order does not entail a right to decide on matters of doctrine.

The right to religious freedom derives from the dignity of the human person. The whole document revolves around this theme, and having considered it in the light of reason, turns then to consider it in the light of revelation. The New Testament gives the example of Christ, who never compelled anyone to follow him; and according to the teaching of the Church the act of faith is by definition always a free act. In the words of the Declaration: 'God calls all men to serve him in spirit and in truth. Consequently they are bound to him in conscience but not coerced. God has regard for the dignity of the human person which he himself created; the human person is to be guided by his own judgment and to enjoy freedom' (sec. 11).

The state is duty bound to maintain a favourable attitude towards religion: 'The protection and promotion of the inviolable rights of man is an essential duty of every civil authority.' Governments are therefore obliged 'to create conditions favourable to the fostering of religious life' (sec. 6).

(It should be noted that the religious freedom referred to by the Declaration is not freedom or autonomy from religion, but rather freedom from coercion either to profess religious faith or to refrain from religious practice. The term refers to the human and social conditions needed to profess faith, not to its doctrinal content.)

This freedom of religious belief and practice has an importance for our times that reaches far beyond the limits of the Church. Pope John Paul II indicated its significance in the life of the Church when he wrote to the signatories of the Helsinki Accord on 1 September 1980 that the Declaration on Religious Freedom contained the fruits of the Catholic Church's deliberations on the subject, and described its publication in terms of 'a document which lays particular responsibility on the Apostolic See' (sec. 3). The importance of the Declaration for non-Catholics can be seen in its influence on the progress of the ecumenical movement, the role of the Vatican in the discussions and final act of the Helsinki conference, the

Vatican's 'Ostpolitik' with its concentration on matters of human rights, and efforts to secure freedom of action for the Church in countries ruled by dictatorship.

In the early stages of the Council religious freedom was discussed in the context of ecumenism. The Catholic Church was widely regarded by outsiders as intolerant, presumptuous, antagonistic towards the ecumenical movement, and isolated from developments in the outside world. A perceived double standard in the Catholic Church's attitude to religious freedom reinforced this negative view: some elements within the Church continued to exercise a nineteenth-century attitude towards non-Catholics, and sought to deny confessional minorities in Catholic countries the same freedom of religious practice which they claimed for themselves in those countries where Catholics were the religious minority on the grounds that error was not entitled to the same rights as truth, and that non-Catholic teaching contained elements of error. The weight of conciliar authority behind the Declaration on Religious Freedom established beyond all doubt the Catholic Church's commitment to equal rights for Catholic and non-Catholic faiths. The clarification of the Catholic Church's position on this subject did much to dispel mistrust among non-Catholics; without it the enormous advances in ecumenism made since the Council would hardly have been possible. The Prefect of the Sacred Congregation for the Doctrine of the Faith has written of the present attitude of the Catholic Church, 'One of the most significant consequences for theology of the Second Vatican Council is that its thought and language are now totally orientated towards the ecumenical dimension'; Catholic theology now draws as much on the resources of other Christian traditions as on its own heritage (J. Ratzinger, *Theologische Prinzipienlehre* 1982, 5).

Article 7 of the Final Act of the Helsinki Conference on European Security and Cooperation (1973–75; the signatories include the USSR) acknowledges a universal human right to freedom of religious belief or conviction: their human dignity entitles all men and women to freedom to profess and practise any religion, whether alone or in community. That the Vatican was invited to send a delegation to this conference at all shows the considerable weight attached to the Declaration on Religious Freedom in international relations. But article seven also shows the influence of the Vatican representatives at the conference. The moral weight of the Vatican II documents on religious freedom, ecumenism and the relation of the Church to other faiths (including Judaism) together with the Catholic Church's general stand on human rights issues gave the Church's leadership an authority in world affairs without which they would hardly have been invited to attend. Once there the Vatican delegates referred the conference in the preliminary discussions to the Declaration's definition of religious freedom; and throughout the following debates the Apostolic See regarded its particular contribution as bringing into the foreground of discussion the hopes and fears of modern man, while other delegations spoke almost exclusively of international relations and their own national interests.

On the subject of the Marxist-Leninist attitude towards religious liberty, which initially prompted the Declaration, I personally would add that apart from the fact that theory and practice frequently diverge, Marxism-Leninism often understands by 'religious freedom', merely freedom of conscience or thought on religious matters. Those who wish to give practical expression to their faith in Marxist-Leninist states often find themselves denied opportunities in higher education, the media, politics, and the armed forces.

Finally, we must never lose sight of the fact that religious freedom is a vital aspect of tolerance of one another in human society, and, even more important, an essential element of the dignity of man. In the words of the Council: 'This demand for freedom in human society is concerned chiefly with man's spiritual values, and especially with what concerns the free practice of religion in society' (sec. 1).

19

RELIGIOUS FREEDOM:
AN AMERICAN REACTION

JOHN TRACY ELLIS

Summing up the Declaration Dignitatis humanae *on what some call 'Religious Liberty' (perhaps a more American translation) two days after its promulgation, V. Gorresio wrote: 'The schema which deals with religious freedom constitutes by itself a genuine development of doctrine, perhaps the greatest and most characteristic progress achieved by the Council' (*La Stampa, *Turin 9 December 1965). Its evolution has been traced in its phases by Mgr Pietro Pavan (in H. Vorgrimler, *Commentary on the documents *IV. 49–62), from* De Ecclesia *to* Ecumenism, *from* declaratio *prior to* textus emendatus *and* re-emendatus, *from* textus recognitus *to* textus denuo recognitus. *Finally, on the last day of the Council, the last text received 2308 votes placet, 70 votes non-placet with eight void: that high vote was the culmination of dramatic struggle, during which a most important doctrine was deepened and clarified. One of the United States bishops remarked that without their support, 'this document would not have reached the floor'.*

The opening lines are key to the whole document: 'Contemporary man is becoming increasingly conscious of the dignity of the human person (whose actions) should not be subject to the pressure of coercion but be inspired by a sense of duty...' The Fathers claimed for everyone today religious freedom as a personal right, not in virtue of historical circumstances or social custom but in virtue of the dignity of the human person. This is clearly a doctrine very near to the heart of the present Pope in his Polish experience and his encyclical teaching; just as it was near to the heart of Paul VI who called it 'one of the major texts of the Council'.

Monsignor John Tracy Ellis has long taught Church History at the Catholic University of America in Washington, where, though he was not directly involved at the Council, he has been called to exercise a close interest. His writings at about the time of Vatican II include A guide to American Catholic history *(Milwaukee 1959),* Perspectives in American Catholicism *(Baltimore 1963) and* Documents of American Catholic history *(2 vols, Chicago 1967). His most recent publication is* Catholic bishops: a memoir *(Wilmington 1984). We should also recall his timely article, 'Religious Freedom in America: changing meanings in past and present', *Wiseman Review 496 *(Summer 1963), 128–38.*

'It was, of course, the most controversial document of the whole Council, largely because it raised with sharp emphasis the issue that lay continually below the surface of all the conciliar debates – the issue of the development of doctrine.'[1] These words of John Courtney Murray SJ, principal architect – so to speak – of the Declaration on Religious Freedom, more than merely suggest the distance that the Church has travelled since sec. 15 of the Syllabus of Errors (8 December 1864) condemned the proposition that, 'Every man is free to embrace and profess that religion which, guided by the light of reason, he shall believe true.'[2] When Newman published *An Essay on the Development of Christian Doctrine* in 1845 a shadow was immediately cast over the name of the new convert, a shadow that was not entirely lifted when he was made a cardinal in 1879. Even after that signal of official approval conservative theologians continued to frown, and some were still frowning in 1965. As Murray expressed it shortly after the Council's close, 'The notion of development, not the notion of religious freedom, was the real sticking-point for many of those who opposed the Declaration even to the end.'[3] And this was only one of several reasons why historically-minded persons have referred to Vatican II as 'Newman's Council'.

If as an American the present writer thinks instinctively of Father Murray in regard to the Declaration on Religious Freedom, he does not wish to create the impression that the achievement was owed to Murray alone. Many others made their contribution, notably Emile-Joseph de Smedt, then Bishop of Bruges, to name only one. The struggle for religious freedom in de Smedt's native Belgium had long since been won when the constitution of 1831 ushered in a unique settlement of the delicate relations of Church and State in the new Kingdom of the Belgians. The matter was far otherwise in the United States where in spite of the Bill of Rights which came into force in 1791 the first article of which read, 'Congress shall make no law respecting an establishment of religion, or prohibiting the free exercise thereof...', the Catholics were subject to repeated campaigns against their Church on the score of its 'foreignism', and especially because of its teaching that the ideal situation was that of a union of Church and State. To their embarrassment, American Catholics were reminded more than once of that teaching in statements from the Holy See. For example, in Leo XIII's encyclical, *Longinqua oceani* (6 January 1895), addressed to the hierarchy of the United States, the Pontiff had many complimentary things to say of the progress of the American Church which he attributed in part to 'the equity of the laws' and to the freedom the Church enjoyed to pursue its mission. 'Yet, though all this is true', said Pope Leo: 'it would be very erroneous to draw the conclusion that in America is to be sought the type of the most desirable status of the Church, or that it would be universally lawful or expedient for State and Church to be, as in America, dissevered and divorced'.[4]

While American Catholics refrained from open defiance of papal teaching in this regard, they were not persuaded to change their traditional acceptance of their country's separation of the two powers. When once again attacks on the Church were stepped up the chairman of the Administrative Board of the National Catholic Welfare Conference, Archbishop John T. McNicholas OP, issued a statement in which he declared: 'No group in America is seeking union of Church and State; and least of all are Catholics . . . If tomorrow Catholics constituted a majority in our country, they would not seek a union of Church and State.'[5]

Several years after the McNicholas statement of January 1948, an American Dominican priest told me that he was going to Rome: was there anything that he could do for me there? I replied that what I would most eagerly desire would be a statement from an authoritative Roman source that would permit American Catholics to live in comfort with both their Church's teaching and their country's Constitution in respect to relations of Church and State. When my friend asked for a statement he could submit at Rome I forwarded the McNicholas remarks quoted above. Some months later I received a letter that brought keen disappointment. The American priest had given over the McNicholas statement to his confrère, Michael Browne OP, Assessor of the Holy Office under Cardinal Alfredo Ottaviani. In substance Browne stated that the McNicholas statement could not stand and that if Catholics came into a majority in the United States it 'would be taken for granted' – or words to that effect – that they would work for union of Church and State.

Thus American Catholics went on striving in vain to quiet the anxieties of their fellow citizens on this score. With the presidential campaign of 1960 the issue became acute when John F. Kennedy, a Catholic, became the candidate of the Democratic Party. Religious prejudice rose to fever heat and coloured much of the national debate. Over and over again Kennedy sought to convince the voters that he would not be influenced by his Church's teaching on Church-State relations, his most important declaration being expressed on 12 September before the several hundred Protestant ministers and laymen of the Ministerial Association of Greater Houston (Texas). 'I believe in an America', he said, 'where the separation of Church and State is absolute – where no Catholic prelate would tell the President (should he be a Catholic) how to act and no Protestant minister would tell his parishioners for whom to vote . . .'[6] If the Houston speech made painful reading to certain members of the Roman Curia, it helped to allay non-Catholic fears, and two months later Kennedy was elected by a plurality of 118,000 votes (indeed the narrowest presidential victory since 1888).

If Catholics in the United States breathed a bit more easily after

Kennedy's election in 1960, there still hovered the shadow of their Church's official teaching to becloud their relations with their non-Catholic fellow citizens. True, from the forthright acceptance of the American position on Church-State relations of John Carroll in 1784, soon to become the first Catholic bishop of the new Republic, on to the 1960s the bishops had held steadily to their nation's law in that regard. But their efforts were constantly nullified, quite understandably, by the official teaching of the Church. That was why in part the American delegation of over two hundred bishops at Vatican Council II were united on this one issue as on no other topic that entered into the conciliar debates. They broke ranks on other matters, for example, on the liturgy; but on religious freedom they were solidly united with the arch-conservative Cardinal James Francis McIntyre of Los Angeles as much committed to the principle as the free-wheeling Cardinal Richard Cushing of Boston.

To be sure, the Americans had powerful support from Council Fathers and *periti* of other nations who were as much convinced as they were that the issue was of paramount importance for the Church's future in a world where pluralism had become so pervasive. Yet the American contribution in this debate constituted what might be termed their finest hour in the Council. That fact was recognized by Monsignor Pietro Pavan a decade after the close of the Council when in a lecture in Washington, DC he stated that he had attended the Council as a *peritus* from beginning to end of the debates. 'Hence', said Pavan: 'I feel able to say with full assurance that the impact of the American episcopate – above all the Bishops of the United States – was decisive (1) in bringing about the Council document *Dignitatis Humanae*, i.e. the Declaration on Religious Freedom and (2) in ensuring that its main line of argument should be what it is.'[7]

Writing as an historian of American Catholicism, I can say that no document of Vatican Council II was of more significance to me than that of the Declaration on Religious Freedom which was formally promulgated on 7 December 1965. Some months before the Final Session of the Council I was invited by Bishop Francis F. Reh, Rector of the North American College, Rome, to deliver a series of lectures on the history of Catholicism in the United States for the students of that College. I had been invited in 1962 by Robert E. Tracy, Bishop of Baton Rouge, [who made a memorable speech on No Racial Discrimination, Ed.] to accompany him to the Council [as his *peritus*] but I had declined his kind invitation due to my teaching obligations at the University of San Francisco. Bishop Tracy was understanding of my position and when I arrived in Rome in September 1965, he facilitated my entrance to Saint Peter's Basilica for the opening of the

Fourth Session where he ushered me to a seat just above that of the non-Catholic Observers with a splendid view of the main altar where Paul VI offered the Mass. Each day thereafter I rode with Bishop Reh to the morning session where I was well placed to hear the debates. I made up for my deficiency in catching all that was said in the various interventions by attending the press panel in the afternoons, a device that had been set up by the American bishops for the press.

By far the most memorable day for me came on 21 September. Upon arrival at the basilica I was informed by an American priest that there was widespread gloom among many since the steering committee the night before had voted sixteen to nine (if my memory does not fail me here) to postpone the debate on the Declaration on Religious Freedom, a tactic brought about by the conservatives to prevent the document's enactment if at all possible. As I made my way to my seat I looked down and saw Cardinal Amleto Cicognani, Secretary of State, crossing the pavement. I thought nothing of that, believing that for some reason or other he was simply late in arriving for the Mass. Later in the day I learned the reason for his tardiness – he, Cardinals Gregory Agagianian and Eugene Tisserant, and Archbishop Pericle Felici had been summoned above to the papal apartment to be told that there would be a vote on religious freedom, true to Paul VI's promise made to Cardinals Emile Léger (Montreal), Albert Meyer (Chicago), and Joseph Ritter (St Louis) at the close of the Third Session the previous year.

Meanwhile Felici as Secretary of the Council rose to the podium to announce that the vote on religious freedom would be taken that morning after all. It is easy to let one's imagination take over on such an occasion, but I honestly felt that there was an audible sigh from the Council Fathers at the announcement. The debates then began and the one I remember most vividly was the intervention of Cardinal Joseph Beran, exiled Archbishop of Prague, who had spent years of confinement in prison under both the Nazis and the Communists for his defence of the rights of the Church. Who among the more than 2,000 conciliar Fathers had a better right to speak in behalf of human freedom? If the Cardinal's Latin spoken with a Bohemian accent left me wondering about certain passages, I had no uncertainty about the significance of the intervention for his fellow bishops as they broke into thunderous applause as the rotund churchman descended from the podium. I made it my business to seek out an English translation and felt a thrill in reading the text, a part of which contained the following:

So, in my country, the Catholic Church at this time seems to be suffering expiation for defects and sins committed in times gone by in her name against religious liberty, such as in the 15th century the burning of the priest John Huss and during the 17th century the forced reconversion of a great part of the Czech people to the Catholic faith . . .

So history also warns us, that in this Council the principle of religious liberty and liberty of conscience must be enunciated in very clear words and without any restrictions, which might stem from opportunistic motives. If we do this, even in the spirit of penance for such sins of the past, the moral authority of our Church will be greatly augmented for the benefit of the world.[8]

Here, it seemed to me, was the voice of a Church that had finally been won to the principle of *semper reformanda* and admitting openly and honestly her past sins in the spirit of the Council's initiator, Pope John XXIII. It was a spirit that carried through to the final vote of that morning when the Declaration on Religious Freedom in the draft under consideration was voted in by 1,997 to an opposition of 224. The revision of the text thereafter deprived the document of no essential quality as the final draft promulgated by Paul VI on 7 December made clear.

No one welcomed *Dignitatis Humanae* more warmly than the man who, in my judgement, was the outstanding American bishop of that generation, Paul J. Hallinan, Archbishop of Atlanta. Ever alert to the 'signs of the times' in contemporary society, he stated in his intervention four days before the critical vote of 21 September, that the teaching of the Declaration on Religious Freedom was not only solid in itself but, he said, 'it is precisely *suited* to our times. For it depends upon the doctrine of the Church, recently evolved, concerning the juridical State, or, as we say in English, "constitutional government" . . . Moreover, the schema corresponds not only to the truth, but to the deep aspirations of people all over the world, especially in those nations which recently have happily achieved their own independence.'[9]

NOTES

1. Edd Walter M. Abbott, SJ and Joseph Gallagher, *The Documents of Vatican II* (New York: America Press, 1966), 673. Cf J. C. Murray SJ, *We hold these truths: Catholic reflections on the American proposition* (New York: Sheed & Ward 1960).
2. Raymond Corrigan SJ, *The Church and the Nineteenth Century* (Milwaukee: Bruce Publishing Company 1938). Appendix A, 290.
3. Murray, *op cit*, 673.
4. Ed Claudia Carlen IHM, *The Papal Encyclicals, 1878–1903* (Wilmington, North Carolina: McGrath Publishing Company, 1981), 364f.
5. Wilfrid Parsons SJ, *The First Freedom: Considerations on Church and State in the United States* (New York: Declan X. McMullen Company, Inc, 1948), 83.

6. Theodore H. White, *The making of a President: John F. Kennedy* (London 1962), Appendix C, 391–3. Remarks of Senator John F. Kennedy on Church & State, delivered to Greater Houston Ministerial Association, Houston, Texas, 12 September 1960. 'I believe in an America where the separation of Church and State is absolute – where no Catholic prelate would tell the President (should he be a Catholic) how to act and no Protestant minister would tell his parishioners for whom to vote. I believe in an America that is officially neither Catholic, nor Protestant nor Jewish – where no public official either requests or accepts instructions on public policy from the Pope, the National Council of Churches or any other ecclesiastical source – where no religious body seems to impose its will directly or indirectly upon the general populace or the public acts of its officials – and where religious liberty is so indivisible that an act against one Church is treated as an act against all.

   I am not the Catholic candidate for President. I am the Democratic Party's candidate for President, who happens also to be a Catholic. I do not speak for my Church on public matters – and the Church does not speak for me . . .' [Ed.] Cf. Lawrence H. Fuchs, *John F. Kennedy & American Catholicism* (New York: Meredith Press 1967), 179.

7. Monsignor Pietro Pavan, 'Ecumenism and the Declaration of Vatican II on Religious Freedom', a paper read at a meeting in Washington, DC, 16 November 1975, 8f. Pavan likewise paid tribute to the work of John Courtney Murray on this document (pp 34, 47), with whom he was a close collaborator in every phase of this document.

8. Ed Floyd Anderson, *Council Daybook, Vatican II, Session 4* (Washington: National Catholic Welfare Conference, 1965), 36.

9. Ed Vincent A. Yzermans, *American Participation in the Second Vatican Council* (New York: Sheed and Ward, 1967), 661.

PART FIVE

CONCILIAR POSTLUDE

20

PRO ORIENTE IN VIENNA: A FRUITIO OF THE COUNCIL

FRANZ CARDINAL KÖNIG

The Archbishop of Vienna is the Western bishop nearest to the East; that is the simple key to the Cardinal's influence. He is a window onto the Church of Silence behind the Iron Curtain, Vienna having been the capital of the Austro-Hungarian Empire that still survived into this century. New lines are drawn thin, new barriers are not absolute; and old customs have not been wholly contained behind them. Vienna, in touch with the Secretariat for Promoting Christian Unity in Rome and the Orthodox Churches of the East, promises – in the Cardinal's words – to be 'not merely a bridgehead but an entire bridge'.

The Orthodox Churches had been invited to send Observers to the Council, but the long centuries of separation and suspicion had rendered John XXIII's invitation suspect: was the Pope luring the Orthodox into a union that was really a submission? It was the Anglican Bishop John Moorman (see p. 155) who, in the spring of 1963 (as Pope John lay dying), journeyed to Istanbul to tell the Ecumenical Patriarch that Rome asked only restored relationship on a basis of equality. The Bishop's simple message was that 'They are in earnest'. As a result, Orthodox Observers from Constantinople attended all the Pauline Sessions of the Council, and official dialogue was soon begun. When Paul VI visited Patriarch Athenagoras in 1967, he attributed to the Orthodox the view that local Churches are united by 'family ties' and so 'like to call themselves sister Churches'. The work thus begun from Rome was equally taken up from Vienna.[1]

At the time of Vatican II, people in Vienna were also busy wondering how ideas which came to the fore during the Council could be made a practical reality. The contribution of the Archdiocese of Vienna to the Council had been marked by such things as the liturgical apostolate of an Augustinian from Klosterneuburg, Pius Parsch, popularizing the vernacular and evening Mass; the pastoral experiments of a Mgr Karl Rudolf; the parish theology of a Karl Rahner, who was active in Vienna during the war. Vienna had no special ecumenical tradition, unless one recalls the ecumenical initiative of Cardinal Piffl when he reported to the Holy See the findings of the joint session of the Leo Society and the Görres Society of May 1926 which included affirmation of the enrichment which would come to Catholic theology through the study of Orthodox theology,[2] or the surprise which

Cardinal Innitzer (of Vienna) gave to his fellow bishops by his first-time participation at Fulda at a Bishops' conference in greater Germany of 1938.

For Vienna, the period after the War had considerably altered the frontiers between the West and the Communist East, as also their geographical and historical significance.

EAST-WEST DIALOGUE, 1920–1964

From the very beginning, the Church was involved in any discussion which took place between East and West. For her, the establishment of an atheist-Communist State in one of the biggest countries in the world was an immediate, deeply felt, shock. Thus, the war of defence against militant atheism had the support of the Church; but there were also circles within the Church and the Vatican which saw, in the huge reorganization of the East, an opportunity for the Church. It also thought that the never abandoned dream of Catholic missionary enterprise among Orthodox Russians might be revived. Attempts to infiltrate Jesuit missionaries into Russia (*Einschleusung von Jesuitenmissionarien*), the creation of a secretly consecrated hierarchy, ended for those caught in death, imprisonment or exile. The humanitarian measures undertaken by the Church to alleviate hunger in Russia at the end of the First World War remained without response from the new rulers in the Kremlin.

The era of Pope Pius XII, which includes the period of his activity as Secretary of State, was marked by a complete break with the East, and an absolute refusal to enter into any kind of discussion. Although the idea of a crusade against atheist Bolshevism was hardly born in the Vatican, it was not rejected there at this time. Perhaps this crusading ideology weakened any power to resist National Socialism, in preferring to press on with the struggle against Bolshevism. The common struggle of the allies of the capitalist West and of the Marxist East against Hitler's Germany during the Second World War could only temporarily suppress East-West opposition. Communist attempts at expansion, the creation of a circle of Communist satellite States after the Second World War, led to the cold war in which the Church also had to play its part. Dean Acheson's 'roll-back policy' which aimed at pushing back Communist influence in Europe awakened diverse reactions within the Church. For within the Church there were also those who thought one only had to wait for the day X, the day of the collapse of the Communist-controlled regimes of Eastern Europe, and prepare for this day, in order to proclaim the faith of Christendom once again to the millions of people in the East. Pope Pius XI [d. February 1939] founded the

Russicum in Rome in order to prepare priests for the day when the frontiers would open, and the way for the proclamation of the Christian message would again be free. There were other attempts of a similar kind made in other countries.

Today the whole matter appears in a somewhat different light. At least two countries of the Communist-Marxist East have an excess of priests and nuns whom we in the West could urgently use. When one day the frontiers do indeed open, then they can come and missionize us here!

The culmination of the spiritual, religious and ecclesiastico-political defensive struggle against Communism was the Decree on Communism of Pius XII, which threatened with excommunication any Catholic who was an active and militant member of the Communist Party. Culmination in this case also signified a turning point, for although Pius XII's Decree on Communism has never been rescinded, today it is hardly ever mentioned.

The turning point came with John XXIII. It was not that he countered anything that had been said earlier: he tried to follow another, a new way. His tremendously outgoing personality sought dialogue and a personal meeting with all people, even the representatives of militant atheism in Communist countries. He believed in the value of dialogue and in new possibilities through personal contact. In his encyclicals he invited Catholics to work together with all people, including those of different views, even those whose philosophies and doctrines were condemned by the Church, in the interests of a common goal, above all that of peace.

It was also John XXIII who enabled me to play a tiny part in the relations of the Church with the East. During one of my audiences with him he spontaneously invited me to go to visit Cardinal Mindszenty in his exile in the American embassy in Budapest. When I objected that this could not be done so easily, he immediately replied: 'What is the difficulty? Go to the railway station, buy yourself a ticket to Budapest and set out on your journey!' In the event I went not by train but by car, and I went not only once but many times, from 1963 onwards.

For the first time in 1960, in a very dramatic way, I became aware that the Archbishop of Vienna has for geographical and historical reasons a special duty to make contact with his Eastern neighbours, the bishops and Catholics of those countries. In February 1960 Cardinal Stepinac of Agram died and I was keen to attend the funeral: I requested a visa through our national Chancery and the very next day heard that I was to be given a single journey visa. In fact I did not reach my destination. Just short of Agram, close to the town of Varazdin, I and my secretary accompanying me were involved in a serious motor accident. We had to stay in hospital there for over a week and received good medical nursing attention until transport back to Vienna was possible.

I had then thought in a joking sort of way, that having shed my blood for Yugoslavia, it was evident that the Iron Curtain could no longer be a line of division between a Church of the East and of the West. Through my own experience I began to understand how important it was to strengthen, through personal contacts and visits, awareness of the cohesion of the Catholic Church, of Christians in the East and in the West. When, as Archbishop of Vienna, I made the first attempts to establish contact with the bishops and dioceses of the neighbouring Communist countries, I was greatly assisted by Austria's position as a neutral state, the extent of the Viennese network of radio and television reaching far into the East, together with all the magic associated with the name of Vienna and the many historical links between Austria and her Eastern neighbours. The experience I gained through my first hesitant attempts confirmed me in my resolutions. It is scarcely surprising that not everyone understood the meaning of my first visits to neighbouring Communist states; I was sometimes fiercely attacked. Some years later, an Austrian Minister of State told me: 'By your journeys to our northern, eastern and southern neighbours you have reminded us politicians that we too have a duty towards the East.'

Since then, I have repeatedly travelled to Poland, Hungary, Czechoslovakia, Romania and Yugoslavia. I also accepted an invitation from the Armenian Katholikos of the Soviet Union. However, shortly before my departure I was informed by the Soviet embassy in Vienna that the Katholikos regretted that my visit was not acceptable. Not long afterwards, I discovered – as I thought – that the Katholikos had been as much surprised by this cancellation as I was.

These journeys have mistakenly brought me the reputation of being an 'expert' (*Ostexpert*) on Eastern affairs and even that of being the Vatican Eastern diplomat. I have always protested – but in vain – against this mistaken reputation. For only the Vatican Secretariat of State or its diplomatic representatives embark upon official dealings and talks with States and their governments; and this of course also applies to Eastern countries. My journeys were undertaken with the knowledge of the Vatican and/or of the Holy Father; but they have never included any official task or mission of a Vatican 'diplomat'. So the whole thing has always been much simpler: the Archbishop of Vienna is the Western bishop nearest to the East: in this fact I found the primary basis of my authority. I was in any case frequently able to confirm the fact that more than half a century after the end of the Habsburg monarchy Vienna still has a good name among the peoples of the East. Even the young people who know nothing more about the past associate the name of Vienna with certain expectations, hopes, dreams. At first it was easier for a bishop of a neutral State to travel in a Communist country than it was for the bishop of a NATO State. Indeed little Austria owes its revival largely to the co-operation of East and West; it can exist only if there is peace in Europe and if the relations between East and West are peaceful ones. If my journeys as an Austrian bishop have helped a little to strengthen this idea, then my efforts have not been entirely in vain. And if they have contributed to the bringing about of certain changes – positive changes – in the climate in which the Catholics of these countries live, then here too I have also been of service to the Church. Only about fifteen years ago it was thought that every journey to the East would simply serve to enhance the value of a Communist government. A journey to the East was regarded even by the Catholics of these lands as betrayal, as a dagger in the back. Nothing is more mistaken than that. During every one of my journeys I have been aware of thankful joy among these people. The Catholics of these lands have taken these visits as proof that we have not forgotten them or written them off. Through my visits in the East and through discussions that I was able to hold here, I have had to correct many a rigid Western preconception.

One matter must be briefly mentioned. All Communist countries have guaranteed religious freedom in their constitutions, but what Communists understand by 'religious freedom' is not what we understand by this. Religious freedom in Communism is freedom of worship; that is, only what is limited to church services is allowed. But even this limited freedom of worship is itself bound up with very important restrictions. Certainly nowadays no priest is executed out of hand and normally the faithful are not arrested when they go to church on Sunday. Yet there are always situations, depending on the position of the Church in any particular country, where one is watched if one goes to church, and one then runs the risk of being summoned and politely but firmly told about the 'unscientific' (*das Unwissenschaftliche*) nature of one's behaviour. One runs the risk of getting into professional difficulty because one's children attend religious instruction; and religious instruction itself can also be an obstacle to obtaining permission to proceed to higher education – all this even though religious instruction is not officially forbidden. Certainly it is not possible for a citizen who openly avows his faith and his religion to aim at high position in State service, become an army officer, write about his religion in a newspaper, or speak about it on radio or television.

And now for a personal reflection relevant to this first section. The

Church in the East and the Church face to face with the East knows that she has to live with Communism: and Communism knows that religious faith is not merely something transitory. Now, should we call this co-existence? It depends what is meant by the word. Communism itself strongly maintains that there can be no co-existence between Communism and religion. But if co-existence means living together – shared lives of opposition – then at least Catholics, and all Christians, in Communist countries with Communist doctrines of State have to co-exist. That may not seem right to us, nor is it pleasant for them: maybe Communism does not want to recognize this in theory, but that does not change the facts. We can help Christians in those countries to exist only in such co-existence. This, then, is what it is all about: the possibility of existence, spiritual breathing space, relief from pressure. What we are waiting for is neither a collapse of the system nor an official change in Communist doctrine, but rather we await further development within an already existent discrepancy between theory and practice, doctrine and actual life in these countries.

THE FOUNDATION OF PRO ORIENTE

In another respect Vienna has been a meeting-place, a centre of dialogue between East and West. In 1964 Pro Oriente was founded here in Vienna with my encouragement. Its task was mainly to revive discussions between the Orthodox Churches of the East and the pre-Chalcedonian Churches with the Catholic Church, which had largely broken down. Even if it is found that the political opposition between East and West does not have real roots in the historic rift between Rome and Byzantium, it did seem to me that at the level of discussion and contact some contribution – however indirect – could be made towards bridging over opposition, reducing tension in a new ecumenical climate.

The society Pro Oriente established the following bases of its activity:

1. In view of the situation that the Eastern partner had for various reasons been reluctant to make contact with the Catholic world Church, Vienna puts herself forward on historical and ecclesiastical grounds as a local Church, ready to initiate and build up contacts with the Eastern Churches.

2. The independence of the Eastern Churches requires that a direct approach to individual autocephalous Churches be made.

3. Pro Oriente avoids making contact with State departments or political parties.

4. For historical reasons, Pro Oriente makes no official contact with the

Catholic Eastern Churches, the so-called united or uniate Churches. The intention is to avoid any kind of resentment which could prejudice contact with Orthodox or pre-Chalcedonian Churches.

5. The official partners for Pro Oriente are in all cases the official Church authorities on the Orthodox side.

6. It has proved advantageous to begin with unofficial or personal contacts as a preparation for official meetings.

7. Pro Oriente alone is responsible for preparing the programme of activities.

8. The non-Catholic Christian Churches of Vienna, or respectively their theologians, are invited to all the multi-lateral activities of Pro Oriente.

It was the aim of Pro Oriente, in touch with the Holy See or the Secretariat for the Promotion of Christian Unity, to co-operate outside Rome and at the level of the local Church over matters that could only be dealt with at a later stage at world level. At the first symposium of 1965 I was able to point out that Vienna was the easiest place from which to reach all the Orthodox Church centres. Eastern Churches might imagine that there were secret expansionist ambitions hidden behind various discussions, but in the present Viennese climate of opinion there is certainly nothing left of that. Vienna offers not to be merely a bridgehead, but to be an entire bridge. Metropolitan Meliton, the representative of the Ecumenical Patriarch, on the occasion of the first meeting, expressed his joy that Vienna was the meeting place of this first ecumenical Symposium to continue what had begun so well at the Second Vatican Council. He then went on to say that after nine hundred years of estrangement a fraternal love was beginning to develop – causing considerable astonishment. Awareness that the Churches of East and West had so much in common was gaining ground. If in the past many hostile or aggressive theologies had been developed, this was caused by such a long period without mutual love. Today neither side wanted to over-simplify problems of belief, but both sides were prepared to meet each other in a spirit of love and understanding.

In 1964 ecumenism was something new and unfamiliar in Catholic Austria. Only the main goal was clear; the methods were untried, every step taken was an adventure.

Somewhat later, during an audience of 30 March 1979, John Paul II called the foundation of Pro Oriente 'a heartening and at the same time apposite answer to the special ecumenical mission of the Second Vatican Council'. He encouraged Pro Oriente to continue its future efforts with the same zeal.

When *Osservatore Romano* assessed new ecumenical ventures among

Catholics during the Unity Week of January 1975, it placed Pro Oriente at the head of it all,[3] and in view of the world outlook of the Papacy and Rome's sense of balance and order, this had considerable weight. The diocesan efforts of Vienna were given first place, coming before the by no means negligible activities of the French bishops' Conference. If we now consider what, in terms of Church politics, could be considered as the success of this Viennese ecumenism, three achievements could be selected:

New initiatives towards Romania

The first concerns the adoption of ecumenical contact with Romanian Orthodoxy. The relationship between Rome and the Romanian national Church was very brittle, marked by the forcible incorporation of Romanian Catholics of the Eastern rite into the Orthodox Church and by the reluctance of a national Church to enter into dialogue with a world Church. Accordingly, the Romanian Church refused to send *observatores delegati* to the Council, prevented participation in theological dialogue and rejected any direct contact with Rome. (This was evident in the case of the visa refused to the President of Rome's Secretariat for Unity.) Yet, it was precisely this Church which was so important on account of its mediating position between Hellenic and Slav orthodoxies, its own high theological level of clerical formation, its deep anchorage in the loyalty of its faithful, its own historical achievement for the preservation of the Romanian nation and the development of the Romanian State, and finally its own numerical strength. (After the Moscow Patriarchate, it is the second largest autocephalous Orthodox Church, with fifteen million faithful.)

In this situation it was the Church of Vienna which enjoyed the two preconditions enabling it to perform the services necessary to ecumenism and the Church at large. As a local Church it lessened the fears often felt by smaller unities in their experience of large, imperial machines of government. When an important Romanian Church leader addressed Cardinal König as 'Patriarch of Austria',[4] this was full of promise for closer understanding between the Churches. And so I visited him in Romania in 1967, the first Roman Cardinal to do so; and then Patriarch Justinian came to Vienna in 1968. Exchange sermons at a different church service were at that time not so self-evident. The Patriarch was extremely moved when he was invited to preach in St Stephen's Cathedral at the ordination to the priesthood which took place on the feast of SS Peter and Paul. Since then ecumenical hospitality, exchange of bursaries and lectures given by visiting professors of theology have all led to a situation where even visits to and from Rome became possible. Through this, the opposition to theological dialogue which came to a head in Patmos and Rhodes in 1980 could be surmounted: an argument used by Orthodox hierarchs friendly to dialogue against initial Romanian opposition was this: 'First you meet the Viennese Cardinal officially and now here you favour a veto.' Up till now all metropolitans of the Romanian Church and many others of their bishops have been guests of Pro Oriente. They have contributed great theological and historical experience to Pro Oriente's efforts; and they have taken away with them an impression of the Austrian Church which has influenced their view of Catholicism as a whole.

New initiatives towards the Orthodox Churches

Another achievement: in an unofficial way Pro Oriente has given considerable impetus to the beginning of theological dialogue with Orthodox Churches. In 1964 the fourteen Autocephalous and Autonomous Orthodox Churches in communion with one another and recognizing the Ecumenical Patriarch of Constantinople as *primus inter pares* decided at the Third Pan-Orthodox Conference at Rhodes (Rhodes III) that on the one hand theological dialogue with the Catholic Church could only be entered into by all the Orthodox Churches together and at the same time; but on the other hand that the time for this was not yet ripe. By this means, the Orthodox Churches of Antioch, Romania and Greece, which had both theological and non-theological reservations about Rome, had achieved a power of veto. But also those Church authorities who wanted to reduce the leading role of Constantinople, and who (with the line of 'one Vatican is enough for us') wanted to prevent the creation of a central role for the Phanar within Orthodoxy and likewise within Orthodox ecumenism, had their own ground for manoeuvre.

In the early seventies there were signs that this decision of Rhodes III was no longer fully effective. Pro Oriente – once again using its well tried method of making contact with individual theologians – invited to a conference with specific theological themes those theologians who in all other pan-Orthodox ecumenical conferences had represented the current Church authorities, but on this occasion came only as individuals. The themes selected dealt with the question of the unity of faith and the different ways in which this could be expressed; with the ecclesiological inferences of a conception of Sister Churches; and with the suspension of the anathema of 1054; as well as with the actual prospects for sacramental and canonical communion. This unofficial meeting was presided over jointly by an

FRANZ CARDINAL KÖNIG

Orthodox theologian and a Catholic theologian, both invited by Pro Oriente; these were no less than Metropolitan Damaskinos of Tranoupolis (General Secretary for the Preparation of the Pan-Orthodox Council) and Fr Pierre Duprey WF (the Pope's 'Minister for Orthodox Affairs' from the Secretariat for Unity). Limited lesser officialdom was also in evidence on this occasion, for the Secretariat for Unity and the Orthodox Centre of the Ecumenical Patriarchate in Chambésy took part as co-organizers. The outcome was already made certain by the successful invitation and participation of many prominent theologians, also very representative of their Churches. Thus Pro Oriente had fulfilled its function as a thermometer to gauge the temperature of the ecumenical climate. In addition, the fact that theologians of the calibre of a John Meyendorff (from St Vladimir, New York), Josef Ratzinger (subsequently a cardinal) and Evangelos Theodorou (Deacon of Athens) participated, gave this enterprise a substantial further effect which was this: a solid preparation was made for pursuing theological dialogue and perceiving ecumenically significant theological themes.[5] Without the 'unofficial ecclesiological colloquium Koinonia' organized by the society Pro Oriente in Vienna-Lainz (1–7 April 1974), the beginning of official theological dialogue six years later would not have been possible.

New initiatives towards the five pre-Chalcedonian Churches

In the third place, the beginning of theological dialogue with the five pre-Chalcedonian Churches should be mentioned, viz the Coptic, the Syrian, the Armenian, the Ethiopian and the Syrian Church of India, with which full Church union has been interrupted since the Council of Chalcedon in 451. Perhaps the four discussions between Roman Catholic and non-Chalcedonian theologians which took place in 1971, 1973, 1976 and 1978 in Vienna-Lainz should be considered the most important single result of the work of Pro Oriente up to date.

We are concerned here with the five Churches which are in sacramental communion with one another and which the Emperor Haile Selassie I, like a new Constantine, summoned to a closer co-operation in 1965. Earlier, at the Council of Lyons in 1275 and the Council of Florence-Ferrara in 1438, the Catholic Church had had individual theological discussions with the pre-Chalcedonian Churches. Following the pattern set by the consultations between Chalcedonian and non-Chalcedonian Orthodoxy which took place under the aegis of the World Council of Churches in Aarhus 1964, Bristol 1967, Geneva 1970 and Addis Ababa 1971, Pro Oriente again succeeded in

310

gathering together the most important theologians and the most ecumenically open representatives of these Churches as private experts in Vienna. A Coptic bishop played an important part in contributing to what became known in journalistic and inexact parlance as the Vienna Christological Formula; this he later still maintained firmly and openly, when a few weeks later he came to the throne of St Mark as Shenouda III Pope and Patriarch of Alexandria. The so-called 'Christological formula' states:

> We believe that our God and Redeemer, Jesus Christ, is God's Son become Man, perfect in his divinity and perfect in his humanity. His divinity was not for a single instant separated from his humanity. His humanity is one with his divinity, without admixture, limitation, division or separation. In our common belief in the one Lord Jesus Christ we contemplate his mystery as inexhaustible and unspeakable, not able to be fully understood or expressed by the human spirit.
>
> We confirm that by reason of our diverse ecclesiastical and theological traditions there are still differences in the theological interpretation of Christ's mystery. We are convinced that in spite of this, the different formulae on both sides can be interpreted as being in accordance with the spirit of Nicea and Ephesus.
>
> Despite the statement that there can be different theological and dogmatic modes of expression used in the interpretation of the mystery of Christ's person, we all intend, in accordance with our various Church traditions, to press ahead in our common efforts aimed at reaching a deeper and more comprehensive understanding of this mystery.[6]

With this text, all participating theologians unanimously endorsed the view that the Antiochean (Severius) as also the Alexandrian (Cyril) Christological formulae could be recognized as orthodox. It stems from this that the reciprocal accusation of Monophysitism levelled from time to time against the pre-Chalcedonians, or the charge of Nestorianism levelled against the Catholics, may be allowed to fall into oblivion as a polemical exaggeration of warring theologians devoid of Christian gentleness.

This Vienna formula also received special confirmation through its strong influence on the declarations signed during the first visits to Rome in modern times paid by a Patriarch of Antioch in 1971 and a Patriarch of Alexandria in 1973; and so obtained an official ecclesiastical confirmation. The declaration signed on 27 October 1971 by Pope Paul VI and Patriarch Mar Ignatius Yacoub III runs as follows:

> The Pope and the Patriarch have recognized the already existing deep spiritual community of their Churches. The celebration of the Sacrament of the Lord, the

common confession of faith in the Lord Jesus Christ made flesh, the Word of God made Man for the redemption of mankind, the apostolic traditions which belong to the common heritage of both Churches, the great Fathers and teachers of the Church, among them St Cyril of Alexandria, who are their common teachers in the faith; all that is testimony to the work of the Holy Spirit who continued his work in their Churches, despite human weakness and mistakes. The time of mutual accusation and condemnation has given place to the will to meet each other and to make a common effort to lighten or entirely set aside the burden of history which still presses very hard on Christians.

Progress in this sense was an immediate goal. Pope Paul VI and Patriarch Mar Ignatius Yacoub III agreed that there was no difference in their belief in the mystery of the Word of God made flesh and true man, even if over the centuries difficulties had arisen by reason of different theological modes of expression used in their confession of faith.[7]

The Vienna Formula is quoted word for word in the declaration of Pope Paul VI and Patriarch Shenouda III:

In harmony with our apostolic traditions which have been handed down to our Churches and preserved in them, and in agreement with the three early ecumenical Councils, we profess belief in the one threefold God, in the divinity of the only begotten Son of God, the second person of the Holy Trinity, the Word of God, in the brightness of his glory and the explicit image of his being, who for us became flesh in that he took to himself a real body with a rational soul and shared our humanity, except for sin; and that our Lord and God, redeemer and king of us all, Jesus Christ, is perfect God as to his divinity and perfect man in respect of his humanity. His divinity is with him in his humanity in a truly complete unity, without admixture, confusion, mistake, change, partition, separation. His divinity was never for a moment or an instant separated from his humanity. He who is the eternal and invisible God became visible in the flesh and assumed the form of a servant. In him are all the attributes of the Godhead and all the attributes of humanity preserved together in a true, complete, indivisible and inseparable unity.[8]

Amba Shenouda recalled his participation at the first Vienna meeting when, standing under Bernini's canopy, he turned to Pope Paul VI and said: 'We have attended many conferences together, but here in particular we have to remember the theological meeting in Vienna between theologians of the pre-Chalcedonian Churches and the Roman Catholic Church, where in September 1971 a tentative formula of faith concerning the nature of Christ was proposed and approved by both parties.'[9]

This is not the place to present the theological results, which take up four volumes.[10] A short summary and assessment of the content of the four meetings has been made by Otto Mauer for the first meeting in 1971,[11] Aloys Grillmeier for the second in 1973 and the third in 1976[12] and by Wilhelm de Vries for the fourth in 1978.[13]

The beginning of official theological dialogue between the Copts and Rome was also influenced by these four meetings. The results of the four conferences were officially transmitted to the Pope in Rome and to the heads of the five pre-Chalcedonian Churches. One of the participants, the Syrian Archbishop of Baghdad and Basrah was meanwhile elected to the see of Peter in Antioch as Patriarch Ignatius Zakka I Iwas. The chief Patriarch and Katholikos of all Armenians has announced that a council of all four Armenian Patriarchs is to take this up.

It is not among the least of the successes due to Pro Oriente's initiative that representatives of all five pre-Chalcedonian Churches have gathered in Vienna. This was not easy in view of the political situation in Ethiopia, the tension between the Coptic and Ethiopian Churches after the removal of the patriarch in Addis Ababa, or the Indian schism with reciprocal excommunication of the followers of the Antiochean and the autochthonous party. The participation of Chalcedonian-Orthodox observers helped to avoid an impression which Orthodox of the Byzantine party might possibly have had, namely that through the increasing unity between Rome and the pre-Chalcedonian Churches a wedge was liable to be driven in between Chalcedonian and non-Chalcedonian Orthodoxy. The invitation of Observers also came about through the conviction that, if the five pre-Chalcedonian Churches and Rome drew closer together, this would also bring them nearer to Constantinople; and the other way round, if the two Orthodoxies drew closer together, this would also bring them nearer to Rome.

The ecumenical progress made in the three spheres considered – the opening of the door to Romania, the emergency help given in the preparation of theological dialogue and the surmounting of the Chalcedonian quarrel – is certainly the most important yield or *fruitio* (*Frucht*) of the work undertaken by Pro Oriente.

NOTES

1. The official documents concerning Vatican relations with the Orthodox Churches during the period 1965–1980, i.e. with six separate ecclesial communities, is set out in English translation (full sources being cited) in Edd Thomas F. Stransky CSP and John B. Sheerin CSP, *Doing the truth in charity:* Ecumenical Documents I (Paulist Press, NJ 1982), XI. Relations with the Orthodox Church, 177–251. Fr Stransky is now engaged on a more complete documentation from 1958 (death of Pius XII) to the present.

2. Michael Lehmann, 'Österreichischer Beitrag zur Ökumene', in F. Klostermann-H. Kriegl-O. Mauer-E. Weinzierl, *Kirche in Österreich 1918–1965*, Wien-München 1966, 1. Band p. 162FF.

3. *Osservatore Romano*, 25 January 1975.

4. Cf. Archbishop Vsilij Krivocheine in the *Messager*, Brussels.

5. Emmanuel Lanne OSB, 'Ein Ereignis, das Epoche machen könnte', in *Pro Oriente, Konziliarität und Kollegialität* (Innsbruck-Wien-München 1975), 48.

6. Otto Mauer, 'Christologischer Disput heute', in *Pro Oriente, Konziliarität und Kollegialität* (Innsbruck-Wien-München 1975), 14. Original English text in *Wort und Wahrheit, Revue for Religion and Culture*, Supplementary Issue Number 1 on the Non-official Ecumenical Consultation between Theologians of the Oriental Orthodox Churches and the Roman Catholic Church (Vienna 1972), 182.

7. Original English text in *Wort und Wahrheit, Revue for Religion and Culture*, Supplementary Issue Number 1 on the Non-official Ecumenical Consultation between Theologians of the Oriental Orthodox Churches and the Roman Catholic Church (Vienna 1972), 184.

8. Original English text in *Wort und Wahrheit, Revue for Religion and Culture*, Supplementary Issue Number 2 on the Second Ecumenical Consultation between Theologians of the Oriental Orthodox Churches and the Roman Catholic Church (Vienna 1974), 184.

9. *Osservatore Romano*, 7/8 May 1973.

10. *Wort und Wahrheit, Revue for Religion and Culture*, Supplementary Issue Number 1 on the Non-official Ecumenical Consultation between Theologians of the Oriental Orthodox Churches and the Roman Catholic Church (Vienna 1972); *Wort und Wahrheit, Revue for Religion and Culture*, Supplementary Issue Number 2 on the Second Ecumenical Consultation between Theologians of the Oriental Orthodox Churches and the Roman Catholic Church (Vienna 1974); *Wort und Wahrheit, Revue for Religion and Culture*, Supplementary Issue Number 3 on the Third Ecumenical Consultation between Theologians of the Oriental Orthodox Churches and the Roman Catholic Church (Vienna 1976); *Wort und Wahrheit, Revue for Religion and Culture*, Supplementary Issue Number 4 on the Fourth Ecumenical Consultation between Theologians of the Oriental Orthodox Churches and the Roman Catholic Church (Vienna 1978).

11. Otto Mauer, 'Christologischer Disput heute', in *Pro Oriente, Konziliarität und Kollegialität* (Innsbruck-Wien-München 1975), 33ff.

12. Aloys Grillmeier SJ, 'Christen aus Ost und West', *Pro Oriente, Konziliarität und Kollegialität* (Innsbruck-Wien-München 1975), 42ff; Aloys Grillmeier SJ, 'Kirche-Christus-Konzil', Vol VI, *Pro Oriente Publication*, Innsbruck 1982.

13. Wilhelm de Vries, 'Der Primat als ökumenisches Problem', Vol VI, *Pro Oriente Publications*, Innsbruck 1982.

21

THE COUNCIL CAME TO AFRICA

ADRIAN HASTINGS

Because the Council was such a major advance in ecclesiology and so much else – in enlightenment under the Holy Spirit – it was especially difficult for the young Churches to grasp and absorb its complexity. Conservative as they naturally are before they reach theological and cultural independence (and the fortunes of Mgr Emmanuel Milingo, former Archbishop of Lusaka surely substantiate that), young Churches also find the medium of the message difficult. For example, the Latin word precepta, *happily translated by Italians as* insegnamenti *(i.e. teachings), is translated by the English as 'directives' and by the French as 'orientations'. Africa is predominantly Anglophone or Francophone, and so left puzzled. How much more is this so then in confronting new theologies or recovered ecclesiologies embedded in major documents – such as that of* Lumen Gentium II, The people of God?*

At Christmas 1965 the prelates of Africa took home their memories and their documents, and asked theologians in Africa to make due sense of both, not only for themselves but for communication to their people. The four year revolution at the Vatican had to be turned into a steady evolution over say twenty years that would bring Catholicism in Africa to a cool and controlled embrace of the spirit of the Council. A principal theologian in East Africa at the time was this author, then in his mid-thirties.

Adrian Hastings was born in Kuala Lumpur in 1929 and educated at Douai Abbey School. He studied History at Oxford and Theology at the Urban College of Propaganda Fide, Rome. Ordained in Rome for the Ugandan diocese of Masaka in 1955, he worked in Africa from 1958 to 1971, after which he became a Reader at the University of Aberdeen and then Professor of Religious Studies in Zimbabwe. He is now Professor of Theology at the University of Leeds. Of over a dozen books to his name (see references below), the author holds in especial place what accrued from his 1958 Rome doctoral dissertation, One & Apostolic *(DLT 1964); and what accrued from his years in East Africa,* A history of African Christianity, 1950–75 *(Cambridge 1979), a pioneer work.*

Probably in no other continent did the Vatican Council coincide quite so neatly and sympathetically with a major process of secular change as in Africa. 1960 was 'the year of Africa' in which more than a dozen countries became politically independent while others followed in the coming years: Tanzania in 1961, Uganda 1962, Kenya 1963, Malawi and Zambia in 1964. The excitement of the Council was, then, closely paralleled by a secular excitement. In each case a quite decisive change seemed on the way. Pope John had announced that there was to be a Council in 1959; at almost the same time European statesmen were declaring to colonial Africa that its independence was in sight. Black prime ministers and black archbishops appeared almost simultaneously. Thus the Catholic Church's suddenly discovered enthusiasm for renewal, for *aggiornamento*, fitted easily within and benefited greatly from a far wider renewal of consciousness. There seemed a natural harmony between the two. The conciliar themes of localization and pluralism, of the recognition of the positive values of different cultures and even other religious traditions, the new use of the vernacular in the liturgy, ecumenical *rapprochement*, all this conformed with the general early 1960s stress on African political and cultural values, on decolonialization, on the social necessity of cooperation and unity across the divisions of tribe, race and religion. On both sides there was the sense of a fresh, rather optimistic, new start, and the two were easily allied. The young states expected the Church to change with the new political order and so a change which, theologically and ecclesiastically, owed little in commencement to any African development, in fact spoke to the moment in a way that would not at all have been the case if it had happened ten years earlier.

In the Council itself the large majority of bishops representing Africa were still white missionaries, but black and white cooperated with dignity – perhaps indeed more closely and effectively than any other continental group. They were led in particular by Joseph Blomjous, a Dutch White Father, the Bishop of Mwanza in Tanzania, Jean Zoa from the Cameroon, Denis Hurley, the Archbishop of Durban (still much in the news). They had almost no theological advisers of their own but, as so many of these bishops came from western Europe, they easily made use of the theologians of Holland, Belgium, France and Germany. They took, for the most part, a moderately progressive line, particularly in pastoral matters, and helped to consolidate that left-centre consensus which so effectively shaped the Council's later sessions.

When the Council was over in 1965 and the bishops returned home, those from Africa could not but notice that in some ways, while the Council was so opportune for their continent, it had hitherto made particularly little impact therein. A lack of available literature and of local *periti* was clearly part of the problem. It was also true that the Council Fathers – both its leading bishops and their theologians – had had the needs of Europe and North America far more in mind than those of Africa or Asia. The bishops returned to their dioceses with a heap of Latin documents to redirect a clergy far less informed about what had been going on than their counterparts in Europe but also, for the most part, far more willing to be redirected. The laity, of course, were still more uninformed. Yet it was clear

316

as day that the condition of Africa and of the Church in Africa cried out loud and clear for something to be done.

It was here that I came into the story, almost by accident. Throughout the Council I was uninvolved. I managed to write one or two articles on conciliar topics for the *African Ecclesiastical Review*, but for the most part I was very fully involved teaching History and English to minor seminarians in Uganda. My bishop in Masaka never showed me a single conciliar draft, never asked for a comment upon anything, and I had been almost too busy to mind. Then in 1965 I was on leave in England, returning to Uganda just at the moment the Council ended. I was available for a new job. Bishop Blomjous proposed to AMECEA, the association of bishops of Eastern Africa, that a quite ambitious programme of post-conciliar re-education needed to be undertaken without delay. The plan was agreed, but who was to do it? Fr Robert Gay, at that moment editor of the *African Ecclesiastical Review* and today Superior General of the White Fathers, suggested my name and so it happened that in May 1966 I left Uganda for Kipalapala Seminary in central Tanzania to spend the next two years responsible for a programme of post-conciliar reorientation for Kenya, Malawi, Tanzania, Uganda and Zambia. As I sailed across Lake Victoria from Port Bell to Mwanza, leaving Buganda behind, its Kabaka was overthrown by the troops of President Obote – just one indication among a number that the rather peaceful, optimistic phase of early 1960s history in Africa or elsewhere was passing away.

Part of that optimism, in Church terms, was expressed by something of a working alliance, based on some mutual confidence, between bishops and theologians. The confidence had been lacking in the 1950s and would be again by the late 1970s, but from the latter years of the Council men like Rahner and Congar were no longer silenced by Church authority but rather used, even eulogized. Two or three leading conciliar theologians later became cardinals. In a much lesser way something of the sort was happening to me. In the rather untheological world of the Catholic Church in Africa I had already been under some suspicion, perhaps just because I wrote at all on theological themes. There was still, in point of fact, some rather painful opposition to my appointment. It was therefore laid down, a little oddly, that all I wrote would be anonymous, that I should have two assistants, and that all my drafts must first be sent for inspection and approval to the various major seminaries and pastoral institutes of eastern Africa. The two assistants were never found. The first material was painstakingly duplicated and distributed to Katigondo, Ntungamo, Kachebere, Bukumbi and wherever. I noted the dates of mailing and sat down to wait. A few weeks later I had received one mild page of suggestions and a couple of postcards urging me to carry on the good work. No more. I sent the data, neatly tabulated, to Fr Flynn, General Secretary of AMECEA at his office in Nairobi. I was ready and able to do the job entirely alone. Otherwise they might as well pack it all in. Fr Flynn agreed and loyally supported me, and so for the next two years I despatched twice a month some five thousand copies of *Post-Vatican II* in bundles to every diocese of the area, nearly seventy in all. In some cases, I suspect, the bundles were never distributed but in most dioceses they were used extensively for clergy conferences – some of which I attended – and regular seminars.

I worked in those two years through all the conciliar texts, making use especially of the great pile of Latin drafts which Archbishop Mihayo of Tabora, one of the most delightfully simple and wise of prelates, put at my disposal. My only real collaborators were the Brothers at the Kipalapala Press who printed and despatched my work most efficiently. My name never appeared from first to last which merely increased the authority of the commentary effectively issued in the joint name of the bishops. One good archbishop from Malawi, unaware of the way things had worked out, did write to Fr Flynn requesting that the names of the various authors should be attached to the different articles which the bulletin contained, issue by issue. Naturally I tried hard to make my comments as careful and objective as possible, as I had been ordered to do, and only one bishop wrote once to complain that a non-conciliar view had been expressed – a view, he thought, drawn from Teilhard de Chardin. Fortunately I was able to point out that the passage in question had been drawn almost verbatim from *Gaudium et Spes*! When it was all over John Todd, who had seen the hundreds of pages produced, asked if Darton, Longman & Todd could reprint it, as the Church in Britain had produced nothing comparable. In consequence a revised edition, *A Concise Guide to the Documents of the Second Vatican Council*, was published under my name in two volumes in 1968 and 1969. It is still selling. I may well be, I suspect, the only person who has had the temerity to comment in print upon all sixteen documents of the Council, but then I did it, I may plead, in obedience to the members of five episcopal conferences.

At Kipalapala I also completed a book which I had been working upon for the last couple of years: *Church and Mission in Modern Africa* was published by Burns & Oates in 1967. Its *imprimatur* was provided by Mihayo, its *nihil obstat* by Theo Van Asten, Rector of Kipalapala seminary and – by the time the book was published – Superior General of the White Fathers: I always believed in making use of these things to good effect to increase the weight of a book's authentication! It was dedicated to the memory of Joseph Kiwanuka, the first African Catholic bishop of modern times and my own former diocesan in Masaka, who had died the year before. It was intended as a sort of trumpet blast for post-conciliar renewal and did in fact work rather well in that regard, becoming – I suspect – the most influential book of the decade for the Church in Africa. John Taylor, at that time General Secretary of the Church Missionary Society (the most important Anglican society at work in Africa as the White Fathers were the most important Catholic one) and since then Bishop of Winchester, described it on the cover as 'Quite the most important study of the problems and prospects of Christianity in Africa to have appeared for many years'. I will quote here, to illustrate its general spirit but also the mood of many people at work in the African Church in those years, some lines from its final page:

> I hope that it is in no spirit of carping criticism that I have tried to assess both the strength and the weaknesses of the Catholic Church in modern Africa. At least my own heart is in the business. I am sure that in the ways of God, both more twisted and more straight than human brain can hope to unravel, this Church of ours has a great part to play, but I pray also that we who have been called in this generation of such stupendous growth and unexpected challenges to live and minister in it will not fall beneath the judgment of God and of coming generations as unworthy stewards. Threatened, both by those who question the point of all we do, and by those who would identify that point with ways of thought and behaviour belonging to ages that are past, we must not falter in our old faith nor in the painful effort to maintain its relevance to a new world.

Both *Church and Mission in Modern Africa* and *Post-Vatican II* were quite effective tools for African Church *aggiornamento*. There were, of course, lots of other tools, in particular the Gaba Pastoral Institute, established in 1967 as a centre of training and publishing. To it the editing of the *African Ecclesiastical Review* (founded in 1959 by Fr Joop Geerdes, its first editor, Bishop Blomjous and others, including myself) was now attached. Gaba has had a quite enormous influence for renewal over the years, especially in the field of catechetics, both from its first base in Uganda and – when the Amin regime made its continuance there difficult – from its second in Kenya. Together such things helped to trigger off a real wave of pastoral renewal. At Katigondo, already late in 1964, there had been a large and decisive Pan-African Catechetical Study Week, at which Fr Höfinger from Manila had been the main speaker. It was a great success and opened many doors; but it had nearly not been because Höfinger had wanted to do almost all the talking and this was really rather boring. Fortunately, Archbishop Hurley was persuaded to lead a mini-coup: he replaced Höfinger as chairman of the plenary sessions (it had cunningly been explained to Höfinger that our African sense of hierarchy would not allow us to have him preside with an archbishop present) and this greatly enlarged the opportunity for free discussion, as Hurley was a most excellent chairman. The proceedings were subsequently published in full in the *African Ecclesiastical Review*.

The most important resolution at Katigondo had been one calling for full cooperation with Protestants in the area of biblical translation into African languages. With some people there, both white and black, this was still a sore point and that resolution took a lot of fighting for, but it pointed the way to one of the most important developments of the next years – the entering of Catholics into the work of the Protestant Bible Societies. I was pleased to be present at the meeting in Rome in January 1966 between the Secretariat for Promoting Christian Unity and representatives of the Bible Societies at which the new relationship of cooperation was formalized. Soon people like Fr Adrian Smith in Lusaka and a good many local African priests in many parts would be busily at work organizing, revising or translating afresh the rendering of the Bible in scores of different languages.

With the Bible went the liturgy. At the great Irish National Mission Week at Navan in August 1968, held to celebrate the fiftieth anniversary of the founding of the Columban Fathers, one speaker declared that it was important to stress that the Churches of the third world had still much to learn from countries like Ireland. I got up, a little provocatively, to remark that if Ireland wanted to teach us (I came at the time from Tanzania) it had first to catch up with us: in Ireland the canon of the Mass was still in Latin, in East Africa it was already being said in Swahili, Luganda or whatever. The importance of the liturgical revolution of the sixties for Africa was immense, of a practical and pastoral significance far beyond that attained in countries like Britain. With translation into the vernacular there went in many places a quite new approach to music and singing – an exuberant acceptance of African tunes, a pattern of words and the repetition of key phrases, a use of instruments, all very different from the old missionary importation of rather straightly translated European hymns, sung to their western tunes and accompanied on the harmonium. I remember how desperately anxious the first African priest I met from my Ugandan diocese, back in the early 1950s, was to take home with him a small harmonium. That was the symbol of Catholic liturgical correctitude for pre-conciliar Africa. But the drum was the great symbol of post-Vatican II liturgy – a symbol at once of cultural pluralism and popular participation, the arrival of an active laity, but still more the arrival of Africa in all its vibrant, populist, rhythmic vitality as a major reality within Catholicism.

Add to all this the new ecumenism. In some few places differing missions, Catholic and Protestant, had long cooperated cordially enough, but in very many others the record of inter-Church relations had been a very sour one. When Fr Vincent Donovan wrote, in one of the first issues of the *African Ecclesiastical Review*, an article entitled 'the Protestant-Catholic Scandal in Africa', a good many missionaries took umbrage at his remarks; they felt he was letting the side down disgracefully. But what he said was essentially true and most people knew it and were beginning to be ashamed of it. There is a flexibility in a young Church which is often remarkable, and the sixties saw in many countries an amazing change-round in Protestant-Catholic relations. Things had earlier been particularly bad in southern Tanzania between the Salvatorians and the Anglican UMCA; but when in 1968 Bishop Trevor Huddleston resigned the see of Masasi, clergy on both sides proposed that his successor should be jointly consecrated by Catholic and Anglican bishops. It was only higher and more remote authority which could not countenance such a thing. Non-Catholic students were admitted to Gaba and to several major seminaries. For a few years in that relatively brief but blessed post-conciliar period barriers seemed to be breaking down on every side and a new inclusive Christianity, biblical, sacramental, Catholic, African, immensely confident in the strength of its popular support, its rate of growth, the riches of faith in its materially ever so poor village congregations, seemed palpably to be emerging. Its best leaders, bishops like Joseph Malula and Christopher Mwoleka, Peter Sarpong and Patrick Kalilombe, Peter Dery and Emmanuel Milingo, were well educated enough but they were far more than that, they were men of imaginative commitment, exuberance and charism. In 1969 Pope Paul visited Africa for the first time and declared in Kampala, in words which have been repeated again and again since that day, 'You may, and you must, have an African Christianity.'

That was a high point in African ecclesiastical history, and no subsequent papal visit to Africa has had in any way comparable significance. The trouble here, as elsewhere, was that the post-conciliar momentum, often not too well thought out theologically anyway, was bound to strike against all sorts of hard walls – denominational prejudices, tribal mistrust, the already deep conservatism of many older evangelized areas, the sense of clerical privilege, and so forth – but especially the barriers of canon law, curial control and an ultramontane model. Africa would not be allowed what was forbidden to Holland. The use of drums is fine but it does not really take you very far along the road of Christianity's Africanization. How far may one advance? Where wheat does not grow, must wheaten bread be imported by a poor Church from Europe for the celebration of every Eucharist? Could not our 'daily bread' be of maize or millet or rice? So many questions were quickly being raised, but one more than any other: how to cope with the sacramental ministry for the growing millions of the faithful, when local priests were few and missionary numbers declining? The Council had stressed again and again that the local Church should be centred upon the Eucharist, but in rural Africa the shortage of priests in many places was now so acute that many a village community would be lucky to celebrate Mass together even once a year. By 1970 the crucial pastoral issue for the Church in Africa had become the ordination of married men.[1] Hierarchy upon hierarchy requested permission to be allowed to go ahead. These requests were rejected by Rome, emphatically, even rudely. Dependence upon Rome, legal, psychological, financial, destroyed the momentum for Africanization at this pastorally crucial, and theologically not questionable, point. A lack of theological and ecclesial confidence ensured that few would continue to propose openly a line which drew on them the disfavour of Rome.

By the later 1970s the period of post-conciliar innovation was well-nigh over. The numbers in traditional seminaries were increasing; ecumenical relations were becoming rather less warm; the vigilance of the papal nuncios was unceasing. Bishop Kalilombe[2] was dismissed for one reason, Archbishop Milingo[3] for another. Moreover the increasingly disturbed and impoverished state of large parts of the continent left little time and energy for extended discussion or sustained planning. There were fewer conferences. At the most local level, however, as control diminished and the presence of the clergy became in many a village still more of a rarity (the sheer cost of petrol helped to ensure that) innovation proceeded willy nilly – congregationalist, biblically rather fundamentalist, quite unclerical: it was the African equivalent to the Latin American 'basic community'. Clericalism at the top but congregationalism at the bottom proved the *de facto* compromise of the post-conciliar African Church.

The spirit of the Second Vatican Council may not seem, on the institutional surface, to matter so much today to the Church in Africa, twenty years after it all happened. Yet in fact it was an absolutely decisive moment in its history, not so much for the hierarchy as for the reshaping of the grass-roots community. It came at a singularly opportune moment. It swept the Church forward for ten years or so on a wave of enthusiastic renovation. No one would go back on that. The Catholic Church of Africa of the 1980s is unthinkable without Vatican II and the many great endeavours which followed close upon it.

NOTES

1. See, in particular, my *Mission and Ministry*, Sheed & Ward, 1971. I first raised the issue of the ordination of married men, especially better trained catechists in areas of acute priest shortage, in an article in the *African Ecclesiastical Review* in 1964, reprinted as the final chapter of *The World Mission of the Church*, Darton, Longman & Todd, 1964.

2. Patrick Kalilombe WF, after being Rector of the regional seminary of Kachebere, became Bishop of Lilongwe, Malawi and chairman of the Episcopal Conference. For mysterious reasons President Banda forced his departure from Malawi and the Church insisted on his resignation from Lilongwe. He is now a professor at Selly Oak, Birmingham. [Ed]

3. Emmanuel Milingo, after being Zambia's 'Radio Priest' for some years, became Archbishop of Lusaka. His ministry of healing attracted increasing ecclesiastical criticism, and he was forced recently by Rome to resign from his see. Cf. E. Milingo, *The world in between: Christian healing & the struggle for spiritual survival*, Ed Mona Macmillan (C. Hurst 1984). He is now with the Pontifical Commission for Emigration and Tourism, in Rome. [Ed]

22

SOCIAL TEACHING SINCE THE COUNCIL: A RESPONSE FROM LATIN AMERICA

MARCOS MCGRATH CSC

The social teaching of the Church, first dealt with as a 'subject' by Leo XIII with his encyclical Rerum novarum (1891), developed by subsequent encyclicals up to Paul VI's Populorum progressio (1967) and rather less directly by the encyclicals of the present Pope, rested principally on the propagation of 'natural law' theology rather than the richer theology brought forward by the Council – biblical theology. In this change, the Dogmatic Constitution Dei Verbum on divine revelation has been crucial, though its impact was not at all immediate. Its effect, in so far as it was felt in the Council, was most evident in the last of all the conciliar documents, the Pastoral Constitution on the Church in the world (Gaudium et Spes).

Gaudium et Spes, as the last work to come from the Council Fathers, benefited from their maturest understanding; and, perhaps not uncharacteristically, it has been regarded as the least 'finished' of the documents. The scope was ambitious beyond others, the capacity to bring it to a tidy solution by no means the clearest. Among the five volumes of Herbert Vorgrimler's Commentary on the documents, none dealt simply with a single document except the last, giving 413 pages to Gaudium et Spes. That is some indication of its outreach. It was the only major document to have arisen from a suggestion made – by Cardinal Suenens – at the lectern of the Aula: it has been called 'the most characteristic achievement of an essentially pastoral Council', a quintessential period piece which is truly a sign for our time. The most amazing thing about it is that it had no place in the preparatory commissions' plans. But then, it is a document without conciliar precedence, needing much time to build and much more to absorb into the Church's life.

A member of the Congregation of the Holy Cross, the author, a Panamanian, completed his clerical education at the Institut Catholique in Paris and the Angelicum in Rome. At the tender age of thirty-seven he was made an auxiliary bishop in 1961 in good time to attend the whole of the Council. During 1964–9 he was Bishop of Santiago de Veraguas, and since 1969 he has been Archbishop of Panama. At the 1967 and 1972 gatherings of the Episcopal Conference of Latin American bishops (CELAM) he was Vice President, being also a member of both steering committees and doctrinal councils for Medellín (1968) and Puebla (1979).

Pope John Paul II frequently exhorts us to read and study the documents of Vatican II. Addressing the bishops gathered for the General Conference in Puebla[1], and referring to our previous General Conference[2], he stated: 'Without Vatican II, the Medellín Conference would have been impossible.

For the Medellín Conference sought to be an impulse for pastoral renewal and a new ''spirit'' in the face of the future, while displaying fully ecclesial fidelity in its interpretation of the signs of the times in Latin America.'[3]

Vatican II is the Council of this century, the Church's response to 'the out-standing problems of our time'[4]. A response formulated by the Council after 'scrutinizing the signs of the times and . . . interpreting them in the light of the gospel. Thus, in language intelligible to each generation, (the Church) can respond to the perennial questions which men ask about this present life and the life to come, and about the relationship of the one to the other.'[5]

In his opening address at the Puebla Conference on 28 January 1979, Pope John Paul II showed himself very conscious of the importance of 'this hour that I have the happiness to experience with you', in the wake of the Council and of Medellín. 'How far humanity has travelled in those ten years! How far the Church has travelled in those ten years in the company and service of humanity!' The Pope goes on to remind the bishops that the times call for them to work with 'calm discernment, opportune criticism, and clear-cut stances'.[6]

With regard to Medellín, Puebla produced all this. It took it forward, deepened and particularized its teaching, applied it with the experience of those ten years – the experience and reflections of the Churches of Latin America, local and national, in active communion with the Holy See and the universal Church. Those ten years were a time of growth, of surer and more dynamic orientation. This process must continue, so that we can carry out the spirit of Vatican II, so that we can be the vision, experience and dynamism of Christ in the world, be the Church living the Gospel, the People of God for the human race at this 'new stage of its history.'[7]

I should like in these few pages to point out one central aspect of the Council, which marked a decisive step forward in the history of the Church and of its presence in the world – and a step that was to have a particular impact in Latin America, so that the Holy See and the universal Church have taken a very serious interest in developments there.

THE SIGNS OF THE TIMES

At the second Vatican Council, we, the bishops of the world, were initiated into a way of searching for and discerning the saving will of God in 'the signs of the times', Pope John XXIII's famous phrase, understood as the main characteristics and events, including secular ones, of each age and place, which reveal the actions and will of God in history, and in peoples.

At the time, this could have seemed a simple way of proceeding: just listing the main problems facing the Church in the modern world, and devising pastoral strategies to deal with them. This could be one sense, though a somewhat hasty and superficial one, in which the *aggiornamento* sought by the Council was to be understood. But it was much more than this, and I want to go on and point out some of the effects of this 'conciliar approach' and show their impact on the life of the Church, particularly in Latin America. This should leave us in a position better to try to apply the same approach to the future of the Church on that continent.

SEPARATION OF RELIGION FROM LIFE

The first point to note is the interest the Council took in questions of the 'temporal order'. It noted that: 'This split between the faith which many profess and their daily lives deserves to be counted among the more serious errors of our age.'[8] This refers to the fact that the twentieth century is perhaps the least 'religious' in the history of humanity, in the sense of the amount of interest taken in religious affairs by the world and humankind in general. But there is more to it than that: the 'spirit of the age' (*Zeitgeist*) has succeeded in creating a basic separation: on one side are technology, science and social progress, which have their own values, with no necessary reference to religion, which, if it has to exist at all, should only concern itself with 'the beyond'[9]; on the other, is religion, wrapped up in its world of rites and sacraments and personal conversions, offering a salvation to individuals alone and then only in the 'next world', a salvation that means retreating spiritually from this world: an *atemporal* religion.

There were of course, many pressures operating against this dichotomy, which produced their fruit in the Council, which gave its blessing to secularization, but not to secularism. These pressures came from all the movements for renewal – *aggiornamento* – which made their presence felt in the generations leading up to the Council, both at the head of the Church, the Pope and the Holy See, and in its members, the local Churches and their faithful. There was a renewal from the sources, a renewal directed towards the world, especially during the pontificate of Pius XII, and inspired by him.

The efforts directed at overcoming the separation between faith and life in our day, in this double movement of return to the sources and insertion in the world, inevitably brought about a new sort of theological pastoral thinking, one that brought the 'word of God' and 'secular life' much closer together. This new form of pastoral thinking started from reality – always seen in the light of faith – and the social teaching of the Church received a new and richer expression, at once closer to the changing nature of human problems and more directly impregnated with the sense of God acting in history and in our lives.

This way of thinking – and acting – 'Church' and 'Church in the world' became characteristic of many movements of the lay apostolate[10], and of the work of numerous theologians, and of the magisterium itself. It provoked a fine flowering of doctrine, theology and pastoral work, all of which found expression in the Council.

VATICAN II: A DIFFERENT COUNCIL

The second point is that no Ecumenical Council in history had ever, in its formal agenda, dealt with questions of the temporal order. The themes and motives for the great Councils of the past had always been of a doctrinal or disciplinary nature. They were usually summoned to deal with a new heresy or schism. This meant that studies of the Councils had evolved a whole hermeneutic for interpreting their decisions: conciliar definitions were not held to exhaust the theme they dealt with, nor even to give a positive exposition of it; they rather defined, that is delineated, one aspect of it, setting aside erroneous interpretations. This meant that faith and theology could continue on their course of understanding revelation with certainty on these points. It also meant that Councils did not claim to produce either theological or pastoral treatises embracing the whole of religious affairs, let alone of temporal affairs.

In their expositions of the faith, and their use of theology – or rather, of 'sound doctrine' – in making magisterial pronouncements, the Councils proceeded in a 'deductive' manner. From revealed data, or definitions already made by the magisterium of the Church, they were able to derive or deduce new conclusions. The idea of starting from intellectual and social currents ('signs of the times') in order to reach doctrinal considerations was simply unknown and unrecognized as a possible way of proceeding, either for a Council, or for theologians, or in pastoral work.

This posed real difficulties for the Council Fathers, and for the experts who advised them. In the first session several intuitions and interventions produced an entirely new way of approaching matters, quite different from that used in the preparatory 'schemas' produced by the Commissions. The new order, approved by Pope John XXIII in January 1963, examined the Church *ad intra*, in itself – its faith and own life – and *ad extra*, in its relationship with the world. This second aspect was to find expression in the last document to be issued, bringing the Council down to earth, as it were, which was initially just known by its number, 'Schema XIII', owing to the difficulties of deciding on the right title for it.

It took a long time for this document to come into existence. It was not till the end of November 1963, in a plenary session of the 'Mixed Commission' (made up of the Commission for the Doctrine of the Faith and the Commission for the Lay Apostolate, with sixty members, plus another fifty advisers), that there was a deep debate on the nature of such a document and its right to exist as a conciliar document. For one Eastern bishop, a member of the Commission, it was unthinkable that an Ecumenical Council should turn its attention to such ephemeral matters as culture, economics, etc. For a great Western theologian, Karl Rahner, even if the Council did consider such themes, it should do so theologically, that is, only reaching doctrinal conclusions on the basis of revealed truth. However, several bishops argued forcibly that 'in view of the profound impact made in the world by the two great encyclicals of Pope John XXIII (*Mater et Magistra* and *Pacem in Terris*), any document aiming to address the modern world had to start with a consideration of the problems of the world and speak to mankind at large in its own terms and with arguments that it could understand and accept.'[11] In the end, it needed the pressure of debate in the conciliar Aula, together with the growing interest shown in the subject by the Press and the world at large, for this Constitution (as it became) to be given the importance it merited in the overall perspective of the Council.

MATERIALIST VIEWS OF HISTORY

In his history of theology in the nineteenth century, Edgar Hócedez observed that the theologians of the time were almost completely devoid of a sense of history.[12] This applied both to the development of doctrine and that of theology, but even more basically to a sense of God's action in history, both in the 'history of salvation' and in what we call secular history. It is no mere coincidence that the same century produced two materialist views of history, directly opposed to the biblical vision.

The first was that secular progress, through the advances of science and technology, would create ever greater prosperity for humankind. In his book *Religion and Progress* Christopher Dawson aptly names this 'The Religion of Progress', whose promised earthly utopia took the place of Christian values and the Christian view of history. The human catastrophes of the twentieth century – two world wars, the atom bomb, East-West tension and the North-South divide – have undermined any faith this 'progress' could inspire. Nevertheless, as an internal 'ethos' it still clearly suffuses Western capitalism, in the so-called 'consumer society'.

The second was the Hegelian view of history, with its later development into Marxism, which was to have such a powerful impact on the philosophical and social thinking of the West (and then of the whole world), particularly in its application to anything connected with social change. Its continuing influence was recognized at a meeting organized by CELAM in Lima, Peru, in 1975, between theologians and experts in the social sciences. This produced general agreement that Catholic thinkers of the time lacked an adequate framework for expressing a view of history, above all a philosophical or theological view. This lack favoured the predominance of the Hegelian dialectical view, with its general use of Marxist categories, especially in the social sciences.

The utopic vision of justice proclaimed by Marxism, despite its materialist presuppositions and lack of absolute moral values, would often seem to produce a more favourable response among idealists, including many Christians, than the cold egoism so much in evidence in capitalist theory. In Latin America, the polarization between these two ideologies, without adequate Christian critique of either, has apparently pushed many Catholics in the direction of Marxist analysis, and thence to Marxist practice.

THE BIBLICAL VIEW OF HISTORY

Vatican II, which produced the Constitutions on the Church (*Lumen Gentium*) and the Church in the Modern World (*Gaudium et Spes*), also gave us the Dogmatic Constitution on Divine Revelation (*Dei Verbum*). For the Church, this double emphasis meant that it was not only bringing itself up to date with the modern world (*aggiornamento*) but it was also returning to its very sources of life, in the Sacred Scriptures and the life of the early Church, and in the biblical view of the universe and of history.

Our basic view of history comes from biblical revelation. We can now see, however, that 'late scholasticism' which has dominated Church thinking for so long, favoured the presentation of doctrine and theology in 'themes' (expressed in theses or treatises) divorced and abstracted from their historical and literary context in the Bible. It was Karl Rahner who, at a lecture given in Rome during the closing weeks of the second session of the Council (at the end of November 1963), observed that perhaps the most influential measure proposed by the Council, which hardly anyone had noticed till then, could be that put forward in the Decree on Priestly Formation, published a month earlier, in which was stated: 'In the study of

Sacred Scripture, which ought to be the soul of all theology, students should be trained with special diligence. After a suitable introduction to it, they should be accurately initiated into exegetical method, grasp the pre-eminent themes of divine revelation and take inspiration and nourishment from reading and meditating on the sacred books day by day. *Dogmatic theology should be so arranged that the biblical themes are presented first . . .*'[13]

The biblical view of history, which lies behind this text and is responsible for it, not only inspires the Constitution *Dei Verbum* but also this Decree and, more generally, all the conciliar documents, which show a gradually maturing appreciation of the centrality of this theme. This great return to the sources of faith, the first impulse of the Council, allowed it to tackle the problems facing the world of today with confidence and force, and post-conciliar documents have taken up and continued this vital impetus.

SOCIAL TEACHING SINCE THE COUNCIL

In Latin America, this dynamic view of history has made some progress within the Church. Since 1964, CELAM (General Conference of Latin American Bishops) has organized a series of meetings whose purpose was to apply the conciliar outlook to our continent. This supposes a Church acting in the world for the world. The extraordinary session of CELAM which took place in Mar del Plata (Argentina) in 1966, was typical of this endeavour in both its theme and content. The theme was: 'The Church in the Integration and Development of Latin America', and in an important message to the assembly, Pope Paul VI stressed that the Church, which had been so prominent at the outset of the continent's history, could not fail it at this stage of its development.

At the time, Medellín produced the best expression of this active presence of the Church in our history, as evidenced in the title it gave to the overall publication of its conclusions: 'The Church in the Present Transformation of Latin America in the Light of the Council'. All the elements seemed to be present to produce a vision capable of integrating the biblical view of history and of salvation, combining a spirituality of the Church *ad intra* with an effective presence of Christians in the world. In other words, the renewed biblical vision of Church and World, plus the active and inductive methodology of *Gaudium et Spes* to carry this vision to the world and to the building up of the world.

All this should have produced a Church confident and secure in its social teaching, and more effectively present, through lay people, in all reaches of the secular world. This was the direction pointed out by the lively forces of renewal that found expression in the Council; this was the hope of the Council Fathers, and of Medellín. But in practice, neither the vision nor the presence proved so easy to achieve. For many years we had to witness the decline and omission of the social teaching of the Church, and of the vision it should have given us, with consequent tensions and divisions, especially among lay people, over how the Church should be present in the world.

Now, twenty years after the closure of the second Vatican Council, we can take more accurate stock of the changes it brought into the Church, beginning with the liturgy, and moving on through biblical criticism, the primacy of the Word and of evangelization in the Church, ecumenical relations with our separated brethren and the search for links with other religions and even with non-believers: all this leading to a more effective Christian presence in the world. And within the Church, the Council has initiated a relationship of greater equality and dialogue between hierarchy and laity, a fuller role for religious of both sexes in the process of evangelization, etc.[14]

All these changes, of presentation and of content, carried out in full fidelity to the doctrine of the Church and its return to its sources, and at the same time with great care for the world of today, are what constitute the greatness of Vatican II. Their very scope is also the reason why all the implications of the Council for the Church will take several generations to reach fulfilment. It is also the reason why it is normal to expect that they should have left a certain amount of disorientation in their wake.

The years of and since the Council have been a necessary period of discernment and of some experimentation. The fact that lay people, religious, priests and even bishops had very little experience of a changing situation in the Church produced some false starts, sometimes through losing the balance to be struck between different aspects of pastoral practice, sometimes through rushing fences in preparing and carrying out changes, sometimes through lack of personal resources and of the necessary organization required for *aggiornamento* in each local church. I do not wish to dwell on such problems in general, but to concentrate on the area covered by this paper, the social teaching of the Church.

The 1970s were a decade in which these questions could be posed with greater maturity of judgement and of experience. The process of renewal in the Church went on, and this always means changes, but it went on with greater clarity and confidence concerning the relationship between old and new, between what is permanent and what is transitory in the Church, with greater fidelity to the Church in its sources, its service to the world and its hierarchical community.

The 'social teaching of the Church' was criticized by many people during the years of the Council. *Gaudium et Spes* avoided using the term 'social teaching'. Why was this so?

Basically, for two reasons. First, because the previous social teaching had relied too much on mediating the 'natural law', with a consequent diminution of direct inspiration in the Word of God. Second, because it was given out without the sympathy needed and the flexibility required to take account of and discern new situations and problems. So, in the Council, the 'social teaching of the Church' as presented in many texts and manuals was criticized as being 'pre-conciliar' in the sense of being insufficiently grounded in the sources of Faith and insufficiently immersed in the real world. For these reasons, the critics said, it accorded badly with both the spirit and the approach of the Council, and especially with those that inspired *Gaudium et Spes*.

These criticisms are clearly not lacking in substance. Equally clear is that the social teaching of the Church must share in the whole process of renewal that the Council implied.[15] What is also clear is that, by going to extremes, the critics have unwittingly supported those who would deny the Church any right to pronounce on social questions. Ironically, then, this produced the unfortunate result of eclipsing, for a time, the Church's very reflections on history and the temporal order which are at the heart of *Gaudium et Spes*. This is largely the reason why the social teaching of the Church was over-shadowed in the decade following the Council. For the critics, all the Church's thinking in this field had to be reduced to evangelical, and often abstract, 'vectors' or 'values'. This attitude is described in this text produced by the Conference of Latin American Bishops: 'There would not be any universally valid or permanent social teaching. Only the Gospel is permanent: by its light alone the Christian communities confront the challenges of the situation in which they find themselves, seek to discern their meaning and to discover how they should deal with them, with no commitment to any tradition of social thinking, which is seen as irremediably obsolete from the moment it is formulated as a doctrinal framework.'[16]

The result of this approach is to leave Christian groups active in the temporal order, or 'frontier' groups of Catholic Action specialized in this field, such as the Young Christian Workers, without formulated criteria of Faith and Morals in the field of politics, economics and social questions. And so many Christians, individually or as groups, fell back on various ideologies, of the right and the left, without any adequate Christian criteria for judging them. Hence the politicization, and consequent polarization, of committed sectors of the Church, especially among lay people. Hence also the express tendency among the most active lay movements of recent years to concentrate on aspects such as spiritual formation and ecclesial ministry.

This is a very difficult point. The great ecclesial movement represented by the Council invites us in Latin America to renew ourselves in the Gospel, and to carry its message of liberation to all, evangelizing the poor in a very special way. It invites us to apply the same process, in the light of faith and in the spirit of the signs of the times, to 'individual nations and mentalities...under the guidance of their pastors'[17] that *Gaudium et Spes* had applied to 'the Church in the modern world'.

This is what Medellín did. Its reflections produced a clear call for the liberation of our peoples, while at the same time beginning to draw the outlines of a 'theology of liberation'. One of its earliest exponents wrote that this was not a new theology, 'not so much a new theme for reflection as a *new way* to do theology',[18] one that seeks its basis in contemporary reality. In essence, *Gaudium et Spes* had set us on this way: *seeing reality, in the light of faith, so as to discern the ways* to follow. This, for many, was indeed a new way of doing theology, though one in fact practised in different ways and at different times throughout the Church.[19] For the present time, it is a new way of doing theology that can complement traditional theology and enrich it.[20]

The problem comes when what is included in 'reality' is already an interpretation of that reality. This leads, by what is an abuse of theological method, to a 'Christian' interpretation of reality, which pre-judges faith itself as well as politics, and then radicalizes them along lines suggested by one ideology or another. Puebla points to three such ideologies prominent in Latin America: capitalist liberalism, Marxist collectivism and the Doctrine of National Security.[21] All these have a tendency to absolutize the values they uphold, even in the name of Faith.

This is not the place to go deeper into this problem as it affects theology and theological method. I mention it because it largely explains the earlier *decline* and now the new *appreciation* of the social teaching of the Church in this post-conciliar time.

PUEBLA: MATURING THE COUNCIL

Puebla certainly represented a great step in the mature orientation of the conciliar movement in the countries of Latin America. I should like to end by showing this in two aspects: the preparation for the Conference itself, and its formulation of the social teaching of the Church.

Those of us who took part in the preparation and the Conference itself saw them as being a continuation of the dynamic process at work in the Council. This was the great strength of Puebla. It was we the bishops of the Conference, helped by experts both clerical and lay, who debated and approved the final document. It thus was and is an act of the pastoral magisterium. But its preparation involved the broadest consultation that had ever taken place in the Church in Latin America: in every Church group, at every level, over two years. As the process of consultation advanced, during 1977 and 1978, the conciliar renewal of a Church whose mission was at heart evangelizing was confirmed; the options expressed by our Churches – the same ones as expressed at Medellín (Colombia, 1968), but more practised, richer and more mature – were reinforced. And without this conciliar experience – the thousands of groups living and discussing the Gospel in their lives, in communion with the Church – Puebla would not have been possible.

The conciliar renewal we experience should be a whole: it should apply in the religious sphere as well as in the social. Puebla noted the tensions produced in the Church by groups that stress one aspect at the expense of the other.[22] It is an undoubted fact that the enormous evangelizing efforts made by the local Churches of the continent already constitute a decided option for the poor, in the process of bringing the Gospel to them and in their incorporation into the ministerial life of the Church. It is equally obvious that the social stance of the Church has been expressed in strong 'position statements' made by bishops and other ecclesial groups against social injustice, corruption, abuse of human rights, and so on.

In most of our Churches, however, we still lack:

(1) Participation of the whole Christian community in working out and applying the social teaching of the Church to specific options and their effective implementation.[23]

(2) An active presence of trained and committed lay people, working within the temporal structures of labour, business, politics, etc, who, conversant with the problems of their environment, strong in their Christian life and well grounded in social teaching, can find not just one Christian model in temporal affairs, since they will know that there are many alternatives, but rather historical models that can effectively express the Christian values they profess.[24]

(3) The training of lay people, especially young people, in doctrine and

social action, particularly in working class areas, on the lines of the Catholic Action movements already referred to. These would form an indispensable source of Christian leaders in these fields in the future.

CONCLUSION

In these pages I have tried to describe the religious dynamic of Vatican II in the area of social questions, and its application – and vicissitudes – since the Council, especially in Latin America, which (as is well known) presents a number of social problems in their most acute form. The 1972 Synod of Bishops dealt with the matter, and the Popes of and since the Council have produced a number of catechetical guidelines. These and other documents have helped orientate the post-conciliar life of the Church in Latin America. The forthcoming Synod called by Pope John Paul II to review the twenty years that have passed since the Council should be another important stage in this process of faithful implementation of the spirit, content and dynamic of the Council.

NOTES

1. The Third General Conference of Latin American Bishops (CELAM), held at Puebla de los Angeles in Mexico, 27 January – 13 February 1979. Pope John Paul II attended the opening sessions, giving an opening address and two homilies. These, together with the 'final document' of the Conference, are published in *Puebla: Evangelization at Present and in the Future of Latin America* (Washington, National Conference of Catholic Bishops; Slough & London, St Paul's Publications and CIIR, 1980).
2. The Second General Conference of Latin American Bishops, held at Medellín in Colombia in 1968. Its documents, particularly that on social justice, with its call for the 'integral liberation' of the oppressed masses of Latin America, had a profound effect on the course taken by the Churches of Latin America in social affairs, and made the rest of the world aware of the current of thought known as 'theology of liberation'.
3. John Paul II, Homily in the Basilica of Our Lady of Guadalupe, 27 January 1979, in *Puebla, op cit*, 19.
4. Pastoral Constitution on the Church in the Modern World – *Gaudium et Spes* (GS), sec 10.
5. GS, sec 4.
6. *Puebla*, 1. The Pope was in fact sounding a note of caution with regard to what he saw as 'incorrect interpretations' of the conclusions of Medellín.
7. GS, sec 4.
8. GS, sec 43.
9. Cf. GS, sec 19: 'Modern civilization itself often complicates the approach to God, not for any essential reason, but because it is excessively engrossed in earthly affairs.'
10. Typical of these were the specialized branches of Catholic Action, such as Young Christian Workers, with their well-known method of approach: 'see, judge, act'.

335

11. M. McGrath, 'The Constitution on the Church in the World Today' in *Vatican II, an Inter-Faith Appraisal* (Notre Dame, 1966), 401.
12. Cf. E. Hócedez, *Histoire de la théologie au XIXe siècle, I, 1800–1831* (Brussels–Paris, 1949), 13–26.
13. *Optatam Totius*, sec 16.
14. M McGrath in *Los Signos de los Tiempos en América Latina hoy* (The Signs of the Times in Latin America today) – Contributions to the Medellín Conference, 79.
15. Cf. CELAM, *Fe Cristiana y Compromiso Social* (Christian Faith and Social Commitment) (1981), 149–54; SEDOC, *Nuestra Salvación es Cristo* (Christ is our Salvation) (1984), sec 162.
16. CELAM, *op cit*, 152.
17. GS, sec 91.
18. G. Gutiérrez, *A Theology of Liberation* (New York, 1973; London, 1974), 15.
19. Cf. Gutiérrez, *op cit*, 6: 'The Augustinian theology of history which we find in *The City of God*, for example, is based on a true analysis of the signs of the times and the demands with which they challenge the Christian community.'
20. CELAM, *op cit*, 136, 139.
21. Puebla, sec 542–9; cf also sec 536 for the tendencies of all ideologies.
22. *Ibid*, sec 90.
23. *Ibid*, sec 473.
24. *Ibid*, sec 553.

23

A LAST LOOK AT THE COUNCIL

YVES CONGAR OP

This chapter first appeared in French as a paper given at the University of Fribourg on 23 January 1979 entitled 'Vatican II: Contributions made by the Council'. It has since been published in the collection Le Concile de Vatican II, Théologie Historique 71 (Beauchesne, Paris 1984) 49–72.

Three months after he had become Pope, John XXIII looked at two areas of his pastoral care: Rome, which was very different from the Rome of his own youth, and the world, which was a prey to the forces of evil, but also full of those released by the grace of Christ. He made a decision which was the cause of a double celebration: to hold a diocesan synod for the city and an ecumenical council for the universal Church.[1] This decision was proclaimed on 25 January 1959 in no more than six words. No explanation was given. This brief announcement, however, aroused a tremendous echo because of the already existing context within which it was made. The new Pope had already made several very meaningful decisions and his image was beginning to emerge, with the result that there were expectations. There were also powerful apostolic and theological movements in the Church. Finally and most important of all, there was a lively ecumenical consciousness.

The same word is, of course, applied on the one hand to the Church's Council and, on the other, at least in French, to the World Council of Churches, as well as to the vast ecumenical movement. The Pope announced the first on the 25 January, significantly the last day of the universal Week of Prayer for Christian Unity. On the same day, we were informed in an official commentary: 'In the mind of the Holy Father, the aim of the Council is not simply the spiritual good of the Christian people. It is also an invitation to the separated communities to seek the unity to which so many souls aspire today throughout the whole of the earth.'[2] From then onwards, the meaning of the word 'invitation' gave rise to many questions. Would the Council be a council of union or at least a first step in that direction?

337

There was quite a rapid response to this very widespread questioning. John XXIII made many declarations about the terms on which the Council would offer, invite and attract the separated brethren to rejoin unity.[3] The term 'return' appeared several times.

Speaking to the diocesan leaders of Italian Catholic Action, for example, on 9 August 1959, the Pope said:

> The idea of the Council is not the fruit of lengthy reflection. It is rather the spontaneous flower of an unexpected springtime . . . With the grace of God, we are convening the Council. And we are intending to prepare it, bearing in mind all that is most essential to bring strength and new vigour in the union of the Catholic family, in conformity with our Lord's plan. Then, as soon as we have accomplished this formidable task of eliminating everything that may at the human level be an obstacle to more rapid progress, we shall present the Church in all its splendour *sine macula et sine ruga* and we shall say to all the others who are separated from us, Orthodox, Protestants and other Christians: 'Look, brethren, this is the Church of Christ. We have tried to be faithful to it . . . Come! The way is open for the encounter, the return. Come and take your place or take it again . . .'[4]

A few days after this, on 15 August, Cardinal Tisserant expressed himself in very much the same way: 'The Council is an internal affair on the part of the Catholic Church, but its aim is nonetheless to work usefully in the direction of unity, in such a way that, after the Council, it will be possible to approach the problems of unity in a new and more favourable manner.'[5] Finally, Cardinal Tardini, the president of the ante-preparatory Commission, declared that, even though the Council was to be an internal event within the Catholic Church, members of the other religious confessions who wanted to be present would be welcome to attend as Observers.[6]

The ante-preparatory period came to an end and we need consider it no further. I should like to look at the Council as it took place and in particular at the following four aspects: 1. The fact of the Council; 2. An 'ecumenical' Council – in what direction and in what way?; 3. A 'pastoral' Council; 4. The post-conciliar period.

THE FACT THAT THERE WAS A COUNCIL

In 1819, Joseph de Maistre asked: 'Why is an ecumenical council necessary, when it is enough to have a pillory?'[7] All the same, in 1869–70, there was Vatican I, which proclaimed the infallibility of the papal magisterium in precise terms. After that Council, the question was still asked: Is a council really useful?

This continued questioning, however, is certain evidence of a simplistic ecclesiology and a lack of understanding of what a council really represents. A negative or hesitant reply to such a question is in fact based on a mechanical conception of the life of the Church and even of the life of faith. Pius XI even thought for a moment of reopening the Vatican Council that had been declared suspended on 20 October 1870. This is clear from an allusion to it that he made in the Encyclical *Ubi arcano* of 23 December 1922.[8] Pius XII had a similar plan, but this was developed in secret, within the framework and subject to the guidance of the Holy Office between 1948 and 1951.[9] Preparations were sufficiently advanced, however, for certain ideas to appear in the Encyclical *Humani generis* of 12 August 1950 or in various plans considered by the preparatory theological Commission of Vatican II, of which I was a member in the capacity of 'consultor'. Pius XII was, it seems, thinking of resuming and completing Vatican I, whereas John XXIII made it clear that his council would be Vatican II.[10]

I do not intend to outline here a theology of conciliarity and the 'conciliar' reality. Many elements of this theme have been discussed and many attempts have been made at a preliminary draft, although the final synthesis has still to be formulated. I would simply like to point, without going into too much technical detail, to one extremely important datum. It is this: Not only was there a council – there was really a council! Not only were the Fathers able to express themselves with complete freedom (that was also the case at Trent and, with certain restrictions, at Vatican I) – the decrees and teachings of Vatican II were really the decrees and documents of the Council. Whereas Vatican I had made use of the formula of the mediaeval councils and its decrees had been those of 'Pius, sacro approbante Concilio', those of Vatican II were promulgated according to an extremely interesting formula that was conciliar, collegial and pontifical.[11]

A council is an event and not only in the sense in which General de Gaulle called Vatican II the greatest event in the twentieth century and in which the Secretary-General of the United Nations, Charles Malik, wrote that it might also be the greatest event in several centuries. It is also an event in the philosophical sense of the term, in other words, it is different from regularly recurring natural phenomena or expected institutional manifestations. It is a datum which, once it has occurred, changes something both in the present and in the future. The great power of the datum of Vatican II has to do with the fact that it represents a moment when the Church's collective cons-ciousness was concentrated on the act of experiencing its faithfulness to Jesus Christ and his Spirit in confessing and celebrating its faith.

'*Concilium episcoporum est*' – a council is a gathering of bishops.[12] This does not mean that it is a more prestigious kind of meeting, because of the predominance of mitres and violet garments. It means the coming together, with the aim of performing the same action together, of the centres of communion and guidance of the local Churches. The collegial act is above all one and the same action performed by a large number. The college is there, gathered together, at a council.

I remember reading, a long time ago, in the classical manuals, about the distinction between the episcopate dispersed and the episcopate gathered together. It was a very ordinary subject and I had no suspicion that it dealt with such an important reality. In fact, it refers to two different levels of thought – the sociological and the theological levels. At the sociological level, there is, in a gathering of bishops, a communication of ideas and convictions and each participant is taken by the others beyond what he is alone.[13] At the theological level, a council is not simply a conference. It consists of men, of course, so that there are tensions and there is manoeuvring. It consists of pastors. It is a reality of the Church, a celebration and a time when God acts on his people. The Holy Spirit is active at a council and makes this sociological communication into a communion and a unanimity that is concerned with the City of God.

Catholic consciousness is concentrated and expressed in two dimensions at a council. These can be described as the horizontal and the vertical dimension, although we should be careful not to be deceived by the very material aspects of these terms. The horizontal dimension points to a decentralization at a council of the *Urbs* and its extension to the *Orbis* and to the fact that the latter as it were takes possession of the former. At a council, in other words, the Church speaks. During the pontificate of Pius XII especially, it was the Pontiff himself and the Roman authorities, congregations and faculties that spoke. They enjoyed a monopoly. Great and vital movements were carefully watched rather than freely promoted. These included, for example, the liturgical movement, biblical research, the movement back to patristic sources, ecumenism and the movement forward towards pastoral care. At Vatican II, all these voices made themselves clearly heard.

Many believed that it was the wicked German, French and Dutch theologians who would bring their controversial ideas to the Council, where they would replace the reliable texts edited by the preparatory commissions in the spirit of the previous pontificate and the Roman Curia. But then, when he heard that Vatican I was to be convoked, Cardinal Pitra had groaned: 'What! Convoke a council! But the French and German theologians will come and overthrow our congregations!'[14] Nothing was over-

340

thrown, but the whole life of the Church was expressed at a higher level at Vatican II and there was no monopoly. At the time, I wrote quite frequently that it was the contribution of the minority that kept the balance in the conciliar documents.[15]

What do I mean by the vertical dimension? Simply the presence at a council of the past. The treasures of Tradition are there in the totalization of Catholic consciousness and its expression at a council. The new aspects of Vatican II were frequently stressed during and after the council. That there were such aspects is undeniable, but it is equally necessary to emphasize the conscious reality of continuity. It has always been a tradition at the early councils of the Church to interpret the decisions made at the previous councils. They have accepted the datum of those councils, with the result that their ecumenical nature had a vertical and qualitative dimension.[16] In the documents of Vatican II, for example, there are 93 quotations from the texts of previous councils, 21 from Tridentine texts and 24 from those of Vatican I. There are also no less than 201 quotations from or references to 92 of Pius XII's acts.[17] In a session commemorating the opening of Vatican I, Paul VI insisted on the continuity between that council and Vatican II.[18] One clear example of this continuity is that the teaching of Vatican II about the episcopate and its collegiality is thought to have restored equilibrium to the purely papal emphasis of Vatican I, as Paul VI declared on two occasions (29 November and 21 December 1963) that it ought to do. The continuity between the two councils was demonstrated by the evidence that the teaching of Vatican II had already been sketched out in the plans of Vatican I.[19]

The fact that there was a Council was, for those who gathered together at that Council, an experience with its own dynamic impetus. Those who took part in the Council were able to discover the many different values that it brought into play. This was very obvious in the case of such important realities as the liturgy, which was revealed in all its variety in the daily celebration of the Eucharist. All the local Churches and their theology were also encountered at the Council, together with the fact of collegiality, since the college of bishops was assembled at the Vatican. It was also clear that it was episcopal ordination as a sacramental reality that made certain men members of that college, since as many as two-fifths of the bishops present at Vatican II were auxiliary bishops. Finally, the conciliar experience reopened the chapter in the Church's book of conciliar life itself. Let us consider briefly what this means.

On 15 September 1965, Paul VI promulgated his Motu proprio *Apostolica sollicitudo* instituting the synod of bishops. One of the reasons that he gave for this was that he had been moved to act thus by his happy experience at the Council of the advantage accorded by close union among the bishops. Chapter III of the Decree *Christus Dominus* on the bishops' pastoral office (28 October 1965) outlined the programme for a renewal of conciliar life in this respect. Since that time, four synods of bishops have been held at Rome, several diocesan synods have taken place and there have also been national synods in the Netherlands, Chile, Austria, Switzerland, Federal Germany and in other countries.[20] It is even possible that the proclamation, followed by the event of Vatican II may have had a certain impact either on the Orthodox Church in its decision to prepare for the 'great and holy Council' to which we are looking forward now or on the development of the idea of 'conciliar community' within the World Council of Churches. An event such as that of the Second Vatican Council continues to have a dynamic effect for a long time. The word 'shock' is, I know, ambiguous, but, using it in its more positive sense, it can be applied to effects of Vatican II, which have not yet been exhausted.

AN 'ECUMENICAL' COUNCIL
IN WHAT DIRECTION AND IN WHAT WAY?

Vatican II was ecumenical in the first place in that it represented the Church and its ideas or rather made the Church universally present by the breadth of its realization. This was possible from the time of the ante-preparatory consultation of the pastors onwards. In the case of Vatican I, there were 244 replies to that consultation, whereas there were more than two thousand in the case of Vatican II.[21] Vatican I brought together 744 Fathers, with an overwhelming majority from Europe, 200 coming from Italy alone, and only one black bishop. I counted, in the 1965 Elenco, the names of more than 2900 Fathers at Vatican II, including about a hundred who were black. 'For the first time in history, all the peoples on earth and all the traditions of the Church were able to make their voices heard at the Second Vatican Council.'[22] Paul VI mentioned this fact on several occasions, saying that no other council had had such breadth and scope.[23] With this in mind, he once said that, in certain respects, Vatican II was even more important than the Council of Nicaea.[24] This was not a very fortunate comment and those who were critical of Paul VI and Vatican II were scurrilous in their misinterpretation of it. It is a comment that should be taken in the sense in which it was intended, the sense in which I have interpreted it above.

I have already spoken above about vertical and qualitative dimensions of ecumenicity and would like to return to this now. In the first place, it is important to note that John XXIII rediscovered the early patristic meaning of reform based on the reform of Christian man, a renewal of Christian life and a reshaping of man in the image of God.[25] Everyone wanted Vatican II to be a reforming council and a reform is 'an appeal made by a less profound tradition to a more profound tradition, a movement back on the part of tradition and a going further in depth and a search for deeper sources'.[26] One of the most decisive aspects of Vatican II was that it went beyond the Middle Ages, the Counter-Reformation and the anti-modern restoration of the nineteenth century and established a connection with the inspirations of the undivided Church. This question was frequently discussed and the phrase 'end of a millennium' was often used in this sense. R. Rouquette even said that 20 November 1962, the date when the Fathers voted to reject the schema on the two sources, Scripture and Tradition, marked the end of the Counter-Reformation.[27]

It was this aspect, I am convinced, that gave Vatican II its greatest ecumenical value. There were, of course, the observers from other Christian communities and there was the splendid Decree *Unitatis redintegratio*, but it is possible to regard the documents produced for internal use in the Church as contradicting these initiatives. A careful study of the history of the divisions in the Church has strengthened my conviction that first the Eastern Church and then the Reformed Churches rejected many of the developments that have characterized the Middle Ages in the Western Church. These include, for example, scholasticism, various devotions, clerical triumphalism and a powerful and political papacy. A return to the sources in the direction of an undivided Church in addition to a vertical dimension in ecumenicity consequently had great ecumenical value.

The references made by Vatican II to the Church Fathers were not simply ornamental.[28] We have in this case to think of the influence exerted by Eastern Christians and the reacceptance by Western Catholics of ideas and realities that have always been valued in the East. Among the latter are local eucharistic Churches, epicleses, the sacramental basis of the structures organized by the law, pneumatology with a Trinitarian emphasis, a personalized view and a cosmic dimension of faith.[29] Finally, a very serious attempt at integration was made at Vatican II. There was, for instance, no Scripture without Tradition and no Tradition without Scripture. There was no sacrament without the Word. There was no Christology without pneumatology and no pneumatology without Christology. There was no hierarchy without the people and no people without the hierarchy. There was no episcopate without the Pope and no Pope without the episcopate.

343

There was no local Church that was not missionary and no mission that was not ecclesial. There was no Church which was not mindful of the whole Church and which did not provide universality within itself and so on.

In his audience of 19 January 1966, Paul VI said: 'It is possible to say that the Council was permeated with that ecumenical spirit which has tended to fill the heart of the Catholic Church outside the framework of its effective hierarchical communion in such a way as to give it the universal dimension of God's plan and the charity of Christ. A potential ecumenicity filled and shook the concrete ecumenicity of the Church assembled in Council.'[30] These words show that the Holy Father was concerned with the problem of the encounter between two and even three kinds of ecumenicity – that of the Vatican Council, that of the ecumenical movement as given concrete expression in the World Council of Churches and finally that which the World Council has formally in view and which it understands in calling itself – in French if not in English – the 'Ecumenical' Council, namely ecumenical in the sense of the entire inhabited world.[31]

The Second Vatican Council was an ecumenical council in the technical sense of the word. It was also open to the other two forms of ecumenicity in its dynamic understanding of the Church. This is clear from a reading of the very first lines of *Lumen Gentium*, its chapter on the People of God, its idea of the Church as the 'sacrament of salvation' and the words *subsistit in* that occur in sec. 8 of the text. These words affirm the authenticity of the Roman Catholic Church as the Church of Christ and the Apostles without devaluing the obviously different ecclesial quality of the other Christian communions. For a long time, the Catholic Church not only practised, but also professed in theory a logic according to which unity consisted in submission to the authority of the Pope. This was something that the other Christian communions refused to accept. With Vatican II, however, the Catholic Church, without losing its Roman centre or its papal head, began as a demanding but open partner to take part in the search for unity. Since that time, what has happened is that many Christians have been speaking of a universal ministry of unity that they attribute without further discussion to the Bishop of Rome as something very desirable. Who would have dared to hope before 25 January 1959, when Vatican II was announced, that the Catholic Church would ever become so committed to ecumenism and would ever have gone so far along the ecumenical way? In the address that he gave at Uppsala in 1968 Fr R. Tucci observed that the open and dynamic view of the Church expressed by Vatican II was clearly a response to the need to understand unity not exclusively in a backward-looking, but also in a forward-looking way. Such a view would help, he claimed, to throw light on the Catholic Church's participation in the ecumenical movement, which was itself open to the dimensions of the world.[32]

This third world-wide aspect of the Council's ecumenicity was expressed in its first 'Message to the World' of 20 October 1962 and continuously until the Constitution *Gaudium et Spes* on the Church in the Modern World of 7 December 1965 and the seven messages at its closure delivered on the following day in the public place and under the vault of heaven. All these documents form part of its ecumenicity.

A 'PASTORAL' COUNCIL

From the moment that it was proclaimed, the Second Vatican Council was presented in fairly fortunate language as a 'pastoral' council.[33] John XXIII said that a council was not a *coetus speculativus*, but a gathering of pastors.[34] He expressed himself in a way that was intended to avoid any false contrast between 'doctrinal' and 'pastoral'. In his opening address on 11 October 1962, for example, he said that the Council 'aimed to transmit, in its purity and integrity and without any dilutions or alterations, the doctrine that has become our common heritage for twenty centuries'. He went on to say:

> Since this doctrine embraces so many spheres of human activity at the individual, family and social level, it is above all necessary for the Church never to cease to look at that sacred heritage of truth that it has received from the past. It is, however, equally necessary for it to turn towards the present time which leads to new situations and new forms of life and opens new ways to the Catholic apostolate . . .
>
> Our task is not simply to preserve that precious treasure as though we were only concerned with the past. It is also to dedicate ourselves resolutely and fearlessly to the work that our times are calling for, in so doing following the path that the Church has followed for twenty centuries.
>
> The essential object of this Council is therefore not to discuss one or other of the Church's fundamental articles . . . The Christian and Catholic spirit throughout the whole world is expecting a leap forward towards a doctrinal penetration and a forming of consciences that will be more perfectly and more faithfully in accordance with authentic doctrine, which should, however, be studied and explained following the methods of research and presentation used by modern thought. The substance of that early doctrine that is contained in the deposit of faith is different from the formulation within which it is clothed and which takes as its example for its forms and proportions the needs of a magisterium which is above all pastoral in character.[35]

There was no opposition or difference here, but difficulties certainly arose very soon at the Council in connection with the schema that bore the unfortunate title *De duobus fontibus Revelationis*. This schema was debated between 14 and 20 November 1962 and the text was so sharply criticized that it was finally sent back to be completely refashioned, because it was regarded as insufficiently pastoral and ecumenical. Those who defended it were equally convinced of its positive value and argued that 'doctrine' was both the most pastoral of acts and the basis of any true ecumenism that aimed to avoid a 'false eirenicism'. By 'false eirenicism' they meant a minimizing of Catholic positions.

The critics of the schema were, however, no less convinced of the strength of their arguments. The difference between the two parties was based on two distinct ways of understanding 'doctrine' and can be traced back to the fact that there were at the council two groups with radically different thought-processes.[36] The members of the first group used an analytical method to arrive at a definition, made firm affirmations in form-ulae that they regarded as objects or things in their minds. Their ideal was to arrive at statements of the same kind as the 'canons' of the Council of Trent or Vatican I. They felt therefore at home in the *Nota explicativa praevia* with which the Theological Commission of the Council had prefaced its examin-ation of the modi of Chapter III of *Lumen Gentium*. The doctrine put forward in this Nota was not different in substance from that outlined in the chapter itself. The only difference was that it was expressed in more concep-tual and scholastic language that was closer to that of the early 'canons'. For those who belonged to this first group, 'a failure to think in purely conceptual terms meant a departure from the truth'.[37]

The members of the second group at the Council, however, approached the truth in a more existential, synthetic way, along a road that was more open to search and research and to new contributions. Their approach was, in a word, more all-embracing. It was certainly also more 'pastoral' and more 'ecumenical'. And this was the approach followed by the Council as a whole. As a consequence, its outline of God's great plan was again and again situated within the 'economy'. Similarly, no attempt was made to 'define' any particular doctrine – although it certainly produced two 'dogmatic constitutions' – or to formulate 'canons' with the *anathema sit* of previous Councils. Points of doctrine such as the sacramental character of ordination to the episcopate were, however, stated quite clearly and certain errors were rejected.[38] But, as John XXIII had said in his opening address and as Paul VI repeated later: 'The Bride of Christ prefers today to apply the remedy of mercy rather than that of severity. She wants to provide for the needs of the present time by pointing to the value of her teaching rather than by renewing condemnations.'[39]

Mgr Marcel Lefebvre proposed that there should be two types of text edited in parallel, in order 'to express doctrine in a dogmatic and scholastic manner for the formation of scholars and to present the truth in a more pastoral manner for the instruction of other people'.[40] This suggestion, which was made to the President of the Assembly, was not accepted. I do not know what reasons were given for this decision or even if any were given. If it had been accepted, it would certainly have 'hardened a dualism of a kind that was spontaneously rejected by those whose pastoral training had been based on the Word of God as something to be taken out into the world'.[41] This dualism was in fact effectively repudiated both in the Assembly and in particular by Mgr Guerry[42] and soon afterwards in various interviews and articles[43] in an allocution given by Paul VI on 6 September 1963[44] and by a number of theologians.[45]

A pastoral approach is not without doctrine. It is doctrinal, but in a way that is not satisfied with conceptualizations, definitions, deductions and anathemas. It intends to present the truth of salvation in a way which is close to men and women of today and which accepts their difficulties and tries to answer their questions. It even does that in a doctrinal form of expression. Vatican II was undoubtedly doctrinal. The fact that it 'defined' no new dogmas does not in any way minimize its doctrinal value, according to the description of doctrine given by classical theology, in a differentiated manner, to the documents promulgated by the Council.

Some of those documents are 'dogmatic' in that they express a common doctrine and can even be compared with the great doctrinal encyclicals (which they frequently cite), except that they express, following the way of (and through the medium of) the extraordinary magisterium, the teaching of what Vatican I called the 'ordinary and *universal* magisterium'.[46] That is the status not only of *Lumen Gentium* and the doctrinal parts of *Dei Verbum*, the Constitution on the Liturgy and *Gaudium et Spes*, but also of many of the decrees and the Declaration *Dignitatis humanae personae*. Other conciliar texts and parts of these documents are more purely 'pastoral' in character, that is to say, they provide, in accordance with the supernatural prudence possessed by pastors assembled in Council, directives of a practical nature. Karl Rahner recognized that *Gaudium et Spes* had this epistemological status in those parts of it which provide classical doctrine and truth that is to some extent outside time.[47]

In the 'pastoral' parts of the Council's teaching that is based to a greater or lesser degree directly on Revelation, there is a content which goes beyond the development of the deposit of faith as such and which is not derived from a pure deduction from the articles of that deposit. This is what the pastors who were united in prayer and reflection at the Council took the risk of saying when discussing historical situations that traditional Faith has to explain in ways that go beyond its classical statements. In so doing, they entered the sphere on the one hand of human information and assessment and on the other of induction. This presupposes that they had first accepted the facts as facts and that they also accepted that the praxis of Christians was to some extent the source of doctrine.[48] It is clear that this was the case in the Decree on Ecumenism, the Declarations on Non-Christian Religions and on Religious Freedom, the second part of *Gaudium et Spes*[49] and many parts of the Decrees on the Ministry of Priests, Priestly Formation, the Renewal of the Religious Life, the Apostolate of the Laity and the Church's Missionary Activity. All this is in accordance with the programme outlined by John XXIII in his opening address, of which I have quoted certain important passages above.

It is also, I am sure, precisely this aspect of openness, induction and detailed words of guidance that many of those at Vatican II could not accept. They left the Council saying: 'It aimed to be pastoral and it was only pastoral'. We are not compelled to accept this. The matter is open to discussion. But what I have said here shows that the attitude of this group is unacceptable. Other participants at the Council, coming from various environments, regretted that the pastoral emphasis of the Council led it to provide only 'flabby' texts and to display a certain timidity with regard to doctrine.[50] Whether that criticism is true or not remains to be seen. In my opinion, neither *Lumen Gentium* nor the first chapters of *Dei Verbum* are 'flabby'. But the fact remains that the language employed by Vatican II was often descriptive and expansive and therefore not comparable to the dogmatic style of Vatican I and above all that of the Council of Trent. It was richer and more wordy and it was also the language of teaching in the widest sense.

In the volume of the *Conciliorum OEcumenicorum Decreta* published by the Istituto per le scienze religiose of Bologna, Vatican II fills 316 pages, Vatican I only 15 and Trent 130. The seven ecumenical councils held before Trent take up 138 pages. Were we very wordy at Vatican II? Similar comments could be made about the non-conciliar magisterial texts found in Denzinger!

THE POST-CONCILIAR PERIOD

It would be foolish to try to deal fully with the enormous and complex problem of the post-conciliar period in the space available to me here. I would have to take into account the dynamic impetus of the Council itself, everything that it set in motion, its results, its responsibility at a time of crisis and the ways in which it was betrayed. There would be enough material to fill a book! All the same, something has to be said, however incomplete. I apologize for the incomplete nature of this last section.

Let me begin by saying with Newman – and the more I come to know him, the more I admire his wisdom and his balanced attitude – that 'it is rare for a council not to be followed by great confusion'.[51] Newman made a detailed study of the Arian crisis. The First Council of Nicaea (325), which defined our fundamental faith, was followed by fifty-six years of contentions punctuated by synods, excommunications, exiles (notably that of Hilary of Poitiers), interventions and imperial acts of violence. Chalcedon (451) called for many explanations and further formulations. Monophysitism, which had been condemned by Chalcedon, reappeared later in the form of Monothelitism, which was condemned only in 649 (Rome) and in 681 (by Constantinople III). It has been demonstrated that iconoclasm was the last of the great Christological heresies. This was condemned in 787 by the Second Council of Nicaea, the last council which we in the West shared with the Orthodox Christians.

In the case of a number of councils, there has been non-acceptance by part of the Church. National feelings or politics have played an important part in this. Ephesus (431) was not accepted, for example, by the Nestorians. Chalcedon was not accepted by the Monophysites. (The Monophysite Christians of Egypt and Abyssinia refused to attend the council of the Byzantine emperor, but their Christology is not heretical. This is clear from their recent confessions of faith.) Nicaea II was rejected by Charlemagne and his Council of Frankfurt (794), against which Pope Hadrian I protested. Trent was, of course, not accepted by Protestant and Anglican Christians and Vatican I was rejected by von Döllinger and the Old Catholics.

Because it incorporates and conveys in a very concentrated form the consciousness and the life of the Church, a council such as Vatican II has great dynamism, but does not have an immediate effect. The case of the Council of Trent is instructive here. It was at once accepted in Spain, but only gradually accepted in France, at least as far as its disciplinary decrees were concerned. The provincial synods were the first to accept it (Besançon in 1571, etc) and they were followed in 1615 by the assembly of the clergy in Paris. Charles Borromeo, who had taken part in the Council, founded a seminary almost at once, but similar initiatives were delayed in France because of the religious wars and for other reasons. The first real seminaries were not founded until 1635 (Saint Vincent de Paul's Bons-Enfants) and 1642 (Jean-Jacques Olier's Saint-Sulpice).

All the Church's councils have had an assured future, but they have acted slowly and it has taken a long time for them to penetrate into the consciousness and life of the Church. The whole of the thirteenth century was influenced by the canons of Lateran IV (1215).[52] These were incorporated into Gregory IX's collection of decretals. Their effects are particularly noticeable in the first two chapters, which formed the basis and acted as a test of theological knowledge for priests, and in the legislation concerning the holding of regular diocesan synods. M. J. Gaudemet has pointed out that there were at least ninety notable councils held in France alone in the thirteenth century.[53]

The Catholic Church was conditioned by Trent for no less than three hundred years. There were many reasons for this. It reaffirmed the received doctrine of Catholicism. Its impetus was continued and strengthened by the energetic activity of the Jesuits. The Council also evolved many programmes, such as the Index, the catechism, various reforms, Pius IV's profession of faith and Pius V's Missal, and these were set in motion by the papacy. Finally, the Roman congregations were set up after Trent and became instruments of a centralization, the full effects of which were not produced until the Catholic restoration in the nineteenth century, after the Revolution and Napoleon and the victories over episcopalism and Gallicanism.

Finally, the two constitutions promulgated by Vatican I dominated Catholic life until Vatican II. *Aeterni Patris* led to a more educated clergy, especially in the spheres of revelation, the supernatural, the question of faith and reason and apologetics. *Pastor aeternus* had an effect on the concrete life of the Church and ecclesiology, particularly affecting the Catholic attitude towards papal infallibility and authority, centralization and the part played by papal encyclicals and the Roman colleges.

It is therefore quite certain – or at least very probable – that Vatican II will also condition the life of the Church for a long time. A high concentration of faithfulness and wisdom drawn from the whole of the Church is, after all, present in a Council. A Council is also a Pentecostal type of event. John XXIII was not wrong to speak about Vatican II in terms of '*cum essent omnes congregati in unum*' – 'When . . . they were all together in one place' (Acts 2:1) – and a visit of the Holy Spirit or a kind of new Pentecost.[54]

It was a strange kind of Pentecost at Vatican II, making us overflow in many directions. That at least is the opinion expressed by some who were present, in a tone of sarcastic joy (*sic*) that often hurt. Those who belong to the renewal or 'charismatic' movement, on the other hand, are conscious of Pentecost spreading everywhere like a forest fire.

Let us admit that there were negative aspects. I deplore these and am very critical of them. It is, as we have seen, normal for a council to have a dynamism that goes beyond itself and for many to have recourse to that dynamism to give support to their initiatives. There was at Vatican II a rather simplistic practice of applying the pattern 'before' and 'after' to the Council, as though it marked an absolute new beginning, the point of departure for a completely new Church.[55] I was at the time and still am anxious to stress the continuity of Tradition. Vatican II was one moment and neither the first nor the last moment in that Tradition, just as Trent, Pius V and Pius X were neither the first nor the last.

I do not believe that the present crisis in the Church is the result of Vatican II. On the one hand, many of the realities that preoccupy us today were already present or beginning to appear in the 1950s and even in the 1930s.[56] The Council did not give rise to them. On the other hand, the current crisis is clearly due in quite an important degree to causes that have revealed their strength since the Council. Indeed it warned against them, warding them off rather than bringing them about. Vatican II has been followed by socio-cultural change more extensive, radical and rapid and more cosmic in its proportions than any change at any other period in man's history. The Council was conscious of this great change – this is evident from the introduction to *Gaudium et Spes* – but not of all its aspects or of its violence. Many questions have arisen in the past ten or twelve years of which the Council was not aware or which it might at the most just have suspected. These include, in the sphere of thought, the collapse of metaphysics as an acceptable philosophy, the feverish pursuit of hermeneutics, the triumphant emergence of critical methods and the all-pervasive influence of the human sciences. It has also become apparent that man can be manipulated in many ways. We have also witnessed the revolt of young people, who form a semi-autonomous world of their own, and the resulting break in continuity with the past. Women are also taking an increasing part in social activity and various initiatives. Secularization has continued and has become more radical. And our society has rapidly become even more completely urbanized. In the Church, we have since 1968 been passing through a crisis of the magisterium and a loss of interest on the part of many Christians, including the clergy, in what the Church is. We are increasingly absorbed by the things of this world, by politics and by Marxist categories.

I do not deny that Vatican II was to some extent responsible for this crisis. In fact I have already pointed out on several occasions how that was so and to what degree.[57] The mere fact that there was a Council and open discussion has contributed to it. Then there were repercussions, brought about and amplified by the modern means of communication. The simple fact of 'council' has changed the conditions established in the exercise of authority since the time of Pius IX.[58] The publicity given to the Council has shown that the 'Church' does not have a reply to every question and that it does have internal tensions.

There was, however, great freedom in the debates. The Council was open to contributions that had for so long been overlooked, excluded or condemned. It was also healthily self-critical in the light of the demands made by the Gospel and the Church's essential mission. These factors meant that the unconditional nature of the system inherited from the Counter-Reformation and the anti-revolutionary restoration of the nineteenth century was completely overcome at Vatican II. The result of the collapse of that system was that ideas and attitudes that had for too long been held at a safe distance entered the Church through the open doors and windows of the Council. And the crisis also entered that way.

But I would like to end on a positive note. The Council produced many very substantial fruits, consisting to a great extent of promises. At present we have only the first crop of these fruits. Many local Churches are displaying great vitality. Charisms and basic ministries are everywhere in evidence. Ecumenical efforts are gradually coming to maturity. Christians are everywhere committed to their fellow men, especially those who are crushed or put to the test. One does not have to look far to find countless examples of total spiritual generosity. Does this not make our period one of the most evangelical in history?

I must admit that it makes me very sad to see so many of the great and fine structures that I loved so entirely fall into ruins or get put up for auction; but I am at the same time astonished to see so many worthy initiatives and so many new beginnings prompted by the Gospel and the Spirit of God. Mgr Etchegaray said at a recent assembly at Lourdes that when a tree falls it makes a great noise, but when a forest is growing nobody hears anything. That Chinese proverb expresses very well what is happening and that can be interpreted in terms of ecclesiology, since what is taking place is a movement from one view of the Church to another.

The earlier view was dominated until the time of Vatican II by a juridical definition of the Church as a *societas perfecta* or a 'complete society' that was unequal and hierarchical. The first article of that unequal and hierarchical structure was the difference by divine right between clergy and laity.[59] Vatican II, however, taught an ecclesiology of Christian existence structured as a Church that is basically sacramental. The vitality of such a Church comes much more from its base, consisting of people who, filled with enthusiasm for the Gospel, create more or less formal communities.[60] This encourages not individualism, but a situation of personal choice motivated by deep conviction.

Will it result in a 'protestantization' of the Catholic Church? In the preconciliar juridical Church, everything was accepted without question. Now, however, it is not possible to manage without much questioning. The institution is still alive, as the events that took place in Rome in the summer of 1978 show. Its vitality is a condition of its health, but its health is traceable to its life at the base, that of a Church that is the People of God on its pilgrim way, that of a Church that springs up in groups of people matured from the seed of Christ, the Word made flesh, Word and Sacrament, brought among them by the apostolate.

'I tell you, lift up your eyes and see how the fields are already white for the harvest' (Jn. 4:35) – 'The harvest is plentiful, but the labourers are few, pray the Lord of the harvest to send out labourers' (Mt. 9:37–38; Lk. 10:2). My last words are simply a prayer in the words of Psalm 80: 'Turn again, O God of hosts . . . and have regard for this vine, the stock which thy right hand planted'.

NOTES

1. The official publication will be found in the *Acta et Documenta Concilio oecumenico Vaticano II apparendo*, Series I (*Antepraeparatoria*) I (Vatican, 1960), 5; and in *DC* LVI, No 1300 (29 March 1959), 388. *DC* = *La Documentation Catholique*.

2. *Osservatore Romano* (26–27 January 1959); see also *DC* LVI, No 1297 (15 February 1959), 197–198.

3. See, for example, 1 April 1959, *Acta et Documenta*, 15 and *DC* (1959), 515; Encyclical *Ad Petri cathedram* (19 June 1959), 36 and 38 and *DC* (1959), 910 and 911; Prayer to the Holy Spirit, 48; Address to the Priests of Bologna (7 February 1960), 76; *Motu proprio* setting up the Preparatory Commissions (5 June 1960), 93.

4. *Acta et Documenta*, 46. See also 14 February 1960, 74 and *DC* LVI, No 1311 (6 September 1959), 1098 and 1099.

5. Quoted in my *Aspects de l'OEcuménisme* (Brussels, 1962), 71.

6. Interview on French television (24 January 1960); *Acta et Documenta*, 160 and *DC* LVII, No 1325 (3 April 1960), 394.

7. *Du Pape* II, Chapter 15 (1869 ed), 276, n. 1. It has not only been Protestant historians who have called the Church's councils pointless; see P. Hinschius, *Kirchenrecht* III (1883), 630; C. Mirbt, *Realenzyklopädie* XX, (3rd ed, 1908), 470. Catholics have also said the same. Even before Vatican I was convoked, some Catholics said, for example: 'Have we not the Pope? Does the Pope not have the power to decide every question?'; see R. Aubert, *Le Pontificat de Pie IX* (Paris, 1952), 312, quoting F. Lagrange, *Vie de Mgr Dupanloup* III, 55. After Vatican I, Bismarck commented that the dogma that it had promulgated had deprived the councils of all reason; see *Eglise et Unité* (Lille, 1948), 24f.

In his preface to *Le Concile de Trente*, Hefele and Leclercq, *Histoire des Conciles* IX, 1 (Paris, 1930),7–9, P. Richard wrote: 'There is less need for a general council today than there was in the past . . . There is even less need in that no one now speaks of convocation except perhaps as an article of publicity . . . The Oecumenical Council of the Vatican has reduced the importance of such convocations to nothing. Whatever may happen now, whether there is another assembly or whether the Holy See undertakes the task of completing its unfinished work, that will be the end of the series of nineteen oecumenical councils . . . The work is completed and future councils, if there are any, will contribute no more to the monument than a few improvements or additional adaptations, the scope of which will not compensate for the difficulties that convocation will involve.' See also J. Nauvecelle, 'Eglise capitale Vatican', *NRF* 36 (1954), 205–206. In *Esprit* (December 1961) ('Voeux pour le Concile'), J. Meyendorff wrote, 793: 'Many of those who belong to the Roman Church and many outside it believe that the decisions taken in 1870 could not be reconciled with the conciliar institution . . .' and S. Neill added, 806: 'A few years ago, I had the opportunity to make a very detailed study of the Council of Trent and the Vatican Council, which led me to conclude that a new council would never be convoked . . .' Daniel-Rops, *Vatican II. Le Concile de Jean XXIII* (Paris, 1961), said: 'Many people, even Catholics, thought that such assemblies of the Church had become useless, simply because of the proclamation of papal infallibility.' G. Huber, *Vers le Concile: Dialogues sous la colonnade de Saint-Pierre* (Paris, 1961), 22, asked: 'It seemed to me that the proclamation of the infallibility of the Pope by the Vatican Council had made it superfluous to hold oecumenical councils. Why, then, have recourse to a slow and complicated procedure when it is possible to use a simple and rapid method?'

8. See G. Caprile, 'Pio XI e la ripresa del Concilio Vaticano', *La Civiltà Cattolica* (2 July 1966), 27–39; French translation in *DC* LXIII, No 1484 (18 December 1966), 2175–88.

9. See G. Caprile, 'Pio XII e un nuovo progetto di Concilio ecumenico', *La Civiltà Cattolica* (6–20 August 1966), 209–27; French translation *DC* LXIV, No 1485 (1 January 1967), 49–68. What is revealed in the article documented by Fr Caprile shows that the Curia played a dominant role here.

10. Allocution of 7 December 1959; *Acta et Documenta*, 60. Cardinal Tardini had already said this on 15 July 1959. Holding the Council at Saint Paul extra Muros and calling it Ostiense I had for a time been considered; see P. Felici, *L'Avvenire d'Italia* (28 January 1960), 4.

11. G. Alberigo, 'Una cum patribus. La formula conclusiva delle decisioni del Vaticano II', *Ecclesia a Spiritu Sancto edocta* (*Mélanges Gérard Philips*) (Gembloux, 1970), 291–319.

12. I have simply taken this formula materially as it is from the *Acta* of the Council of Chalcedon, because it is clear and striking. For its historical meaning, see P.-R. Cren, 'Concilium episcoporum est. Note sur l'histoire d'une citation des Actes du Concile de Chalcédoine', *RSPhTh* 46 (1962), 45–62.

13. 'What many a bishop kept to himself within his own diocese or only made public hesitatingly and with great prudence was, at Rome, whispered at the beginning in a timid and muted way. Bishops in this way discovered that all their colleagues had similar ideas and this led to a moral unanimity that had already existed before the Council, although it was only latent. The contact that the bishops had with each other . . . released something which had for a long time clearly been calling for official expression'; E. Schillebeeckx, *L'Eglise du Christ et l'homme d'aujourd'hui selon Vatican II* (Le Puy, Lyons and Paris, 1965), 37 (text of 5 January 1963).

14. Quoted by Aubert, *op cit*, n. 7 above.
15. T. Raymondos and R. Prévost have provided a good assessment of this situation in 'Vatican II, ligne d'arrêt et de départ', *Dieu n'échoue pas*, No. 6 (1969).
16. See P. T. Camelot, *Le Concile et les conciles* (Paris and Chèvetogne, 1960), 65; the Fathers of the Seventh Oecumenical Council, Mansi XIII, 776C; my own contribution in *1274 année charnière. Mutations et continuités* (Paris, CNRS, 1977), 439 and n. 7; H. J. Marx, *Filioque und Verbot eines anderen Glaubens auf dem Florentinum* (Steyl, 1977), 300f.
17. See the *Indices* of the various editions of the sixteen documents of Vatican II. For Pius XII, see E. Innocenti, 'Le citazioni pontificie nei documenti conciliari', *Concretezza* (16 July 1966), 6–10. This is cited by Caprile. The notes accompanying the Constitution on the Liturgy, *Sacrosanctum Concilium*, published in MD 76, clearly illustrate the continuity between this excellent document and the work of Pius XII and Pius X.
18. Address given on 8 December 1969; see *DC* LXVII, No 1554 (10 January 1970), 10ff.
19. See J.-P. Torrell, *La théologie de l'épiscopat au Premier concile du Vatican* (*Unam Sanctam* 37) (Paris, 1961); G. Dejaifve, *Pape et évêques au Premier concile du Vatican* (Bruges and Paris, 1961).
20. Attention has also been drawn to the conciliar aspect in the structure and the life of the Church. See W. Aymans, *Das synodale Element in der Kirchenverfassung* (Munich, 1970); J. Neumann, *Synodales Prinzip. Der grössere Spielraum im Kirchenrecht* (Freiburg, 1973).
21. Figures supplied by Cardinal Tardini in his interview on French television (24 January 1960); *Acta et Documenta*, 160.
22. G. Marc, *Le Supplément* 124 (February 1978), 85.
23. Discourse given at a public session (18 November 1965); see *DC* LXII, No 1460 (5 December 1965), 2046.
24. Paul VI in a letter to Mgr Lefebvre (29 June 1975). If it sets anyone's troubled mind at rest, it is worth recalling that, at the time of the centenary of the Council of Trent, the Fathers of the Gregoriana expressed the view that 'di tutti i Concili' Trent was 'forse il più importante'; see *Gr* 26 (1945). P. R. Régamey has written of Vatican II, *Ce que croyait Dominique* (Paris, 1978): 'No other oecumenical council has ever thrown such a full and certain light on the areas of faith from which the human spirit should receive its orientations and on the spheres of life which should be influenced by that spirit today'.
25. G. B. Ladner, *The Idea of Reform: Its Impact on Christian Thought and Action* (Cambridge, Mass, 1956). This aspect of John XXIII's plan has not been sufficiently emphasized.
26. This text is from Charles Péguy (1 March 1904). I applied the same text to my subject matter in *Vraie et fausse réforme dans l'Eglise* (Paris, 1950), 602; (Paris, 1969), 543.
27. See J. Corbon, G. Alberigo, W. Kasper, Y. Congar and R. Rouquette, 'Bilan du Concile', *Etudes* (January 1963), 104. See also E. Schillebeeckx, *L'Eglise du Christ*, 115.
28. It would be good to have a study on this subject. Some aspects of it were discussed in *Seminarium*, New Series IX/2 (April–June 1969), 145–50, 186ff, 287–90.
29. See Maximos IV, *L'Eglise Grecque Melchite au Concile. Discours et notes* (Beirut, 1967); J. Corbon, 'Les catholiques à la redécouverte de leur âme orientale', *POC* 15 (1965), 145–158; 'Bilan orientale du Concile', *POC* 16 (1966), 19–28; Emilios Inglessis, *Maximos IV. L'Orient conteste l'Occident* (Paris, 1969).
30. *DC* LXIII, No 1466 (6 March 1966), 421.
31. See W. A. Visser 't Hooft, *The Meaning of Ecumenical* (London, 1953); see also E. Fascher, 'Ökumenisch und katholisch: Zur Geschichte zweier heute viel gebrauchten Begriffe', *ThLZ* 85 (1960), 7–20; H. van der Linde, *Wat is oecumenisch?* (Roermond and Maaseik, 1961); H. Stirnmann, ' "Catholic" and "Ecumenical" ', *ER* (July 1966), 293–309.

32. See A. Wenger, *Upsal, le défi du siècle aux Eglises* (Paris, 1968), 305f; text by Tucci in *DC* LXV, No 1523 (1 September 1968), 1471–89, see especially 1482f.

33. For example, when Cardinal Tardini said in his interview on 24 January 1960, *Acta et Documenta*, 159: 'At present, it is possible to say that the main aim of the Council will be more especially Church discipline, those aspects of Canon Law that can be modified and then the whole of the Catholic way of life. As far as one can know now, it will be a council of a real, practical kind rather than a council concentrating on doctrine. But doctrine will not be entirely excluded . . .'

34. Allocution to members of the central preparatory Commission (20 June 1961), *AAS* (1961), 501.

35. *DC* LIX, No 1387 (4 November 1962), 1381–1383; cf Ed W. M. Abbott SJ., *The documents of Vatican II* (London 1966),715. In his communication of 5 December 1962 to the Secretary of State, giving directives for the carrying out of work, the Pope reproduced the text quoted above and asked that 'we should devote ourselves fearlessly and vigilantly to work that consists in drawing conclusions from the early doctrine and applying it to the conditions of our own period, that is, we should continue along the Church's way forward in time'. See *DC* LX, No 1381 (6 January 1963), 21.

36. See R. Laurentin, *Bilan de la 1ère Session* (Paris, 1963), 27f; G. Philips, 'Deux tendances dans la théologie contemporaine', *NRTh* 85 (1963), 225–38; E. Schillebeeckx, 'Impressions sur une divergence de mentalité' and 'Malentendus au Concile', *L'Eglise du Christ*, 37–61; my *Le Concile au jour le jour* I, 67f, IV, 104 and 142–6, and 'La théologie au Concile. Le "théologiser" du Concile', reproduced on files entitled *Vérité et Vie* (Strasbourg, 1965) and reprinted in *Situation et tâches de la théologie* (Paris, 1967), 41–56.

37. E. Schillebeeckx, *L'Eglise du Christ*, 42, who also writes, 57 (19 January 1963): 'During the debates in the Council, I have often noticed how the "progressives" have fought exclusively against this way of imprisoning the truth, while the others have believed that the essence of the truth was being called into question.'

38. P. B. de la Margerie, *La Trinité chrétienne dans l'histoire* (Paris, 1975), 144, n. 137, refers to *Gaudium et Spes*, 47, 2; 58; *Apostolicam actuositatem*, 6, 4; 7, the condemnation of racism and total war, etc. Errors may have existed and Vatican II may have rejected and excluded them by formulating a positive teaching, but it was not, like Trent and Vatican I, conditioned by an obsessive need to condemn them. It had not been convoked in order to speak against teachings; that would have denied its pastoral character.

39. *op cit*, n. 35 above. See Paul VI, Allocution, 6 September 1963, *DC* LX, No 1409 (1963), 1266; see also n. 44 below. See also his address given on 4 February 1970, *DC* No 1559 (15 March 1970), 252f.

40. Intervention, 27 November 1962; text in Mgr Lefebvre, *J'accuse le Concile* (Martigny, 1976), 18–21.

41. M.-D. Chenu, 'Un Concile "pastoral" ', *Parole et mission* 21 (15 April 1963), 182–202, reprinted in *La Parole de Dieu* II: *L'Evangile dans le temps* (Paris, 1964), 655–72, especially 661.

42. See A. Wenger, *Vatican II: Première Session* (Paris, 1963), 111f.

43. Mgr Guerry, the Archbishop of Cambrai, in *La Croix* (1 and 2–3 December 1962). Long extracts will be found in *DC* LIX, No 1390 (16 December 1962), 1582f, and A. Wenger, *op cit*, 112. See also Cardinal Liénart, *La Croix* (8 December 1962), quoted by A. Wenger, *op cit*, 75f.

44. *DC* LX, No 1409 (6 October 1963), 1266f.

45. M.-D. Chenu, *op cit*, n. 41 above; Y. Congar, *op cit*, n. 36 above; E. Schillebeeckx, *op*

cit, n. 36 above; A. Wenger, *op cit*, 111; J. Ratzinger, *LThK.E* I (Freiburg, 1966), 348–59, especially 350.

46. Dogmatic Constitution, *Dei Filius*, 3; DS 3011.

47. K. Rahner SJ, 'Réflexions sur la problématique théologique d'une constitution pastorale', *Gaudium et Spes. L'Eglise dans le monde de ce temps.· Schéma XIII. Commentaires* (Paris, 1967), 13–42. The Conference of German Bishops (22 September 1967), *DC* No 1511, 1698, 323, can be compared with the Note made by the Spanish Episcopal Commission for the Doctrine of Faith (15 February 1978), 31; *DC* LXXV, No 1753 (7 December 1978), 1026f. The difficulty of deriving religious freedom from the revealed deposit of faith illustrates clearly the fact that something is here involved 'quite different from developing in a doctrinal manner the deposit of faith as such'.

48. M.-D. Chenu wrote, *op cit*, 670f: 'This means that apostolic praxis is the proper place for theology. Pastoral theology forms part of the theological knowledge, not simply as a lower sphere of applied knowledge, but as the principle by which faith is understood...' The word 'praxis' also means more than a merely practical application of conclusions already formulated theoretically. It means that the facts and their carrying out are, at their own level, a datum of thought to be elaborated.

49. The status of this second part of the Constitution in theological and conciliar criteriology was the subject of very difficult discussions in the mixed Commission responsible for the document and in the assembly. This is hardly surprising as it was without precedent. This passage from the *Praesentatio generalis textus* is worth citing in this context: 'Scopus praecipuus huius schematis non est directe doctrinam praebere, sed potius eius applicationes ad condiciones nostri temporis necnon consectoria pastoralia ostendere et inculcare.' ('The particular scope of this schema is not the direct presentation of doctrine, but rather its application to the circumstances of our time; and also to indicate and indeed drive home its pastoral consequences.')

50. The term 'flabby texts' was employed by Fr Bruckberger. Mgr Graber, however, remarked that, because of its 'pastoral' character, its wide vision and its absence of canons terminating with *Anathema sit*, the Council tended to produce documents that could be disputed. See *Athanase et l'Eglise de notre temps* (Paris, 1973), 68. The *Praesentatio generalis textus* of *Gaudium et Spes*, for example, said: 'Notandum est insuper, quod, attenta indole essentialiter pastorali textus, schema hoc non indiget disceptatione tam rigorosa cuiusque vocabuli, ut fieri deberet in re stricte dogmatica.' ('It is further to be noted that, given the essential pastoral character of the text, it does not require so exact a debate upon each word as would be demanded by a strictly dogmatic context.') The criticism of 'doctrinal timidity' was made by Mgr H. Denis, *Les chemins de la théologie dans le monde de ce temps* (Paris, 1977), 66f.

51. Letter dated 7 August 1870, written to O'Neill Daunt; see *Lettre au duc de Norfolk (1874) et Correspondance relative à l'infaillibilité (1865–1875)*, translated by B.-D. Dupuy, DDB (1970), 457.

52. See the excellent book by R. Foreville, *Latran I, II, III et Latran IV* (HCO 6) (Paris, 1965).

53. J. Gaudemet, 'La vie conciliaire en France', Lot and Fawtier, *Histoire des institutions françaises au moyen-âge* III (Paris, 1963), 314, n. 1.

54. John XXIII often spoke in this way. See his address on 17 May 1959, *DC* (1959) 769f; Pentecost 1960, *DC* (1960), 806; Constitution *Humanae salutis* of 25 December 1961, *DC* (1962), 104; discourse at the end of the first period of the Council, 7 December 1962. Paul VI also spoke of the need for a lasting Pentecost in his audience of 29 June 1972; see *DC* (1972), 1105.

55. See J. F. Six, *Le courage de l'espérance: Les dix ans qui ont suivi le Concile* (Paris, 1978), 85: 'The Council appeared to many Christians to be a reformation or even a revolution, in other words, a new beginning.'
56. I have begun to collect material on such matters as the decline in the number of vocations, spontaneous groups, liturgical renewals, philosophical questionings, 'new' theology, the worker-priests, ecumenism and the increasing spread of ideas and attitudes favouring individual autonomy and spontaneity.
57. See *La crise dans l'Eglise et Mgr Lefebvre* (Paris, 1976), 60f. (2nd ed, 1977), 62; *Eglise catholique et France moderne* (Paris, 1978), 49f.
58. 'It was not the positions adopted by the Council that brought about the crisis. It was the very fact that a Council was held that caused a deep change in the Church's organization and its pattern of relationships with the world . . .', in *Vive notre histoire: Aimé Savard interroge René Rémond* (Paris, 1976), 144. See also M. Légaut, *Panorama chrétien* aujourd'hui 96 (November 1976), 27.
59. See K. Walf, 'Die katholische Kirche – eine "*societas perfecta*"?', *ThQ* 157 (1977), 107–118; N. Timpe, *Das kanonistische Kirchenbild vom Codex Iuris Canonici bis zum Beginn des Vaticanum Secundum* (*EThSt* 36) (Leipzig, 1978); H. M. Legrand, 'Insertion des ministères de direction dans la communauté ecclésiale', *RDC* 23 (1973), 225–54.
60. Italo Mancini has noted: 'The success of the Council of Trent can be attributed largely to the work of the religious congregations that followed it. Similarly, the success of the change of course initiated by Vatican II will depend on whether the basic communities [communautés de base] which make Christian love visible do flourish and grow': see G. Zizola, *L'homme du septième jour* (Paris, 1978), 126.

APPENDIX

DELEGATED OBSERVERS AND GUESTS AT THE SECOND VATICAN COUNCIL FOURTH SESSION 1965

Ecumenical Patriarchate of Constantinople

His Excellency the Most Reverend Emilianos, Metropolitan of Calabria

Very Revd Archimandrite Maximos Aghiorgoussis, Rector of the Greek Orthodox Parish of Rome

Very Revd Archimandrite Andrew Scrima, personal representative of His Holiness Patriarch Athenagoras to the Secretariat for Promoting Christian Unity

Greek Orthodox Patriarchate of Alexandria

Very Revd Archimandrite Nicodeme Galiatsatos, Great Protosynkellos of the Patriarchal Throne of Alexandria, Patriarchal Pro-Vicar in Cairo

Dr Theodore D. Mosconas, Director of the Patriarchal Library, Editor of the official review *Pantainos*

Dr Vasso Canavatis, Legal Counsellor of the Patriarchal Throne of Alexandria

Russian Orthodox Church (Patriarchate of Moscow)

Very Revd Professor-Archpriest Vitaly Borovoy, Vice-Chairman of the Department for Inter-Church Relations of the Moscow Patriarchate and Representative of the Russian Orthodox Church at the World Council of Churches

Very Revd Archimandrite Juvenaly, Vice-Chairman of the Department for Inter-Church Relations of the Moscow Patriarchate

Very Revd Archpriest Livery Voronov, Member of the Department for Inter-Church Relations, Professor at the Theological Academy of Leningrad

Bulgarian Orthodox Church

Very Revd Archimandrite Joan, Protosynkellos of the Metropolitan See of Sofia

The Orthodox Church of Georgia

Very Revd Professor-Archpriest Vitaly Borovoy (proxy)

Coptic Orthodox Church of Egypt

His Excellency the Rt Revd Amba Antonios, Bishop of Sohag and Secretary of the Holy Synod

Revd Yuhanna Guirguis, Rector of the Church of St Mark, Hadaek-Choubrah

APPENDIX

Ethiopian Orthodox Church

Revd Abba Petros G. Selassie, Rector of the Ethiopian Orthodox Church in Jerusalem

Dr Sergewa H. Selassie, Professor at the University College of Addis Ababa

Syrian Orthodox Church

Very Revd Saliba Shamoon, First Secretary to His Holiness the Patriarch

Syrian Orthodox Church of India

Revd Dr C. T. Eapen, President of the Syrian Christian Congress and Member of the Managing Committee of the Orthodox Church

Apostolic Armenian Church (Catholicate of Etchmiadzin)

Right Revd Bishop Parkev Kevorkian, Delegate of the Catholicos in Moscow, Bishop of the Armenians in Moscow

Mr Krikor Bekmezian, theologian, member of the Supreme Spiritual Council of Holy Etchmiadzin

Apostolic Armenian Church (Catholicate of Cilicia)

His Excellency, the Rt Revd Bishop Karekin Sarkissian, Dean of the Armenian Theological Seminary, Antelias (Lebanon)

His Excellency, the Rt Revd Bishop Ardavazt Terterian, Bishop of the Armenians of Southern France

Russian Orthodox Church Outside of Russia

Very Revd Archpriest Igor Troyanoff, Director of the Russian Orthodox Churches of Lausanne and Vevey (Switzerland)

Very Revd Archimandrite Dr Ambrose Pogodin, Rector of the Russian Orthodox Church in Rome

Substitute

Prof Dr Serge Grotoff, of the International University for Social Studies (Rome)

Old Catholic Church (Union of Utrecht)

Very Revd Canon Peter John Maan, Professor of New Testament at the Old Catholic Seminary of Amersfoort and Vicar of the Cathedral Church of Utrecht (The Netherlands)

Substitute

Revd Prof Dr Werner Küppers, Rector of the Old Catholic Seminary at the University of Bonn (Germany)

360

APPENDIX

Mar Thoma Syrian Church of Malabar (India)

His Excellency the Rt Revd Bishop Thomas Mar Athanasius

Anglican Communion

Right Revd Dr John Moorman, Bishop of Ripon (England)
Right Revd Dr Najib Atallah Cuba'in, Bishop of the Diocese of Jordan, Lebanon and Syria
Revd Dr Eugene R. Fairweather, Professor of Divinity, Trinity College, University of Toronto (Canada)
Revd Dr Canon Clement W. Welsh, Canon-Theologian of Washington Cathedral and Director of Studies, College of Preachers, Washington, D.C. (USA)

Substitutes

Dr Peter Day, Ecumenical Assistant to the Presiding Bishop, Protestant Episcopal Church in the USA, New York
Dr John W. Lawrence, Editor of *Frontier*, London (England)
Revd Canon Bernard Pawley, Canon-treasurer of Ely Cathedral (England)
Revd Prof Howard Root, Fellow and Dean of Emmanuel College, Cambridge, and Lecturer in Divinity, University of Cambridge (England)
Revd Canon John R. Satterthwaite, General Secretary of the Church of England Council on Foreign Relations, London
Revd Canon John Findlow, representative of the Archbishop of Canterbury, President of the Lambeth Conference of Bishops, Rome/London

World Lutheran Federation

Revd Prof Kristen E. Skydsgaard, Professor of Systematic Theology, The University of Copenhagen (Denmark)
Revd Prof Warren A. Quandbeck, Professor of Systematic Theology, Luther Theological Seminary, St. Paul, Minnesota (USA)
Revd Dr Vilmos Vajta, Research-professor at the Institute for Ecumenical Research Strasbourg (France)
Right Revd Dr Sven Silen, Bishop of Västeras (Sweden)

Substitutes

Dr Seppo Teinonen, Lecturer in missiology and ecumenics at the University of Helsinki, and General Secretary of the Ecumenical Council of Finland, Helsinki
Revd Dr Jerald C. Brauer, Dean of the Divinity School, University of Chicago (USA)
Revd Prof Haggen A. K. Staack, head of the Department of Religion, Muhlenberg College, Allentown, Pennsylvania (USA)

World Alliance of Reformed and Presbyterian Churches

Revd Prof Vittorio Subilia, Dean of the Theological Faculty of the Waldensian Church, Rome
Revd Prof John K. S. Reid, Professor of Christian Dogmatics, The University of Aberdeen (Scotland)
Revd Dr Richard H. N. Davidson, Minister of the United Church of Canada, Fairlawn United Church, Toronto (Canada)

APPENDIX

Evangelical Church in Germany

Prof Dr Edmund Schlink, Professor of Dogmatics at the University of Heidelberg (Germany)

Substitute

Revd Dr Wolfgang Dietzfelbinger, Pastor in Erbendorf (Germany)

World Methodist Council

Right Revd Fred Pierce Corson, Resident Bishop of the Philadelphia Area, President of the World Methodist Council, Philadelphia (USA)

Revd Dr Albert C. Outler, Professor of Theology at Southern Methodist University, Dallas, Texas (USA)

Revd Dr Harold Roberts, Principal of Richmond Theological College, Richmond (England)

Substitutes

Revd Dr José Miguez-Bonino, Director of the Evangelical Theological Faculty of Buenos Aires (Argentina)

Revd Dr Emerito P. Nacpil, Professor of Systematic Theology, Union Theological Seminary, Manila (Philippines)

Revd David Alan Keighley, representative in Italy of the British Methodist Church of the United Kingdom and of the Methodist Missionary Society, Rome

Revd Dr E. Gordon Rupp, Professor of Ecclesiastical History in the University of Manchester (England)

Revd Dr William R. Cannon, Dean of the Candler School of Theology, Emory University, Atlanta, Georgia (USA)

Revd Dr Robert E. Cushman, Dean of Duke University Divinity School, Durham, North Carolina (USA)

Revd Max Woodward, British Secretary of the World Methodist Council, London (England)

International Congregational Council

Revd Dr Douglas Horton, former Moderator of the International Congregational Council, Randolph, New Hampshire (USA)

Revd Prof George B. Caird, Senior Tutor at Mansfield College, Oxford (England)

Substitutes

Revd Edgar H. S. Chandler, Executive Director, The Church Federation of Greater Chicago (USA)

Revd Dr Stuart LeRoy Anderson, President of the Pacific School of Religion, Berkeley, California (USA)

Revd Prof Ralph D. Hyslop, Union Theological Seminary, New York

Revd Dr Ruben H. Huenemann, President of the United Theological Seminary of the Twin Cities, New Brighton, Minnesota (USA)

Revd Dr Heiko A. Oberman, Professor of Church History at Harvard University Divinity School, Cambridge, Massachusetts (USA)

APPENDIX

World Convention of Churches of Christ (Disciples)

Dr Wm Barnett Blakemore, Dean of Disciples Divinity House, The University of Chicago, Chicago (USA)

Dr Basil Holt, Administrative Field Secretary of Disciples of Christ for South Africa and Minister of Linden Christian Church, Johannesburg (South Africa)

Friends World Committee for Consultation

Prof Douglas V. Steere, Professor at Haverford College, Haverford, Pennsylvania (USA)

International Association for Liberal Christianity and Religious Freedom (IARF)

Prof L. J. Van Holk, Professor at The University of Leiden (The Netherlands)

Revd Dr A. W. Cramer, Executive Secretary of the IARF, The Hague (The Netherlands)

Substitutes

Revd Prof George Williams, Professor of Divinity, Harvard University Divinity School, Cambridge, Massachusetts (USA)

Dr H. Faber, former President of the IARF, The Hague (The Netherlands)

Church of South India

Right Revd Pereji Solomon, Deputy Moderator of the Church of South India, and Bishop in Dornakai

United Church of Christ in Japan (Nippon Kirisuto Kyodan)

Dr Tetsutaro Ariga, Director of the National Christian Council Center for the Study of Japanese Religions, Osaka (Japan)

Protestant Federation of France

Revd Hébert Roux, Minister of the French Reformed Church, in charge of inter-confessional relations, Paris (France)

World Council of Churches (Geneva)

Revd Dr Lukas Vischer, Research Secretary of the Commission on Faith and Order, Geneva, Switzerland

Dr Nikos A. Nissiotis, Director of the Ecumenical Institute of the WCC, Bossey (Switzerland)

Substitutes

Revd Dr Paul A. Abrecht, Executive Secretary of the Commission on Church and Society, Geneva

Revd Dr Victor E. W. Hayward, Secretary of the Commission on World Mission and Evangelism, Geneva

APPENDIX

Revd Dr Patrick Rodger, Executive Secretary of the Commission on Faith and Order, Geneva

Revd Dr Paul Verghese, Associate General Secretary of the WCC, Geneva

The Australian Council of Churches

Revd Frank Cuttriss, Rector of St James's Church, Sydney

GUESTS OF THE SECRETARIAT

Orthodox Theological Institute, St Serge (Paris)

(represented alternately by:)

Very Revd Archpriest Alexis Kniazeff, Rector, Professor of Old Testament and Mariology

Very Revd Archpriest Nicholas Afanassieff, Professor of Canon Law and Early Church History

Prof Paul Evdokimov

St Vladimir's Orthodox Theological Seminary (New York)

Very Revd Archpriest Alexander Schmemann, Dean, Professor of Dogmatic Theology

Community of Taizé

Revd Pastor Roger Schutz, Prior, Taizé (France)

Revd Pastor Max Thurian, Sub-prior of the same community

The Lutheran Church – Missouri Synod

(represented alternately by:)

Revd Dr Oswald C.J. Hoffmann, Speaker on The Lutheran Hour, St Louis, Missouri (USA)

Revd Dr Carl S. Meyer, Director of studies and professor at Concordia Seminary, St Louis (USA)

Revd Dr Walter F. Wolbrecht, Executive Secretary of the Lutheran Church – Missouri Synod

National Council of Churches of Christ in the USA

(represented alternately by:)

Revd Dr Robert C. Dodds, Associate Secretary for Christian Unity and Director of Ecumenical Affairs, NCC, New York

Revd Dr William A. Norgren, Executive Director of the Department of Faith and Order, NCC, New York

APPENDIX

Revd Pastor Marc Boegner, of the French Academy, Honorary President of the Protestant Federation of Churches in France

Revd Prof G. C. Berkouwer, Professor at the Free Protestant University of Amsterdam (The Netherlands)

Revd Prof Oscar Cullmann, Professor at the Universities of Basle and Paris

Revd Pastor Wilhelm Schmidt, Vicar of the 'Evangelische Michaelsbruderschaft', Bremen-Horn (Germany)